The Creation of the
Southern Dairy Industry

LAND OF MILK AND MONEY

ALAN I MARCUS

Louisiana State University Press
Baton Rouge

Published by Louisiana State University Press
www.lsupress.org

Designer: Barbara Neely Bourgoyne
Typeface: MillerText

Cover images: Cows in stanchions in dairy barn, ca. 1938. Photographs courtesy
Library of Congress.

Library of Congress Cataloging-in-Publication Data
Names: Marcus, Alan I, 1949– author.
Title: Land of milk and money : the creation of the southern dairy industry /
   Alan I Marcus.
Description: Baton Rouge : Louisiana State University Press, [2021] | Includes
   bibliographical references and index.
Identifiers: LCCN 2021013740 (print) | LCCN 2021013741 (ebook) | ISBN 978-
   0-8071-7605-4 (cloth) | ISBN 978-0-8071-7670-2 (pdf) | ISBN 978-0-8071-7671-9
   (epub)
Subjects: LCSH: Borden Company—History—20th century. | Dairy products industry—
   Southern States—History—20th century. | Dairy products industry—Mississippi—
   Starkville—History—20th century. | Industrialization—Southern States—History—
   20th century.
Classification: LCC HD9275.U6 M37 2021 (print) | LCC HD9275.U6 (ebook) |
   DDC 338.7/637097609042—dc23
LC record available at https://lccn.loc.gov/2021013740
LC ebook record available at https://lccn.loc.gov/2021013741

to the newest members of our family
Justin Bolivar and Enikő Marcus
welcome with our affection

CONTENTS

ACKNOWLEDGMENTS

This manuscript was written during the first part of the pandemic. I was fortunate in that I had completed almost all the archival research before the disease hit. Sheltering in place gave me an opportunity I have not had in years: it left me alone with my thoughts. This book is the consequence. But you are never entirely alone with your thoughts, and I had much assistance as I considered and wrote this book.

Our son Greg and his wife Enikõ fought in every way to keep us safe. They ran our errands and met us weekly on the front porch—appropriately socially distanced—for our delightful diversion of International Supper Club. Greg also provided a bit of research assistance, going to the library on several occasions to pick up a book or two or to track down a stray PDF so I would not have to. Along with my wife and our daughter Jocelyn, he also read various aspects of the manuscript as I puzzled over phrasing.

The Mississippi State University Department of History office staff, especially Pamela Wasson and Brenda Harris, kept the department running smoothly while I disappeared into the library during the book's research stage.

Several members of the staff of the Mississippi State University Libraries provided much-appreciated assistance. Jennifer McGillan, Coordinator of Manuscripts, took an active interest in my project. She shared her enthusiasm and went out of her way to help. Aron Bowers, Senior Library Associate, cheerfully retrieved some pages I neglected to copy. Summer Mord, Access Service Coordinator, secured certain journals and newspapers that I could have never accessed by myself. Their efforts made this a better manuscript.

Having other professionals to discuss ideas with is always a treat. It is even better when they are friends. Mark Hersey and Jim Giesen never tired—outwardly at least—when I asked them to read some pages or, enthusiastically, read a section out loud to them. More importantly, they were good enough friends to tell me when they thought I was wrong. I always listened but I did not always comply.

My graduate seminar in the spring of 2020 focused on the history of Starkville, Mississippi. Many thanks to Xavier Sivels, Patricia McCourt, Ryan Reynolds, Max McCaskell, Kymera Sneed, and Jake Gabriele for listening to me hold forth and for pushing back in a way that enhanced my own understanding as well as theirs.

Some years ago, a young graduate student, Josh Camper, needed a seminar paper topic. We agreed that he would focus on the opening of the Borden plant. I remember that Josh and I found the experience frustrating. I am glad to have had the chance to resolve, at least for me, that frustration. It has been a pleasure to write this book.

Dr. Rand Dotson, Editor in Chief, Louisiana State University Press, and his staff have been very helpful and I enjoyed working with them. I would certainly do it again.

Last and foremost is my wife Jean, my lifelong partner as we have pursued our separate and collective endeavors. There is no one I enjoy sharing everything with remotely as much.

LAND OF MILK
AND MONEY

INTRODUCTION

Many years ago, I would occasionally go to my in-laws' house in the northern Wisconsin woods. On several holidays—Memorial Day, July 4th, Thanksgiving, and Christmas—a long-padlocked tavern would open for business. Named the Boneyard, it served to commiserate and celebrate. It mostly functioned to remember. The Boneyard was one entrepreneur's attempt to commemorate the death of the many small towns and communities that had surrounded the tavern. Once a thriving lumber area, the towns, camps and communities of the northern Wisconsin woods had diminished every year. They continue to diminish today. With the means of economic survival vanishing, most residents moved on. Their children certainly did. Trees and brush eroded many of the signs of civilization—where people staked a claim, raised children, buried kin. Proprietors whose businesses served these places did not want them to fail. In many cases, they did everything possible to help the settlement persist. But the failure of a single institution—a mill, the consolidation of schools in some other town, the closing of a Catholic church—could signal the death knell for a community.

This book is not about those failures. It is about fear of failure. It is about the very real fear—in place after place—of becoming a ghost town like the towns of northern Wisconsin. It is about the universal small town phenomenon of fighting off depression, dissolution, and abandonment. There was probably no more chilling prospect for its inhabitants than a town collapsing. Lives would be turned upside down, futures questioned, prospects obliterated.

It is from the perspective of small towns that this book explores a phenomenon quite distant from the demise of northern logging towns. It examines the events that culminated in the southern dairy industry.

The southern dairy industry started in the North, not the South. The New York City–based Borden Co. led the way. In 1926 it established the first industrial milk plant south of the Mason-Dixon line: a condensery, a facility for manufacturing condensed or evaporated milk. After careful deliberation, Borden had selected Starkville, Mississippi, for that experiment. A town of about 2,500 adjacent to the state agricultural college, Starkville garnered international acclaim as a consequence of Borden's decision. Three major newsreel companies came to film the celebration that marked the condensery's opening. American and Western European theaters featured the event. This initial burst of publicity was portentous: the Starkville condensery soon became the mechanism through which hundreds, perhaps thousands, of southern towns learned about industrial dairying. Borden's competitors soon swooped down from the North and established their own facilities in the region's small cities and towns. While in 1925 there had been only a handful of small, often struggling, locally owned commercial milk plants in the South, by 1929 there were over three hundred industrial milk plants in Mississippi alone. These new facilities manufactured condensed, evaporated and powdered milk, ice cream, butter, cheese, malted milk, and a whole slew of other milk-derived products. In that same year, Tennessee, Alabama, Kentucky, Georgia, and Texas all reported vibrant, industrial dairying sectors. Louisiana, Arkansas, and both North and South Carolina soon rushed to join them.[1]

The explosive growth of dairying in the South was so profound that a shortage of dairy cattle soon rocked the nation. Wisconsin, Illinois, and the other traditional dairying states registered fewer cows and less milk as the southern dairies siphoned away their stock. Commentators wondered if the South was poised to replace the Upper Midwest as America's dairyland.[2] In less than four years—from April 1, 1926, to December 31, 1929—the southern landscape had been transformed. The South had become a dairy region.

Such a profound change is breathtaking. It begs the question of whether a major national or regional event propelled the matter. No new technological marvel was introduced. Condensing milk was a mid-nineteenth-century event, and the technology for its large scale production stemmed from the late nineteenth century. There was no sudden economic disruption that caused southerners to gravitate to dairy cattle. The southern economy had been in desperate shape for more than a generation, and reformers had been through the South for decades in vain attempts to make things right. The boll weevil, bovine tuberculosis, and the cattle tick had long plagued southern farmers, and to a degree would continue to do so. Northern capital had flooded into the South since the late nineteenth century. The textile mills of Tennessee, Georgia, North Carolina, and other places are testament to that.[3]

What led Borden and then the others to move with such alacrity and purpose and what led small towns to welcome the advance? That Borden initiated this activity and that the South proved receptive to this sudden "invasion" stemmed from a particular cluster of ideas and events that transformed Borden and soon other industrial firms. It changed the ambitions, goals, and methods of many southern small towns and cities. In a very real sense, the historical drama that resulted in the creation of the southern dairy industry was set in time and circumstance.

What Borden and Starkville had done and what they had encountered in the previous decade positioned these two corporations to pounce on this opportunity. Both functioned as if they were individuals, the legal designation for American corporations since at least the late nineteenth century. Perhaps by virtue of being composed of many human beings, corporate entities are the repository of memories, ideas, and desires. In many ways, they possess human-like functions. Corporations learn, they grow, they change, they mature. Rarely do they stay the same. Their subsequent actions are overwhelmingly based upon previous considerations, coupled with the introduction of new information. What they tried and did not try, what they watched and what they did not see, is where and what they learned. Corporations are each a unique life lived. They hold vastly different experiences, different temperaments and different abilities. Some are sheltered or meek, others aggressive, and some thoughtful. Corporations grow, develop, die, and spin off other corporations in this personified corporate world.

The two pillars of this story, the Borden Company and the town of Starkville, Mississippi, could not be more dissimilar. Yet it was how these two corporations recorded their experiences of the previous decade—and thus learned from them—that enabled them to see the possibilities of a southern dairy industry. What they learned and did during the ten years leading up to the condensery made that milk plant conceivable. In the case of Borden, its experiences as a major fluid milk producer in Chicago and New York, coupled with its condensed milk experience during and after World War I, primed the company to shun its late nineteenth-century moorings and adopt a new set of business initiatives.

The Borden of the 1920s no longer made milk products. It now made profits. It recognized demand as elastic, something that could be molded, formed, manufactured. The modern Borden considered conventional models of vertical and horizontal integration passé when factoring in marketing and distribution. Fundamentally redefining the company's purpose led it to reorganize virtually all its activities and enterprises and set it on a new course to ensure that profits were sustainable. Borden's modernist manipulations of its entire business operation anticipated by about five years that of General Motors and other multinational corporations, which in the mid- and late 1920s actively implemented an exciting array of programs to capitalize on the new insight. An advertising-fueled consumerism was among the offshoots. So too was establishing industrial dairying in the American South.[4]

Borden came to understand that modern business corporations did far more than reduce manufacturing costs and fill demand. Having a stable base from which to maneuver, defusing tensions among newly conceived partners, and fashioning a certain public image or premise all contributed to reliable profitability. Reducing distribution costs permanently enhanced the bottom line as did the vigorous expansion of markets.

Starkville too had its own experiences and its own epiphany. For roughly a decade its commercial elite had failed to coalesce in its efforts to enhance Starkville's quality of life, the town's reputation, or its future. Only as the group learned to incorporate other residents of Oktibbeha County—the county in which Starkville resides—into its vision and calculations did it manage to gain traction. Forging a Chamber of Commerce that embraced Oktibbehans, rather than ignoring, opposing, or disregarding the county's various citizens, emerged as a key concept. Borden's long dalliance with Starkville before agreeing to locate its condensery there cemented the newly formed Oktibbeha community. It firmly established the Chamber of Commerce as the lead organization in the challenge to advance the county, and it quickly spearheaded efforts to improve the lives of Oktibbeha residents.

When the condensery opened, the chamber embarked almost immediately upon a rigorous advertising and publicity campaign. It hoped to further development by focusing on the county and town and their success in securing the condensery. It expected to demonstrate to the American public how that event stemmed from the character of both town and county. Only with a new notion of Starkville as part of an Oktibbeha County community did the city possess the weapons necessary to strive for a stable, sustainable future. It was the story embraced by a vast number of small towns seeking salvation through dairying, each of which tempered and reinterpreted the condensery tale through the lenses of their own personal experiences. Over 30,000 southerners scheduled visits to Starkville and Oktibbeha County just to see the condensery and talk to Starkvillians in the mid- to late twenties. An even larger number likely came without official notification. The story of the Borden condensery at Starkville was indeed legendary. It provided an impetus for the proliferation of industrial dairying in small towns across the American South in the 1920s. These dairy plants facilitated small town survival and frequently granted these places the latitude to craft their own futures.

1 | THE MILK WARS TO END ALL WAR

Borden before and after World War I

In 1899 the Borden Condensed Milk Company of New York City held the title of "largest manufacturer of proprietary food products in the world." It produced condensed milk in large plants in New York State and in the greater Chicago metropolitan area. Borden also made butter, ice cream, and malted milk at its production facilities in New York and Chicago. Regional sales representatives marketed these commodities nationwide.

Borden held a dominant place in the condensed milk trade. But condensed milk manufacture and distribution was small potatoes. True, American soldiers during the Spanish-American war became acquainted with the substance. The war's four-month duration was far too short to provide more than a casual taste. More typically, condensed milk served two main populations. Individuals isolated from a regular fluid milk supply constituted the first. The long shelf life of condensed milk, coupled with its storage at room temperature, made it perfect for miners and explorers and an able substitute for infants when fluid milk was lacking. Southerners—particularly in New Orleans and Texas—constituted the second consumer group. The high heat and the lack of adequate refrigeration made fluid milk storage difficult.

But it was fluid milk, not condensed milk, that made Borden into a juggernaut. Although it also distributed the product to a few smaller cities, Borden ruled the market in the nation's two largest metropolitan areas, New York and Chicago. These localized fluid milk distribution operations were extensive ventures. Borden provided milk to about a quarter of New York's 5 million citizens and a somewhat larger percentage to Chicago's 2.5 million residents. In both cities, the company's thousands of drivers acted as salesmen, each with a designated delivery area. There they would recruit customers for regular milk delivery, receiving commissions for the number of Borden-owned bottles they dispensed. The milk came daily from dairymen in the greater metropolitan areas. Each milk producer had its own contract with Borden to produce a certain quantity of milk at a price fixed by Borden. The milk would arrive via railroad or wagon to Borden-owned storage facilities and then to Borden-owned milk plants in Borden-owned cans. Borden employees would pasteurize the milk, bottle it, and provide it to its drivers for delivery. A smaller quantity of the fluid substance delivered directly to the cities would go to manufacture condensed milk. Evaporated with sugar added and canned in Borden-owned facilities, this milk product remained stable for long periods and could be shipped anywhere. Borden's condenseries—the place where condensed milk was made—in each of the two cities were the company's secondary markets as fluid milk took precedence. Whatever milk was not needed for delivery went to the condensery. Depending on the season, cows produce differentially, with winter showing considerable decline. Borden always contracted for at least enough milk to fulfill its fluid commitments and then used the surplus for its urban condensing operations.

For a turn-of-the-century corporation, Borden was extraordinarily up to date. It labored to control the entire fluid milk manufacturing and distribution process. It had central milk plants near its producers, where milk could be cooled, pasteurized, and stored. It transported that milk to condensing or bottling plants, depending on the milk's final disposition. Its drivers took it from there. The very model of vertical and horizontal integration, Borden maintained that structure even as milk demand accelerated and the company had to sign agreements with producers more distant from its base of operations. There it contracted with the appropriate railroads, making sure to get low rates for volume, based on the regular transportation from one of its farmland milk plants to a condensery or a city bottling plant.

As impressive as this highly articulated system was, several factors undercut Borden's attempt to control its milk operations. Most revolved around capitalistic imperatives, but New York's and Chicago's treatment of fluid milk as if it were a public utility also contributed. Adulteration was not the central issue in the 1910s. That battle had taken place earlier. Milk supply and price emerged as areas of potential governmental intervention and regulation about the time of World War I. To its partisans, milk was as necessary to the body politic as electric lighting, the telephone, and a public water supply. Governments rarely wanted to own fluid milk operations and undercut private and corporate ownership. What they wanted was a constant, appropriate price at a reasonable cost. For their part, city and state governments were under strong pressure to step in and keep prices down and supplies up. This was, after all, the era in which states and the federal government busted trusts and used the bully pulpit to cause changes in policy. In the case of milk, aggressive jawboning and special or standing committees to investigate matters were the methods that cities and states used to rein in corporate entities. No matter the conclusions of these investigative bodies, these pronouncements and institutional annoyances that offered them circumscribed the industry and lessened the freedom in which Borden operated.[1]

Borden, of course, far preferred laissez-faire capitalism. It wanted the freedom to pursue its own destiny and to let the immutable laws of supply and demand have their day. It sought to keep milk, labor, and other costs at a minimum and prices as high as possible to derive the greatest return on its considerable investment in wagons, facilities, and equipment. Like other turn of the century corporations, Borden wanted to wring every possible penny out of its industry. The company was also inherently ambitious. It vigorously sought to gain greater shares of the New York and Chicago markets. Both cities' continually growing populations offered Borden opportunities to expand business and hike profits. The nature of the fluid milk market was immediate, daily, and irresistible. Expansion in a world of classical economics dictated a means to increase supply. As the cities grew and as their metropolitan areas became more densely settled—and as Borden successfully captured some of its competitors' customers—the corporation reached further to find enough milk and milk producers to fulfill the continually relentless demand. For example, in 1913 the company relied on milk from 250,000 cows owned by 12,000 farmers located in 11 states. Its 7,000 employees drove 4,000 horses and 2,500 vehicles to deliver the product.[2]

Borden's imperialist ambitions ran into what was then thought to be the foe of corporate efficiency, the curse of collectivism. Individual contracts with providers, workmen, or salesmen provided the corporation the ability to cut out inadequate performers or to ruthlessly adjust their operations to reflect current demand. To the corporation, collectivism—a group acting as if it were one—had several critical flaws. First, it protected the weakest members with poorest performance by making it difficult to eliminate them from the operation or process. That was the very definition of inefficiency as it undermined productivity. Second, it enabled the group to exert a certain leverage over the corporation. By binding together, the collective could withhold any critical function or service essential to the manufactory. It could force the corporation to pay what it deemed usurious rates and therefore reduce the moneys going to stockholders or into corporate coffers for further expansion.

Borden was not immune to collective intrigue. Ironically, its first major faceoff was with what had historically been identified as America's yeomanry, its strong-willed, independent farmers. Trouble for Borden began in Chicago. Area dairymen, beset by the low prices offered per hundred pounds of milk in their individual contracts, formed themselves into a collective, the Milk Producers Association, to stand up to the milk distributors. In its 1913 annual meeting, the group threatened a "milk famine" strike that would deprive the entire city of the precious fluid. Its members strenuously objected to an ordinance, sponsored by the Chicago Board of Health, that required straining milk at the dairy as a prelude to bringing the raw milk to a distributor-owned milk plant for pasteurization. Maintaining certain health and safety standards at dairies and performing an additional technical operation before having the milk enter the hands of dealers increased production costs dramatically. To these producers, these straining costs were rightly those of dealer/distributors, not dairymen. Claiming the board was "working for Gail Borden, the milk trust owner," they threatened to "reorganize the Boston Tea Party."[3] Citing health concerns, the state quickly entered the fray. It upheld pasteurization and sanitary methods, including milk strained at the dairy. Illinois women's clubs also backed enhanced sanitary measures at dairies and offered their solution. They favored the producers' demand that distributors double the price they paid producers for milk to defray the enhanced production cost "as simple justice," but maintained that the dealers should absorb the costs and not pass them on to a beleaguered public. Distributors remained unmoved.

A year later, dairymen took a different approach to gain their increase. The group contended that distributors constituted a trust and that Borden set the price for all Chicago cartel members. The producers called on the federal government to investigate the alleged combine as violating the Sherman Antitrust Act. Distributors countered by claiming that the Milk Producers Association itself was an illegal combination in violation of the Sherman Act, acting monopolistically by cornering the milk production market. Federal agents investigated both possibilities, but also entertained a third, that the whole milk price raising matter was a scam, a conspiracy between the producers and distributors to enhance their profits at the expense of the citizenry.[4]

The Justice Department filed no formal charges, but antitrust investigations would be renewed every time there was a milk supply stoppage. Lack of indictments and absence of strikes did not signify labor peace. Borden in particular tried to vanquish its irritants. For example, it retaliated against some of its accusers by purposely closing a milk plant that had received the milk from a particularly belligerent segment of the producers' group. Unless the dairymen immediately found another outlet, their milk spoiled.[5]

World War I emphasized condensed milk and changed the dairy industry equation. Europe had always served its population's fluid milk needs. With the war, that no longer became possible. Dairy farms often sat idle as their farmers became soldiers and joined the battle. Milk cows were butchered, their meat used to fuel armies and prevent starvation. But even if there had been dairy cows enough for European needs, the food required constant refrigeration and the cows daily milking. Evaporated and condensed milk, the former differing primarily from the latter by not adding sugar, proved perfect war rations for soldiers as well as nonbelligerents. With Europe a vast battlefield and farmers comprising a considerable portion of the military, a vibrant new market and potential profit center opened for Borden and other American canned milk companies. In 1914 American condenseries shipped three million pounds of their product abroad. At the end of hostilities, exports of American condensed milk had exploded to more than two billion pounds a year, a nearly 700-fold increase. During the war, two-thirds of the Chicago area fluid milk purchased by Borden went to processing condensed milk.[6]

Mobilizing production to meet the wartime condensed milk need required Borden and the other manufacturers to consider how to achieve that grand goal. Making condensed milk in small portions is a fairly easy process but to manufacture it to feed entire armies and civilian populations was something very different. In its simplest terms, condensing milk is evaporated under pressure until roughly 60 percent of the water is gone. Sugar is then added to preserve the mix. Condensing tens of thousands of pounds of milk daily in a single facility introduced complexity of scale. Industrial condensed milk production became an assembly line process, similar in spirit and thrust to those that manufactured the Ford Model T. Large plants, regularly more than 100 feet long, contained massive coal-fired boilers to provide the heat necessary for evaporation. Huge pressure chambers and vacuum pans permitted workmen to evaporate large quantities of milk at a single time. Single-purpose machines guided can manufacture. Assembled in precise order, the machines took sheet steel and then slit, rolled, tinned, or soldered cans to ship the final product. Automated machines on conveyor belts poured the appropriate amount of milk into each of twenty-four vessels. The filled cans were carried to the next station where lids were placed, crimped and soldered. Pallets of the full, completed cans then traveled to pressurized heating chambers to sterilize the condensed milk. After the cans cooled, machines printed and affixed the appropriate labels.

While the milk was being condensed, filled, and sterilized, an exacting series of chemical measurements was underway. A random organism or bacteria could doom the entire batch. Milk improperly cooled at the dairy produced an unfortunate taste in milk processed this way. Sometimes batches could be saved. Milk chemists were well versed in the mysteries of their art. But a dangerous or off-flavored shipment of poorly prepared milk was nearly as deadly to the firm as it was to consumers. Condensed milk marketing depended on reputation. Consumers in America and Europe demanded that the product be as promised. Any single aberration sullied its reputation and undermined that faith.[7]

Creating what was in essence a giant new export industry required capital but also two other things: facilities and raw materials. Condensed milk operations in wartime took over every available creamery and cheese factory, even those dilapidated and aged, and retrofitted them as condenseries. These out-of-date facilities had depended on area milk supplies, which now could be expanded and redirected to condensing. Much of the World War I condensery expansion by Borden and the other big condensed milk manufacturers (Carnation and Pet[8]) took place in the Old Northwest, but some distance from the region's major metropolitan areas. These small farm communities and cities truly became America's dairyland as condensed milk manufacture dominated these regions during the war. Land prices were dear in that area so Borden also looked beyond it to other small rural dairy communities. Its condensed milk empire extended west as the company gobbled up failing small condenseries in British Columbia, Logan, Utah, and Modesto, California. At its height during the war, Borden ran forty condensing plants.[9]

The company's attempt to increase the condensed milk supply led it in another direction. It attempted to create prime dairy country and therefore the places where the firm could secure enough milk for industrial condensing. In addition to converting or acquiring condenseries in established dairying areas where fluid milk was often spoken for or otherwise limited, the company manufactured and cultivated new dairylands that could supply fluid milk to new condensing facilities. Fort Scott, Kansas, proved its most ambitious effort.

In the early twentieth century, many rural communities were on the make. Threatened by declining economic bases, with adult children moving to cities for increased opportunity, these communities struggled to find some way to be viable, and even to persist. Often railroad lines helped. They understood that their economic well-being depended on have freight to carry, so they actively sought to improve the economic character of areas bordering their lines. Entrepreneurs in these small places also tried to ensure that no business opportunity was missed. Town elders visited places that had become somewhat successful to determine their secret, and scoured the newspapers in hopes of finding some economic activity to strengthen their community. At Fort Scott, both were in order. Fields of wheat and other grains surrounded this southeastern Kansas town of about 10,000. Its depleted soil yielded fewer bushels each year. Fort Scott was stock country: its animals went to market as meat. The only dairy animals in a twenty mile radius supplied milk for their owners' use and that of Fort Scott residents. With Kansas City only 80 miles away, the Frisco Railroad (the St. Louis–San Francisco Railway) tried to interest local farmers in fluid milk dairying to service that large city, but to no avail. The railroad even employed a dairy agent to show wheat farmers how to convert to dairying. Few took him up on the offer.[10]

This desperate community had for decades spent countless dollars hoping to find some industrial concern that would guarantee its survival. Its leaders—generally members of its Chamber of Commerce—now recognized that the condensery boom necessitated by the war might well serve its purpose. They coveted the success of the Illinois-Wisconsin dairy industry, visited Borden condenseries in Monroe, Wisconsin, and Dixon, Illinois, and contacted the company to explore the economic miracles that dairying could bring.[11] Buoyed that the company responded but aware of the limited dairying near Fort Scott, the city's commercial leaders enumerated by name all persons located near Fort Scott engaged in any aspect of dairying and purchased two purebred bulls to improve and increase the area's dairy stock.

Whether because of the community's initiative and persistence or just serendipity, Borden did a detailed study of what the place had to offer. Land there was dirt cheap, unlike Wisconsin and Illinois. As a contemporary put it, Fort Scott offered Borden "the very great economic advantage of cheap lands to compete with the high priced lands in all developed dairy districts." The corporation also recognized that the soil was limestone abundant, an important ingredient for growing pasture grasses and silage. In November 1916, J. G. Waters, who oversaw the condenseries west of Chicago, hopped the outbound Frisco to check out Borden's western milk plants. He stopped at Fort Scott on the way.[12]

There Waters outlined Borden's predicament. "In selecting a site . . . we, of course, investigate technical matters." Fort Scott has "water, drainage, railroad facilities, a proper site, good roads, soil for dairy crops," all "essential to factory operation." But "we cannot operate a condensary without milk." The "big question is 'will farmers here supply milk enough?' If they agree to do this we'll talk to you: if they do not agree to do it we cannot talk to you." He further outlined the company's terms. Unlike other business concerns that Fort Scott had dealt with requiring special economic perks, Borden asked for "no bonus. We have no stock for sale." The company drills "its own well and we buy our own sites." All Borden asked, according to Waters, "is that the community get behind us . . . and produce the milk." We "would not invest $150,000 to $200,000 in a factory . . . unless we can have some sort of assurance that the first day we are open for business we will receive the minimum requirement of raw material—milk." Farmers must answer the milk question "before there is any opportunity to secure a condensery and make this a permanent dairy community."[13]

Those were the company's nonnegotiable terms. Even then, it did not promise a condensery. Waters would report the outcome of his investigation to Borden in New York for the final decision. In effect, Borden was requiring Fort Scott residents to buy a pig in a poke. It asked them to abandon their livelihoods as grain and stock farmers—as questionable an undertaking as that had become—to plunge into dairy farming. Within four days of Waters's visit, area farmers were asked to fill out and sign the following document: "Providing that the Borden Condensed Milk Company builds a Condensary at Fort Scott, I promise to deliver or have delivered to them on September 1st, 1917" a specific number "of pounds of milk." Farmers were to testify to the number of cows they had at present. They also were to pledge that they would keep at least a certain number of cows in the future to produce the milk they promised. They then had to give their address, note the miles distant from Fort Scott and finally to sign the document.[14]

The de facto contract Borden demanded of dairymen and its acknowledgment that a condensery's success rested on milk producers' participation exposed a fundamental dichotomy whenever rural cities or towns sought to bring industrial agriculture into a region. The idea that Fort Scott or any other rural place was a community with the farmers and others in the surrounding areas only went so far. City leaders, however defined, pitched and promised to seduce industries to come to their place and transform its future. But that transformation depended on others located miles distant. Each farmer evaluated his/her course of action not by an appeal to community spirit but by whether the civic leaders' plan made good hard economic sense. These goals—the city's and the farmers'—frequently conflicted. Sometimes they required a group to shuck generations-long practices to embrace what could very well be a pipedream foisted upon them by city folk. To be sure, there were common points of unity. Small city and town banks tended to be run by people with direct ties to farming. Certainly the persons called upon to adopt the promoted agricultural practice relied on the banks and often the railroads. That is a very different thing, however, than to say that their interests were identical. Merging the divergent agendas of the two groups sometimes seemed an intractable problem.

For the next couple of weeks, Chamber of Commerce members went near and far—stopping at every conceivable place within a hundred miles of the city in every direction—urging farmers to get on board, for their own sake and for the future of Fort Scott. The chamber also prevailed upon the state agricultural college to draft some circulars to help teach long-standing grain farmers the particulars of successful dairymen. The chamber got some pushback from the proud Kansans, who bristled at being held hostage by Borden. "If the Bordens don't want to come here," noted H. Brown, an irate farmer, "let's get cheese factories. If not this then a first class creamery." The Frisco Railway took a more conciliatory approach. It sent its dairyman to reside in Fort Scott for a time, to circulate among the farmers and teach them their new business of dairying. To up the number of quality cows in the immediate area, the chamber purchased a railroad car full of premium dairy cows bred at Borden facilities, to sell to farmers at cost.[15]

The number of farmers willing to sign the document and the number of dairy cattle within 100 miles of Fort Scott proved more than adequate. After another visit by Waters and Borden Vice President A. P. Johnson and three days of negotiations with the Chamber of Commerce, Borden agreed to build the plant. It then sent Waters again, this time with the company's chief engineer, who was to supervise construction. Borden brought one of its dairy experts to Fort Scott to teach the new dairy farmers how to run, manage, and plan a dairy; how to grow alfalfa and make corn ensilage; and, most importantly to Borden, how to run sanitary operations. Clean, good sweet milk made the best condensed milk.[16]

Six railroad cars bearing condensery machines made at a Pennsylvania steel mill came to the new facility on a railroad spur from the Frisco line built by Borden. It was followed over the months by many, many more. When the condensery opened its doors in mid April, 1918, America had already been at war for a year. A great deal of the area around Fort Scott had dairy cattle. The local Fort Scott newspaper contended that it seemed possible "to ship milk to the condensery here from points more than a hundred miles distant." Borden championed the Fort Scott endeavor "as an entirely new field" for the company. It had no condenseries in "Iowa, Nebraska, Colorado, Texas, Oklahoma . . . or Missouri." The company carried its expansionist ideology to its natural conclusion. The new plant would stand as the central facility. Around it would spring "other condenseries. Any community may get in on the benefits of an unlimited dairy market by intelligently developing its dairy possibilities." Waters simply stated the obvious: "We are building the Fort Scott plant for the purposes of developing the dairy industry in Kansas." Farmers would adopt dairying and the areas in Kansas that develop "fastest and insure the greatest volume will receive preference" when locating additional condenseries. Fort Scott promised to be to Borden what Dearborn was to Henry Ford and the automobile industry.[17]

Opening the Fort Scott facility took Borden seven months longer than it had planned. The delay in construction led to a delay in production, which exacerbated the condensed milk–fluid milk dilemma once America entered the war. Yet it was not balancing the domestic fluid market and the European export market that drew the company's interest. It was the initial surge given to American-produced condensed milk by the collapse of the European milk industry that proved most illustrative to the corporation. As Borden scurried to meet as much of the skyrocketing stable milk demand as it could, the company gained a substantial taste for and exposure to export markets. Borden recognized a new vista. Condensed milk was the perfect agricultural product for worldwide distribution. It could be manufactured in Chicago or any place else and sold everywhere.

Although Borden redirected 66 percent of its midwestern milk production and 55 percent of its New York purchase to the export trade, it was not nearly enough to saturate demand. That wartime strategy of seeking as much of the highly profitable export market initially worked for Borden but it had consequences. Coupled with Chicago's and New York's population growth, wartime demand for condensed and fluid milk severely challenged Borden's metropolitan suppliers. They expanded herd sizes to increase the milk and the company reached even further from its bases of operations to secure more of the fluid substance. A 1913 law ending milk tariffs against Canada led the company to recruit that country's dairymen for the New York City market and to establish a condensery near Montreal.[18] Adding new dairymen to the mix enabled Borden to expand its business but it also placed the firm's fluid milk operations in a vulnerable position. With supply lines so attenuated, the margin for error so slim and the market so immediate, any fluid milk supply disruption could be catastrophic. In short, now more than ever before, what the company feared most was collectivism.

In 1916 the Chicago Producers' Association took advantage of the dealers' exposure. Declaring "this is a fight to the finish," they sought to create a subsidiary to distribute milk themselves and thus replace and ruin established distributors. Lacking the equipment and distribution channels necessary to carry out this project made it a hollow boast. At the same time, they accused Borden and non-Association dairymen of signing agreements that would circumvent the Association's leverage with the dealers. In early April, association members dumped their milk in roadside ditches or fed it to hogs rather than send it to the dealers who refused to pay higher rates. They also picketed bottling plants and blocked highways so nonstriking milk producers could not bring milk to the dealers. At milk plants, deliverymen were egged, their full wagons dumped. Armed deputy sheriffs tried to stave off the mob. An estimated million quarts of milk were destroyed on the first day. Dealers declared that they had milk enough on hand to last two days but feared that they would only be able to meet fifty percent of demand thereafter.

Borden diverted much of the available milk used for the condensed trade to the fluid market but even then it closed three local plants on the strike's second day.[19] The city's health commissioner declared that if the strike were not resolved in a few days, milk distribution would be restricted to families with babies. He also called for arbitration, arguing not to "forget . . . the baby" in the dispute. Dealers asked for increased police protection to protect farmers who ignored the strike and deliverymen within the city. They also suggested using condensed milk in lieu of the fresh product. The Milk Producers Association had its corresponding claims, maintaining that every day its numbers grew as more dairymen joined the strike.

By the fourth day, some of the smaller dealers buckled and agreed to pay an extra twenty-two cents per hundredweight for fluid milk. Borden was having none of that. Claiming it had to shutter four of its plants and was losing in excess of $5,000 daily, it sought injunctive relief, asking a federal judge to bar the producers' group from interfering with the collection or delivery of milk. Other area dealers acted without Borden. Under the auspices of the health commissioner acting as mediator—yet another manifestation of viewing milk as a public utility—the dealers met with the producers' association to hammer out a deal, the final terms of which signaled a capitulation. Not only did the distributers pay the same twenty-two-cent increase, but they also pledged not to pass their costs onto consumers. Milk prices would remain the same as dealers' profits shrunk.[20]

Or so it seemed. Borden finally surrendered but within two weeks it violated its pledge, raising the cost of a quart of milk by a penny for consumers, an increase of 12.5 percent. Other milk distributors immediately followed. The health commissioner conferred with the dealers, hoping to convince them to relent. He was greeted by a counterproposal from one of the city's smaller dealers, who urged formation of a huge corporation of producers, transporters, distributors, drivers, and consumers to set uniform prices at every operational stage and thus serve the public interest. The lack of autonomy in the proposition appealed to almost no one. The Chicago Producers Association rejected it most emphatically. It formed its own corporation, a corporation of dairymen, to be capitalized at $500,000, to manufacture and distribute milk products. Promising milk at six cents a quart, the new cooperative would put Borden and the other distributors out of business.[21]

The whole chaotic mess drew the attention of the assistant secretary of the US Department of Agriculture. He came to Chicago and spent weeks investigating the strike and its aftermath. Dealers continued to argue that the producers by acting collectively had engaged in illegal restraint of trade and used the across-the-board, twenty-two-cent price hike as evidence. Borden went further. It abrogated another of the agreements it made with producers, refusing to negotiate rates for more than a month at a time and argued that it needed that flexibility to keep consumer prices stable.[22]

Before any of these issues were resolved, New York City emerged as Borden's new flashpoint. There the pattern was similar. Borden was whipsawed between several competing entities. The first volley came from Borden employees, its driver-salesmen. They threatened to strike for higher wages and used the possibility of affiliating with the American Federation of Labor or the International Brotherhood of Teamsters as their cudgel. Borden relented, gave the drivers a higher wage, and labor peace ensued.[23] Milk producers were not so easily placated. A group very much like the Chicago Producers Association, the Dairymen's League, agitated in New York City for higher prices for hundred pounds of milk. Rather than let the situation devolve as Chicago's had, Commissioner John J. Dillon proposed that the entire milk supply be placed under state supervision and control. Borden and the other firms argued that the "law of supply and demand" governed milk prices and any artificial attempt at control was destined to fail.[24]

Things came to a head October 1, 1916. Contracts expired on that date and League members, who controlled roughly 80 percent of the supply, demanded a 45-cent increase. Distributors offered 20 cents. The League demanded to bargain as if it were a single entity and the dealers balked, taking out ads in the city's papers contending just how expensive milk distribution was. In the face of this public relations campaign, Commissioner

Dillon had a truly novel suggestion. He urged the dealers to turn over their plants and distribution lines to the League, to see if it could deliver milk cheaper than the dealers. The dealers adamantly refused. The League initially proposed to distribute milk directly from farms but that proposition ran afoul of the health code, which required pasteurization and certain sanitary measures. To curry consumer favor, the League argued that its requested increase would not lead to a per bottle price increase. Distributors could pay it out of their already obscene profits.[25]

In this heated environment, New York City distributors arranged to bring in additional milk from other states and Canada. League dairymen stopped all wagons approaching the city, took off milk barrels and poured the contents on the road. Pickets were everywhere. Night riders raided the cooling houses of unaffiliated farmers and spilled the milk. Sheriffs swore in special deputies and violence broke out. Distributors demanded that the state attorney general declare the League a trust and disband it. Only about 10 percent of the usual amount of milk reached the city the first day. The city made preparations to have the distributors supply hospitals and well-baby stations before serving private customers. The mayor met with the distributors, who sent a letter to the Governor demanding that the League be disbanded. The League, for its part, maintained that its boycott was gaining strength. It cited a growing number of new members and claimed that they came from the new areas where the distributors found their milk. They also gained the support of the National Housewives' League. Five hundred mothers, many with infants in arms, stormed two health department milk stations in Harlem.[26]

Negotiations continued for nearly a week, generally with the mayor or district attorney as mediator. Both sides offered poison pill compromises that were rejected. The Governor tried to pressure both sides into an agreement but to no avail. After a week many of the smaller dealers caved to the League's demands. Borden did not. It bought several large parcels in the metropolitan area and set about establishing dairies there to provide the company the necessary milk. The League countered by planning to build large pasteurizing plants to distribute the milk itself, promising to undercut the cost of dealer-distributed milk.[27]

Two weeks into the strike, confusion ensued. The League's president announced agreement with Borden and the other large manufacturers, and directed dairymen to ship milk to those concerns. Its board of directors asserted that the president had no such power to proclaim the strike ended and prohibited delivery. Producers followed the executive committee at which time Borden withdrew its willingness to settle. The company then announced the terms to which it had agreed. The settlement would last only until January 1, 1917. At that time, a nine-member committee would set "a fair price for both producer and distributor." The mayor, governor, merchants' association, commissioner of health, and Chamber of Commerce would each make an appointment to the committee. The distributors would appoint two as would the League.[28]

Those terms were not what the League had struck for. A spokesman put it succinctly: "There is not enough money in Wall Street to make me sign such a contract." If "these people want milk they must agree to every one of our demands." Recognition that the distributors would be signing the contract with the League, not individual dairymen, was paramount. The League's executive committee then ousted its president. Negotiations resumed immediately after the ouster. After a marathon session, the distributors and the League agreed to the League's price hike but with individual contracts and limited the agreement to only three months. The subsequent three-month period would be determined by a committee of two distributors, two league representatives and a fifth member agreeable to all. The dealers also received the League's blessing to raise milk prices by a penny a quart. During the nearly two-week strike, over 11 million quarts of fluid milk never reached market.[29]

New York City distributors raised the price of all milk products one cent within days after signing the agreement.[30] Successes of the dairy combines in New York City and Chicago emboldened dairymen in other places to copy their methods. Boston-area milk producers and those in Virginia and Maryland, just to name a few, banded together for collective action against milk companies. Progress towards this end seemed so encouraging that the Chicago producers took it upon themselves to call a nationwide meeting of milk producers. The call proclaimed that the "production and distribution of whole milk is undergoing a remarkable transformation, and milk producers in areas close to large cities must either reorganize their methods . . . or go out of business." They must "take it upon themselves" to establish "fair and equitable methods for the collective sale of milk."[31]

The national meeting generated predictable results. Producers could only "smash the milk trust" by acting collectively and marketing their own milk. To that end they created the National Federation of Milk Producers to unite the nation's dairymen as if "from one factory," arguing that this organization would eliminate strikes and provide milk at the cheapest price nationally. Organization began almost immediately. Local and statewide chapters were designated and officers elected.[32]

The Chicago group figured prominently in the new organization. To show its mettle, the Windy City association quickly reopened its pricing demands, this time demanding over a dollar per hundred pounds of milk increase. Distributors strenuously objected, claiming the higher rate would necessitate 12 or 13 cents per quart, about a 25 percent boost. Borden finally accepted the hike and immediately made preparations to sell 13 cent milks in a few months when the new agreement kicked in. The other distributors followed suit.[33]

Six months later, the Chicago association demanded yet another nearly dollar increase from the distributors. That gambit ran the producers afoul of Herbert Hoover, who as head of the US Food Administration (USFA) was charged with ensuring the nation's food needs during the war. The Chicago group deliberately dismissed Hoover's request that they delay any increase until his team could investigate the producer-dealer nexus. Their rejection contrasted starkly with the condensed milk manufacturers, who at Hoover's behest voluntarily turned supervision of their businesses and price setting to the USFA. Despite the exploding market in the United States and in Europe, they promised that for the war's duration they would sell their wares to the public at the same price that the Federal Trade Commission determined they should offer the Army and Navy.[34]

The Chicago producers' anticipated price hike angered Hoover because it would be the prelude to higher military and public costs. His ire proved only one of their problems. In late September 1917, the Cook County State's Attorney, aided by the assistant attorneys general of Illinois and Wisconsin, raided the offices of the Chicago headquarters of the Chicago Milk Producers Association, secured their records, and began a price-fixing, antitrust, conspiracy, bribery, and influence-peddling investigation. The grand jury returned indictments for all association officers. Prosecution was delayed by the war and persisted into late 1919. Distributors and milk producers squabbled and occasionally squared off as the case wound its way through the courts. Tensions simmered but did not flair as the wartime food administrator for Illinois mediated emergent disputes.[35]

The war dampened passions in New York but did not eliminate them. To be sure, the Dairymen's League cited rising production costs to demand a significant price per hundred pound increase. Borden and the other distributors reluctantly agreed and passed on the increases to consumers. Both sides hurled Milk Trust charges at each other. City and state officials marked out ground upon which both sides could compromise. Hoover's intervention further calmed the waters. The milk antagonists accepted Hoover's oversight and regulation of prices and methods for the war's duration. That was not the case with Borden's workers, however. Its wagon driver-salesmen struck for higher wages and union representation. The company yielded to the demands and the militant International Brotherhood of Teamsters represented the drivers who opted to join a union. Higher wage costs and fluid milk prices led the company to close several pasteurizing and distribution plants and scale back hours at others. Essential workers balked at these rollbacks and struck, demanding restoration of salaries and an increase to a nine-hour day.[36]

This continual back and forth with producers, workers, and union organizers—both in the company's headquarters city and in Chicago—led Borden to reevaluate its business. It had become increasingly complex. Introduction of the Teamsters into the operation stretched the company and established another threat to profitability in the form of inefficiency. The fluid milk imbroglios contrasted dramatically with Borden's condensed milk operations. Its condensing centers were booming, dynamic. They also had labor peace. That facet of the industry was not directly located in giant urban areas yet it had national and international scope. Fluid milk distribution was local, wracked by unrest, and subject to the capricious nature of the producers as well as the public and its representatives. It was, by its very definition, highly unstable. Fluid milk had immediacy and a daily imperative. Everything each day was in effect a crisis. Producers needed to produce, plants needed to pasteurize, and deliverymen needed to deliver. Any single failure on any given day doomed that day's milk, which undermined confidence and profitability.

The unpredictability of fluid milk became increasingly impressed on Borden. So too did the taint, the poison, the chaos of operating in large metropolitan areas. In these venues, collectivism was rampant. When coupled with fluid milk's inexorable immediacy, collectivism was especially threatening. It seemed a proverbial sword of Damocles hanging precar-

iously over the head of the corporation. That was intolerable and it demanded action. To isolate the consistently profitable condensing from the
turbulent and dramatically dangerous fluid milk situation, the company
restructured itself. It spun off fluid milk as the Borden Farm Products
Company, while maintaining its condenseries under the old name, Borden
Condensed Milk Company. The condensed milk company owned all the
Farm Products Company stock.[37]

Condensed milk exports enabled Borden to expand its practices, hori-
zons, and profitability. Two factors limited Borden's ability to reap even
greater profits from that sector. First, German U-boats made transporting
condensed milk across the ocean dicey. Some product was lost while other
shipments were delayed. A more immediate constraint stemmed from the
firm's agreement with Hoover. Rising prices for wartime milk had so raised
Borden's costs that the price it pledged Hoover seemed insufficient to yield
the projected profits that were guaranteed as part of the deal. The company
faced two choices: produce less condensed milk and close plants or raise
prices beyond what it had promised. It discarded the first as "unpatriotic"
and chose the second of the two options. Even thus limited, Borden's condensed properties generated considerable moneys. Its fluid milk operations
barely broke even during the years that Americans fought abroad as condensed profits blossomed.[38]

Condensed milk's tremendous wartime boom in both production and
profit attracted notice. Recurring fights in cities between farmers, dealers,
consumers, and governments had kept the industry in the news. Greed,
prices, strikes, and stoppages had drawn public ire. It was not surprising,
then, that the explosive new growth of the canned milk industry became
one of many sectors to attract the attention of the Federal Trade Commission (FTC). Charged by the United States Senate to investigate war
profiteering, this watchdog group concentrated on those industries fundamental to the war's pursuit. Its overarching conclusion was dismal: many
of the "great industries vital to the nation's war program" used the war as
an opportunity to secure "unfair and extortionate profits." The commission
recognized that some profitability was merited and stemmed from "war
pressure for heavy production." The rest came from "inordinate greed and
barefaced fraud."

The canned milk industry appeared before the FTC, claiming that it
belonged to the first group, not the second. Borden went unquoted in the

report but one of its competitors explained how enormous profits resulted from conscientiously serving national goals. Demand by the military and among European combatants and their peoples became so overwhelming that the firms struggled "with great difficulty" to keep the price "from going much higher." All price hikes were made, according to the industry spokesman, "for self-protection" and "to keep orders from piling up on us beyond our capacity to fill." On a few occasions, the condensed milk trade took drastic action and refused orders it knew it could not meet. The FTC apparently accepted that explanation and dropped any further canned milk inquiry.[39]

Freed from the trade commission's scrutiny, the condensed milk industry was left to contemplate what had been unimaginable prior to 1914. It immediately recognized that during the war it had left tremendous profits on the table. It had lacked capacity to make as much money at it could have had it been able to provide all the condensed milk that it could have sold. What the war demonstrated to the American condensing industry was fundamental. The explosive possibilities of the wartime export trade suggested to Borden and the others that their goals had been shortsighted. For decades, they had primarily targeted the domestic market. They had ignored the rest of the globe. There was an entire world out there from which to profit. While the situation in Europe was temporary, a wartime aberration, the lessons learned about the possibilities of export trade were not. The war showed them conclusively that demand was essentially elastic, the consequence of vision, ambition, and daring. It could be discovered, uncovered, and perhaps even created. The old model of demand being fixed and supply being adjustable now came face to face with a newly revealed, nonclassical model. Here demand was as huge as you could imagine it or actively create it.

Borden positioned itself to capitalize on this exciting new economic metric by closing outdated condensing plants and planning to bring new units online. The significant population growth of Lansing, Michigan, increased demand for fluid milk and placed whole milk in direct competition with the 35-year-old Borden condensery there. The company opted to close the condensery and to leave the state's static milk industry. Conversely, it prepared to erect a new facility in Belvidere, Illinois, right in the heart of midwestern milk country. It also explored adding a second condensery in Kansas. Although quite distant from Fort Scott—the dairy area that

Borden seeded, nurtured, and established as the hub of its Kansas properties—the anticipated new plant reaffirmed Borden's commitment to further
developing the state's dairying.[40]

Before Borden had a chance to significantly revitalize its condensing
properties, problems exploded in New York City, the corporation's headquarters. Fluid milk's prewar labor troubles quickly resurfaced. Hostilities
among producers, workers, and unions in New York flared to new heights.[41]
Consumers also got involved. Right after yet another fluid milk price increase, an exposé in New York's *Evening World* charged that Borden reaped
outlandish profits from its condensed milk export trade at the expense of
the city's working men and women. Investigated and written by Sophie
Irene Loeb, a reporter whose previous career included advocating for the
rights of women and children, the paper's argument revolved around two
main points. First, that the insatiable demand of the export trade created
an artificial milk shortage and forced up fluid milk rates. If the milk supply
to the city increased as it did in the summer, Borden simply diverted the
excess to its condenseries, which kept fluid milk prices intolerably inflated
year-round at the same artificial rate.

Loeb's second point was more complicated. *The Evening World* maintained that Borden and a few smaller concerns siphoned off the nearby
New York fluid milk to make the highly profitable condensed milk for export. That manipulation of the market meant that milk shipped to New
York for home and store delivery had to come from further away—neighboring states and Canada. Borden then foisted the increased transportation
costs off on New Yorkers in the form of even higher milk prices. New Yorkers, then, unwittingly propped up corporate profits, which the newspaper
considered unconscionably high. Looking back at Borden finances, it de-
duced that the condensing company had offered a dividend to stockholders
of at least 8 percent for seventeen of the last twenty years. Coupled with the
idea that a certain percentage of profits was plowed back into the business
to expand operation or to undertake new product line, the *Evening World*
charged Borden with unethical if not monopolistic behavior.

There was one additional charge. The newspaper claimed that the Borden Condensed Milk Company always paid dividends but the Borden Farm
Products Company never had. The only way that could conceivably occur,
the paper concluded, was for the fluid milk group's earnings to be funneled
into the condensed milk coffers. Borden refuted that charge, claiming that

the high wage it was forced to pay its drivers was the culprit. The public dismissed that contention and called for action. Governor Al Smith's Fair Milk Price Committee announced state and city investigations into the fluid milk brouhaha. The city's Board of Aldermen voted 54 to 4 to take over milk delivery, no doubt a threatening proposition given the New York City machine's long dominance of city politics.[42] The city's civic and charitable organizations promised to boycott milk unless prices were lowered, a move the city's health commissioner opposed as detrimental to health.

Arthur Williams, who during the war had headed the federal Food Administration Board in New York State, called for a nonpartisan group similar to the Public Service Commission to regulate fluid milk sales and pricing. Several legislators introduced measures to establish fluid milk as a public utility, with the state maintaining the distribution network and a state board setting prices all the way through consumption. The "policy of fixing food prices under police power" drew the *Evening World*'s emphatic endorsement. Borden heartily backed state involvement because it promised to stabilize on a profitable footing an otherwise chaotic industry. In fact, Patrick D. Fox, vice president of Borden Farm Products, outlined a meticulous plan to bring what he saw as sanity to an otherwise confused process. It was an update of a proposal offered a year earlier by Charles A. Weiant, president of Borden Farm Products.[43] Noting that his two-year-old company had issued no dividends despite gross annual sales of $50 million, Fox pushed for a new corporation, the stock in which would be distributed to reflect each dealer's assets as determined by the city's Board of Appraisers. This entity would limit itself to fluid milk, cheese, butter, and cream to "conserve the fresh milk products so as to conserve the fresh milk supply adjacent to New York for the fresh milk requirements of the population." Directors would manage the corporation and be comprised of dealers, producers, and consumers. The corporation was to guarantee one-half cent profit for each quart of milk delivered, and to file annual reports to ensure transparency.

The plan would go into effect when a second major producer joined Borden in signing on to the venture. Through this corporation the fluid milk industry in the city would have "sound capitalization, limited profits, full publicity, [and] participation of producers and consumers" among the directors. It could enact essential cost cutting measures "through limitation" of "duplicated investment and service." Fox argued the corporation would eliminate "unnecessary points of operation," require deposits on milk bottles to insure "cooperation of the consumer" in their return, increase wagon size to decrease the number of delivery wagons and drivers, and increase the amount of fluid milk at each milk plant to reduce labor costs. A 20-year Borden employee who would become company president the next year, Fox emphasized that his plan would "conserve . . . individual initiative." By opting for corporate ownership rather than municipal or state operation, "the skill of men long experienced in the conduct of a specialized business" could be retained.[44]

Such a plan would have provided Borden a resolution to almost every problem that fluid milk dealers had faced. It granted the company an almost controlling stake in the venture, since Borden remained the largest New York City distributor and would thus receive the largest amount of stock. It kept the new entity out of the much more lucrative condensed milk trade. It focused local dairymen on fluid milk. The new corporation mandated profitability, a profitability fixed no matter the cost of milk or labor. Economies of scale would enable the new entity to secure tin for its transport cans. Bottle deposits would rid the corporation of replacement costs and increasing wagon size and production per plant would reduce labor and equipment costs.

Despite the self-serving nature of the proposal, it was Borden's first publicly offered holistic conception of the fluid milk trade. That was an important intellectual Rubicon to cross. Because corporate success relied on the presence and performance of others, a corporate strategy that aimed for total victory and vanquishing one's enemies made little business sense. Profitability stemmed from consistency and reliability. Peace through participation was a primary means to achieve predictability.

2 | BECOMING MODERN
Borden Pioneers the Union of Advertising,
Marketing, and Manufacturing

With the war in Europe over, Borden seized the opportunity to continue the journey it initially began when it moved fluid milk to a separate corporation. Borden changed its corporate name to rebrand itself as a modern, progressive food production corporation, one fit for the new post-war economy. Claiming that the old name was "restrictive," that it implied "the manufacture of only one product," the company jettisoned the condensed from its name and became the Borden Company. The new name reaffirmed that it manufactured a series of products and planned to expand even more. It was about the Borden of the future, not the past. The new Borden was to be nimble, flexible. The company's adoption of a series of modern business practices furthered the thrust towards modernity. It issued financial reports and annual reports to stockholders and changed its reporting period to the calendar year to conform to the schedule of other corporations using modern methods. The calendar change enabled the firm to coincide with the accounting protocols then used for federal and state statistical reports.[1] What it would do in the next several years is to redesign its institutions and conventions to match its new, modernist ethos.

Among the first things that the Borden Company did was to extend the lesson it learned about demand and market creation in the First World War. This time it focused on the domestic trade. Over 4.7 million doughboys served in the year and a half that the United States was a combatant. They ate Army rations and drank condensed milk. No doubt many gained a taste for that convenient shelf-stable beverage. They brought that taste home to their families and friends. These were people that Borden and the other condensed milk companies had not traditionally served. They were young, most under thirty years of age. This was a vibrant, thriving potential market that had not yet been tapped. Borden aggressively entered it through what had become the conventional way to engage an audience: advertising.

Several themes predominated, all of which sought to capitalize on the American soldier's wartime experience. Under the heading, "serving the cause," an ad recounted how in the Civil War, the Spanish-American War, and World War I, Borden "provided America's Armies [*sic*] with milk—pure, safe and dependable." For those sixty years, the ad continued, "the American consumer, like the American soldier," found Borden to "provide milk in practical, convenient forms" with the "highest possible purity and quality."

Harkening to the past was no accident. Borden attempted to establish a venerable reputation for reliability, a reputation that placed their products in the first rank of consumer goods. Another advertisement addressed the company's long-standing commitment to the public weal. Arguing that now state and municipal laws dictate product safety, the ad maintained that it was Gail Borden, the company's founder, who "over 60 years ago formulated the sanitary code which served as a basis for all later protective regulations." Yet another ad stressed how Borden was founded upon democratic precepts—"pure milk the year round and pure milk for all—this was the ideal upon which Gail Borden" started the company 60 years ago. Now, Borden "nation-wide in its scope, faithfully lives up to the same ideal." The "name 'Borden' on the container is an absolute assurance of purity and quality." Borden, according to a final example, has taken milk and milk products and been "developing them, perfecting them and placing them within the reach of every one since 1857."[2]

The patriotic tone of the advertising strategy played on how Borden condensed milk personified the American experience. Its primary goal was to expand domestic demand for condensed milk, something that seemed possible after the war. It soon became imperative.

Borden (and condensed milk generally) banked on the world's great need for milk and increase in cargo space after the hostilities to further fuel the export industry. The industry blithely produced the commodity at near wartime rates. The war's aftermath was not as planned. Condensers anticipated the return of standing armies to their homesteads and the subsequent restoration of European dairy industries, but they did not suspect that the transformation would happen so swiftly. Even if that had not been the case, the export trade was in trouble. Foreign countries erected import restrictions to rebuild their own dairy industries. Credit in Europe was exceedingly tight. A tiny number of importers could finance and take the size of shipments that American manufacturers had contemplated. What had been highly profitable condensing operations faced a new economic reality as European demand cascaded downward and crashed. American exports were sliced by far more than half, to about 968 million pounds. The industry's failure to anticipate the sudden drop led in 1920 to a stockpile of hundreds of millions of pounds of the product. A stellar earner had now became a huge economic drain.[3]

At the milk section of the 1919 annual meeting of the National Canners Association, discussion focused on how to get on top of the export situation. Sentiment gathered for "a master export company," which included all condensers. That company would allocate "orders that come in from foreign territory, and send the milk out under one brand." Arguing that no single entity had the resources to scour the world, develop connections and push its milk, the proposal favored the master corporation as "the best way to go after the foreign trade." While the group failed to create such an entity, Borden's two largest condensed milk rivals, Carnation and Helvetia (renamed Pet in 1923), took advantage of a 1918 act permitting combinations for export purposes, and formed the American Milk Products Corporation to jointly market their milk overseas.[4] Pooling resources as a means of drawing down the stockpile of condensed milk did not find favor with Borden, which sought to establish its own export connections. But the company increasingly recognized that at least in Europe, American condensed milk products were going to run up against indigenous production. Condenseries in Europe had few shipping charges and lower wages. Borden concentrated instead on Asia, Mexico, and Africa, less wealthy areas but ones lacking highly developed milk industries. Heavily populated island nations, such as Singapore, Cuba, and the Philippines, or areas with little developed farmland, like Thailand, offered better export opportunities.[5] At the same time it pursued overseas markets, Borden saw the advantage of concentrating on the new, growing domestic market. Selling things in the United States is something that the firm knew. It had been the vast part of its condensing business for nearly sixty years.

Borden's immediate postwar advertising certainly had a theme. The company was as American as mom, apple pie, and the girl next door. Touting its Americanness in an era of foreign wars and Bolshevism proved an effective strategy, but not one likely to expand markedly its penetration within the American marketplace. As product sat in warehouses, Borden contemplated how it might transform the domestic market. What it settled on was a profound intellectual sea change, a fundamental reconception of the place of advertising in the corporation. Borden determined, then embraced, a new form of advertising and new advertising goals. It started with the merchant and the consumer. Rather than design signage, cutouts, and window trims extolling the time-honored virtues of its product—quality—[6] the new advertising department at Borden divided the nation into sections and sent young men into the field to talk with dealers and consumers in their areas. Their research uncovered what consumers and dealers liked about the product, what could be improved, and why other products were superior. Put simply, the young men in the field wanted to know what dealers and consumers wanted Borden's condensed milk to be. Armed with that knowledge, this advertising sales force sent the information back to corporate headquarters and the advertising sales manager, a new title befitting the now fundamental inseparability of the two functions. There and in conjunction with other executives something different than plotting a sales campaign and designing ads to appeal to consumers was taking place, something more raw and visceral. They literally changed the nature of production to ensure that the finished product reflected what their public wanted.

Claiming that there were three legs to the advertising dollar, A. H. Deute, who came to Borden to establish the advertising sales department after working at a small Oregon candy company, maintained that "unless production was properly connected with the advertising, the chances of making advertising pay were slim." He recounted a story of a small manufactory. The owner showed his workers what consumers and dealers wanted in the product and asked them if they could achieve those goals. Everything, he claimed, was in these workers' hands. "They could make or break the advertising and selling and . . . they could make or break their own futures." He capitalized on their esprit de corps and pride to motivate his workers to manufacture a product that conformed to public and dealer aspirations. From then on, Deute continued, "every advertisement, before it appeared," was shown to the department heads and workers. "Man after man was asked if he could do his part to make the merchandise come up to those claims." And, Deute, who later became regarded as the "oracle of the selling world," concluded, "man after man gravely stated that he could."[7]

Borden's new understanding of advertising's centrality to everything the company did reflected the partnership and interdependence that characterized the emerging business model. It was not just old wine in a new bottle. It was a basically different way of seeing the operation and of conducting all aspects of the business. It redefined options and strategy for corporate or product expansion or contraction. It held the potential to redefine products themselves. It redefined factory management. It redefined the corporation. It redefined demand as malleable, plastic, the fulfillment of consumer desires. Most of all, it redefined profitability.

Among the first things that Borden did was secure a whole series of new trademarks for its condensed milk to signify its new advertising approach. The corporation even named these new images and what they portrayed. There was Darling, a smiling picture of a child; Sunny Side, with cows; Tip Top, with a top hat; a Magnolia, the tree; Pioneer, with a man in coonskin; Silver cow, self-explanatory; Winner, a jockey on a race horse; Bell, a dinner bell; and a Rose, which by any other name would smell as sweet. Taken as a whole, only the pioneer image was backward looking. The others spoke to a bright future, one fueled by Borden condensed milk and its cows.[8]

These trademarks appeared on cans and in ads. A quick examination of some of the new advertising campaigns inaugurated by Borden suggests how these new trademarks combined with the new advertising ethos— and market research—to foster a new vision of Borden products. In the case of its fluid milk trade, Borden ads featured its "Prize Rhyme" contest. Open to any child under the age of fourteen, the company published in the local papers winning entries with the child's name and address. It then piggybacked a pitch for the product based on the piece of doggerel. For example, Rose Bloch, 340 West 26th St., New York City, won the $5 prize for "Children with faces round and pink, Every morning have Borden milk to drink." The text claimed that "the surest way to make your cheeks glow with the that pinkness of good health" was to drink "plenty of Borden's rich wholesome milk." The beverage makes "your blood richer and redder than any other food." Having "your kiddies drink a quart of Borden milk every day" gives "them the proper chance to grow and thrive."[9]

Having authentic neighborhood children testify, not to the quality of milk, but to its benefits, spoke directly to their mothers, those largely responsible for ensuring the health and growth of children and the community to which those mothers belonged. As another ad stated, "children all over the country—thousands and thousands of them—owe their vigorous and robust health" to Borden's condensed milk, the key to good health, good development, and especially good motherhood.[10]

Borden ran best-baby competitions in each state. Winners received $500 and had their pictures and addresses posted in large quarter-page advertisements prominently displayed in the state's newspapers. Competing against "many thousands of fine, healthy children," the mother of each winner claimed that the child was "raised on" Borden condensed milk. It makes them "strong, robust, sturdy children—perfect physically and keen and active mentality [*sic*]." In addition to targeting mothers of small children, Borden also went after mothers of babies. The ads reminded readers that "mother's milk is best for baby, of course. But if for any reason you cannot nurse your baby, don't take risks with him." Borden condensed "has been standard baby food for sixty-four years."[11]

Clearly, Borden salesmen-advertisers had reported that their market was mothers with small children, anxious to raise them properly during these troubled times. It was on mothers that the company fashioned its advertisements, and in a particular way. It did not so much discuss safety or purity, and never price. It aimed only at helping each mother raise her child as perfectly as possible. Its Cream Pitcher advertisements also aimed at mothers but as home economists. Borden's Recipe Club seemed to cater to a subset of women, part of the new middle class. Reportedly over 25,000 strong, these women shared recipes "for the pleasure and profit of the rest of the members." Cream of Watercress Soup, Spanish Crabmeat in Ramekins, Tamale Chicken Pie, Lobster Patty, and Cromesquis were typical recipes shared by club members. These women were the vanguard. "In these scientific days the thoughtful housewife gives careful consideration to the planning of nourishing meals." Use of Borden products guaranteed "healthful food can be made the most delicious in the world."[12]

Vignettes—narrative aphorisms—engaged readers as they recounted unusual situations that yielded the fundamental "truth" of the relationship of Borden's condensed milk to impeccable motherhood. One such story, nearly a thousand words, appeared under the headline "the Indian mothers . . . marveled at such a baby as mine," and detailed how an American missionary couple went to South Dakota and raised their "husky little chap, sturdy and full of life" among "the grandchildren and great-grandchildren of old Sitting Bull." On the reservation, "Indian babies are not healthy because they are usually not properly fed."

The missionary couple's son had not always been so vibrant. In fact, the ad went on, he was born premature. His mother had undergone a Caesarian, and the child's "chance of life had been slim." The reservation's Indian mothers kindly visited the missionary house daily to help. They watched attentively as the tiny white baby was fed Borden's condensed milk and quickly started to become a chubby, happy, heathy, vigorous child.

Some months later when the boy was flourishing, the missionary was called to the home of an Indian family where the mother had just given birth. Much to his surprise, he saw the new mother open a can of Borden condensed and bottle-feed the baby. By feeding her sickly baby condensed milk and having her Indian compatriots watch him grow large, the missionary mother had taught "the Indian mothers to give their babies" Borden. The ad then reminded readers that Borden condensed was "more used than all other infant foods together." It not only "brought vigorous health to a million babies," it also "helps to build bone and muscle for growing children." If "you cannot nurse your baby, start him on . . . [Borden's] and keep him on" it. "You can buy it anywhere," the ad concluded, "whether you live on an Indian Reservation or in the heart of the metropolis."[13]

There were other similarly engaging true-to-life scenarios in this genre of Borden ads. Borden also managed to ingeniously design a domestic aid that would help the company gain a foothold in the Middle East. In 1919 Congress established a corporation to "fight against malnutrition, starvation, and disease among children of the Near East countries." Named Near East Relief, Borden used the organization in an ad to talk about the death and deprivation that agency hoped to counter. Borden's plea to the public was that of Christian charity; it urged consumers to assist those unfortunates by purchasing "one, two, or three cans—as many as possible" of Borden's and donating it to the group to ease Middle Eastern suffering. Borden got more than increased sales, however. Near East Relief's associate director wrote baldly, "I wish there was some way that the people of the United States could learn of the great value of condensed milk," a statement that Borden liberally used in its advertisements. After making all sorts of claims about the efficacy of the product, Borden reminded the audience that its condensed milk was the only milk substance "produced especially for the feeding of children." It was "exceptionally rich in energy producing foods," of "special quality," scientifically formulated and "carefully blended to give the right butterfat content." Its "vitamins . . . aid in promoting and regulating growth." The same factors that make Borden "the best condensed milk for use with your own children" also makes it "the most useful and valuable brand you can give to the Near East Relief."[14]

Borden's print advertising budget exploded after the war. In 1890 it was $513.75. In 1922 it was a few dollars short of $1 million. And the mix changed. In 1918, 70 percent of the company's advertising was in magazines. In 1922 over 50 percent was newspaper ads. Ads in the newspapers spoke more directly and more immediately to the group upon which Borden now concentrated its marketing—mothers, especially those with babies and children still at home. America in the 1920s remained a nation of immigrants, a factor that Borden acutely recognized. It designed ads with text in Lithuanian, Russian, Polish, and Spanish, to name a few. Equally significant, Borden planned out its advertising campaigns a season at a time. By planning ahead, Borden made campaigns roll out with military precision. Ad followed ad at the perfectly appropriate time to fortify and build to a crescendo. But the company purposely refused to look too far into the future. In that fashion, it could respond seamlessly to whatever intelligence its salesmen/advertisers found on their trips through their territories. Messages and means could be changed, updated, or confirmed with only a slight time lag. These techniques were "an important factor" in producing "top-notch sales."[15]

Print ads were not the sole means by which Borden carried its message to mothers. Put another way, the company's sales/market research generated other means to demonstrate that Borden did and had become what its customers had wanted it to do and become. It established a welfare department and negotiated with school systems in poor areas to provide milk daily to indigent students at a pittance. It even purchased time on the new medium of the radio to offer advice on the "feeding of infants in the summer." Not ignoring print, the welfare department composed a book "for mothers" on "the care and feeding of babies," which it distributed free of charge. In blistering heat, a shelf-stable milk product—Borden condensed milk—no doubt proved a benefit. The Borden Nutrition Department hired several young women "nutritionists" to travel across the United States to talk to women and children about Borden's centrality to proper development and growth. The goal was to put a "cow in the pantry" in every case, but venues differed considerably. In one instance, a Borden representative met Jewish high school and college girls for a "health talk." A "round table talk" at the Women's Guild of the Episcopal Church focused on nutrition for the entire family. Each woman was "to bring her own problems for discussion." Borden's expert then gave her "advice gained through her wide experience in special nutrition work."

Listening to the nutritional problems of mothers was certainly a passive market research form. Sometimes Borden nutritionists tackled problems head on after learning of concerns firsthand. That often stood as a consequence of Borden's technique of embedding its nutritionists within communities for several months. There they could engage in a wide variety of activities, becoming almost big sisters to the mothers, young women, and children they met. Cooking classes, child-rearing meetings, and general nutrition talks each brought the Borden brand to the fore. These nutritionists also attempted to modify behavior. For instance, Borden sent Miss Dorothy Randolph to Scranton, Pennsylvania, for five months in late 1922. A graduate of Columbia University who had majored in nutrition, she held meetings three days a week in the city newspaper's offices "to advise . . . without charge" women seeking to learn about baby and child-rearing. She also gave numerous talks on a wide variety of health- and nutrition-related topics. She talked to several Girl Scout troops, including a troop of African American scouts, about the "rules of the game," the eight health rules promulgated by the Child Health Organization of America. With two representatives of the Tuberculosis Society, Randolph opened a nutrition clinic where twenty-five severely underweight children came daily for a mid-morning glass of Borden condensed milk. Once a week she held a nutrition class for the group. There she established an honor roll for children ages six to twelve who would swear off coffee and tea and substitute milk for a month. Those successfully completing the challenge got their name listed prominently on the wall the first of each month. Coffee or tea had been the beverage of choice for 16 of the 22 students.[16] While in town Ms. Randolph also talked to Scranton Bolt and Nut Works, the Scranton Anthracite Bridge Company, and the "Americanization group" of Jewish immigrant women. She shared her knowledge and then led "a round table discussion of health matters." It was at the round table portion of the proceedings where Randolph learned of the women's fears, concerns, and expectations. Many of the revelations certainly found their way into shaping Borden advertisements.[17]

Deute and Frank G. Cover, Borden personnel department head, took every opportunity to spread the gospel. They talked at men's clubs, business organizations, and advertising workshops. They gave addresses across the United States. Most of the talks focused on what was happening in modern business, with Borden as the example. Deute's stock slogan was "he profits most who serves the best," a shorthand way of saying that market research was the key to creating a much desired product and high profitability. But they often celebrated modern business in novel ways. When finding out he was sharing the platform with an Episcopal bishop, Deute scraped his talk entitled "keep your sunny side up" and instead talked about how the Bible was the manual for modern business. Follow its lessons as Borden did and your organization would surely be successful.[18]

Deute's sermon was delivered years before Bruce Barton published the two greatest sellers—to that point—in American history, the Bible excepted. *The Man Nobody Knows* and *The Book Nobody Knows*, published in 1925 and 1926 respectively, told how the life of Jesus and the Bible were guides to commercial and corporate success in the modern world. Not surprisingly, Barton, like Deute, earned his living in advertising.[19]

None of this new advertising blitz was idle chatter. It all drove to the same end—to establish a significantly larger domestic market. That was to be Borden's corporate panacea. It had made inroads in the Far East and Mexico and other places, but the domestic market was to be the company's salvation. When the new advertising was first implemented, it promised to extricate Borden from the condensed milk surplus. No doubt the folly of overproduction and the subsequent economic hardship had awakened the company to the virtue of fiscal responsibility based on meticulous, broad-range planning. It was evident in Borden's dealings with the New York area Dairymen's League. Ironically, it would be the first step in transforming that contentious relationship.

Like Borden, the League found itself in quite a postwar quandary. It too suffered from the war. In order to fuel the tremendous increase in milk production necessitated by World War I, dairymen doubled and tripled the size of their herds. When the war concluded, they were stuck with an overabundance of milk-producing cows. Fluid milk cannot be stored in that form for long. Borden disingenuously urged the League to bring the milk to market where the laws of supply and demand would operate and reduce the consumer price. New York City's milk commissioner followed up with an offer "to start an educational campaign in the poorer sections of the city to encourage more consumption of milk, with the idea of preventing waste of surplus milk" due to the collapse of the export market. The League dismissed both recommendations out of hand: selling milk below cost was economic folly and would lead to bankruptcy. It demanded that Borden buy the fluid in the same quantities it had done during the war and at close to the same war-inflated prices. The League even passed a resolution asking Hoover to take over management of Borden to compel it to purchase the milk according to its dictates. Borden's huge condensed milk overage led it to refuse to buy anywhere close to its wartime milk allocation. The company even shuttered several condenseries that were closer to New York City. A series of strikes, disputes, riots and government interventions followed but resolved nothing. The matter came to a head when Borden and other manufacturers said that as of October 1, 1920, they would buy no more milk for condensing purposes until they had drawn down the surplus. League members could slaughter their cows or find ways to handle surplus milk. They chose the latter.[20]

Incorporating themselves as the Dairymen's League Cooperative Association, Inc., the group aimed to create a web of association-owned milk plants to make cheese, butter, powdered milk, and other shelf-stable, milk-based goods. The association claimed that it would provide for each of its members "an assured market for his milk, stability of business, and a more equitable distribution of proceeds." The United States Department of Agriculture (USDA) favored this sort of stabilization, especially after the war, and provided loans to cooperatives to help translate that vision into reality.

The association quickly lined up potential production facilities throughout the greater New York milkshed. A key requirement was established in the interests of the association as a whole: farmers must purchase the milk plants and bear much of their operating cost.[21] The Borden Farm Products Company greeted this development in a way that reflected the company's newly modernist ethos. Even as it fought tooth and nail with the milk producers, it recognized them in some sense as partners. League members ultimately provided the raw material on which Borden depended. Stability, consistency, and reliability were all factors that enhanced Borden's operation. The cooperative's entry into the manufacturing business did just that.

It made League members' operations adjustable, acutely susceptible to demand. They would always cater to their largest customers, members of the milk industry. When fluid milk was needed, the cooperative could decrease its processes that preserved milk. With overproduction of milk, it could be turned into product to be sold at a later date or to a different market.

Borden no doubt had thought about establishing a new relationship with producers for some time. In fact, Weiant, its president and the incoming president of the International Milk Dealers Association, witnessed the organization's previous president argue almost the exact same thing. John Le Feber, a prominent Milwaukee dealer, urged dealers in December 1918 to "bring more power, influence, and success" to the fluid milk dilemma by simply ending that dilemma. He urged cooperation with "every component element that can be used to our mutual advantage." Acknowledging that this was no easy task, he singled out producers as the first target for the dealers. No one could deny them the right to a "just profit" nor should producers "begrudge the dealer his meagre profit." We, he continued, "must do everything in our power to help one another." The dealer and the producer, Le Feber concluded, "are necessary to each other and must work together, or success is impossible."[22]

Borden's recognition of its interdependence with the Dairymen's League quickly acquired a tangible manifestation when the Association hired Weiant, who had in August 1919 left Borden Farm Products Company to run the group's newly acquired milk plants. Weiant's selection as assistant general manager proved interesting. He had pushed hard the idea of producer-dealer interdependence soon after passage of a New York statute granting protection from monopoly prosecutions for cooperative farm organizations. Weiant lost favor within Borden as he urged the company to absorb some of the costs associated with the dealer-producer nexus and not pass them on to consumers.

The Cooperative Association actively worked to increase its flexibility and to prepare for expanded production. Old facilities were adapted to new purposes. Dated or abandoned dairy stations near railroad lines as well as pasteurization plants became cheese factories or powdered milk manufactories. The co-op's thirteen milk factories in June 1920 had become twenty-seven by November. Ten of these had been Borden rural receiving stations. Rather than shut and discard them, it sold the properties to the Cooperative. By the end of the year, one of the smaller distributors of milk in New York City sold its entire operation to the the co-op. Rather than undertake house-to-house delivery and therefore compete directly with the distributors, it sold its milk in 40-quart cans to hotels, restaurants, and delicatessens.[23]

The Cooperative Association quickly ran into problems with some League members and unaffiliated dairymen. With the large condensed milk manufacturers sitting out until the condensed surplus had dissipated, much of the huge overage of fluid milk remained. While the Cooperative scurried to build, acquire, and/or convert milk-modifying units to handle massive amounts of unspoken-for fluid milk, that took some time. Meanwhile, there was significantly more product than required. The co-op was faced with the responsibility—and it was not necessarily a welcome one—of setting the price at which it would purchase milk from its members for the co-op to render and sell. Oversupply drove the price down, some producers howled, and investigations and lawsuits claiming restraint of trade and price-fixing ensued.[24]

In its first end-of-the-year annual report to stockholders, Borden had a more optimistic assessment. The cooperative brought cost and quantity dependability to the fluid milk trade as well as a modicum of profitability. Condensed milk proved especially profitable. Refusal to purchase milk for the last quarter of the year meant that all sales of the product were from the wartime stockpile. The corporation had accrued relatively few new costs. The result was that even as gross sales significantly dropped, the company offered investors a full 8 percent dividend.[25]

Borden also built a new corporate headquarters, one befitting a successful modern major corporation. For decades, Borden had been located in a ten-story building designed in the style of Louis Sullivan, at 110 Hudson Street in lower Manhattan. Its offices were clustered among produce companies as well as a few other agriculturally based businesses. Built in 1904, that building reflected the old Borden. The company even left its subsidiary, Borden Farm Products, housed there, while the new, dynamic corporate entity relocated to its new facility. The Borden Company set up shop at a most fitting place—at Madison Avenue and the northwest corner of 45th Street, right in the midst of the exploding advertising industry. The twenty-three story building, marked by intricate brickwork, was reminiscent of a Gothic cathedral, as its separate wings culminated in a single grand tower. Costing about $4 million, the elegant design befitted its impressive address. It resided across the street from what in two years would become the palatial Roosevelt Hotel, an epic of luxury and grandeur.[26]

Borden's celebratory building reflected the corporation's modernist bent. It confirmed that advertising was essential to market creation and the corporation's success. The first annual meeting of the Borden Company's managers, supervisors, and executives—from New York, New Jersey, Pennsylvania, and Connecticut—also shouted out modernity but in a different fashion. The gathering had much in common with the retreats of the 21st century. Its members were ensconced in a locale—in this case, rustic Binghamton, New York—for two days. Informal meals bracketed four specific sessions. Conversation and discussion characterized the meeting, not addresses by leadership. At this conference, "every phase of the dairy industry and the problems of milk distribution will be up for discussion." Two templates dominated the conversations. Changes had to enhance standardization and utilize "every development of science" as its participants tried to "still further perfect" Borden operations.[27]

Both science and standardization were clear paeans to modernity's central notions. So too was the idea of partnership as replacing the deliberately hierarchical administrative artifices of the past. The new Borden had shunned its 19th century origins as antiquated relics. It now embarked on new challenges and in new ways.

The company's modernist creed did not end squabbling around the fluid milk trade. In fact, its expansive elegance might have exacerbated it. While Borden increasingly accepted its milk producer partners, it chafed at unions, especially among its drivers. The cost of living sank in the years immediately after the war. Borden and other dealers lowered their fluid milk prices to prewar levels. In January 1921, its union drivers went to arbitration, seeking a $10-a-week raise. Citing the reduced cost of living, the federal judge serving as arbiter turned them down. That ended the matter until October. This time the union did not seek arbitration but chose to strike. Dealers offered a decrease in base salary, which they said was consistent with the further decline in fluid milk prices. The drivers demanded a $5 weekly raise. Although not welcomed by the twelve thousand drivers, federal mediators tried to broker a resolution, but to no avail. The strike was not just about money, however. It was about power and control. The union demanded that milk wagon drivers become a closed shop—that only union drivers would work delivering milk. Borden and some of the other firms attempted to end the strike by hiring nonunion drivers and by demanding that the police protect these men and their wagons. But night deliveries made protection hard, and violence ensued. Dealers responded by changing delivery hours to after daylight so that perpetrators could be identified and arrested. They sought and received a writ barring intimidation by the milk drivers' union. Distributors also placed milk wagons on busy streets and encouraged residents to come and pick up their milk rather than get it delivered. Violence became so widespread that the city replaced its traffic and school guards with women police reservists to free up additional male officers to better control the uprisings. The union alleged police brutality and promised to take motion pictures of future incidents.[28]

By mid-December, police escorts of nonunion drivers were working. Nearly 80 percent of milk deliveries were restored. At that time, Board of Aldermen President, Fiorello LaGuardia, asked the dealers if they would rehire strikers to fill their ranks. Borden president Patrick Fox refused any blanket rehire and stood as the staunchest anti-union advocate. He told of demands that were relentless. First came a closed shop and next would come "the demand that all equipment and supplies necessary to the business bear the union label." That meant that Borden could only buy necessary commodities from companies that had already undergone unionization, which wastefully caused higher prices and rewarded inefficiencies. Fox maintained the demands went further. He was "informed that the union leader would advise our purchasing agent where to secure supplies." Such conditions could not be negotiated or compromised, he argued. "To temporize . . . is but to invite a later outbreak. Such an issue must be settled some time. We know of no better time than the present," said Fox, who had begun his career as a Borden wagon deliveryman more than two decades earlier. Referring to the union and the strike, he maintained that Borden was engaged in "one of many battles between democracy and a vicious autocracy." "Corporate management [is] always answerable to law and public opinion," he concluded. It "will serve the [public] better and longer than Soviet rule."[29]

The strike petered out in the bitter cold of January 1922. Borden hired back some strikers but kept all workers who did not strike or who were hired during the strike. While other dealers considered how to mollify workers and tamp down unionism, Borden acted decisively to secure a stable labor force. Making it abundantly clear that its problem was with the unions, not its workers, Borden created an employees' representation plan, which it extended to all the company's employees. The strike was a revelation to Borden. According to Frank Cover, the company's personnel director, it cost Borden "millions of dollars to learn that close personal contact and cooperation is necessary between employe [*sic*] and employer for the greatest degree of productivity." Thus educated, the company sought "a business relationship upon an equitable and durable basis," characterized by "mutual advantage" and "mutual understanding." With some input from company workers, the new plan established a framework that would give "them a voice in the management of the business." It provided "for creation, development, and execution of all policies affecting the personal welfare of the employes [*sic*]" and granted them "an equal voice in the development of operating policies." In a strategy that would become much more famous as the Hawthorne experiment a decade later and Total Quality Management a half century after that, the plan hinged on discussion through "channels," essentially representatives from each subunit. Workers would understand "the intimate problems of management" and management would "recognize the sentiment of the men in relation to policies affecting them." Both employees and the company see the plan as "democratic, inclusive of mutual advantages, and a medium through which mutual understanding and agreement may always be reached." They all would partner in the successful Borden enterprise. This sense of inclusion would "establish a harmonious feeling throughout the plants."

But the chain for discussion and for reporting was tortuous, both up and down the line. Workers in each type of activity elected representatives and discussed matters, conditions, and situations with them. Representatives made recommendations to the appropriate superintendent. If action was necessary and he disagreed or was powerless to undertake the correction, the recommendation went to the district manager, then the personnel department, then the district committee, and finally to the company president, whose decision was final. Information from the president trickled back down through the same byzantine network.[30]

Though complicated, this labor-centric formulation held much in common with Borden's new advertising scheme initiated a year or so earlier. At their heart was the idea that the consumer in advertising and the worker in labor were both essential parts of progress and profits. Both advertising and labor relations depended on listening, observing, and asking, an

acknowledgment that the opinions of both consumers and workers mattered since they helped determine profitability. Their thoughts, wishes,
and objectives deserved respect because they were partners, instrumental
to Borden's corporate success.

Borden's personnel management mechanisms aimed at restoring and
retaining labor peace, but the Teamsters Union wasn't buying it. It decried
the Borden discussion-based employee representation system as a "lollypop
union," a "company union scheme designed to crush organized labor." They
asked union members not to participate but virtually all of Borden's drivers
did. The four thousand drivers that Borden and the others did not rehire
because they took part in the strike also left the union. They decertified
the Teamsters, who they blamed for the catastrophic strike, and sought to
become a corporate body in the State of New York. Calling themselves the
Independent Milk Workers' Union, they claimed a very different purpose
than the Teamsters. The new union's stated objectives listed in the articles
of incorporation were "to foster co-operation with employers in order that
the lot of employees may be bettered, the businesses of the employers improved and the public benefited generally." To further distance itself from
the Teamsters, its elected officials were to carry on all labor negotiations
for the group.[31]

These were noble goals, of course. The corporate objectives outlined the
terms of a partnership rather than groups in perpetual opposition. Borden drivers did not opt for the new organization, however. In addition to
remaining loyal to the employee representation plan, Borden drivers also
formed their own group. Named the Mutual Aid Association of the Employes [sic] of Bordon's Farm Products Co., Inc., members pooled dues to
protect employees and families during illnesses or injury and "to promote a
social and fraternal spirit among the members." On its first anniversary, the
association held a grand dinner for members and their wives. Seventeen
hundred "members and friends of the Borden family" attended. Its guests
of honor were the officers of the Borden Co. and the Borden Farm Products
Co. Each corporate notable praised "employer-employee cooperation" and
saluted the workers as the backbone of the Borden effort.[32]

A few months later, Fox complimented one delivery crew for the increased productivity of its members. He asked them to draw up a new
salary scale that rewarded their prowess. *Collier's Weekly* reported that
the workmen had embraced Borden's corporate capitalistic ethos: they had

truly bought in. What emerged was a progressive wage rate. The "slower man can make forty dollars a week, while the hustler can earn as high as seventy-five." To Collier's, these drivers were "not lost in a big corporate organization: they are running it."[33]

Within a month of announcing its new employee relations apparatus, Borden squared the circle. Again acting alone, it shunned the institutions that had enabled dealer/distributors to act in unison—in fact, it resigned membership in the dealers' group—to make a unilateral agreement to purchase all its milk in the greater New York area from the recently created Dairymen's cooperative.[34] Borden notified the cooperative of its new policy through Weiant, who had recently completed a total overhaul of the cooperative's business and record-keeping systems. No other New York dealer followed Borden's lead. The company's stunning decision to buy only from the co-op in the New York market was the corporate culmination of the modernist view that Borden had been working through in the previous several years. It was a powerful, definitive acknowledgment that amity and comity were critical to maximum, sustainable profitability. Harmony and tranquility were not feelings. They made good, hard-headed business sense that showed on the bottom line. Maximum profitability over time, not maximum immediate profits derived from cutthroat competition, served corporations and their stockholders. Supply certainty, wage certainty, labor certainty, and market creation and intelligence marked the essence of a streamlined, forward-thinking corporation. Put more baldly, corporations did not deliver milk, make condensed milk, manufacture cars, or make telephones. All successful modern corporations made one thing and one thing only. They made profits, the greatest sustainable profits. Costs did not matter. Nor did prices. The only thing that counted was profits, not onetime profits but ongoing profitability. Modern corporations were successful when they determined the road to making the greatest consistent profits. Borden learned during the time of First World War and its aftermath. Its new policies—the institutional mechanism and procedures that it enacted—reflected that education.

Borden reexamined its Chicago fluid milk dealings in the wake of its arrangement with the Dairymen's cooperative in New York. In short order it recognized that they were impossibly outdated and promised to remain so. There Borden had to deal with independent, ornery, capricious milk producers, individual entities upon which one could not absolutely rely.

To mitigate the impact on the rest of the organization, Borden broke its Chicago-based fluid milk away from the Borden Farm Products Co. It created the Borden Farm Products Co. of Illinois. It isolated that fluid milk concern, which continued to be subject to work stoppages and violent interactions among participants,[35] from the rest of the of the Borden enterprise. The new Borden Company was ready for business.

The bold Fort Scott experiment was among the ventures that Borden watched with keen interest. Its original plans to have the condensery be the seed that would create a great new dairy region that Borden could milk failed to account for a most common human foible—greed. Even before the facility opened in April 1918, land speculators gobbled up a significant part of the area and raised land values sky-high. With Borden placing a condensery there and publicly announcing plans to make the area a new Illinois/Wisconsin, residents owning land jacked up prices while outsiders purchased adjacent land as an investment. Holding the land meant that until speculators got their price wheat and other grains prevailed. These investors refused to purchase cows or dairy equipment. They did not establish milking barns or grow alfalfa for winter feeding. Lack of dairy improvements, combined with the artificially high land values, made it even more difficult to attract dairy farmers, who would need funds enough to purchase and improve the land before they could benefit from the condensery.[36]

The war worsened the financial constraints. Fewer farmers worked the land and even fewer had the funds to buy into the Fort Scott environs. The weather also proved a problem. A fine rock road was one of the factors that led Borden to place the condensery at Fort Scott. The road held up in all sorts of weather, but the smaller roads feeding into it did not. Incessant rain and winter snows made them impassable, reducing the milk carried to the condensery. The daily number of pounds of milk promised to Borden totaled over 40,000. The company claimed it took from 20,000 to 25,000 to make the plant a going concern. The new building could serve more than six times that amount, but the day it opened a meagre 7,500 pounds of milk was brought by about 75 farmers. Two weeks later the number of dairy farmers and quantity of milk merely doubled.[37]

While the paucity of product no doubt disappointed Borden, especially in the second half of 1918 when demand for condensed milk reached astronomical heights, it remained committed to making the experiment a success. One of its most useful and sustained initiatives was to offer an artificially high price for milk delivered to the condensery. This tactic helped Borden attract distant dairymen, including some who served the far Kansas City market, as well seducing those reticent others to take up the challenge. Premium prices for raw milk would be a recurring strategy as the company struggled to convert southeastern Kansas into the "Wisconsin of the West" with Fort Scott as its hub.[38]

Chambers of commerce and other small town and progressive organizations chipped in during the years right after the war. In the case of Fort Scott, its Chamber took out ads in *Hoard's Dairyman* appealing for "dairymen to come here with their herds and locate." When the ads did not get the anticipated response, the group sponsored a trip to the Wisconsin and Illinois dairylands. The Chamber hoped to entice farmers to move their operations to Fort Scott, but they also opened the trip to local Kansas farmers interested in becoming part of the dairy industry. The group returned with twelve boxcars of purebred dairy cattle. This trip, which had been essentially a short course in dairy agriculture, led the Chamber to create a four-day dairy show in the city. Its purpose was clear. It would educate area farmers and dairymen about dairy farming, introduce first-rate breeding lines into the county, and promote the extensive new possibilities of Borden's condensery. An Amish group from Minnesota relocating in Fort Scott was among its notable successes. Chambers of commerce and others fostered dairying in Kansas by purchasing prime Wisconsin and Illinois dairy cattle and selling them at cost to local aspiring dairymen. Sometimes these groups encouraged cow-testing campaigns. Recording the daily output of each cow helped the dairyman cull unproductive stock, sell it for beef, and purchase prime dairy cows. To further milk production, the Fort Scott Chamber of Commerce favored the highly prolific Holsteins. It convinced area farmers to form a Purebred Holstein Association, dedicated to adopting these cows, improving the breed, and spreading these heavy milk producers throughout the region. Calving and selling the offspring enhanced purebred dairying farming profits.[39]

High-level Borden officials, usually accompanied by Waters, came to Fort Scott at least three times a year. While there, they reassured Fort Scott and its surrounding dairymen that the company would work patiently to develop dairying for everyone's mutual interest. At the same time, the Borden group undertook reconnaissance for the firm. It made surveys of area dairies, seeking first hand, up to date information about the experiment's progress and what Borden might do to hasten dairy development in south-eastern Kansas. Almost invariably, surveyors reported that "the development of dairying in this section . . . has been very pleasing to the company" but reminded audiences that "more rapid and wider development in the future is anticipated." And so it went. During its first several years of operation, the Fort Scott condensery expanded its base and produced additional product. At the end of two years, the condensery received an average of 35,000 pounds of milk daily, more than enough to sustain the operation. Five hundred dairymen brought milk there and received an average $1,100 for a year's work, a rather significant total. But growth had come not nearly as quickly as Borden had wanted or the area had promised.[40]

Still, the company gave its seedling every opportunity to prosper. It urged culling of herds and reminded farmers of the great need to bank grasses in the summer for winter cattle feeding. It also pushed additional rock roads as the surest way to increase milk to the plant. It recognized that muck and mire were the enemy of routine transport and a critical factor in whether farmers chose to adopt dairy farming. One Borden official put it succinctly. "muddy roads . . . demoralize milk transportation."[41]

Despite the company's optimistic public statements and Fort Scott's frantic efforts, the condensery faced several challenges. One was the introduction of the American Federation of Labor (AFL) into its factory. At about the time that the Teamsters struck the New York milk dealers, eighteen of the fifty-four employees at the Kansas condensery established a branch of that union, demanded a minimum wage of 50 cents per hour, an eight-hour day, and a union shop. The plant supervisor—after contact with the New York office—offered a compromise and a statement reaffirming that any unionist would always find the door to the superintendent's office open, which was the "same respectful consideration and hearing" that all nonunion employees received. The AFL then appealed to the Central Union of Fort Scott, a collective of all local unions, to join the strike. The strikers drew picket lines and some violence ensued.

Interests in this became increasingly muddled. The strikers demanded "a square deal" and denied trying "to paralyze this young industry which we know and admit is a good thing" for Fort Scott. The Central Union acted as a sounding board, little more. It did not join the job action. Borden offered a compromise—45 cents per hour minimum, nine-hour days, time-and-a-half for overtime—but adamantly opposed a union shop. It remained for a group of dairy farmers to enter the fray. Indeed, it was their ox being gored if the condensery failed, so they formed a committee to investigate the melee. It found for the company in all particulars and contended that the strike had been unwarranted in view of Borden's counterproposal.

It was, however, the committee members' apologia that proved most enlightening. They found Borden policy toward employees had always been "most liberal." It had "retained employees through slack periods rather than ruthlessly cutting down the pay-roll." Many of the strikers had become unnecessary at the plant before the work stoppage, they argued, but Borden kept them on. They also offered a prescription. "We dairymen . . . have investments" in the industry. We "call upon the level heads in union labor and upon the business men of Fort Scott to use their influence" to end scurrilous talk. Workers and businesses alike must "stop the untrue statements and vicious . . . practices of the 'strikers.'" Continued verbal assaults on Borden "bid fair to prejudice Fort Scott for years to come in the upbuilding of the dairy industry."[42]

The labor issue receded as all parties recognized that their futures depended on the condensery. That kind of unity sustained them during the farm depression of 1920. Borden refused to take any new milk for its eastern condenseries as of October 1 and soon closed them. It kept its Wisconsin and Illinois facilities going not as condenseries but as separators to make butter. At Fort Scott, the status quo persisted. Borden bought all the milk and at a significantly higher price than anywhere in the country, including Chicago. The matter was clear. "The company knows that anything that discourages" local dairymen "will tend to retard expected development here." It retained its commitment—its "permanent interests"—to make the area's dairying blossom—"its big plans for development"—even though it had at least fifty million dollars' worth of product in company warehouses. The only changes made at the Kansas plant were that once condensed milk filled the local storage facility, the company shipped the remainder out for storage elsewhere.[43]

The company's frequent refrain that it favored Fort Scott through higher milk rates because the area's dairy development matched the company's long term interests worked two ways. Certainly it provided immediate solace. The company was not going to leave anytime soon. But it also was a frequent reminder that patience did not last forever. The area needed to show the kind of growth and profitability that Borden representatives had projected in 1916–17, when the company began its region-transforming effort. Pressure fell to the entire community. The condensery had provided to an economically dissolute town the prospects for a better day, but its owners required that goals be met.[44]

A certain shrillness characterized the Fort Scott community's actions even before Borden reopened its eastern condenseries. Locals redoubled their efforts to fashion new rock roads to tap additional areas adjacent to Fort Scott, claiming that new roads would increase milk delivered daily to 100,000 pounds. It then averaged close to 60,000 pounds during the peak spring season, but less than half that for much of the year. From as far away as 35 miles in every direction, 700 dairymen brought milk to the condensery. Regularly scheduled milk trucks would be contracted to cart the milk once the anticipated roads were finished. The Chamber of Commerce took a more cynical approach. To achieve success, it declared success and initiated a campaign to press that message. In an article entitled "Fort Scott's Five-Year Program Almost Realized," it breathlessly proclaimed that the city had a "remarkable record" that "you can not conceive of . . . until you read this." Not everyone was on board. Fort Scott's achievements could be taken in a different direction. One man wondered why so few farmers "take advantage of the great opportunity." We should "produce five times as much milk." If every farmer had "fifteen to twenty paying milk cows," we could reach that figure. We are ignoring the "wonderful advantage . . . of limitless possibilities" provided by Borden's condensery. Another commentator wondered why Kansas had not surpassed Wisconsin in dairying. Kansans can grow grass "at least three months longer than Wisconsin. Barns need not be so expensive here, as the climate is milder."[45]

By late 1922, the condensed milk stockpile had become depleted. The industry ramped up production. Borden Co. became even more anxious to expand its Kansas operations. The condensery had not yet averaged 50,000 pounds of milk a day over the course of a year, the figure guaranteed by the Chamber of Commerce in 1916 to entice Borden to the region. The firm had proven that new dairy areas could be cultivated, even as the process moved remarkably slowly. Now was the time to profit from the experiment. Waters told the Chamber that the sales department had set a goal of a 15 percent production increase for 1923 and that "the Fort Scott factory must produce her share." The time for nurturing the experiment had passed. Both "the farm employe and business man" have been "getting the benefit of outside money sent in by the Borden." It was time now for consistent, continuous profitability.

Borden's relative Fort Scott success also had a downside. The company's biggest competitors, Carnation and Pet, both seized on Borden's experience to scout out areas to establish condenseries in the state. Fort Scott was proof of concept. Parts of Kansas's wheat fields made excellent dairyland and its farmers could be taught to take up cows.[46]

While Borden showed the other manufacturers Kansas's profound possibilities, newspapers worked overtime to make willing local partners. They told Kansans what dairy farming meant to local communities. Fort Scott as nirvana—the living embodiment of the "old dream of a rich farming community for contented people"—became a local newspapers staple. Often these small town publications simply republished grandiose stories first appearing in the region's big city papers, such as the *Kansas City Journal-Post* or the *Kansas City Star*. The myth of Fort Scott spread quickly. "The milk condensery has been a godsend to the community," the myth began. With dairying came cash, which "soon put new blood into the arteries of business. Farmers began to have ready cash in banks. Business firms were getting old accounts settled. Sentiment for more rock roads grew rapidly." Since the "coming of the dairy cow," the town "has been growing in every way. Business is good, all houses occupied, cash from milk is flowing everywhere." Farmers benefited mightily. "The old plan of selling the wheat crop (if there was one) is in the discard forever." Manure from cows, when applied to the land, resulted in "the fields . . . getting richer and crops . . . getting better." Crop failures, "which used to be all too frequent, are never known since the advent of the dairy cow."[47]

Such a miraculous story whetted the appetite of many Kansas small towns. Each desired success, and Fort Scott provided the roadmap. Bitterness and disappointment over their present situations were frequent themes. "The country around Caney is better than the country around Ft. Scott," matter of factly stated one observer in a piece titled "what dairying has done." Yet "the farmers around Caney are complaining bitterly about their crop returns," while Fort Scott farmers are "laying up money." Through their civic or governmental leaders, small town and city residents worked to attract a condensery nearby to create prosperity. Pitting small town against small town and condenser against condenser promised to turn the state into a twentieth-century Bloody Kansas. Pet targeted Borden and southeastern Kansas directly, placing a condensery in Iola, a scant forty miles from Fort Scott and surely well within the pioneer city's milk-shed. Other condensaries were considered near two of Kansas's main cities, Wichita and Topeka.[48] But even before these condenseries got beyond the planning stage, Borden made a consequential decision. It discontinued its plan of establishing its personal milk fiefdom in southeastern Kansas but retained its condensery at Fort Scott.[49] While the area failed to reach the lofty goals and profitability that the company set, it was indeed sustainable and marginally profitable. Borden continued the property and hoped it would expand but ended its policy of Fort Scott exceptionalism to devote itself to other ways to generate profits.

Attempting to create a new arena from which to secure supply was a daring innovation. Southeastern Kansas had neither dairying history nor tradition. Borden established its condensery there to capitalize on an antic-ipated dramatic upshot in worldwide demand. It was a preemptive attempt to secure the lion's share of what would become tremendous new mar-kets: markets producing regular, consistent profits. It was not Borden's sole anticipatory maneuver. The company labored hard to expand its market penetration by refining what its markets were, in this case by diversifying its product line. It engaged in diversification, but not in the way that pro-gressive, turn-of-the-century firms had. It chose not to establish idea labo-ratories as had Bell Telephone, General Electric, and others. Borden opted to diversify by absorbing and purchasing companies. That too had been a common turn-of-the-century practice. General Motors bought out com-panies to own their patents, to both eliminate competitors and to be able to employ some technical process. That was not Borden's goal. It bought or absorbed companies to capture their distinctive markets, to expand the condenser's product line. Markets and products mattered only because they resulted in profits: it was profits that truly mattered. Borden aggressively seized markets and then worked to expand profitability further.[50]

The company had taken care to place itself in this position. During 1919 and 1920, it accrued debt that approached the company's worth. By December 1922, it emerged debt free. It had paid off its spectacular build-ing that, with its 97 percent occupancy became a prolific moneymaker. By closing facilities as it spent down its condensed milk stockpile, the com-pany reduced expenses significantly without ruining profits. It persisted in paying stockholders at least an annual 8 percent dividend. By December

1923 the firm had accumulated over $12 million in cash. With its house in excellent financial shape, the company did the logical thing as it began to think about acquiring product lines and their markets. It recapitalized itself, moving from $22.5 million to $35 million.[51] The now-unleashed corporate leviathan was ready to pursue whatever opportunities for profits came its way.

Borden's acquisition and merger campaign began after the company took stock of the Fort Scott experiment. That experiment succeeded, just not to the degree that its designers had anticipated. The company took what it learned and resolved to try it again, albeit with modifications. Rather than look towards land in the west, it focused on a region. That region was the South.

3 | THE STATE OF THE COTTON SOUTH
The Failure of Capitalists, Scientists, and Governments to Remake or Replace the Region's Farmers

Well before Borden officers turned their attention to the South, commentators both inside and outside the region claimed it was in severe economic trouble. Almost always their critiques focused on farmers. Farmers were the problem of the South and of rural America generally. As a group, they were a fickle, intransient lot. They almost always opted for the status quo, preferring to adopt the tried and true even if it were really the tried and failed. They often persisted in planting crops that depleted the soil or failed to provide them with the income they felt they so richly deserved. Change was often viewed with suspicion, almost as an enemy. The devil they knew was almost always preferable.

The South's peculiar landholding conventions merely reified past practice. Sharecroppers farmed what they knew and landlords chose the dependability of the status quo and the income it consistently would generate. Tenant farmers had more apparent latitude but that was a mirage. Their futures may well have been tied to a single harvest. Either the crops came in or they could lose the relative freedom of tenancy.

The problems that faced farmers made hash of rural America, and were especially devastating to small towns and cities. Almost every activity there depended on farmers in some capacity. Grocers and other small merchants needed farmers to spend money in their stores. Farmers were their markets. Others relied on farmers for their raw materials. Railroad lines needed freight to keep freight costs down and truckers needed to carry products to have jobs. Bankers needed farmers' funds to invest and their debt to profit from. Success was more beneficial to banks than failures. It was frequently difficult to resell what were proven dubious properties.

In each instance, farmers possessed all the agency. Except for the most downtrodden sharecroppers, they pursued the agriculture they chose and that was within their means. The rest of the community served at their mercy; its members blossomed when farmers prospered and lived small when they were strapped. From this essential relationship came a series of programs. Each ostensibly aimed and was structured to help the farmer. In reality, however, each was designed to move farmers in particular ways to further the interests of the group doing the maneuvering or the prosperity of the community generally. Farmers certainly would have welcomed additional largesse if unencumbered by change but were reticent to undertake programs that would have challenged or revamped established precepts.[1]

The twentieth century, then, saw tremendous impetus to redesign, modify, change, and reorient the crops and practices of farmers. As rural cities and towns stumbled and as rural Americans moved to the industrial cities of the North, citizens who remained in their southern small town and city homes worked to improve their quality of life and their economic interests. As the sole independent agents, farmers provided targets for these grand plans. The goal always was to modify farmers' habits and practices to assist those who demanded alterations. These changes in farming often provided advocates with leverage, money, standing, or legitimacy. It was the modifiers who were to be the ultimate beneficiaries.

Farmers were a canvas with which to redraw rural America. To be sure, any number of calamities were called into service to argue that farmers needed assistance. Invariably, those approaches favored the skills, knowledge, or interests of those raising the propositions. In some instances, those advocating change were the same lot that had appeared as bugaboos to the previous farm generation. They themselves had been identified as culprits in the farmer's dilemma, as explanations why farmers lost lands or had not been as prosperous as farmers thought they ought to be. Accepting long-standing villains as partners—the way they now presented themselves— proved difficult for farm men and women. Proponents of change found the transition much easier. Using the verbiage of assistance and sometimes claiming disinterest, they now sometimes portrayed themselves nobly as they pursed their agenda of farmer modification.

Perhaps because their palette of options was so limited, these marketers of change painted farmers with a single brush. Farmers in the South were lumped together as if one group with predominantly one problem that could be resolved in one manner. This monocausal diagnosis simplified the aid onslaught. Even though it rested outside the South, the events surrounding the Borden condensery at Fort Scott proved illustrative. Soil worn by wheat production failed to provide residents of Fort Scott their desired economic future. Its progressives—its Chamber of Commerce—contacted Borden to see if a milk plant might be started there. Borden's interest spurred the chamber to mount a tremendous campaign to change farmers from grain producers to dairymen. The chamber even purchased prime dairy cattle by the railroad car, contacted the state agricultural school, and went farm to farm in an attempt to compel a goodly share of farmers to get on board. It established tours of Illinois and Wisconsin dairylands and worked strenuously to bring in dairy farmers from elsewhere to convert the area.

The pressure ratcheted up when Borden signed on. The Frisco Railway sent its dairy agent to train farmers. Borden joined with the Chamber of Commerce to travel the countryside to convince farmers to abandon wheat for milk. The two groups also helped secure prime dairy stock. The company dangled the prospect of a condensery and the considerable income it would bring months before they approved it, which created considerable anxiety and freneticism borne of that anxiety. It was an impressive battle to get farmers to participate in a shared Fort Scott future.

During World War I, southern farmers were in high cotton, both figuratively and literally. The war had eliminated competitors and provided additional markets for the South's food and fiber. Commentators cited the war as cause for the southern economic resurgence. Two basic interpretations emerged. One aimed to establish mechanisms to have the boom persist after the war. The other congratulated southerners for making substantive changes and assumed that they would persist when the war concluded.[2] But the war masked economic pitfalls. Like condensed milk, which benefited from an artificial export market, the war conflated southern agriculture's new virtues. Critiques of southern agriculture, similar in tone but not specifics to those that preceded the war, reemerged periodically during the war and exploded during the agricultural depression of 1920. Entrenched interests generally outside the South brandished these analyses. While the boll weevil, climate, and worn-out soil served as proximate causes, the fundamental prewar problem was farmers. They lacked the vision for success, wedded as they were to old, outmoded ways. That may have been suitable for previous times, but it now became a social crime. Farmers' inability to change doomed or diminished the South.[3]

Two tropes characterized efforts to correct farmers. Some promoters employed terminology most closely associated with the military. They embarked on a campaign, undertook an onslaught, and sought victory. Others likened their work to a religious revival—"farmer uplift"—where they aimed to get farmers to come to Jesus through "the gospel of diversification," often a "revelation to the farmers of the South."[4] Goals were likewise somewhat different. To be sure, both groups aimed to get farmers to adopt the new practices they offered. But the militarists wanted to "conquer" ignorance and outmoded tradition, while the religionists sought conversion to the communitarian gospel and adherence to the golden rule.

No less an industrial light than International Harvester (IH) devoted years and millions to changing southern farm practices. Yes, the implement maker had profound financial reasons to push and pull farmers into a modern present. There is no doubt that it profited extensively from the success of these efforts, since the company made virtually every variety of farm implement. But those motives did not undermine the character of Harvester's campaign. Its initial appearance was somewhat timid. In 1910 Harvester created a service bureau within the advertising department. It employed experts whose job it was to respond to farmers' questions and to offer advice. Not satisfied with farmers' tepid response, it planned to establish a series of demonstration farms to carry its message through the South. Working in conjunction with railroads, the USDA, state agricultural colleges, and state governments, the head of International Harvester's new service bureau, J. E. Waggoner, formerly professor of mechanical and agricultural engineering at Mississippi A&M, toured the South to spread the twin gospels of diversified farming and best practices, as well as to identify possible sites. Three farms—one each in Mississippi, Alabama, and Georgia—became the company's first demonstration farms. Superintending the farms was G. H. Alford, former editor of *Southern Farm Gazette*, Mississippi legislator, and graduate of Mississippi A&M.[5]

In 1912 IH decided to expand its farmers' reclamation projects and to separate them from its advertising division. Cyrus H. McCormick explained the company's decision. For two years, "we have been experimenting" taking knowledge of "scientific farming from the library shelves" and bringing it "direct to farmers in their own homes." We are now "step[ping] into this work in a larger way." As Clarence S. Funk, the company's general manager put it, "this is not exactly philanthropy." Although not immediately, "we expect to sell more agricultural implements as a result" of our new initiative.

Creation of Harvester's Agricultural Extension Department marked the company's new foray into agricultural modernization. Headed by Perry Holden—a leading agricultural science promoter who had worked at the agricultural colleges in Michigan, Iowa, and Illinois—the department started with a million dollars but was promised whatever it needed, even "five million." Holden worked with established journalists and agricultural science and technology promoters to write articles, take photographs, make lantern slides for schools, offer lectures, and present "motion pictures . . . at fairs, land shows, granges, farmers' institutes, teachers' institutes, and Chautauquas." Holden was bullish on the South. It was "at present passing through a great agricultural awakening," engendered by the trauma of the boll weevil to embrace "diversified farming." That "character of farming" made "country banks, good schools, good roads, and rich communities."[6]

Holden's primary delivery method was to barnstorm. Whether by automobile, horse and buggy, or train, he carried his message of improving the soil and diversifying crops. In his first full year at the department, he sent "experts and literature by automobile throughout the entire country." His most sustained effort during its early years was "the alfalfa delegation," which aimed to "visit every farmer in the corn and cotton belts this year." At each stop he arranged "alfalfa days in schools and alfalfa editions of newspapers."

Chambers of Commerce or bankers invited Holden's group, who arrived on railroad-donated trains. Usually the processional was large enough that two locomotives were necessary. County schools were called off for the days when the proselytizers were in town. The whistlestop tour went from county to county a day at a time, sometimes for weeks on end. Always there were lectures, glossy pictures, bright colors and demonstrations of the benefit of crop diversifications and the techniques to achieve excellent yields. African Americans were generally welcomed to these events and sometimes a special set of activities was added for students at the state's African American agricultural colleges.[7]

In addition to traveling through the South and Midwest, the department created an extensive pamphlet literature through which to teach rural living and farming. Titles included *How to Prosper in Boll Weevil Territory; The Farm. The Greatest Purchasing Power; Diversified Farming Is Safe Farming; How to Vitalize the Teaching of Agriculture in the Rural Schools; The Liberty Book;* and *We Must Feed Ourselves.*8 Each aimed to redirect agriculture not simply to assist farmers but also the community in which they farmed. In the 1915 pamphlet, *Every Farm Is A Factory. The Opportunity of the Town Lies in the Country,* sets out the goal in detail. "The opportunity of the town lies in the country," began the pamphlet. "The old fashioned Chamber of Commerce . . . is rapidly passing away. Rather than attempt to seduce industry to an area, we now must realize that our opportunities lie hidden in the fertility of the soil." Something as basic as "a successful hay campaign will bring factories to town. Hay means beef and pork, which beckon the packing house and storage plant." Corn "means cereal mills, glucose factories, starch factories." After running through a series of other agriculture-community processes, the author concluded with this plea: "Every farm is a factory, and . . . in every state there are thousands of these factories which need our best thought and effort to make them productive."9

The contention that farms needed "our best thought" directly challenged farmers. It demanded that they understand the interrelationships between excellent farm practice and community success. Farmers must adopt the most progressive methods if they wished their neighbors well and wanted to advance their communities.

Roughly contemporaneous with the heyday of the International Harvester Extension was the State of Mississippi's 100th anniversary. Entering the Union in 1817, the state took the opportunity provided by Harvester's 1914 crusade in southwestern Mississippi to devise its own program of agricultural modernization. It slickly combined state pride and a celebratory atmosphere to launch its "Grown in Mississippi" initiative at the state's capital in Jackson. That slogan masked the initial agenda—to diversify the state's agriculture.

Holden provided the impetus. During the 1914 campaign, he claimed that Mississippi sent two out of every three dollars out of state to import food. That he recognized as entirely wasteful and recommended that Mississippi emulate Iowa, which turned around its economic prospects through a twofold approach. First, its citizens committed to eating only Iowa-grown products. Second, it took pride in what it produced, so much so that it affixed the label, "Grown in Iowa," to each product it shipped out of state.

"Very patriotic Mississippians" greeted the suggestion enthusiastically. At its heart, however, was a central tenet. If Mississippi were to consume only its own agricultural products, it would need to grow far more diverse and far more plentiful crops. Holden suggested that "Grown in Mississippi" be placed in every school room, printed in every newspaper, and preached in every sermon. Bankers, railroad men, and "everyone else interested in the development" of the state needed to cleave to the motto. Generating luster and fervor, "Grown in Mississippi" would also create wealth through diversification.[10]

In the next few weeks, "bankers, merchants, stockmen, farmers, professional men, teachers, [and] manufacturers" all rallied behind the movement. A veritable who's who of Mississippi agriculture endorsed the strategy. USDA representatives in charge of the tick eradication campaign, agricultural college professors, the superintendent of education, and editor of the *Progressive Farmer*—though now based in Memphis—issued hearty assent. So too did H. E. Blakeslee, state agricultural commissioner. He called a meeting of representatives of "organizations of every character" and various other individuals to start an association for "encouraging our people everywhere to grow those things they are now buying from" the Midwest, including pork, beef, butter, lard, eggs, canned goods, and livestock. The meeting also sought a means to ensure that every product that left the state would have a "Grown in Mississippi" tag attached to it.[11]

An impressive number of interests heeded Blakeslee's call. Many spoke at the meeting. W. H. Smith, state education superintendent, guaranteed that schools in the state would each devote a week to studying the variety of products in Mississippi. R. S. Wilson, the US farm demonstration work director for Mississippi, pledged to use his fifty agents to remove any "skepticism" from Mississippians who did not believe that every necessity could be grown in the state. R. H. Pate, director of the agricultural college's farmer institutes, promise to hold 600 institutes to spread the message. The director of the US Bureau of Animal Industry's campaign to rid cattle ticks from the state, the head of the industrial and immigration department of the Illinois Central Railroad, and the president of the Mississippi's Farmer Union each stated they would place stickers in prominent places on their wares. Pate and Wilson gained places on the "Grown in Mississippi" executive board. The group laid out two major objectives in its constitution: "to promote the diversification of crops" and to engage in "a state-wide campaign for producing on every farm as far as practical the needs of that farm and home." The organization agreed to tax local business clubs one dollar for each one thousand inhabitants in that community to generate working capital.[12]

Tremendous optimism greeted the meeting. "If everybody will lend a helping hand and co-operate," reported one newspaperman, then Mississippi will "be one of the greatest producing states in the Union." He hailed its "fertile soil and unlimited capacity for . . . pastoral pursuits." Mississippi had "broad acres of stock raising . . . inexhaustible mineral resources [and] oil production." Officers began their work almost immediately. They chose to go after businesses, corporations, and organizations rather than farmers. They quickly got endorsements from the Mississippi Press Association, a consortium of fruit jobbers, and the state society of retail merchants.

Blakeslee enumerated what he expected from the initial phase of the movement. Every public speaker was "expected to devote a portion" of their talk to the campaign. Each minister was to give one sermon each year to the cause, which "offers so much . . . increased prosperity and happiness." "Grown in Mississippi" would supply textbooks to each school for the Grown in Mississippi week. It would culminate on Thanksgiving with a basket dinner for 730,000 school children, serving only Mississippi products. He also broadened the campaign to include the slogan "Made in Mississippi," to incorporate things manufactured in the state. Blakeslee urged every state newspaper to print a "Made in Mississippi" edition and called on fertilizer manufacturers to place a label with the same words on every bag they produced.[13]

He also inaugurated a monthly bulletin of events and achievements but that came a cropper when it was discovered that it was printed out of state. Rebounding from that embarrassment, Blakeslee partnered with the agricultural college to send a train full of speakers to the Hattiesburg area to deliver four different programs. These lecturers stuck to the script. They told the tale of Mississippi sending millions of dollars yearly out of state to purchase foodstuffs that could be grown in the state, and offered to assist in developing those crops. While USDA and college personnel addressed the topic in roughly the way it was proposed, other groups did not. They opted for enthusiasm over substance, hoopla over facts. For example, the public school program aimed to inspire and entertain, not merely educate. Its statewide "Grown in Mississippi" program was organized as follows: 1) all singing "America, the Beautiful"; 2) ten young children reciting "We Thank Thee; 3) ten older children reciting "Ten Modern Discoveries"; 4) address: "Our Community Resources"; 5) recitation: "When the Frost is on the Pumpkin"; 6) recitation: "Delights of Farm Life"; 7) song: "Home Sweet Home"; and 8) dinner composed of Mississippi products, accompanied by recommended songs: "Bringing in the Sheaves"; the "Star Spangled Banner"; "Dixie"; "Mississippi"; and "Down Where the Cotton Blossoms Grow."[14] Railroads also deviated from the initial plan. Four separate railroads—the Illinois Central, Southern Pacific, Union Pacific, and the OWH & N—agreed to hold a "Grown in Mississippi" week as a marketing tool and to follow that up in the second week of November by serving only Mississippi products in their club cars. Retailers hung banners inside their stores. They also competed for a loving cup, presented to the business organization that held the best dinner or luncheon made with Mississippi products during that second week of November. The state board of trade even prepared to enter the culinary competition. Mayors were urged to sign "Grown in Mississippi" proclamations the week of Thanksgiving.

In a moment of reflection, Blakeslee talked about the hard work ahead. This year's labor, he began, will only "impress upon the people" the program's importance. In the next year he planned to implement what Mississippians had learned this year. "Our whole plan is to make Mississippi a diversified farming state: to grow live stock; build silos; practice a sane system of crop rotation with legume crops, and thereby maintain the fertility of our soil." Blakeslee recognized that working with farmers directly was hard work. They needed to be inspired, not appealed to directly. Farmer rigidity and intransience would almost certainly doom direct calls to abandon monoculture. They required a grander purpose to manipulate them. William Ward, editor of the *East Mississippi Times*, told the old Sidney Lanier tale to drive home the point. A Georgia farmer had read all the diversification literature and listened to lectures. He was convinced that farmers absolutely must diversify and figured that hogs, corn, and fruit were best. And, the farmer continued, "everybody'll grow 'em, and quit growin' cotton; and cotton'll fetch 'bout a dollar a pound—Therefore, I'll plant more cotton!"[15]

R. S. Wilson, head of the USDA farm demonstration effort in Mississippi, appealed to farmers directly. The state offered excellent opportunities to raise livestock, Wilson noted, and the USDA presented unparalleled aid to those who sought it. Yet those two objects did not guarantee success. "A man must also be a good farmer" if he is to be a good livestock man, he concluded. H. L. Whitfield, president of the Mississippi Industrial Institute in Columbus, argued something similar. Citing unprecedented natural resources for farming, he argued that "the paramount problem is the training of people for the work they must do." The battle for excellent husbandry "must be won by men and women." He despaired that the status quo would persist "until a new generation, educated for this better life," emerged. An unnamed contributor put it bluntly. "A one-crop system will ruin any country. It means poor soil and poor people. . . . Do you know what it means to waste a large share of revenues purchasing out of state goods? . . . No country in the world can withstand such a drain from year to year. The South cannot prosper under this system."[16]

As the "Grown in Mississippi" movement approached its second year, fewer persons began to publicize it. Blakeslee worked to keep up the momentum, but even the schools seemed to lose interest. There was no "Grown in Mississippi" week, no basket dinner of Mississippi food. The loving cup drew no press coverage. But Blakeslee was not idle. He thanked newspaper editors for their support and welcomed groups, stressing the construction of good roads. "Grown in Mississippi" did convene to mark its first year of existence as the president of the Farmers Union railed against "the land-hog demagogues and politicians." Holden made a return appearance but almost all meeting attendees were small town apparatchiks. They mostly championed the new "spirit of cooperation between town and country, between merchant and farmer [and] between banker and producer." Despite the fine rhetoric, enthusiasm for Grown in Mississippi had dissipated. Various marketing cooperatives replaced it, each of which claimed that the interests of merchants and consumers must be preserved. They reasoned that farmers might be persuaded to give up on king cotton if other roads to profitability lie before them. As a member of the Columbus, Mississippi, Chamber of Commerce asserted, farmers are "anxious to find a way out of the wilderness of uncertainty caused by the war and the boll weevil."[17]

Some of these methods were remarkably local, such as neighborhood or community retailing associations. Advertising was very much part of the marketing, sometimes indistinguishable. Indeed, advertising under-scored the whole "Grown in Mississippi" campaign. Mississippi products, noted one commentator, "must be brought to the favorable attention of the great consuming public, until there is a demand for them that will ac-tually exhaust the yearly supply." In other cases, more ambitious contracts were sought. With these bigger contracts came a subordinate question: a minimum standard of quality. The issue was not quality per se, but a floor that all representatives of the product would be expected to exceed. That standard became the agreement upon which a marketing contract was based. For example, such a contract might require livestock to be purebred and to weigh a certain amount. For a farmer to participate, his products would have to at least meet that specification.[18]

Merchandising—marketing—took over in other ways. Discussants re-alized just how little of Mississippi was under the plow. They sought to correct that deficiency, not by selling additional land to Mississippi farmers or landowners but by soliciting and bringing in farmers from the North. They attempted to resolve the problem of ignorant and stubborn farmers by replacing them with farmers without similar deficiencies. Selling the state's livestock and vegetable possibilities was the attractant. As an ob-server argued succinctly, Mississippi's advantages "for the good white man seeking a home must be brought to the favorable attention of the people throughout the United States. Millions of acres of land lie idle awaiting the hand of an intelligent and energetic man." The state, wrote another, "needs all the good people with good moral and financial standing, industry and thrift it can get to develop its conceeded [sic] wonderful natural resources." Without better farmers, complained a third, Mississippi must be "content with being fed from the back door of a wiser people."[19]

Collapse of "Grown in Mississippi" did not mark the end of passion in Mississippi. The IH agricultural extension rekindled the fires, albeit for a short time. In 1915 the Memphis Business Men's Club saw monoculture, worn out the soil, and the boll weevil as conditions that afflicted the Arkan-sas and Mississippi Delta region. Slavish adherence to cotton meant that already-strapped farmers were repeatedly forced to spend whatever mea-gre incomes they generated to purchase food to live. Bad harvests led to demands for money from the banks as well as high interest rates. Indepen-dent farmers became tenants. Inept farm practice showed in "poor schools, poorly equipped farms, bad roads, poorly paid teachers and preachers, and finally that the people were becoming poor."

Club representatives went to Chicago and asked the IH Agricultural Extension Department for help in reorienting farmers' practices. Even though the company had engaged in a diversified farming campaign in Mississippi the previous year,[20] they committed to sending thirty trained agricultural lecturers, numerous lecture charts, and at least one million pamphlets to assist the Memphis businessmen. Five railroads, led by the Illinois Central, promised to provide transportation. Arkansas and Mississippi agricultural colleges, Memphis business schools, the *Memphis Commercial Appeal,* and the *Progressive Farmer* all pitched in.

All together there were 3 speaker crews of 20 each. The campaign, sometimes referred to as a "big agricultural revival," lasted 28 days. None of the meetings were held in cities. Speakers, accompanied by local businessmen, went to farms, country schools, and rural churches. The consortium held 2,100 meetings and over 220,000 farmers attended lectures. It distributed 1.25 million free agricultural bulletins that in the aggregate weighed 40 tons. Speakers and the accompanying businessmen traveled 80,271 miles by railroads and 28,642 by automobile, buggies, or wagons. Looking back at the event, the International Harvester people congratulated themselves for "service well performed in behalf of community building." The effort was a triumph "in citizenship-making and character building."

The IH department knew that the vast majority of farmers they encountered on the Memphis project were born in the United States. But citizenship and character required something more than place of birth. Action defined those qualities and it was exactly those qualities that the improvers approached with religious fervor. Farmers must adopt the most modern practices because their failure to do so would damage those who depended on them. It was their community and national responsibility, their obligation, to practice agriculture in a manner that differed from what their fathers and grandfathers had done. In this context, citizenship demanded a group perspective rather than an individual one, and practices that would enhance others as well as oneself. Anything else would injure others.[21]

Like the religious revivals of the time, the IH work aimed at conversion. For a brief time, representatives of the organization came to a place, preached charismatically to audiences to forsake cotton monoculture, accept diversification, and farm properly, according to best practices. Then the IH team went on to the next venue. It labored to transform farming one farmer at a time. The special Chautauqua in Crystal Springs, Mississippi, the same year was radically different. Everything there was practical, oriented toward specific programs that could be applied exactly. There were directions for model farm accounts, home demonstrations, plant disease exhibits, canning, poultry raising, farm clubs for young children, fertilizer application, hay, grain and forage crops, and care of livestock.[22]

The Crystal Springs Chautauqua had much in common with the Smith-Lever Act passed by the United States Congress the year before. The act established the public agricultural colleges and their experiment stations as the locus of knowledge for agriculture and rural life in each state, their minions as disseminators of that knowledge, and helped pay the salaries of those disseminators.[23] The act clearly prioritized practical education, not conversion, as the mechanism for bringing farming into the twentieth century. While potentially folksy, neighborly, and chummy, extension agents brought rules and procedures. Their approach and methods were logical, rational, dispassionate. One of the first programs in the state tried to add an additional one million acres of corn to the agricultural mix for 1915. To be sure, enthusiasm figured in the calculus but their approach brooked no hoopla. Through step-by-step instructions and coldhearted statistics, farmers would be taught, shown the latest techniques and practices.[24]

Sporadic enthusiastic campaigns quickly gave way to bureaucratic entrenchment. The touring efforts of the IH Extension Department produced little movement. As early as 1915, it sometimes had difficulties finding suitable local partners. It suffered a major embarrassment in 1917. The IH team appealed to the Monroe, Louisiana, Chamber of Commerce to inaugurate a campaign near the city. After some negotiations, the "Feed Yourself" initiative took shape. Scheduled for December 3 and 4, it concentrated on Ouachita Parish and considered livestock, dairying, home building, and food production and conservation. The chamber arranged a wide variety of activities, including public lectures, meetings with school children, and trips to the rural environs for their guests.[25]

The IH visit proved a dismal failure. Few locals bothered to attend the sessions. Their "value [was] not appreciated" and the "importance of the lectures were not fully understood." The chamber was embarrassed and voted to ask Harvester to reprise the campaign. The Harvester people greeted the proposal coldly. They would agree to return only if "good audiences for them to speak are assured." For ten days the chamber appealed to the citizenry. At the end of that time "only one man has taken the occasion to express hope that the lecturers would return." Even though there was no enthusiasm to get the show back to Monroe, the chamber issued another invitation. Harvester again asked for a commitment that a large audience would attend the lectures. A few days later, the chamber conceded it could not guarantee adequate attendance, and the matter was canceled. Spectacle, at least when it came to farmer revitalization, lost the luster that it had just a few years earlier. The IH Extension Department persisted, but it virtually retired from barnstorming and devoted its efforts to pamphlets and other literature as well as some occasional lectures.[26]

The disastrous agricultural depression in the years after the war did not bring a return to farmer conversion. Rather, advocates of a new southern agriculture did not seek to remake individual farmers but to act through permanent institutions to teach farming principles that would yield profitability. Teaching why something would be profitable replaced showing how something would be profitable. Even so-called demonstrations demonstrated less and taught more. The term demonstration merely catered to farmer stubbornness; they accepted being shown, but not taught.[27]

Certainly the immediate post war years provided dramatic evidence that the prewar campaigns to diversify farming achieved much less traction that initially thought. Combined with the earliest years of the Black migration to the industrial north, King Cotton seemed quite troubled. Prices per pound lurched from 5 ½ cents one year to 40 cents the next. In this context, southerners and others urged creation of methods to protect cotton producers economically—bonding bank debts, establishing protective tariffs, moratorium on loan repayment, passing anti-foreclosure laws, guaranteeing loans for next year's crop, and the like. Farmers themselves withheld cotton from market when they felt the price had fallen too low, and even threatened to torch gins who dared to clean cotton during those desperate times. Cotton farmers attempted to manipulate the market by cutting back on the number of acres when cotton prices were reasoned to be low, but rarely did any of these measures work.[28]

Observers now called on monoculturists to add a second crop to the mix and perhaps a third. This approach was to indemnify producers from market fluctuations. It differed in character from the prewar diversification mania. It was not about redrafting farmers. The new thrust sought to enable cotton to remain king by provided the surety that producers had traditionally lacked. It rejected remaking individual farmers for the grander remaking of the cotton farming economy, which would go far to remaking the rural South. They sought to achieve economic stability and vitality for cotton growers by establishing on each farm a second cash crop. That meant taking some cotton land out of cultivation and swapping it for the other market product. Abandoning cotton production or nearly so was no longer a goal. Enhancing it with a second market crop meant that southern monoculture would yield to the more stable "duoculture."

State extension agents proved adept at providing this information. Agricultural colleges generally organized their personnel by specialists, experts in a particular crop or species of animal. Traditional farm classifications, such as insect pests and farm accounting, also found representation. A third class of specialists worked specifically in marketing. They facilitated the acquisition, production, and demand-creation of agricultural commodities. They guided and sometimes participated in cooperative purchasing, sharing, and marketing agreements, reducing overhead and benefiting from economies of scale.[29]

Clemson, for instance, identified the specialties of its extension agents in this way. Its "purebred hogs, cattle, and forage crops" unit "encourages and aids" the importation of purebred stock. To support these animals, the division "stimulates permanent pastures and the growth of forage crops." It also assisted in the "cooperative feeding and marketing of cattle." The "silos, dairy, barns, dairy schools, and bull associations" specialists devoted themselves to development work—feeds, purebreds, dairy schools, and construction of dairy barns and silos. The "corn and cotton breeding work" section taught farmers methods for field selection of seed corn and relayed to them the newest methods to combat the boll weevil. Its "orchards, gardens, and potato storage houses" specialists advised how to make these facilities and worked to establish "cooperative canneries" to prepare that produce for market. Clemson's "poultry work" people both created an industry and then a market for it. They fostered "reliable breeding centers" for "pure bred poultry" and then planned to "establish and develop representative poultry plants" throughout the state to butcher them. Its "marketing" agents worked with the state's truck farmers to form "local marketing associations" to mitigate individual risk. The "boys' club work and short courses" unit sought to enlist "the intelligent interest of boys" in agriculture and to use that interest to engage "their parents." The final specialty, "rural organizations," sought to encourage "community organizations" and to lend "the full support of the division . . . toward making them a continued success."[30]

Little of this bore resemblance to the campaigns to change farmers and hence rural life. These initiatives were highly articulated, profoundly so. They dug deeply. They were about establishing industries, permanent markets in rural environs. Their goal was not explicitly to make each farmstead a bastion of self-sufficient sustainability. The end product was to be economic stability through production of a subsequent crop to partner with cotton. These initiatives required planning, knowledge, insight, and dedication. They were highly bureaucratic, formalized, and structured. Their dependability was the virtue. Their promise of elevating an area to consistent, permanent, economic viability held out hope for southern rural America.

Commentators sometimes appeared oblivious to the visible hands of the southern agricultural colleges and extension agents.[31] Most national publications in the early 1920s focused on two southern phenomena. The first, the Black Migration, was presented from numerous perspectives. The lure of northern factories and the dearth of agricultural advantage produced by the boll weevil invasion were most usually mentioned.[32] Others posited the horrid Jim Crow conditions in the rural South and the rise of the odious Klan as causal factors.[33] Most wondered about the migration's effects on southern agriculture and the social organization that undergirded it.[34] Some pointed to the easing of Jim Crow's most notorious facets as a reason why migration would soon cease, while some states passed laws making it illegal for anyone to elicit or assist Blacks leaving the state.[35] Southerners sought to remedy the potential labor shortage and social situation by recruiting white labor to move to the region and take over cotton farms. South Carolina even offered white northern farmers free land if they emigrated to the state. One commentator went further. He saw "the racial problem" moving from the South to the North, maintaining that was "poetic justice." After all, he reasoned, "the North is largely responsible for creating" the racial divide "and has kept it alive by almost continuous agitation."[36]

The second issue was cotton growing and the way it was represented rarely had much to do with labor. Cotton discussion almost always took a Washington, DC, bent. Reporters focused almost exclusively on the cotton crop—usually citing governmental figures—and then on its market price. Typical stories suggested that good times would lead to an economically rejuvenated South,[37] while those stories written when cotton prices were low focused on mechanisms to shore up the price, guarantee loans for next year's crop or end the importation of the fiber and fabric.[38] Reporters often cited the boll weevil's activity or lack of activity as the reason why cotton prices deviated. Sometimes, however, they focused on foreign production.[39] Beyond that, they would discuss plans and prospects for next year's crop and various kinds of cooperative and marketing associations.[40] There was remarkably little consideration about the quality of southern farms, the wisdom of devoting farms to monoculture or possible secondary crops.

Cotton too played a prominent part in agricultural newspaper reports and stories but those periodicals were of quite a different character. Like the national papers, they often downplayed agricultural colleges and extension agents as but mere johnny-come-latelys, recent participants in the drive to secure the rural South. Agricultural newspapers had a much longer, firmer tradition. For generations they had been the bastion of information and agitation for rural America. These periodicals reported what they heard and offered their opinions on a wide variety of situations and events. Their editors often had a stake in farming. They certainly established their reputations as tillers of the soil. In addition to their own experience, they tended to rely on correspondents for their material. Well known correspondents were generally the most well-regarded sources, no matter the subject. Success and notoriety in one endeavor were proof of competency in other enterprises.[41]

As a consequence of their vast differences in experience and realms in which they had achieved personal success, their prescriptions for the South varied considerably. Herbert W. Collingwood, editor-in-chief of the esteemed *Rural New Yorker* since 1900, had edited the Starkville, Mississippi-based *Southern Live Stock Journal* in 1884–85. His present periodical cast a particular eye on the South. He was especially interested in the effects of the Black Migration during World War I and after. His correspondence with southerners showed them in two camps. Most believed that the harsh northern climate would chase the emigrants back south but a certain coterie asserted that southern agriculture would excel without Black sharecroppers and tenant farmers. Put bluntly, they argued that white minds would replace Black hands. Farming would be improved and the need for labor drastically reduced. Collingwood took the unusual step of talking to some of the emigres and writing the editors of Black newspapers in northern cities. Their universal assessment was that the flight north had little to do with economics. Black men and women simply seized the opportunity to flee the repeated inhuman treatment and danger of the Jim Crow South. Under no circumstance would they return. Collingwood was left to ponder how the South would carry on without cheap Black labor. He focused on two main thoughts. First, cotton could only be sustained at its previous pace by the invention of a cotton picker; second, reduction of southern cotton fields acreage might be an economically savvy thing. It would force southern landowners to develop a second source of income that was not labor intensive.[42]

In the postwar years, Collingwood proposed the South adopt a series of secondary crops. Clover, yams, and potatoes all made his list. But he returned time and again to an industry he knew well—dairying. When Collingwood first pushed southern dairying, the nation was just entering the war. He mentioned that southern dairying tales were extremely rare. Almost no one reported on that activity. By not keeping cows, southerners played "into the hand of the oleo makers." He found this unfathomable. Having dairy cows on farms not only provided milk and butter but they solved a variety of southern issues. Collingwood flatly proclaimed that "there is no section on earth where the soil and the farmers have more need of the blessings which grass culture and dairying bring." Farmers must grow grasses and lay them up as hay in winter. During the summer months, cows would pasture and provide organic matter to fertilize the soil. As the situation stood now, he complained, southerners must buy their own fertilizer. Those fertilizer costs taxed small cotton farmers "to the limit." Fertilizer costs recurred yearly. Dairying was ever profitable. Manure repairs the soil, while cow's milk "produces a cash crop surer than cotton." Whenever a southern farmer brought in northern-grown hay or northern-mined fertilizer, Collingwood thought it "looks as if his wagon were a hearse carrying the soul of his farm."[43]

Wilbur Fisk Massey, former editor of the *Practical Farmer* and a frequent contributor to the *Rural New-Yorker* under the moniker Maryland Farmer, refused to countenance diversified farming for the cotton South. He had long ridiculed those commentators who considered corn, wheat, and oats simply as "supplies" for cotton planters to keep profits on the farm. What he advocated instead was systematic farming—"the permanent improvement of the soil through wise rotation of crops." It required growing legumes for feed, feeding it to cattle and making manure. The manure was plowed back into the soil. In that manner, soil fertility could be maintained and the cotton crop stay as bountiful as ever. The cattle could be bred and sold as milch cows or for meat, providing farmers with a second and more dependable source of income.[44]

The *Rural New-Yorker* was hardly the first proponent for dairy cattle in the South. As early as 1902, the USDA published a Farmers Bulletin on the possibilities of southern dairying. Written by S. M. Tracy, a grassman who knew Montgomery well and through that association had become the first director of the Mississippi Agricultural Experiment Station, the pamphlet outlined step by step instructions for dairying and how to build milk houses, barns, and the like. Other than pointing out the South's climatic advantages, Tracy's pamphlet discussed nothing particularly southern. Its utility was as a dairy manual. Four years later, the Dairy Division of the USDA's Bureau of Animal Industry began field work to develop a dairy industry in the South. Among the things that spawned the Bureau's effort was a sense that the milk supplies of southern cities were sadly deficient, a fact that the field work confirmed. Herds were kept in deplorable conditions within city limits among filth "almost knee-deep." Milking and delivery techniques eschewed sanitation. The survey also identified several creameries—places producing butter for market—but noted that these sites were miniscule; farmers for their own use made 250 times the butter as did those manufactories. Few southerners made cheese commercially or for personal use. Ice cream, however, was popular in large southern cities and produced in those places.

The field work concluded that dairying in the South was profoundly unprofitable. Cows produced little milk when compared to their northern counterparts. Their animals were fed poorly and, since a large portion of the region's cows were city-based, rarely pastured. Feed was often brought in from afar. The milk produced in these southern cities was thin and often sour. The report concluded with "three main points." To be profitable, farmers needed "better cows, more homegrown feed, better product." In short, dairying in the South did not exist as a for-profit enterprise.[45]

It would be wrong to suggest that nothing changed in the dairy South in the nearly fifteen years after the Bureau's report. A small number of creameries opened, especially near large cities or in conjunction with agricultural colleges. These schools endeavored to practice what they preached. They provide opportunity—a market—for any nascent dairy movement they might inculcate. A college creamery also served students, acquainting them with all the nuances of the business, and curious farmers by showing them the financial benefits that could accrue to them if they adopted dairy practice.

This began to change in about 1920. Any number of observers began to suggest that the South should become America's dairyland. In fact, J. J. Reasor, a Gallatin, Tennessee, stockman, argued that it was "time to make Nashville the Elgin of the South." Rather than go to Illinois, Iowa, and Wisconsin for dairy products, Tennessee should become the dairy center for the South and East.[46] L. O. Thayer, editor of *Ice Cream World*, a New York City–based publication, chose not to go the optimist's route. He despaired at how little the USDA and the agricultural colleges did since the Bureau's field trials, maintaining that whatever dairy industry existed in the South was the consequence of the ice cream boom the past three years. That market indicated to farmers that money could be made from dairying. Citing a USDA study, Thayer called on cotton planters to "bring in a million high class stock from the north and start a real dairying industry." He was particularly bullish on the Carolinas and Tennessee but predicted that Mississippi "will be about the last state to develop in a dairy way." There "little is being done." He did not fault the land. It was the cows that Mississippians kept. Tours there showed that "they are all the same breed of runts and have the appearance of always being dry." These animals failed even to produce milk enough for those who owned them, he surmised. Retailers in Mississippi conceded that they sold more condensed and evaporated milk than any other item.

Thayer found that shocking fact "enticing." A monopoly selling all the condensed milk in Mississippi would make the salesman "as rich as Rockefeller." While the "natives have other ideas for farming," Thayer called on a northern entrepreneur to establish a southern dairy industry. Once that happened, he concluded, the Midwest would be vanquished from the dairy business. "Illinois would have to look at its corn laurels and the Dakotas to its wheat."[47]

USDA statistics revealed later that year disagreed with Thayer's gloomy scenario. It found in the thirteen years since the last USDA accounting the number of cows had increased by 50 percent, with purebred cattle making up the bulk of the increase. Purebred bull associations now dotted the region. Agents attributed the rise in the number of dairy cattle to the establishment of "a system that would supply the home demand for dairy products and at the same time build up and maintain soil fertility, both by supplying manure and by enforcing a proper rotation of crops." Cotton yields proved greater on less land. To store feed for winter, county agents worked directly with farmers to build silos, jointly constructing nearly two thousand such structures.[48]

USDA and extension specialists worked hard to erect a home dairy operation that would be economically viable, what they called "profitable dairying. The aim was not to produce "the greatest possible quantity of milk" but to produce "the greatest possible quantity of milk at the lowest possible cost." Cost, not gross output, became the guiding principle. Farming, first and foremost, was not about growing. It was about profiting. A basic rule was to feed cows "what the farm produces" rather than purchase expensive grains exclusively. Alfalfa, cowpeas and beans made inexpensive dairy feeds a farmer could grow.[49]

By 1921 it was clear that southern farmers, particularly in Tennessee, had established developing dairying areas. East Tennessee was often hailed for its small but solvent dairying concern.[50]That the region suffered its worst cotton production in thirty-three years no doubt provided some of the impetus. As one observer noted, southern cotton was subjected to "the Boll Weevil, Army Worm, Drouth, and Rain" all in one growing season. Another commentator looked at the economic blight and saw a hopeful sign. "Adversity is the world's greatest teacher," he claimed. "Prosperity only makes men forget." Now was the time for all cotton producers to recognize the benefits of the "Market on Four Legs." He went on to point out that dairy cattle fertilize the soil, as do the silage crops. They produce milk and meat, both of which can be sold. "Now is the time for the South to begin to break that vicious circle." His pointed conclusion: the South's need was "less cotton and more cows."[51]

Dairying combined two economic interests in one cow. Cows produced manure and milk. One enriched the soil and the other enriched the farmer's family and others. Livestock production, especially of cattle, had many of the same virtues. Cattle breeding enabled farmers to employ manure to help cotton. Stock required good fodder, which meant that a portion of a farm served as pastureland for cattle to roam and to grow silage for winter months. As the animals matured, they could be sold either as breeding stock or for meat, producing a renewable income source. While many northerners remained fixated on dairying, southern commentators recognized a significant livestock industry in the region.[52] G. H. Hunnicutt, editor of the *Southern Cultivator*, devoted considerable attention to cattle raising. Arguing that he could not see how farmers are "to prosper without having cattle to convert food into beef and cash," he argued that no matter the economic climate "you can always sell finished cattle for a fair price."[53]

In a decade, the agricultural arsenal of the American South changed markedly. Cotton dominated, as it had for a century. What accompanied that dominant crop, and how it was conceived and justified, took different forms. At the beginning of the decade, interventionists sought to change the nature of farmers and farming. Diversification was their clarion call and they sought to inspire southern agriculturists to redraft enterprises. Significant enthusiasm greeted these efforts—in fact, that was the method of delivery—but they achieved only a modicum of influence. The fundamental difficulties with southern agriculture that diversification sought to address remained. Reconsidering the cotton South—not fighting it—enabled agricultural college and extension agents in the years during America's involvement in World War I and after to plow what had now become a fertile field. They focused explicitly on sustaining cotton agriculture. They aimed to prop up that dominant crop by making farmers' livelihoods independent of it. By fostering a subsequent or secondary income stream for farmers, the nexus of agricultural college, extension agent, USDA, and agricultural newspapermen made it possible for farmers to better weather and survive whatever economic storm befell them. In the case of cattle breeding and dairying, manure also helped farmers restore their land and secure higher yields per acre, which increased farm income. Put quite simply, when cotton farmers grew beef or dairy cattle, the purpose was almost always in service to cotton. Cotton remained king and the new pursuits were to stabilize, develop, and maintain equilibrium for the farm economy. Stock raising and dairying became mechanisms to convert cotton farming into a reasonable, possible business. It was that agriculture that greeted Borden when it began to examine the dairy South.

4 | STARKVILLE?

The Serendipity of Cattle in a Small Town's Search for Economic Salvation

Borden undertook its search for its southern experiment the way it pursued most of its activities—with careful, detailed planning. New to the region, it did not have some preconceived notions about what spots might be the most attractive. The company could pour over USDA and experiment station reports, read agricultural periodicals, and check various statistical measures. But it had a much better set of indicators. Those salesmen employed by the company's sales/advertising arm traveled in the region, lived there, and talked to retailers and others in their territories. They had boots on the ground. Their jobs were to learn the wants, desires, and predilections of both their areas and their clientele and report to the main office. Those reports became the basis of new advertisements and often revamped production practices.

Although these young men almost always came from a town within the region—and therefore might be less than objective about where Borden ought to build—the company trusted them implicitly. It was on their reports—their intelligence—that the company staked its profitability and hence its future. Their understanding of how Borden operated, how Borden approached things, was a fundamental prerequisite for their reports on their territory's desires. They needed to recognize what should be reported and how it should be cast so that the company could best benefit. That confidence placed in a relatively junior group provided an immediacy and dependability that enabled Borden to tailor their sales and manufacturing work quickly and effectively to maximize gain.

In February 1923, Borden's New York City–based officers met with its southern sales representatives in Jacksonville, Florida. From this meeting apparently came recommendations for possible sites for the nation's first southern condensery. Several contenders emerged. Starkville, Mississippi, was among those selected.[1]

Starkville stood as the seat of Oktibbeha County and was situated near its center in east central Mississippi. The county rested on a friable limestone cropping—Selma Chalk—somewhat different that the more famous Black Belt. Numerous streams traversed it and rolling hills marked the territory. Its soils were deep, moderately well drained, and slowly permeable, overlaid with chalky sediments. The county's mild winters and hot humid summers provided an extensive growing season, while its abundant rainfall precluded massive irrigation efforts.

The city of Starkville had long been on the make. Its location adjacent to the state agricultural college, which welcomed its first class in 1880, gave Starkville a permanence and security that most other small rural communities lacked. Its tiny population more than tripled when the college opened, up to about 1,500. Forty years later, Starkville was still small; it had only 2,500 residents. Sluggish growth also marked the area's cotton and corn agriculture. Both crops grew comparatively poorly. Farmers had great difficulty keeping their lands free of grasses, which grew there in abundance but choked the cotton and corn, robbed them of nutrients, and harbored pests.[2]

While cotton and corn crops proved problematic in Oktibbeha County, Starkville grew one thing well—southern agricultural newspapers. In the later nineteenth and early twentieth centuries, Starkville was a hotbed of agricultural newspapers. Since there often existed little distinction between newspaper editors and college professors, several of these men also held positions at the agricultural college. The *Southern Livestock Journal, Southern Farm Gazette, Southern Ruralist,* and *Progressive Farmer*—major journals all—held their main editorial offices in Starkville. These newspapers provided the place with a visibility that belied its size. With the college, Starkville always reigned as a knowledge center of the cotton South. The editors' opinions and recommendations were felt far beyond the state.[3]

The county's agricultural life changed somewhat when W. B. Montgomery returned following the Civil War. Trained in the method of a southern gentlemen at Princeton, he traveled widely even after he resettled on his Mississippi plantations. His many trips included several to England—he was a cotton broker—in the early 1870s. There he was introduced to purebred Jersey cows and imported several to his Mhoon Valley estate, just north of Oktibbeha County. The first several animals died due to "acclimation disease"—probably cattle tick fever. Montgomery continued to bring English Jerseys to Mississippi. He had 3 registered Jerseys in 1872. In 1876, he listed 31 animals on the registry, 13 of which were bulls. Finally, he established his breeding stock and sold their progeny in 1877 "as fully acclimated."[4] As his Jersey herd started to take shape, Montgomery founded and edited the *Southern Livestock Journal*. Its pages traced the history of the new agricultural college—he was a trustee for a quarter century and instrumental in getting the school placed near Starkville—and discussed topics related to farming, particularly livestock. As Montgomery put it, his periodical was "the only paper published in the gulf states, giving special prominence to our grass and live stock interests. It embraces . . . Field, Orchard and Garden." The journal also aimed "to encourage immigration and the development of all the Agricultural and Mechanical interests of the South."[5]

Quite a heady agenda, and one at odds with most of the region's agriculturists. Cows had been anathema to cotton farmers. They still were. They walked where they wished, often trampling crops. If farmers kept any on their land, they raised them incidentally. Extremely lean, they foraged wherever they chose. They cost virtually nothing to raise and potentially served the farm as draft animals. Rarely did they offer the household significant milk and meat.[6]

Scrub cows had little to do with Montgomery's southern agricultural vision. He championed diversified farming, arguing that keeping money at home would transform the cotton South. Farmsteads were to be farmsteads, not one-crop extractive operations.[7] Livestock had to be part of that mix, and Montgomery had recognized southern scrub cattle as woefully inefficient. If kept as part of a livestock operation rather than allowed to wander and graze, their output would not come close to justifying costs. They would need to be fed to produce more than a modicum of milk and beef and their physical limitations would make the economics prohibitive. Montgomery turned to purebreds for that reason. Though more costly initially, they provided dependable, efficient conversion of feed to milk and meat. Their progeny demonstrated the same desirable characteristics.[8]

That set the issue at how to feed these precious animals most economically. Expensive feeds would raise the cost of livestock precipitously. Taking advantage of the climate and soils where he lived, Montgomery accentuated growing various grasses, heretofore the bane of cotton farmers. He quickly put several hundred acres to pasture at his estates around the city, making sure to define what was growing where and identifying its characteristics. He found that he could feed his Jerseys on pasture year-round, and with the exception of Timothy, all the grasses he tried worked reasonably well.[9]

Montgomery resolved the stock feeding problem to his satisfaction, but what he truly mastered was advocacy. As a trustee he lobbied for dairying and livestock raising as important features at the agricultural school, even though both were very minor industries in the region.[10] He used his journal in any number of ways to promote Jerseys over other breeds and ran frequent discussions of the various breeds' merits for assorted purposes. He especially favored the Jersey's small size, its docility, the fact that it gained weight and produced milk at minimal cost. The breed's milk was high in butterfat, which facilitated butter-making.[11] When accused in 1883 of using the journal to profit from his involvement with Jersey cattle, he turned the paper over to his son, Edwin. The substance of the *Southern Livestock Journal* did not change, but Montgomery was shielded from any further claim of impropriety.[12] He pushed diversified farming and championed grass culture at the college. Professor D. L. Phares' classic, *Farmer's Book of Grasses and Other Forage Plants for the Southern United States*, was a tribute to his persistence. Montgomery advised farmers interested in adding livestock to first buy purebred bulls as the way to enhance their herds most effectively. He relentlessly pushed the college to establish a creamery, which it did reluctantly in 1885.[13] His group of Jerseys, which he kept on five of his farms, became the largest collection of purebred Jerseys in the world. He was a regular participant in cattle auctions, seeking always to enhance his herd. He stood as the go-to source for farmers purchasing breeding stock.[14] He sold more purebred cows than any single farmer in the state and probably in the South. When a New Yorker wrote to the *Southern Livestock Journal* that northern butter far exceeded the quality of its southern counterparts,[15] Montgomery established a considerable butter-making operation that distributed its wares to the whole of Oktibbeha County. He funded and acted as chairman of a railroad company to serve his butter delivery area. His butter occasionally made it to Mobile and New Orleans. Montgomery helped to establish county, state, and gulf-coast livestock associations and, after getting the college to erect a creamery, a county dairy association.[16] He opened his farms to skeptics of all stripes—grass-feeding, butter-making, Jersey-breeding skeptics—to make his very specific and concrete points.[17] An inveterate booster of the area, he recruited investors to establish the town's first cotton mill in 1902. By the time of his death in 1904, Starkville and Oktibbeha country were known for their Jersey cattle.[18]

Various parts of Montgomery's program continued after his death. Grasses still held a prominent place in county agriculture, and Jerseys by far outpaced any other breed. His indefatigable spirit brooked no compromise and his persistence, coupled with his sizable wealth that enabled him always to be heard, supported many a venture. With Montgomery leaving the scene, the diversified agriculture drumbeat lessened and commercial buttermaking nearly ceased. The college creamery and its private competitors left the business. Oktibbeha County and Starkville continued to breed cattle but not generally for milking or for local beef consumption. The area became a singularly impressive stockbreeding and stockfinishing operation. In fact, the college created a specialty in "dairying and stock breeding" to help further the local economy. Oktibbeha residents bred prime dairy and beef cattle and supplied them to two distinct major markets. They shipped them to the North and the Southwest to become the stock for dairy operations or to southern cities for butchering. They went in the railroad carloads. In 1906, 129 carloads of Mississippi beef left for the stockyards in St. Louis, just one of the major cities served by Oktibbeha cows. In 1909, the number registered 975 carloads, an increase of more than sevenfold. Oktibbeha cattle were in such demand that some were even purchased for and shipped to the Philippines. Cattle became so ubiquitous within the city limits that the Board of Aldermen passed legislation impounding cattle wandering in the city and fined their owners as they charged them for water and hay during imprisonment.[19]

Oktibbeha County farmers did not raise cattle to supplement cotton agriculture generally. They grew cows rather than bolls. Oktibbeha had become, according to Thomas Wood, editor of the *Starkville News,* "grass and hence a cattle county." In effect, a new kind of monoculture arose next to the cotton monoculture. It prized pasture and well-water. Silos and cattle barns marked its landscape. And like cotton agriculture, which was inflicted with the boll weevil, cattle culture had its own disease. Cattle tick fever sickened and diminished cattle and caused uncountable deaths. Prevention required dipping animals at regular intervals in vats of an arsenical solution to eliminate the pests. In 1906 the federal government appropriated money to treat cattle in the South, but dipping remained voluntary. Farmers had to be convinced to bring their cattle to be dipped about every two weeks. Dipping was critical on two counts. First, ticks could be spread among a farmer's animals. Second, other farmers, many distant, refused animals from areas where the tick was active, or quarantined them before they were slaughtered or integrated into new herds.

There was a certain sad irony in Mississippians shifting to cattle tick–infested cattle to get away from boll weevil–infested cotton. Mississippi engaged the tick only after many of its southern counterparts began to quarantine Magnolia State cattle. Inaction held economic consequences. Some Oktibbeha cattlemen continued to view dipping with suspicion. They heard any number of pleas to get their cattle dipped. The Oktibbeha branch of the Farmers' Union proved particularly aggressive. Meeting in early 1908, this collective of area farmers heard of the disease's devastation from professors at the agricultural college and learned of the movement in the legislature to appropriate money so individual farmers would not bear dipping costs. They also received a call from the state livestock association, an institution that had fallen into inaction with Montgomery's death but had been revived at the state fair in November 1907 precisely to fight the cattle tick, to work together to get this measure passed.[20]

As the state-leading cattle county, the Oktibbeha legislative delegation urged that state government act. J. H. Wellborn, the county's representative, introduced a measure to establish a state tick board and enforce a quarantine against persons refusing to dip animals. It passed in less than a month. Smaller Oktibbeha towns created their own livestock associations to coerce fellow farmers to dip. The new board systematically inspected cattle from north to south in Mississippi. It found the going slow and estimated it would take several years to get the state off quarantine lists.[21]

Things progressed more swiftly than the board had imagined. Neighboring states lifted the quarantine on a county by county basis. By August 1909, several states again accepted Oktibbeha County cattle. With this good news the state livestock association joined with the recently revived Mississippi Dairy Association—an organization Montgomery had helped found—to form a new group, the Mississippi Live Stock and Dairy Association. It met at the state agricultural college near Starkville and devoted an entire day to livestock and dairy interests. E. R. Lloyd, director of the Mississippi Agricultural Experiment Station, put together the program. The dairy association's rebirth reflected that county dairying had rebounded from its previously depressed state, and was recognized statewide.[22] It also indicated that in the fight against tick fever the two industries were inseparable. Both combined to fight and keep away that devastating pest. Three members of the college faculty served as the organization's first officers: Tait Butler, veterinarian and editor of the *Progressive Farmer*, J. S. Moore, professor of dairy, and Archibald Smith, professor of livestock and secretary of the new tick board. The organization undoubtedly chose three agricultural college faculty to head efforts because its members recognized they faced a technical problem. But the choice of leaders showed something more: the rise of the college in the county's agricultural affairs. The school had never been entirely absent. But neither had it been a vital cog in the county's agricultural efforts. Now it pledged to become a full partner. The station asked for the assembled to report on their livestock practices so that they could be disseminated in a station bulletin. "Make it a medium of exchange for ideas and experiences," Lloyd stated. "The experience of a man who has been successful will be worth a great deal to others."[23]

While these sentiments were not usually associated with college personnel who wanted to trumpet their special training over practical experience, they were certainly effective in gaining a hearing—and ultimately power—in the new effort. The college had what the livestock and dairymen desired: assistance in eliminating a scientifically identified widespread pest that was ruining their economic prospects. The college wanted farmers to recognize that doing what their faculty indicated would improve farm economics. In the case of the cattle tick, both sides got what they coveted. College faculty got a bit more, a foot in the door that would be kicked wide open with passage of the Smith-Lever Act.

The college faculty moved almost immediately to extend this cattleman–college relationship. They joined with officials from the USDA Bureau of Animal Industry—who had long tried to create a southern dairy industry—to hold a number of three-day dairy institutes across the state. Lloyd and Smith also purchased a farmstead to serve as a model dairy, which aimed to convert area farmers to the dairying cause.[24]

Neither initiative proved successful. Governor Edmund Noll destroyed any chance to extend the nascent college-farmer livestock union. He fired Smith from the cattle tick board and had his trustees remove Smith from his college post, which also killed the model dairy farm experiment. The Mississippi Live Stock and Dairy Association passed a resolution protesting the Governor's callow act. Butler, then president of the organization, cast the Governor's initiative as pure political cronyism and wondered what it meant for the beef and dairy industries in the state.[25]

He did not have long to wait. The newly constituted tick board did not move aggressively to clear Mississippi of the tick. Both in Starkville and Oktibbeha County as a whole, the situation got much worse. Residents failed to capitalize on the early success of cattle dipping and became lax. Several large breeders objected to the program's cost, and the county board of supervisors revoked its policy of working with state and federal officials to apprehend and punish livestock farmers reticent to clear their cattle of the scourge.[26]

With the near-total absence of enforcement, the disease returned in numbers large enough to place the county back on the quarantine list. Contemporaries wondered if the quarantine would doom the county's beef cattle trade. It profoundly affected the trade in milk cow breeding stock. Separately marked railroad cars transported cattle from quarantined areas. Once at their destination, butchers either slaughtered the animals immediately or placed them in specially marked pens far from "clean" cattle where they were housed and fed for weeks until clearing quarantine. Cars in any of these transactions then needed sterilization to rid them of ticks before they could again become rolling stock. In any case, purchasing quarantined cattle raised costs prohibitively and unnecessarily. The economics seems so perilous that it was feared that markets that had been taking Starkville cattle for years would now seek new livestock suppliers, leaving traditional partners behind.[27]

The restored quarantine provided the backdrop for two agricultural enterprises. The first renewed the call for diversifying the county's agricultural practices. On cotton land, part of the farmstead served as pasture and for forage. Oats, wheat, rye, and corn followed where vetch, crimson and burr clover, and alfalfa were grown. As always, cow manure was plowed into the soil as were corn stalks and other organic material. In this system of agriculture, cattle and grains existed simply for the family, the animals, or the local market. They were not significant for profit additions. Cows ate the grasses, grains, and fodder crops. They fertilized the ground, saving on manufactured fertilizer costs. They produced milk and meat to prevent the farm's owners from squandering cotton moneys purchasing the family's foods. As an unidentified writer noted, "live stock offers the best means for diversification and combatting the boll weevil."[28]

The efforts of the International Harvester (IH) Extension Department and the "Grown in Mississippi" campaign capitalized on this iteration of diversification in a few short years. Appeals for diversification provided a potent rationale for a local livestock market, especially among area cotton farmers. The other initiative seized more explicitly on the quarantine's vagaries. The character of Oktibbeha cattle raising changed significantly from just a few years earlier. Ironically, the cattle tick provided livestock agriculture in the Southeast a visibility and immediacy that that type of farming rarely had had before. These animals stood at the forefront of government policy and in the minds of Mississippians generally. Bureau of Animal Industry and other federal officials regularly ventured to the area to press their programs. That prominence led farmers to investigate cattle-raising possibilities even as it fixed the idea that they might be difficult to ship to market. Quarantining disrupted long-standing distribution arrangements, especially in areas distant from Starkville. But it also opened new marketing venues. Forcing cattlemen to keep their animals within the state or county would require them to find productive uses for these creatures. Diversification of agriculture was one route. Dairying—figuratively converting these animals into butter—was another. The Mississippi Live Stock and Dairy Association talked not only ticks but also milk, and it invited B. H. Rawls, USDA dairy division chief, to address them about dairying in the South. He urged farmers to adopt dairying, noting that after butterfat was skimmed for butter, farmers could feed calves and pigs the residue, in effect providing dairy agriculture a secondary market.[29]

As the county opened itself to dairying in addition to feeding and breeding, Montgomery's long obsession with Jerseys began to find purpose. Oktibbeha's preponderance of purebred Jerseys proved in this difficult milieu what Montgomery had preached them to be—excellent multipurpose cattle. They produced milk high in butterfat, and for their size were quite prolific. Jerseys were efficient in transforming fodder into flesh and did so at a relatively low cost, making them more than suitable as beef cattle. Their relatively short finishing time was a plus.[30]

Whether the quarantine revealed already established local dairy interests or helped promulgate them, dairying was now an acknowledged part of the Oktibbeha landscape. The local dairy farmer churned his own butter and sold it through a Starkville merchant. If supply exceeded demand, which it occasionally did in the summer months, he sent it to nearby cities.

That model changed when Noll left office in 1912. A new college president, G. R. Hightower, took over. A former state legislator and then-sitting president of the Mississippi Farmers' Union—a consortium of cotton farmers—he accepted the office with a notion that the college, including its experiment station, should essentially pay for itself. Its station should not simply experiment but grow crops to help defray experiment costs. Otherwise, what lesson was the station teaching farmers?[31] Moore took Hightower's appointment and its attendant philosophy as an opportunity to propose to operate a cooperative creamery at the college. The college herd already approached a hundred cows and coupled with the area dairymen, he ascertained he could make it a paying concern. A preparatory meeting indicated that the creamery would draw 300 cows at the onset with a promise that the market would expand.[32] Part of Moore's agenda may well have been the idea that a creamery would promote dairying in Oktibbeha. For over a decade, Starkville area dairymen had no easy outlet for their milk. Beyond the small local market and the farm churn, raw fluid milk with butterfat skimmed from that milk with a home skimmer needed to be taken to a center to be processed into butter or cheese. The implications were clear. Without a creamery or some such institution, profitable dairying in Starkville was difficult.

Moore immediately got allies in his creamery venture. It became the focal point of the A&M exhibit at the state fair. The federal government also joined in. Rawls's tour of the area some months before had convinced him of its manifest dairying possibilities. He acted to make the longstanding USDA efforts to introduce commercial dairying into the South a reality. Rawls assigned a dairy division agent who had been working on developing dairying in Lafayette County, W. I. Bleeker, to the college and brought down as his assistant, L. A. Higgins, who was in Brookhaven as part of the Harvester service department's demonstration farm. The *Jackson Daily News* summed up the state-federal partnership succinctly: "The college, aided by the government, is doing much to help novices in the dairy business."[33]

Bleeker and Higgins drew up silo and sanitary barn plans to bring young dairymen into the fold. In less than a month, they recorded twenty-seven requests for plans. Once they finished designing the plans, the real work begun. They took their designs and went to farmsteads with "overalls and intelligence to do the job with dispatch and thoroughness." The college-situated, USDA men "will help you to select your cows, your herd bull, to build your dairy barn or your silo, and will show you how to make a profit out of the dairy cow."[34]

Even with Washington's support, Moore's speculative cooperative creamery placed him at odds with established parameters for a successful venture. Creamery after creamery failed without at least 500 dedicated cows. Butler made the case time and again. "It has proven disastrous wherever and whenever cooperative creameries have been established to encourage dairying," he wrote. "Until we have more dairy cows the cooperative creamery will continue to fail as it has in the past." "Financial loss" was only one consequence of a bankrupt creamery. Its repercussions resonated throughout an area. It would mean nothing less than, claimed Butler, "a set-back to the dairy business" in all of Oktibbeha County. He wanted to make sure that no one misunderstood his objection. Butler backed creameries "when sufficient milk is available," but without that volume "they are as useless as an ice-making plant at the North Pole."[35]

Locals disagreed. They recognized that the venture could not fail because it "will surely create a demand in the county for Dairy cows." Hedging his bets only a bit, the *Starkville News'* Wood called on his fellow citizens to "all see that this department is encouraged." Its success will rebound throughout the county and "demonstrate to the people . . . the possibilities of this work."[36]

The question of which must come first, the creamery or the cows, persisted, but in the case of the agricultural college creamery it remained a false dichotomy. So long as the USDA and the college were willing to pour money to prop up the creamery, it would not fail. It would provide members with the opportunity to sell their milk for profit. The college did its part. It went to state fairs and promoted dairying and creameries. The USDA also attended these venues and erected its own dairy displays. Time after time they trumpeted the area and its dairy cows. In Oktibbeha County, "all grasses and clovers grow to perfection and [are] a great source of wealth to our farmers." The creamery "has proven a great success." In state butter-tasting contests, the college creamery—the state's only commercial creamery—sometimes won. Dairy cows "will redeem the country," gushed an observer, "and make it bloom and blossom as the rose of health and prosperity, whose fragrance of happiness will be borne upon every breeze." The "dairy interests have grown to large proportions," claimed another. Because "it keeps money in circulation at all seasons," the dairy cow is "the best friend to business." To "go to grass" used to be an insult for poor farmers. "It directs one now to a gold mine." Some worried if there would be markets enough for the anticipated deluge of Mississippi butter. Others dismissed those sentiments out of hand. Until there are more creameries in the state "than in the dairy areas of Illinois, there will be no lack of a ready market for the product."[37]

These fulsome statements boosted Oktibbeha County but they did not reflect reality. The college remained so unsure of an extensive butter market that they cautioned dairymen to add eggs and chickens to their dairy concerns to safeguard incomes. It wasn't until 1916, four years after the creamery opened, that the area produced enough butter to send a carload to the north. Rather than expand, the number of cows at the college creamery decreased during its early years.[38] The various rosy statements were fluff but had two main objectives. First, Starkvillians desperately wanted immigration into the county. They wanted young white men to come to the area and seek their fortune. Immigration revived an otherwise somnolent community with new ideas, new energies, and most of all, new moneys. Second, they hoped to create a truly thriving dairy industry in Mississippi. Declining cotton and corn yields, the weevil, and fluctuating cattle prices repeatedly placed farmers on the brink. Dairying, in lieu of cotton and corn or in addition to cotton and corn, promised a more predictable income stream. What really happened in Oktibbeha in the years before the United States entered the war was twofold. First, the number of cattle did grow considerably in the county but for breeding and meat, not nearly so much for dairying, and the legislature made considerable strides to resolve the tick dipping situation and free Oktibbeha of quarantine. It passed legislation in 1916 requiring each county where the tick persisted to dip cattle regularly until such time as the tick board certified the county clean from ticks. The was no option. It was a mandate.[39]

By the mid-1910s, beef and cattle breeding dwarfed cotton in Oktibbeha County. Shipped cattle brought in over one million dollars in 1916. The county's cotton crop that year fetched only $300,000. A year earlier, a single livestock concern purchased a thousand head of Oktibbeha County cattle at one time. It took three engines and thirty railroad cars to transport the animals to the new owner. These figures dramatize the fundamental change in the area's agriculture. Cotton and corn, dominant earlier in the century, had been supplanted by beef and breeding cattle. Raising cattle for beef or for breeding stock required a significant investment not in infrastructure but for the animals. Hardscrabble or tenant farmers and sharecroppers lacked the resources to conduct this type of farming themselves. Manure, which had been at a premium, now was readily available. The county's natural limestone outcroppings resulted in a calcium-rich dirt that sweetened the soil. Little of this transformation came willingly. It was the product of years of effort, publicity, government programs, and other factors. It was borne not from complacency but rather anxiety, at least as much on the part of all persons dependent on the success of farming in Oktibbeha County as the actual farmers themselves. In many if not most cases they had heavy investments in both camps.[40]

During the war, the situation changed dramatically. The massive exportation of condensed milk and butter, coupled with milk producers' strikes in many metropolitan markets, put great strain on southerners. A significant proportion of the region had relied on condensed rather than fluid milk. Because of the war, the supply to the South diminished and the price skyrocketed. Graham T. Golson, editor of the *Starkville News* since 1916, took notice. "Oktibbeha County is conceded to be one of the greatest dairy sections of the world." Yet in Starkville it was "next to impossible . . . to buy sweet milk and buttermilk." Because of this, "there are families suffering for the want of milk." The USDA and county agents confronted similar situations throughout the South and worked to replace the condensed milk and butter that went to Europe and to the north with local products. Enticed by these area and regional markets and the high price for these precious commodities, Mississippians accepted the challenge right away. Dairy surveys of the state at the war's conclusion were remarkably different than those on the eve of America's involvement. Creameries had been established throughout the state. Where there had been one creamery in 1912, there now were 22, most of which were war creations. The amount of butter produced in 1914 was about 200,000 pounds statewide. In 1917, it mushroomed to 1.5 million pounds and in 1918, Mississippi's creameries made 3 million pounds of butter, which sold at nearly a dollar a pound. In 1919, 27 creameries operated in the state and butter output neared 4 million pounds. "A steady and growing market . . . for Mississippi dairy products" existed "in the larger cities of the South," wrote the head of the Mississippi Creamery Association, an offshoot of the Board of Trade in Jackson, Mississippi. Others feared that the butter surge in the state would soon collapse. "Creameries have been organized faster and in a greater ratio than can be properly supplied" for their continued operation, worried one observer. He understood that the dairy boom's consequences went beyond butter. "I watch with astonishment," he continued, at "how much and how rapidly our soils are improved and built up by dairy herds."[41]

Cow manure improved Starkville's soils. The town's business environment had long seemed resistant to fertilization. In the first decade of the twentieth century, the only industry introduced into Starkville capitalized on its major crop, cotton, and its major institution, the agricultural college. The state provided funding in 1900 to create a textile school at the college and a textile mill to train workers to manufacture goods and to design and operate mills.[42] Starkville's civic league, established by 1904, met and worked regularly from the proposition that a clean and modern infrastructure and a cultured population would attract settlers and industries from afar.[43] City newspapers harped on the fact that many nearby localities housed canning factories but remained puzzled that Starkville was unable to attract canners.[44] Few other business initiatives approached the city about establishing facilities there. Increasingly, Starkvillians wrote about neighboring communities, usually with undisguised envy. They did not begrudge their success. Rather, the stories pointed out how inept and lackadaisical Starkville seemed to have been in determining its own success. "Seriously and candidly speaking, good sidewalks are . . . the best indication of the character of a people," protested Golson as he noted the city's lack of sidewalks. In another piece, he wrote about Maben, a small Oktibbeha County town of roughly 500 persons. "We believe for its population," Maben has "more wealth than any other town in the state." The town's genius was its commercial elite. Maben businessmen were "prudent, cautious, diligent, and industrious, and in every way enterprising." Because of these men, Maben "can excel any place." Starkville was an entirely different situation. He considered Starkvillians too often "satisfied with what" they had. "It is up to you," he demanded of his neighbors and friends, "to stand still or grow." Looking around the city, his counterpart at the Starkville-based *East Mississippi Times* complained facetiously that if Starkville had a businessmen's group, "we don't know it." It must create one "by all means." Even neighboring Columbus was on the move. It continued "to grow more metropolitan." Some twenty-five miles from Starkville, the city now had all-night service at the post office, policemen now wore helmets, and the fire department had brand-new uniforms.[45]

Image was important and often synonymous with action, a fact not lost on Starkvillians. At about the time that the college created its creamery, Starkville welcomed D. A. Daniel, who represented the Southern Commercial Congress, a union composed of the secretaries of the commercial organizations in southern cities to create "a greater nation through a greater South." He urged cooperation with the regional congress and his audience agreed. It established the Starkville Progressive Business League and pledged "to promote a healthier and more prosperous business condition" and to encourage "immigration and the establishment of industries" within Oktibbeha County.

Its first act was to call for a paved road near the courthouse. It may well have been the group's last act. Within a year, the newspapers were again calling for a group of businessmen "to help boost Starkville," shaming that community by arguing that virtually every other Mississippi municipality had such a group pursuing their city's interests.[46]

Things remained quiet for years. Four years later, a similarly named entity formed in Starkville. The new Progressive Club acknowledged that Starkville was one of the few places in the region lacking a group "to promote public improvements, better industrial and agricultural conditions, increase trade relations and secure high class and beneficial publicity for Starkville and Oktibbeha County." Like its predecessor, it went on record with only one public declaration before disappearing. It urged the building of a grand hotel, "which will give credit to our city and meet a necessity that every progressive town demands."[47]

No new hotel came from the group's pronouncement. At about the time the second of the ephemeral progressive organizations was established, Starkville created its second Civic League. Unlike the earlier club by that name, women comprised the new organization's entire membership. They looked to update the city's privy system and garbage collection and to clean up any eyesores that might appear. The reorganization sprung from desperation. The college's Field Day was less than a month away and as many as ten thousand people would attend. The women did not want to miss making a statement that Starkville was "a clean, beautiful, and sanitary city." The *Starkville News* celebrated the Civic League's success declaring that "a wave of progressivism sweeps over Starkville and Oktibbeha county." Apparently, storm sewers, gutters and arrangements for paving the city's Main Street put "Starkville in her proper place among the most progressive towns in the state."[48]

With the event that precipitated its formation passed, the Civic League fell into oblivion. A bold attempt to create a commercial league was announced at the end of the year, but it too drew no traction. In the spring of 1917, Memphis business groups held a meeting to inspire smaller cities from that metropolis's hinterlands to create businessmen's organizations. Starkville businessmen attended but there was no carryover on their return to their homes.[49]

A special Illinois Central Railroad train carried the Starkville contingent to and from Memphis. This combination of aspirant and transportation was more than apt. Railroads had been a primary development force in the South since about the turn of the century. Three major railways—the Southern, the Mobile & Ohio, and the Illinois Central—engaged Oktibbeha County residents. Each railway adopted similar objectives and to a certain extent similar methods. Each employed a series of individuals to advise and assist persons along their routes to improve fortunes and prospects. Almost all initiatives required new capital expenditures and involved area banks. At the heart of these endeavors lay a straightforward proposition. Railroads made their moneys carrying freight and to a lesser extent people. New ventures, more successful farmers, and additional settlers all increased road travel and boosted profits for the railroad.

The Illinois Central was a most active promoter of Oktibbeha County. In the decade before the war, it undertook a series of programs and initiatives aimed to transform the prospects of the area and Mississippi generally. A farmers' institute train was among its projects. On this vehicle rode Illinois Central–hired speakers preaching the new gospel of modern farming. It stopped in town after town as experts lectured farmers on the latest techniques and pleaded with the audience to heed their advice. The railroad's immigration agents employed different tactics. They rarely traveled, maintaining an office and mailing out promotional literature in English, German, Hungarian, and Italian. In one two-month period, the immigration office sent out 1,010,500 circulars and 80,000 pamphlets in 11 languages. At about the same time that the IH service department created its demonstration farms, the Illinois Central industrial agents established and ran their own demonstration farms in Mississippi. These farms grew a diversity of products and regularly exhibited their wares at the state fair. They even plastered their goods with "Grown in Mississippi" placards when that campaign had its heyday. The railroad's president sometimes visited sites along the company's tracks to give communities what amounted to a pep talk. In 1913 C. H. Markham, the longtime Illinois Central president, visited the Starkville area and laid out his vision for the area's agricultural future. West Tennessee and Mississippi "in a few years will be the great cattle raising lands in the United States," predicted Markham. Memphis will be transformed into "a city of packing houses." Cattle-loading pens will become as common as "depot cotton platforms are now." The South, he continued, is "one of the greatest grazing sections of the country. Everywhere alfalfa and clover."[50]

Illinois Central even had its own magazine—"a literary gem," noted one commentator—to drum up business. Its feature writers were "devoted to the development of the cities, towns, and country along its lines" and wrote about those places. Starkville was singled out in 1917 for a ten-page piece that was thorough and unsentimental yet positive. It covered the city's history, infrastructure, schools, churches, and the agricultural college. There was no mention of industrial activity. The article focused on the physical geographic character of Oktibbeha County and the types of agriculture practiced there. The writers spent considerable space on the area's cattle industry and discussed the grasses that grew in support of that practice. It did not neglect other agricultural products, highlighting the county's diverse crops and even arguing that cotton might now be only the third most popular crop there. The piece closed measuredly. It invited everyone seeking a home to investigate Starkville and Oktibbeha County "before deciding on a permanent location."[51]

To a lesser degree but in a similar manner, the Mobile & Ohio and the Southern involved themselves in Starkville and Oktibbeha development. The Southern aggressively formed a Cotton Culture Department to assist the USDA in slowing the boll weevil's spread, but in 1912 merged it into its Department of Farm Improvement Work. This department was a joint venture with the Mobile & Ohio as well as other railways. Its immediate goal was to show "farmers what they can do on their own resources." To that end, the department gathered material from local farmers and the agricultural college to publish a pamphlet "exploiting the advantages and resources of Oktibbeha County and the city of Starkville." The railroad consortium's longer term project was "increasing the prosperity of the territory traversed by its lines." The next year the M&O and Southern teamed up again, this time for a "silo train." Officially named the "Forage, Silo and Live Stock Special," it featured a tick eradication proponent joined by silo equipment and livestock. Its dairy agent joined in the tick campaign. That same year, the Southern created a group, Market Agents, to bring "producers" in its territories "into relations with buyers." These agents were touted as especially adept at establishing cooperative marketing and selling combinations, "strictly in accordance with business principles and keeping of accounts."[52]

Railroads carried commodities to and from cities. Roadways—asphalt, macadamized, or dirt—connected farmers to cities and cities to other places not served by railroads. Roads needed to be good—passable in all weather, stable enough not to require constant maintenance. Roads were costly, with the quality and length of the road dictating expense. But roads were also signs of civilization, progress, and prominence. It was not surprising that the quest for good roads accompanied other "progressive" initiatives and emerged frequently in the decade prior to the First World War. It was equally understandable that these thoroughfares were built only hesitantly in Mississippi. A series of entities needed to partner to provide the funding, routes, and techniques for roads. Cities and towns, counties, and the state did these things collectively, sometimes with federal assistance and guidance. While interested parties, industries, and political units often pushed for specific paths, development took time. Nonetheless, rarely did a year go by in Oktibbeha County and Starkville without at least some expansion of the local roads.[53]

Roadbuilding, railways, the college, Starkville, and area farmers had changed the character of Oktibbeha County in the years prior to the war. The county continued its cattle-breeding and beef emphasis during the war but was joined by a strong dairy expansion. Several post-war programs sustained the Mississippi dairy boom. The agricultural college, Oktibbeha County, and Starkville pioneered many of them. During the war and its aftermath, the college had helped farmers choose prime dairy stock—a purebred bull and purebred cows worth nearly $40,000 in toto. It also led six counties to establish cooperative bull associations to increase dairy productivity. In order to qualify, a bull needed to be descended from a cow that had provided at least 500 pounds of butter yearly. This bull, which they purchased together, lived on one farm but served as stud for the county association members' cows. It also had established a series of cow-testing clubs. One 800-pound Jersey ate roughly the same as another 800-pound Jersey. But not all Jerseys (or any other breed of cow) produced as much milk and butterfat as the next. The clubs measured the quantity and quality of the milk over time. The greatest butterfat producers were listed on an honor roll. Farmers culled the least productive cows from the fold, sent them to slaughter, and acquired more prolific animals.

After the war, area banks played an active interest in furthering local dairying. They developed a cooperative plan to "stimulate the pure-bred Jersey industry" in the county. Oktibbeha banks offered to finance purchase of prime purebred bulls. Understanding that many farmers lacked knowledge to discern between a high performing bull and another, and to protect their investment, the banks had farmers sign notes, gave the actual money to a "dairy expert" whose responsibility it was to go to the appropriate sale to select and purchase the most excellent bulls and then to deliver the bulls at cost to their new owners. The banks charged the actual price to the farmers' paper.[54] As the bulls began to arrive—a forty-piece marching band from the college welcomed the first carload—the banks created the Oktibbeha County Cooperative Jersey Association to bring "about rapid development of productive milk cows" through the "use, sale and exchange of meritorious pure-bred bulls" and through the judicious purchase of fine heifers and cows. Chaired by G. Odie Daniel, president of Starkville's Merchants and Farmers Bank, the county's largest cotton planter and the college creamery's biggest patron, the new association promised "to exert every possible influence for the improvement and furtherance of the livestock industry" in the county. To make that point, the group at its first meeting brought E. R. Lloyd to speak. Now director of the Memphis Bureau of Farm Development, a division of the Chamber of Commerce, and formerly the director of the Mississippi Agricultural Experiment Station, Lloyd talked of the economies generated through dairying with only tested purebred Jersey stock and urged his audience to spread that message far and wide.[55]

The college too did its part by creating instrumentalities that would perpetuate the changes made during the war. Even as the county association was getting organized, it acted to expand Jersey interests throughout the state. College dairy extension agent Higgins revived the quiescent

Mississippi Jersey Cattle Club, and to ensure it would move decisively had W. W. Magruder, a prominent Starkville lawyer and dairyman, installed as the club's president. Magruder, who had been a state senator, was in Jackson to address the state legislature on behalf of Oktibbeha County businessmen and the state agricultural college.[56] At the group's first annual meeting Magruder proclaimed that he "never saw a man go broke raising Jersey cattle" and then went on to discuss the virtues of that breed. In attendance that evening was H. J. Schwietert, industrial commissioner of the Illinois Central Railroad and fully vested in the state's dairy industry.

Schwietert's attendance at the meeting was no accident. With John B. DeMotte, who was an editor at the *Starkville News*, he was there to gather information for a new feature on Starkville. Entitled "Oktibbeha, 'The Jersey County of the South,'" the piece in the Illinois Central magazine was published under DeMotte's name. It appeared a mere three years after the initial Starkville article, an unprecedented occurrence. Its authors and the Illinois Central apparently thought a new article essential. Starkville and its environs seemed incredibly different than they had three years before. The new piece reflected the county's new reality. These was some discussion of the virtue of the land and soil but the vast majority of the article concentrated on the area's dynamic and thriving Jersey dairies and the agricultural college, which to DeMotte indicated "high civilization." To the Illinois Central's authors, Starkville and Oktibbeha were no longer searching for an identity. That identity had become the Jersey county of the South.

As he concluded the piece, DeMotte noted that in Oktibbeha County "life and living seem so close to perfection." He wondered why Wisconsin dairymen suffered "through the long and expensive winters . . . when the productive lands of Oktibbeha offer many superior advantages." Local citizens "are clamoring for more real farmers," he argued. Immigration of northern farmers to Starkville would bring "maximum prosperity to all."[57]

Publicity and constant boosterism were important, but institutional trappings were critical. When it came to sustaining the emerging dairy industry, one institution was far more crucial than all the others. The southern dairy industry's health depended almost entirely on creameries within the state—places that purchased milk daily—and the college worked to fortify those businesses. It created a three-month-long creamery short course to train a cadre of skilled creamery workers. Learning practice and theory in the college creamery, these trainees would fill the "demand for helpers, buttermakers, and managers for creameries" since demand for these workers "has far exceeded supply."[58]

Even as the college turned out workers for creameries throughout the state, it began to feel the pinch of too many creameries, too few cows. At the college creamery's annual meeting, Professor Moore outlined the facility's virtues, and the group resolved to recruit other local dairymen as members. Pride in the home institution was always tied to economic realities. A creamery's economic viability was hurt when a dairyman "ships out of the county to a privately owned creamery." By that single action, he "is serving his community poorly." Local dairymen were encouraged to "start shipping to A. & M. now. Get in line. Help your section of the state and yourself."[59]

While this generalized sentiment prevailed, the action of Sturgis dairymen made the situation raw. The second largest city in Oktibbeha County, Sturgis farmers sent their product two counties away to the Aberdeen creamery. For that act, they bore transportation costs for the fifty-mile journey. They received in return a weekly check, whereas the college creamery paid only monthly. The Kosciusko creamery, fifty miles distant from Starkville, also siphoned off customers. "If the members of our [creamery] would get the spirit and enthusiasm" behind it that the Kosciusko creamery has, "profits would be bigger all the way around."[60]

Golson took it upon himself to explain what each patron owed to "HIS creamery." A member's job was to increase the number of cooperative members and increase the quantity of milk. But more than that, every co-op member must "patronize HIS OWN CREAMERY." Cooperative creameries pay for the butterfat that each individual farmer delivers. But they also pay on the total amount of butterfat they turn into and sell as butter. Thus if a dairyman shuns his local creamery for one farther away, he is not only hurting himself but also his fellow co-op members. They will not get a share of the profits from his butterfat. Each co-op member needs to make "HIS cooperative creamery more successful by getting his neighbors interested and seeing that no cream from that neighborhood goes to any other creamery." As in all aspects of life, sometimes things go wrong in a creamery. Golson urged his readers that when such an occurrence took place they needed to come together "and get things straight." The worst thing a patron can do, Golson concluded, was to take the matter public. Do not under any circumstance, "knock your own business." It will discourage others from joining the cooperative. C. P. Barrett, the county's new extension agent, said it simply. The college's cooperative creamery "was the biggest step that has ever been made in the agricultural development of the county."[61]

The plea to support the college creamery at all costs signaled a change in how Starkvillians approached the dairy industry and, ultimately, economic development in general. Economic development meant more than economics. It demanded community, a certain communal spirit that often was antagonistic to the myth of the independent yeoman. The cry a decade of so earlier focused on how poor farmers hurt, even, ruined the communities that depended on them. Resolution was straightforward: Make better farmers by teaching them or replacing them. This new critique did not necessarily depict these men as inept at their trades. They were something worse, more perfidious, willingly selfish, or greedy as they refused to sacrifice their idea of economic mastery for communal success—the success of their neighbors, their town, their friends, themselves. They were asked to temper personal success for community success. This new discourse identified those who trod a different path as social miscreants, not bad farmers but bad or wayward people.

That intellectual reorientation posed numerous issues and ruled out various possibilities. Bad people were much more difficult to "fix" theoretically than bad farmers. What mechanisms, what institutions existed to affect such a transformation? Assuming that repair was unlikely, then communities needed to function without—and despite—these individuals. Metaphorically, they needed to cull these people from the herd. Excising the bad from the good accentuated what made the good, good. Policies, programs, and plans needed to seize on the good—those with, for want of a better word, community spirit—and build around that. Put another way, the cure for a lack of voluntarism and a modicum of self-sacrifice was the creation of institutions to coerce or encourage communal participation.

In Oktibbeha County dairying, newspapers, the college, and others redoubled efforts to press dairying's case. Efforts to convert more farmers to dairying, to have dairy farmers enlarge their herds and to bring in successful dairymen from distant locales took on a new intensity. While the litany of acts looks similar to past attempts to inculcate dairying in the county, the campaign in 1920 and after had a new urgency—the creamery and hence the county depended on it. The A&M exhibit at the state fair was larger than ever before and focused on the creamery. The Starkville exhibit at the county fair was named "The Jersey Show." It announced Oktibbeha, as "the leading Jersey county of the South." Among the wares was "as fine a lot of Jersey milkers as could be grouped at any community center in the country." All this cost money, and the *Starkville News* was proud to list contributors. Three different banks put up funds as did a series of lawyers and dairymen. But so too did a millinery, a drugstore, a café, a candy store, a building supply company, a men's clothing store, several physicians, a general store, the city market, and the A&M Creamery.[62]

Having such a broad base of participation had been a goal for at least a decade, and it had almost always been unsuccessful. Moore too aimed to increase participation, in this case in the college creamery. He took the unusual approach of writing an open letter to Oktibbehans. Under the bold title, "Queen Jersey Reigns Supreme," he addressed the time when cotton was king and the attendant troubles that a fickle market and the boll weevil brought to the county. He contrasted that boom-or-bust agriculture with dairying where "day after day," regardless of the weather, cows produce the liquid. And day after day the milk has gone to the creamery, and Starkvillians have "reaped the reward in good sized checks." Despite the largesse they bring, we think not about dairy cows, he continued. We rarely grow corn, hay, and grain enough to see them through a cold winter. Instead, year after year, we plant cotton. We need to change our farming, Moore continued. King Cotton was the potentate, "his subjects were for the purpose of doing his bidding." Queen Jersey is "the modern idea." She "delights to serve."

Golson wrote a preamble to Professor Moore's piece, making sure no one misunderstood its message. "Here is a letter from a man you know—one whom you can believe—and when he says, 'Give Queen Jersey a chance and she will beat King Cotton,' he knows it is true for he has proven it. What he has done, you too can do if you will only try." Golson made the issue a matter of trying. The process was not hard. J. S. Moore had demonstrated that it could be done. But he challenged Oktibbeha citizens by asking them directly if they would be willing to try. Success and community membership were reduced here to a matter of trying, of changing from established farming practice to a new way for a new day. Those who refused to try were shamed for not being progressive. They were mired in a bygone era with its attendant issues and failures, unwilling to assist their community.[63]

Concern for the creamery soon found a parallel but much more menacing expression in the city and the county. The 1920 census showed that the county had lost more than 3,000 people over the previous decade, about 15 percent of its population. More than a handful of communities and settlements in the county had disappeared, their residents with them. Starkville also had shrunk, but only by a hundred or so. The number of people in the decline was not nearly as significant as the decline itself. After years of puffery and boosterism, the area had not grown. The combined efforts of extension agents, USDA demonstrators, myriad railroad initiatives, and the college all failed to stem the loss of people from the county. Each of those efforts aimed to produce a new day in Oktibbeha, one bright for its citizens and their families. Each was to welcome people and to expand the region's economic base. Schools, churches, grand hotels, opera houses, hospitals, movie theaters and the like depended on the size and wealth of the population. A declining populous put all that in doubt.[64]

Some Oktibbehan residents wrote off the decline as part of the Great Migration of Black people to northern cities. To their reckoning, losing population from that sector of the community was not a tragedy. But others countered by arguing that there had been precious few white folks moving to the county to erase that loss. In that sense, the situation was far worse than it appeared. There would be significantly fewer Black sharecroppers, tenant farmers, and laborers to work fields and milk dairy cows. That population loss was exacerbated by the fact that the county was able to attract only a miniscule number of white farmers. Land, apparently good farmland, just lay there waiting for immigrants from the North to come and develop it. It was a double catastrophe and a potent threat to each county resident's economic and social situation.

In agriculture generally, things seemed even more drastic. The postwar agricultural depression decimated Mississippi. Barrett looked at the census and found "some facts about our county that are not especially pleasant to contemplate." The census showed decline in corn and cotton yields per acre as compared to the 1910 census. It also revealed that the county had not "as many acres of improved land, as many farms or as many farmers as we had in 1910." While the situation was dire, Barrett argued that just knowing these facts was a step towards erasing them. "If you are one of the persons producing corn and cotton at the 1920 average rates, you are a poor man," he noted. If you continue to employ similar methods and get similar yields, "you are likely to remain poor." Fortunately, "we have it in our hands to improve our condition . . . in the next ten years." It simply requires farmers to "only try." That "is no vain illusion. . . . [We] can easily accomplish it if we will try."

Trying was the critical part. Failure by this measure was a result of a lack of effort or interest, an unwillingness to assist the city and county out of its economic decline. Others took a different tack. They refused to believe the census figures and so proclaimed things in the city and county exceptional. We are telling everyone "that you can't judge STARKVILLE or OKTIBBEHA by the census enumerator's report." The next three or four years, Golson reported, "are going to show the greatest progress and growth for OKTIBBEHA ever recorded."[65]

As much of Starkville contemplated its plight, neighboring Sturgis took action. It created what R. L. Hannah, vice president of the Sturgis Bank, called "an active, hustling Business Men's League." Its "progressive spirit" ensured that the town was "ripe for further expansion," growth "wisely directed." Among its first acts was to raise funds to purchase a potato kiln to cure sweet potatoes, converting them from a seasonal to a year-round crop, and to hire an expert to manage all aspects of the potato crop, including marketing. In that sense, the kiln served as a parallel to the A&M creamery. It processed sweet potatoes from all over the region and sold the dried products through the new cooperative kiln. Sturgis should be "an inspiration to every community in the county," claimed the *Starkville News*. Its "spirit of co-operation and civic pride" that will carry Sturgis "into the lime-light."[66]

Sturgis aggressively promoted itself. It soon had its own page in the Starkville paper, a page that the Sturgis business group paid for. Its businessmen's league, now renamed the Citizens League of Sturgis, claimed to have enrolled 75 percent of Sturgis residents within the first month. Its contention that it stood "as one of the livest [*sic*] civic organizations in North Mississippi" did not seem misplaced. Sturgis was among the best farming sections. "We have the land and we have the people—good as can be found." The town understood that it and its surroundings were of one piece. It started with farmers, who realized that "tillers of the soil hold the balance in his [*sic*] grip. Sturgis businessmen are realizing the same thing." Collectively "they are putting their money and influence solidly behind" farmers. The Citizens League managed, enabled and facilitated the initiatives. "We have one of the best organizations of its kind in the country. . . . [and expect] to see many other towns and cities organize on the STURGIS PLAN."[67]

Sturgis's hubris was also prophetic. As Sturgis planned its next enterprise, a front page unsigned letter in the *Starkville News* declared that the time was right to "put over" a businessmen's club. It would be "the best thing that could happen to Starkville." We need to "lay plans for its organization. CITIZENS-LET'S DO IT!" A few weeks later, other unsigned letters appeared. One accused the city of having "some citizens who do not care whether the town moves forward in the march of progress." They would rather "be left alone with what they have got," and have "the town stay as it is, just so long as they get their share of the money." Other "towns in the state, some much smaller than Starkville, are organizing Citizens' Leagues," the author continued in an apparent reference to Sturgis. If Starkville and the area's farmers "just wake up, the county will grow with leaps and bounds." DeMotte commented on the last piece. A Citizens League would "push Starkville and Oktibbeha County to the front and let the world know that we have the best city and the best county in the South." He included a form below his piece and urged "any citizens with the interest of the community at heart" to sign it and send it to the *News*.[68]

That the city was undergoing one of its periodic outbreaks of malaria could not have helped gain signatures.[69] A week later the *News* hammered at its readers: "Other towns and counties with fewer opportunities than ours are putting us in the shade," an obvious reference to Sturgis. "The time is TRULY coming, unless something is done, when we will perforce bow down to those other communities." Every farmer, "property owner and business man among us will suffer." If "you want to stop apologizing for your city—GET BUSY. THE ONLY way is to get together." The *News'* tempestuous display resulted from the fact that only twelve Starkville residents had signed the pledge during the previous week. Another plea and form followed. The next week the total had grown to twenty and the frustrated *News* changed tactics. It told its citizens to use the Honor Roll—the new name for the list of signees—to see who was worthy of their business, reminding them that "more than talk is necessary—sign coupon."[70]

The total did not change the next week and the *News* asked, "Say, are y-o-u interested in Starkville?" The list grew by one the next week. The *News* wondered, "Does the Loss of $2,000,000 Annually Mean Anything to You?" Two more signed on the next week. The following week's screed was entitled "'Let Starkville Rest,' Writes this Man, 'Rest and Rot.'" By the first week of May, thirty-six Starkvillians had signed the pledge. The *News*'s message was, "Lunatics Never Cooperate." During the next two weeks the totals went to forty-seven and then fifty. The scolding was entitled, "Do You Realize This?" and then the written shouting stopped. An initial Citizens League meeting was scheduled for June 4. The Honor Roll did not appear again.[71]

Led by the fabulous fifty, designated as charter members, its initial thrusts included increasing the membership to 250, better county roads, securing a grand hotel, building modern sewerage, and attracting new enterprises to the city. This list of particulars mimicked that of major progressive cities like New York, Cleveland, and Cincinnati in the late nineteenth and early twentieth centuries. For small places to have similar agendas marked them as forward-looking, seeking to become and then join the new urban boom, even as it depended on agriculture and the countryside. Indeed, the 1920 census was the first US census where urban areas, defined as places of 2,500 or more, held more of the population than rural areas. Being part of this progressive nexus was no small feat, and Starkville's commercial and banking elite recognized it as the means to ensure the town's successful future.[72]

To better make its case, the group chose as its formal name, the Starkville Chamber of Commerce, and voted to extend honorary membership "to all the white ministers of the city" because of their abilities to galvanize congregants. The irrepressible DeMotte served as its first president. He pledged that the Chamber would bring "better roads in the county, even if we have to build them ourselves." The group sent the county supervisors—elected individuals in charge of county roadbuilding—a prioritized list of roads needing to be constructed. In the next couple of weeks, the chamber enrolled a total of 150 members. The group endorsed a candidate to be the next president of the A&M college—he did not get the post—and established seven standing committees to guide the collective work. How the Chamber identified its work proved illustrative. Its standing committees were: "Rural Affairs; Retail Trade; Wholesale Trade; Industrial; Civic; Publicity and Conventions; and Traffic and Transportation."[73]

Clearly, the name change had suited the group. It was almost all business. The committees generally worked to put a good face on Starkville and to facilitate attempts to attract new merchants and industries. That it placed "rural affairs" as its first standing committee was no accident. Starkvillians understood that their interests rested in the county and in the country. Agriculture would perpetually be the source of Starkville's and

Oktibbeha's wealth. The Chamber of Commerce both recognized agriculture's importance and how to capitalize on it immediately. It adopted for all advertisements the slogan "The Jersey County" and worked to design a Jersey Cow trademark to appear on the back of all Chamber stationary. The group chose its new slogan because it "naturally presupposes the rich agricultural lands and grasses of which [Starkville] richly boasts." In another advertisement, the Chamber referred to "the farmers [as] the life of the section." The other six standing committees were the mechanisms to place agriculture in such a manner to achieve county and town prosperity.[74]

Extruding that wealth in an effective, efficient way became the long slog that the Chamber needed to embrace. It had to devise plans, pick targets, reach out to groups, and figure ways to generate publicity. What items were too small for the Chamber or too big? In its first few months, the Chamber sponsored a "Style Show" to market its merchants' newest ready-to-wear fashions, purchased a projector and established a Starkville movie night, and dedicated and sponsored a ladies' room to house women's civic organizations. It fostered a local telephone exchange, created a hitch lot for visiting farmers to place their horses and wagons, moved to a new venue, and placed advertisements for the city and county on a billboard at the Artesia railroad depot, a location passed by more than 3,000 train passengers daily. The Chamber also staged a fiddling contest, brought in prominent speakers and conventions, and held a citywide "Bargain Day" to encourage consumers to buy from city merchants. How the Chamber was to harmonize the desires—not the interests—of its members was tedious yet critical work. It was the kind of work DeMotte excelled at. As a consequence, he stepped down as Chamber president to serve as the group's first secretary. He could ride herd on the various committees, ensure that what needed to get done, got done.[75]

An outbreak of typhoid fever greeted DeMotte in his new position. Starkville needed sewers to replace the more than 600 open privies that bred flies and mosquitoes and seeped into wells, poisoning the water supply. Wastewater and discharges from cesspools became standing ponds of "stagnant grossly polluted water," an "almost intolerable" situation. The Chamber helped convince the Board of Aldermen to begin a sewerage system but found the supervisors too cash-strapped to build them and to build roads. To get the situation resolved, the Chamber organized an all-Oktibbeha "Road Day." It divided the county into thirty-one units, each with a captain, and asked each county business to close on August 13 so that employees could fill holes and grade roads.[76]

At the end of its first six months, the Chamber took stock of the publicity it generated for Starkville and Oktibbeha. It claimed over one thousand inches of free advertising in the *Memphis Commercial Appeal* and northern magazines as well as state papers. It received approximately 300 letters, wrote 701, and sent out over 5,000 pieces about the area. It also paid for 1,500 inches of advertisements. DeMotte explained advertising's virtues. It was nothing less than "the backbone of any successful business concern." The quality of a business "does not matter" without advertising. Consumers need to be educated but the salesman must believe in his message. Without belief he will lack "pep" and without belief-generated pep "it is useless to send a man out to sell." After that extensive preamble, DeMotte turned to the Chamber. It was "the selling force" for city and county. You must "believe in the wonderful resources of the county," he argued. "God has blessed this section with wonderful soil advantages. Study the situation; make yourself familiar with the many advantages." These advantages are right here. "Open your eyes, fellow members." Only "when you believe can there be the proper 'pep' into the selling organization of Oktibbeha county—the Chamber of Commerce." "Just as sure as the sun rises every morning . . . Oktibbeha county is the coming county of the South." It was time to make the Chamber "a one man selling organization for Oktibbeha county—the best agricultural section of the United States."[77]

DeMotte's analysis was troubling. It harped on the problem that the Chamber had been created to solve. It demanded that Starkvillians try and try together, lest they all fail. Yet at the most recent Chamber meeting only 35 members attended. At another meeting, the Chamber asked for suggestions of paths to follow but that initiative drew little interest. The group soon ran out of funds to continue the movie nights.[78] Immigrants were not streaming to the county in the numbers that boosters had hoped. Pep and belief, the soul of proselytizing, seemed missing. Without it, Starkville could not emerge as the modern city its Chamber hoped to build.

The Chamber claimed the new year as an opportunity to restart, refocus, and revive the organization. It went back to basics. Remembering that the city's success depended on its neighboring farmers, it reduced efforts to make over Starkville institutions. It used that energy to manufacture programming to enhance agriculture, especially dairying. The Jersey cow and the great expansion of Oktibbeha dairies became the Chamber's way out of the area's morass. "Now let us plant cows in place of cotton," wrote John White, an Oktibbehan in the *Memphis Commercial Appeal*. The college's J. S. Moore agreed. Working jointly with the Chamber, Moore embarked on a campaign to increase the number of Oktibbeha dairies by one hundred before spring's end. The established reasons were recounted for dairying but the economics of cotton culture in 1920 provided a new immediacy. Extension agents determined that dairy farmers—and then only those who conducted their operations rationally—had profited during the past year.[79]

The Chamber's new dairy campaign centered "around the circuit of country schools." Its members, assisted by the college and extension agents, gave a series of five presentations, each "illustrated by immense charts and pictures." Late in January it claimed success "even far beyond first expectations." County residents started five new dairies. While new dairies provided the backbone of the Chamber effort, M. A. Saunders, lawyer and staunch Chamber supporter, purchased—as president of Starkville's Peoples Saving Bank—500 settings of 15 choice hens egg sets to dispense among the grade-school children of the county. Not to be outdone, the Bank of Sturgis followed suit with a similar number, as did the Home Bank of Maben. This was no idle endeavor. The children would have to pledge to raise the chickens from the eggs and then "pay" the bank back later in the year with the two poorest specimens culled from the flock. Efforts to jump start a chicken and egg industry in the county and to increase the number of dairies did not mark the limits of the Chamber's new rural-oriented program. It partnered in a new plant for drying and preserving white potatoes, and established a warehouse to store Oktibbeha commodities as they awaited the most opportune markets.[80]

Concentrating on the environs around Starkville made good practical sense. The devastating agricultural depression and the precipitous drop in cotton prices promised to continue for some time. If Starkville were going to emerge relatively unfettered from that economic collapse, it needed to shore up its rural base. Lack of money among farmers meant an inability to purchase Starkville goods and supplies. It might also lead to foreclosures. Oktibbeha's problem was not too many farmers and people. It was too few. It might be difficult, if not impossible, for banks to find new buyers for foreclosed farmsteads. Banks could avoid immediate foreclosures by extending additional credit far beyond surety, but that did not usually make good business sense. Without a path to change practice and to seek out a new, potentially more profitable path—and guidance to pursue that path—foreclosure became for banks the least economically disastrous option. Granting further loans would only become palatable if the assistance were used to develop the countryside in a far more sustainable way than sole reliance on cotton. The Chamber and the college sought to provide that assistance.[81]

Attempts to create a choice poultry industry demonstrated that dairying and livestock farming possessed limits. Butter only went so far. For the number of dairy animals in the state, Mississippi suffered from too many creameries, not too few. While markets for butter outside the state were certainly increasing, butter seemed to run the same risk that cotton once had and still did. Single crop agriculture always placed farmers at the vicissitudes of the weather, pests, and markets. By attempting to broaden dairy agriculture to include poultry, the Chamber sought to buffer farmers and protect their investment. Poultry also provided another outlet for milk skimmed of butterfat. It could be fed to chickens.[82]

Reporting on the egg aspect of the Chamber's program, the *Jackson Daily News* wondered in jest if Oktibbeha should now change its slogan to the "poultry county of the south." There was no chance of that. But Saunders did set a goal of doubling the poultry business in Oktibbeha during 1921. Activity surrounding the dairy campaign more than kept pace. The creamery added a new employee to lead the program for one hundred new dairies. Included in this task was visiting the new dairies and assisting the novice dairymen in setting up dairy operations, a maneuver that guaranteed the new facilities would be run according to the most modern practices.

In the end, Oktibbeha County boosters clearly recognized it was dairying or bust for the county. They soldiered on without DeMotte, who took a post at a Montgomery newspaper. Before he left for Alabama, DeMotte managed one final editorial. He likened the growing of a town to the growing and marketing of crops. To sell a product requires salesmen to create demand for it. So too with a town. "Its people must talk its advantages, push its good points, and set forth its location." They must show the town's "adaptiveness for whatever purpose it is best suited." In crops, weeds spring up but must be removed. So too with towns. "Someone must work to pull the community out of the slough of lifelessness." No doubt DeMotte, called a "live wire and a good booster" by Ward at the *East Mississippi Times,* recognized himself in that characterization. A town is alive only "because its citizens are alive." Three or four "good workers can raise a town from the dead." He closed on a sad and perhaps sour note. Every leader "from the time of Noah down to the present" has heard the "scoffs and scorns and taunts of the ingrates he was trying to help." The success of naysayers explains "why some towns stand still."[83]

The Chamber missed DeMotte's dynamism and his unwillingness to take no for an answer. It also missed his ability to think big. The Chamber again took up the idea of establishing a grand hotel in Starkville, but lacked the capital for the venture. Saunders suggested they try to raise half and then pay off the rest with five- and ten-year notes. Even that seemed too much for the town. It resolved to advertise for "foreign capital" to put up a "commodious hotel building" in Starkville. If the town were going to get its entertainment palace and signature institution, Starkville or public money would not be funding it.[84]

As the Chamber regrouped after DeMotte's departure, dairying remained in the forefront. The Chamber continued to host groups to show them model dairy farms and the cooperative creamery. It supported Oktibbeha County exhibits at various agricultural fairs. It held its latest iteration of the Jersey Show, now named Jersey Jubilee.[85] These moves kept dairying and the county visible. State banks soon provided another boost. Virtually all state banks held suspect paper, and they agreed to reduce their exposure by denying all cotton farmer loan applications that would use any money to purchase feedstuffs. More baldly, they forced a portion of cotton lands to become grass and grain lands at least to sustain whatever farm animals their farmers owned. This new policy also led cotton farmers to seek an auxiliary crop. Many turned to dairying and livestock, which helped the Chamber and the college get closer to reaching their pledge of one hundred new dairymen. In this county, the "most delightful and favored spot of the Creator's universe," "the 'hub' of the dairying interest of the country," dairying continued to boom. To the college's dairy extension agent Higgins, that should have been anticipated. Dairying's virtue was "stabilizing a southern state against crisis." Despite this serious dairy expansion, the college creamery continued to lag. It enrolled only about 225 dairymen in 1921. Other creameries in the state continued to siphon off a good share of county dairymen.[86]

The cooperative creamery's inability to catch fire led the college to a drastic act. It had the creamery established as a separate corporation. As its own corporate entity, the creamery could set policy outside the college, which could lead it to pay its members at higher rates. But it also removed the college safety net. More than ever, the creamery was on its own.[87]

And so was Starkville or so it seemed. In a letter titled "the Best Town in Mississippi" to the *East Mississippi Times,* "G" asked, "Why is not the opportunity throttle pulled 'wide open'?" His answer was "slackers." He identified "people so jealous of their neighbor's prosperity" that they spread falsehoods about them. "These are dangerous characters," he maintained. "They cause more sorrow, more strife, more bitterness than possibly any other class of our citizenry." He then talked about "another class" but argued that the first two letters of class "should be marked off." This group wanted to keep Starkville as it was. They had "as much love for a stranger coming to our town as the devil has for Holy water." But G reserved his ultimate scorn for "profiteers." He claimed Starkville's merchants and suppliers raised prices artificially high, rendering the city not competitive with its neighbors. He reported on a recent meeting where the Chamber pleaded with the Board of Supervisors to improve country roads. One merchant protested vociferously. He claimed Starkville was already losing half its trade to neighboring cities. If we fix the roads to facilitate travel, then the other half will go and "give their trade to other towns."[88]

Rudderless Starkville came alive again in mid-August. The decision to join the Mississippi State Chamber of Commerce provided new impetus to the local organization. Within days, the local Chamber lobbied the city to extend its sewers and to find a solution to the breeding grounds for mosquito and flies. It went on record opposing what it called "exorbitant rents" in some boarding houses and started its first country club. The Starkville Chamber adopted the plan of its Jackson counterpart and began to lobby to attract more small farmers. Rather than restrict outreach to established dairymen with large herds and to try to lure them south, the group agreed to target smaller farmers with less initial capital to further build Oktibbeha's agricultural base.[89]

Three of the less well highlighted Chamber achievements spoke to its attempt to enrich Starkvillian lives as well as pocketbooks. It first created for the city an Oratorio Society as "a valuable adjunct to civic life." Adept in both "classical and popular music," the society would capitalize on the "abundant and unusually good" talent in Starkville to "make community singing a feature of civic life." The Chamber also initiated Starkville's first volunteer fire company. It was populated with "merchants, ministers, bank cashiers, editors, and business men," not the sort usually associated with rowdy fire companies. The Chamber's endorsement of the expansion of the agricultural college's athletic facilities was another success. It reasoned that with the "completion of the good roads leading to Starkville and the impetus in road building" throughout the state, people from "every section of Mississippi and enjoining states" will want to attend games at the college. The college would become a destination. Larger arenas, enhanced parking, and comfortable seating would make that possible. Certainly some of the visitors would stay, shop, and eat in Starkville and carry their impressions home to families and friends. The Chamber wanted to make that experience a positive one.[90]

Chamber-inspired programs enhanced the city's reputation as a forward-looking place. Its long-term success continued to depend on the health and wealth of the county. Even though cotton prices rebounded somewhat by the end of 1921, that crop remained a dicey proposition. Golson argued that even with the traditional size of cotton planting, the county's agricultural resources had "hardly been scratched. The premier grass lands of the South are right here." Dairying, livestock, and poultry "can easily be doubled or trebled in the next few years." All that was required was systematic, intelligent practice.[91]

Cow testing—determining which cows gave the most milk and which milk possessed the highest butterfat, and culling the most inefficient from the herd—helped create adroit dairy practice. The Illinois Central initiated a program to assist in establishing other aspects of that practice. Members of the Chamber and the college divided themselves into ten groups of seven. On the week of November 7, armed with railroad-owned motion picture projectors, each group descended on a different small community in the county. There speeches, movies, practical lectures and just plain talk took place. The week's topic was efficient dairying but its goal was not simply to create more and better dairy farmers in the state. The meetings were also to acquaint country folk with Starkvillians. Chamber members from all walks of life participated in these exchanges with county men and women. So too did the female relatives of Chamber members. In nine of the ten groups, at least two group members were women. It was right neighborly. The leaflet inviting residents of the small communities outside of Starkville explained that the groups would "devote a part of the time to social diversions."[92]

In this economic struggle with cotton, cow tests became the means to ensure that dairying came out on top. Few prominent agricultural journalists needed confirmation. Butler in the *Progressive Farmer* argued that the only obstacle to dairy farming in the South was "the habits of the people." Dairying required daily tending. Cotton proved much more accommodating. The *Rural New-Yorker's* Collingwood thought the South could produce milk and butter far more cheaply that the North but a southern dairy industry "will not develop till the farmers are taught how." Hunnicutt mentioned that barns, dairy machinery, and prime animals were costly, and urged bankers to take the lead in furthering dairying in the South by providing loans at liberal terms. In each instance, inability to change established policies or practices hampered what seemed likely an easy conversion. Dairying could redeem the cotton South when and if habits, traditions, and practices could be changed.[93]

In the unending series of postwar debates between city and country, urban and agricultural, or dairying versus some other kind of cropping, one feature always stood out. The problem was a lack of effort, a lack of vision, a lack of pep, a lack of something. The same scenarios recurred in 1922. The creamery created an honor roll to show which farmer delivered the largest amount of butterfat the past month, a tacit acknowledgment that farmers were not delivering it as they should. A Chamber analysis showed that creameries in other counties received fully one-third of Oktibbeha County cream. Aberdeen was shipping two railroad cars filled with butter to New Orleans weekly. The co-op creamery board debated moving the operation to Starkville proper to attract more dairymen. Entrepreneurs opened an ice cream plant in town. As it developed its own supply network the new facility threatened the creamery further. A businessman purchased three thousand head of purebred cattle for his Oktibbeha farm but they were Hereford beef cattle, not milkers. Located across the border in Lowndes County, the neighboring city of Columbus, which barely recognized Starkville's existence, suddenly got interested in dairying. Its Chamber of Commerce arranged for a train to tour the dairylands of the Upper Midwest— Illinois, Wisconsin, Indiana, Iowa, and Missouri—and loaded the tour with 125 farmers, bankers and businessmen.[94]

Meanwhile W. W. Magruder, then off from a failed run for Congress, proposed to combat the Columbus dairy gambit by officially renaming Oktibbeha County "Jersey County," thus highlighting the county's most prominent feature. Starkville's business leaders opted for a Jersey show rather than name change. Magruder, the figurative descendant of Montgomery as the largest and most impressive breeder of Jerseys in the state, won several prizes for his animals at the event. The show was at least as much optics as substance, however. Yield per dairy cow in Oktibbeha County was down, so far down in fact that the cow testing association awarded no animal honor roll status for several months. Despite slippage in the dairy sector, Magruder stayed active in dairy's cause. He used his influence to beat back two very real threats to Oktibbeha and the dairy industry. He led the Mississippi Jersey Cattle Club to oppose an attempt to vitiate the mandatory tick eradication program. With Magruder at the helm, the group joined with leading bankers to topple a legislative measure that sought to impose a lien on cattle and other livestock for overdue land rent. For his efforts and because of his clout, the Jersey club again elected him president.

Other Oktibbeha crops came to the fore, and while they did not challenge milk production's centrality to the county's health they did reduce attention to it. The county continued to ship off boxcars full of beef and breeding cattle. Railroad shipments of chickens and of turkeys left Starkville on more than one occasion. In fact, poultry farmers established the Oktibbeha County Poultry Association to better market their product. Over twenty poultry farmers attended the initial meeting. Sweet potatoes and "goobers"—peanuts—became for-market crops in the county.[95]

Establishing a second crop to carry a farmer through bad times made sense but it also meant that he devoted less of his acreage, his attention, and his time to his primary crop. In Oktibbeha, cotton had been that crop until it was supplanted by dairying. In 1922, cotton made a huge comeback in the county. 1921 yields were good and prices adequate. That led farmers to plant more cotton in 1922, and they were rewarded by good prices and a bumper crop, double that of the previous year. Ward acknowledged that farmers opting for cotton had made big money, and knew that they would be enticed to devote even more land to the crop the next year. He appreciated that each bale was extra income for the farmer but feared that they would fall back into old habits. He reminded farmers that "Oktibbeha County is no longer regarded as a cotton county and . . . our chief industries are dairying, hay, and market gardening."[96]

Cotton was a specter, an existential threat to the dairying world that Starkville and Oktibbeha County had created. It was not likely to achieve past glory but it was seductive. It welcomed bad land practices and promised impoverishment. Cotton was boom or bust agriculture, with labor primarily restricted to the picking of the crop. Dairying was regular, cerebral, and relentless, a 365-day-a-year workload as well as paycheck. Cotton farming was tradition, peculiarly southern. Dairying had occurred virtually everywhere except the South.

While Starkville residents worried about cotton's comeback, two small Oktibbeha communities seemed to have placed themselves on firmer ground. Sturgis with its sweet potato kiln and its several grist mills established its industrial base on agriculture. Geographically closer to Starkville and smaller in population than Sturgis, Longview was home to abundant crops and an extensive sawmilling concern. In contrast, Starkville had dairying, the college creamery, and livestock. Its cotton mill training school and factory had become defunct. Only that year did a Jackson businessman, J. W. Sanders, purchase the facility and attempt to revive production and convert it into a for-profit concern.[97]

Starkville, then, was muddling along. William Ward, editor of the *East Mississippi Times,* reminded his readers that a main reason that Starkville did not "get more needed improvement" was because they were "quick to jump at the conclusion that it is going to benefit the other fellow more." That was a narrow view. Starkville was a community. "No matter what part of town we may live in, we are benefited by the improvement of any street or alley or sidewalk in any part of town." Consequently, Starkville's citizens should put their shoulders "to the wheel every time a public improvement is launched." Ward's strong, positive sentiments masked an underlying fear. He wrote elsewhere that Starkville was living in a gilded age. "We may maintain a Chamber of Commerce," certainly a sign of modernity. "We may build big hotels," an unfulfilled Chamber ambition. "We may bring in new people" to the community, "erect many dwelling houses, build business houses" and attract entrepreneurs to fill them. These were all Starkville's desires, its citizens goals. But, he continued, they truly "amount to but a bauble." What Starkville truly needed was many more farmers. They needed people to "produce something to create a market." Only then could they "give permanent life and permanent prosperity to the town."[98]

Starkville's inability to expand its agricultural base paralleled its inability to provide all the amenities that its town residents demanded. The city's newspapers and civic institutions worked to that end. So too did the college and the several agricultural groups that coalesced around a specific commodity. Bankers changed policies, railroads actively recruited far and wide. National agricultural journals sung the praises of the area. Yet Starkville remained mired in the doldrums without any obvious means to progress and economic security.

5 | THE MILKMEN COMETH
Northern Industrialists, Dairying, and
Hope for a Small Town

While representatives from Borden's New York office and young salesmen from the South met in Jacksonville to hear suggestions for the first condensery in the American South, Starkville carried on as it had the previous year. Its Board of Aldermen cut the salaries of the mayor and other city officials to lower costs. County farmers planned to expand cotton planting tremendously. The previous year's soaring cotton prices proved irresistible. To further their economic prospects, cotton farmers formed a cooperative marketing association to get the highest prices when the crop came in. A consequence of renewed interest in cotton farming was a decline in diversification and especially in dairying. Dairying required preparation of crops and grassland, possibly fodder, outbuildings for storage of milking equipment and generally twice-daily milking. Cotton required none of those things. The Merchants & Farmers Bank grew alarmed by what it saw taking place in Oktibbeha County. It cautioned farmers to not let high-priced cotton "turn your head." "Be judicious," the bank continued, "produce as many things to sell as you can."[1]

The bank was not alone. Even with a presumptive revival of cotton's halcyon days, the Illinois Central pushed dairying for the state. It ran a train—the Pure Sire Special—through Starkville and much of Mississippi, touting dairy farming. Its purebred bulls were lent as studs gratis to dairymen on the route. When the train neared the Louisiana border, the bulls had to be left behind. The cattle tick's presence made it too dangerous to bring these stud animals into bayou country.[2]

The creamery remained a point of concern. County extension agent Barrett admonished the partners to stop criticizing the creamery publicly and stop sending cream to the Aberdeen, Macon, and Kosciusko creameries. He reminded them that the A&M creamery was a "splendid institution in our midst." At the same time, he acknowledged that its management had "made some mistakes" and was trying "to clean house." He called on local dairymen to "start the new year right by delivering Oktibbeha County cream to our one and only Oktibbeha County creamery." Despite the hullabaloo, farmers from across Mississippi and Alabama came to inspect the creamery's methods and procedures in expectation of establishing similar enterprises near their farms. Birmingham, while it extolled the virtues of the A&M creamery's butter, bemoaned that an estimated two million dollars yearly left the Birmingham area to pay for the delicious product.[3]

Most importantly, Starkville's entrepreneurial element remained dissatisfied with the city's lack of success in assuring its and the county's fortunes. Lack of success quickly became a lack of effort; with a product such as Starkville to sell, only slough on the part of Starkvillians could conceal that self-evident truth. Claiming that no city in Mississippi could objectively surpass the charms and opportunities of Starkville, the sole explanation became its proponents' failure to spread the message. Starkville's light remained hidden under a bushel.[4]

The city got an apparent chance to right this wrong when in March the *East Mississippi Times* proclaimed "our great opportunity. Will Starkville let it pass?" Editor Ward recounted how thirty years earlier, the city had passed on becoming a way station on the Georgia Pacific railroad. That road would have opened up the city to the east and increased access and trade with that area. Now Starkville was presented with another possibility. A southern Mississippi timber company, the McLean Hardwood Company, planned to establish a railroad that connected directly with the Illinois Central. Its simplest path was through Longview. But Ward wondered if the city would be willing to pick up the tab for the extra three or four track miles necessary to route it through Starkville. He called for a town meeting to move on this opportunity.

Starkville did better than that. Within a week, 318 citizens engaged in the "greatest forward movement ever made for the development of Starkville and Oktibbeha County." They joined together for a "complete reorganization and rejuvination [*sic*] of the old Chamber of Commerce." The huge upsurge in participation showed just how keen attendees were in pressing forward and just how desperate they had become. The movement's backers guaranteed that the new organization would produce "growth, development, increased population, and greater prosperity" for the city, and fixed its first two initiatives as securing the railroad through Starkville and establishing a grand hotel.[5]

Like the aldermen's salary-cutting move, the Chamber election reflected dissatisfaction with the status quo. The officers included none of the stalwarts from the previous few years. All had prominent Starkville commercial ventures. The new president, R. C. Jarnagin, earned his living as an Illinois Central agent, a particularly attractive occupation for Starkville's attempt to acquire the new railway. Three trustees worked as directors of city banks. M&F Bank was not represented. The fourth was a druggist and the final board member sold insurance. Among their first acts was to establish an industrial committee to pursue the new rail line and grand hotel. Mayor H. A. Beattie, owner of an insurance agency who several times served as mayor and alderman, chaired the committee. Its members included Graham Golson, editor of the *Starkville News;* Karl Goodman, a German émigré who ran a dry goods establishment with his brother; F. L. Wier, who operated a drugstore with his brother; and A. W. Reynolds, a merchant and farmer.

Under their tutelage, the Chamber remained true to its promise to first work towards the new rail line and hotel. Magruder traveled to Memphis to lobby the Illinois Central and urge the southern Mississippi lumbermen to set Starkville as part of the route. He returned somewhat pessimistic, but the group resolved to keep up the fight. The hotel posed a different problem. Several East Coast firms offered to fund the facility but wanted a 7 percent fee for loaning the money. The Chamber was unwilling to agree to that type of deal. As Starkville dithered, Aberdeen acted. It planned to sell $75,000 in bonds to finance an elegant, three-story, fireproof, steam-heated hotel. While several maintained that Starkville was far grander than Aberdeen and therefore merited an even more excellent hotel—in reality, Starkville was two-thirds the size of Aberdeen—the Chamber remained at an impasse.[6]

All these concerns faded around May 20 when the Chamber got notice that the Borden Company was looking to construct a large condensery in the South and was contemplating putting it in Starkville. The firm's Dallas, Texas, salesman, J. Wallace Maxwell, delivered the message. Maxwell was a Starkville native. He had run a laundry and raised sweet potatoes, pigs, and milch cows before joining Borden. Quite active in farming, he had even fallen into a dipping vat as he worked to keep his animals free of the cattle tick. When called to the meeting in Jacksonville he pushed his hometown, remembering no doubt the work of Montgomery on Jerseys and grasses and the then-common moniker for Oktibbeha, "the Jersey county."[7] The company's officers mulled over possibilities based on their salesmen's reports and selected potential sites in Texas, Louisiana, Alabama, and Tennessee, as well as Mississippi, for further investigation. H. R. Ryder, supervising veterinarian for Borden's Illinois and Wisconsin dairies who had turned down a Cornell professorship to remain with the company, did the initial surveillance. He left visiting Starkville for his last stop, citing its reputation as the "Dairy County of the South" and its proximity to the agricultural college, which made it the most likely destination for the condensery. Immediately before arriving in Starkville, Ryder apparently visited Selma, Alabama, as well as both Meridian and Macon, in Mississippi, among other places. Moore welcomed him at Macon, as did W. H. Sudduth and A. W. Reynolds, who took him to Starkville, talking up the area on the way.[8]

The choices of Sudduth and Reynolds as tour guides displayed Starkville's occupational diversity. Both were city farmers. They lived in Starkville proper but owned extensive properties worked by tenant farmers and sharecroppers. Both were mid-career, with extensive involvement in city politics and city affairs. Sudduth had invested in the Starkville Lumber Company, which had quickly become defunct. He was a director of both the Peoples Savings Bank and of the Security State Bank, as well as one of the county's largest cotton planters and beef cattle merchants, but he also raised and sold sheep and dairy cattle. Equally diversified, Reynolds grew considerable cotton. He also purchased cotton seeds to process for oil and cattle feed. Most of his fortune was in beef cattle, but he also was a coal merchant. Like Sudduth, he had partnered in a failed business, the Starkville Brick & Tile Company.

Once in Starkville, a group of businessmen and farmers greeted Ryder, who was joined by Maxwell. As chair of the Chamber's industrial committee, Beattie presided. His initial question, "What is condensed milk anyway? They feed it to babies and sick people, don't they?" got the proceedings off to a less than auspicious start. Ryder recounted Borden's westward expansion during the war—including Fort Scott, Kansas—and indicated that the company hoped to reduce transportation expenses to one of its largest markets, the South, by creating a condensed milk manufactory there. The creamery faculty and the assembled businessmen and farmers pointed out Oktibbeha's features. Ryder's response closely followed the script the company had used when it first discussed the Fort Scott condensery with that town's Chamber of Commerce. He wondered if the area did indeed provide enough milk daily to justify what would be Borden's considerable investment. A minimum of four thousand gallons of milk daily would get the plant started, but Ryder acknowledged that the company expected rapid growth in fluid milk delivery. In fact, Borden would promise to expand the plant to meet whatever demand that the area could supply. He also mentioned one other parameter. The site of the condensery would need adjacent railroad connections. The company would sink its own well and establish a waterworks and sewerage system.

Ward and the Chamber understood just how momentous Borden's decision would be. Calling it "the biggest development project that has ever been offered our community in its whole history," Ward gushed that Borden in Starkville "will undoubtedly contribute more to the upbuilding of our city and the surrounding section than any one industry has ever done." Several dairymen committed to dramatically expanding their herds if only the New York company would place its condensery in Starkville.[9]

Ryder possessed no decision-making power, however, and returned to Chicago, saying only that the area's dairy industry was impressive. The company sent another veterinarian, C. D. Pearce, to confirm Ryder's assessment. He too lacked authority to green-light the project. That did not stop Starkville from preliminarily celebrating its great luck. Beattie and the board promised to upgrade or build roads and sidewalks to and from the condensery once the site was chosen. It was anticipated that more than enough open land near the Illinois Central tracks could be used to erect the facility and provide a cutout and a roadhouse to load and reposition trains. Oktibbeha farmers almost fell over each other promising to expand their dairy operations to soar past the 4,000-gallon daily threshold. In fact, Ward argued that the county provided more than enough milk to take care of the entire South. That blatant exaggeration implied that sustaining the creamery and the condensery was no problem. In a fit of misrepresentation, Ward now maintained that the creamery was so overburdened by the county's dairy farmers that it turned away vast amounts of milk, which went to maintain creameries in other counties. In any case, he continued, the city will need "good roads leading to the dairy farms when the big white milk tanks of the Borden Company start out on their daily rounds to gather milk." Ward anticipated that farmers from as far away as ten miles would be using this service.[10]

Almost immediately after Ryder left the city and before Pearce came, the Chamber and Beattie got busy. They compiled a list of prominent agricultural leaders who knew something about Oktibbeha County agriculture, and on May 29 Beattie asked each to send a testimonial to use to press the city's milk-plant case. A great many invitees had been agricultural newspapermen who had edited their papers in Starkville, persons who had lived in Starkville, or former faculty at the nearby college. The *Starkville News,* which soon affixed the phrase, "The Dairy Center of the South," above its front-page nameplate, published excerpts from these letters over the course of a month or so as the Chamber labored to convince area men and women as well as the Borden people on the viability of their site for the proposed new condensery. The *Rural New-Yorker's* Collingwood said the Starkville area was "destined to be the great stock and dairy ground of the Gulf States." Butler of the *Progressive Farmer* argued that he had never seen anyplace "where better pastures exist with so little effort on the part of the farmer." Lloyd, now director of agricultural development for the Memphis Chamber of Commerce, claimed that he had never seen a place where "dairying and live stock could be made more profitable" than Oktibbeha. The Starkville area has "the best pastures I have ever seen in any country." The "lime lands around Starkville are the most wonderful grass lands that I have ever seen," he gushed. If that were not enough, these lands were adjacent to "the greatest agricultural college in the South." W. C. Wellborn—a relative of the Starkville legislator who pushed the tick eradication bill, a former professor of agriculture at the agricultural college, a commissioner of agriculture for the Philippines, and now editor of the *Kansas City Weekly Journal*—compared Starkville to nearby Fort Scott. Claiming to know something about Oktibbeha County because "I have owned enough of it," he found it vastly superior to the Fort Scott area. There limestone croppings and alfalfa grass are in abundance but the land was "much rougher." Starkville grew many different grasses and forage crops. Fort Scott was far more limited. Wellborn mentioned that he had traveled the world and he had found no place that "possesses greater advantages for live stock and dairying than you have." The grasses of Starkville can carry cattle all winter, reducing if not eliminating the need for forage crops. The area's Jerseys are high in butterfat, producing a secondary market when condensing milk. He closed by reminding the Borden Company that Starkville had "cheaper labor on farms and in factories" because of the inexpensive "living" there.[11]

No doubt that last line resonated with Borden. It had expended significant effort trying to keep wages down in New York, Chicago, and even Fort Scott. In those areas, it encountered collectives that pooled their efforts to raise wages and prices. Starkville—with its dependence primarily on sharecroppers and tenant farmers, many of whom were Black and subject to the strictures of Jim Crow segregation—seemed unlikely to offer such impediments. Just as importantly, there existed no mechanism or tradition to enable these minority dairymen and women to function collectively. Labor peace in Starkville and in almost all the South seemed to be assured.

The Chamber's industrial committee followed up the letter writing initiative with a slick pamphlet highlighting each of the letters. The pamphlet, titled "Oktibbeha, The Jersey County of the South—Why," set about to explain why Borden should place its condensery there. In addition to identifying the authors, the committee provided excerpts of the testimonials. It also devoted significant space to many of the things it told Ryder: it described the area's geological prowess for grass growing and the varieties of grass grown, its railroad facilities, its water sources, and the neighboring agricultural school. The volume also provided some demographics about the area— its human and its cow population—as well as a series of homey statements and stories about the county and dairy farming generally. Its folksy, "with good grasses for cows and clover for bees, Oktibbeha is the veritable 'Land of Milk and Honey,'" was among the least hackneyed. When the project was done, the committee tied it together with ribbon and sent it off to Borden headquarters in New York. It followed up the volume with a series of letters further extolling Oktibbeha's virtues.[12]

The committee's bulldog tenacity proved relentless and perhaps tiresome. It sent an endless series of letters to the Borden people championing Starkville's possibilities. The last of these many letters was greeted by a formal reply. It stated that the material that the industrial committee sent was in possession of Borden executives "and their action, if any should be taken, would be announced later." Nonplussed, Beattie opted for good old southern charm. He invited C. C. Lobeck, a Borden Vice President, to join Starkvillians in a fish fry at the pond on A. W. Reynolds's place. Lobeck wrote back that he had a previous commitment, but at least the responses to Starkville's pleas became less brusque.

Although there was great excitement about the condensery's possibilities, some in town remained wary. A certain constituency was not dissuaded by Ward's assertion that the creamery had far more butterfat that it could ever use and openly worried about the institution's future. A bird in the hand—a regular paycheck from the co-op—was certain. The condensery might prove to be a pipe dream and its pursuit might cause irrevocable damage to the reputation of the creamery and area. Moore intervened in this dispute, taking the condensery side and quickly reducing the noise.[13]

Starkville's neighboring places were less than enthusiastic about a Starkville condensery. They saw it as beginning a slow death to their cities as Starkville would begin to siphon off business, interest, and money from these places. One cannot overestimate how tenuous and fragile small town rural life was in the 1920s. Loud, popular, optimistic places aspiring to success could and often did become ghost towns, seemingly overnight. Ripping just one significant institution—a church, a bank, a school, even a grocery—or adding one to a competitor could tip the balance and send a place spiraling into economic insolvency and then oblivion. One less payroll, one less reason to visit the town, one more reason to go to other towns could radically alter a small town's already precarious future. To prevent that from happening because of Starkville's securing the condensery, each engaged in a campaign to have the condensery located in their town. West Point, Durant, Aberdeen, Macon and Tupelo each tried to urge Borden to place the big facility in their cities. It would not stretch the imagination to think that some of these campaigns might have pointed out what they saw as Starkville's flaws.[14]

With uncertainty abounding, the industrial committee prevailed upon Jarnagin to ask the Illinois Central for help. He contacted Schwietert, who had already been involved when Ryder visited, and asked him to intercede on the city's behalf. After hearing the committee, he talked to Ryder in Chicago, who expressed interest in the number of dairy cows within 10 miles of the city. When Ryder had come to Starkville in May, he asked the industrial committee how many cows were within that radius. The group estimated three thousand. That may not have been enough to supply the size of the condensery that Borden envisioned. He asked if the committee could do a cow census and send the material on to the New York office.[15]

On July 16, the Chamber gathered and agreed to undertake the cow census. It organized ten teams to canvas the entire 456 square miles of Oktibbeha County. Their survey recorded the names of each dairyperson and the number of cows then actively producing milk.

As Starkville was taking the survey, Borden was acting in another direction. It sent Ryder on another several weeks' tour to find a suitable southern condensery site. Columbia, Tennessee, a town about double Starkville's size and abutting the Nashville milkshed, was among the places he went. Whether as a failsafe for Starkville, a secondary site, or an outright replacement was not clear, but Ryder pronounced himself suitably impressed. Columbians, who had hosted the first southern dairy congress the previous year, were attune to the same prospects as Starkville—growth of their community and growth of the dairy industry. They expressed their profound desire to shelter the condensery. Ryder also visited Lebanon, Tennessee, which rested north and east of Columbia and was slightly smaller. The New York company had been shipping large quantities of condensed milk to Kentucky, Tennessee, and Alabama, and had found freight rates expensive. He mentioned that the county's reputation for dairying had reached the New York office and how it had tried without success to buy the local co-op creamery.[16]

Starkville's industrial committee completed its survey at about the time that Ryder concluded his recent southern trip. They claimed to find roughly ten thousand viable cows within ten or so miles of the town. Schwietert took the results to Lobeck in New York in late September, and the dubious Borden vice president proposed sending a railroad car of milk to Dixon, Illinois, for analysis. Lobeck wanted the shipment sent in November when dairy production was at its nadir and butterfat content in milk at its highest point. Those were the constraints that Borden would have to contend with in a Starkville condensed milk plant and he wanted to make sure that year-round production remained viable. The purposes of the proposed trial were severalfold. First, the time it took to fill a railroad car with milk would be a fine approximation of how many dairy cattle—and how much milk they produced—were in the area. Second, the quantity of milk delivered would show how much enthusiasm area farmers truly had for the project. Third, butterfat content also mattered. Borden needed to see how much might have to be skimmed before condensing. Conversely, if there were a butterfat deficiency, the milk would prove unsuitable for the company's use.

The parameters of filling a railroad car for shipment mimicked what would happen at a condensery. The milk from the various producers would be pooled, mixed together and cooled as quickly as possible. Hot milk spoils rapidly. The milk also needed to be sweet and pure. If animals had been fed on garlicy or oniony grasses, the taste translated to the milk. Then there was the question of Jersey cattle. Holsteins comprised the great bulk of Borden's dairy cows. Would Jersey milk with its higher butterfat and other slightly different properties taste the same and remain as shelf-stable as Holstein milk, no matter the conditions? That was no idle query. For years, farmers and creameries had been competing for the best-tasting butter. If butter could have different flavors, might not condensed milk made from two very dissimilar breeds also taste or behave differently?

All of this and more was the purpose of Lobeck's test. The company agreed to supply the ten-gallon cans, pay for the milk, and pay cooling costs and freight charges to get the substance to Dixon. To ensure that cooling occurred properly, Borden insisted that one of its experts oversee the cooling process, which would take place at the creamery. The creamery agreed to host that aspect of the test.[17]

From the Chamber's point of view, that was all simple stuff. What remained to be done was to marshal the entire county to act as one on the day of the trial. In a county-wide meeting, Oktibbeha residents evoked their best Tammany Hall imitation. Sudduth was chosen to head the effort. He divided the county into beats and set up a committee to oversee each beat. It was their job to get the milk out, just as Tammany sought to get out votes. Moore gave those at the meeting precise instructions on how to handle the milk so as not to corrupt the city's entire supply. More than a month prior to the test, nature, both environmental and human, intervened. A dry, early-frosting winter hit the area, turning the grazing land brown. Most farmers had not laid away silage to allow for such a contingency. As a consequence, cows were poorly fed, and the quality and quantity of their milk suffered. Dairymen usually furnishing twenty gallons daily might be down to seven or eight. As the date of the trial drew near, the industrial committee feared that a single milking of the county's cattle would not reach the requisite quantity for the test, so they made preparations to game the system by arranging to secure a second milking to add to the mix.[18]

Borden sent J. G. Waters, from the Chicago area, to oversee the Starkville delivery. Twenty-two trucks carried the fluid from farms and twenty-five lead cars went out to make sure nothing on the route would delay delivery. As it turned out, the cow census had been spot on. The nearly 10,000 cows of Oktibbeha County and the over 400 farmers who milked them provided far more than enough milk in one milking to fill the car to capacity. On the morning of November 20, the railroad car festooned with banners hailing "Oktibbeha, The Jersey County of the South" departed for Dixon. It arrived on time the next afternoon. Chicago chemists immediately analyzed the fluid and sent the determinations to Waters. He read the telegram to the Chamber. It identified the milk's constituents, including butterfat. The telegram concluded with the approving phrase "if Mississippi babies drink this rich milk they should weigh a ton each at 21."

Waters then spoke to his Mississippi audience from his heart. Ryder, he remembered, had declared Oktibbeha a "great dairy section" and a prime place for Borden's condensery. He seconded Ryder's assessment and argued that the possibilities for the dairy industry in Starkville "were greater than in any section" he had seen. Waters argued that everything was in the farmers' and businessmen's hands. "You have a splendid country and a fine people." All they needed to do was to take the land and divide it into "small dairy farms." They would "develop wonderfully." Waters went on to say that Starkville did not need more or better farmers, because they had the people they needed right there. "I would like no job than to be down here . . . and watch this country grow."[19]

The story of the Starkville milk traveling to dairy-rich Illinois became the stuff of lore. Newspaper after newspaper across the country simply mentioned it as a considerable yet ironic feat, like carrying coals to Newcastle. But others took a more circumspect turn. While they congratulated Oktibbeha for now officially being regarded as the dairy center of the South, they also wondered why their cities and towns could not replicate the Oktibbeha miracle. Milk was money, good money. It need not be the sole crop but it indemnified any area against catastrophic loss. It stabilized the agriculture of a county and thereby enabled the town or city that depended on the local agricultural practice to survive, even thrive. It was about small town America and what might be. Cotton or most monocultural agricultural production remained a recipe for disaster, representing too precarious a life for town merchants, bankers, and retailers.[20]

Collingwood in the *Rural New-Yorker* celebrated Starkville's apparent selection. "Think of what this means," he asked his readers. Not too long ago there existed "only a small handful of dairy cows south of Tennessee." Flies, ticks, and fevers led experts to conclude "that commercial dairying never could be successful south of the Ohio River." This has all changed "in one generation." Southerners have "begun the mighty work of readapting our soils and climate to suitable crops." It now seemed likely that dairying could progress as "far south as Texas." That had been as unthinkable a short time ago as "cotton growing should travel as far North as Southern New Jersey."[21]

Collingwood marveled at the human implications for the environment reflected in the possible Borden condensery. Waters referred to and Lloyd would highlight human possibilities revealed in the condensery search. Both pinpointed Black tenant farming as a crucial aspect of Starkville's success. Waters insisted that Oktibbeha County needed no new white midwestern immigrants to thrive and grow as a dairy section. Black tenant farmers already oversaw a tremendous number of dairy cattle and did a first-rate job. Although living in Memphis, Lloyd maintained several dairy farms in Oktibbeha County, each of which was run by Black tenants. He expressed his complete satisfaction with the arrangement. To hammer home his point, he undertook a cursory survey of black tenant dairy farming in Oktibbeha, finding it extensive and apt. He claimed that Black tenant farming was a fruitful southern dairying model, conclusions he published in the *Progressive Farmer*.[22]

Despite the widespread interest focused on determining its meaning, Starkville's coronation of the southern milk capital was far from assured. The question of where Borden was going to place the condensery was not yet settled. There also remained the matter of what the properties of Jersey milk would be once condensed. The initial findings were almost instantaneous. But how the material would do over time, how it would do in cold or hot climes, all took time and effort. While Borden performed those tests and shipped condensed milk made from the Starkville shipment across the United States to let it sit for six months, the Chamber and the creamery moved to protect what seemed an inevitable event. They led a dramatic, county-wide campaign to eradicate scrub cattle and thus guarantee the purity of their future purebred Jersey cows. The scrubs were collected and brought to a central place. There, a bizarre public spectacle would ensue. After great fanfare and in front of the whole town, a jury of twelve farmers would vote to condemn the bulls for the crime of being scrubs. One would be killed to symbolize their guilt of this great crime. The other scrubs would be sold and shipped out of the county. Farmers who had owned these animal miscreants split the receipts of the sale. Former scrub owners received the use of prime purebred bulls as stud in lieu of the scrubs.[23]

Borden had more dramatic problems than scrub bulls. Growth of urban populations and creation of dairymen's associations had imperiled the company's condensed milk production. This was especially true in the Midwest. There the growth of Chicago, Racine, Kenosha, Rockford, and Milwaukee, and their burgeoning suburbs put pressure on the fluid milk industry. Consortiums of producers aimed to keep profits high. Workers struck repeatedly for higher wages. To a large degree, cost hikes could be passed off to consumers. That fluid milk demand would only grow. Dealers, such as the Borden Farm Products Company of Illinois, reached further and further into the hinterland to supply this commodity, often pitting fluid milk deliverers against condensers. Because they could easily pass costs off on consumers, dealers could pay more for milk. Condensers did not have that sort of flexibility or fail-safe. They competed against other condensing operations, such as those in the west and Kansas, where fluid milk demand and fluid milk competition was low. They refused to match the prices paid by big city fluid milk dealers.

Borden Company manufactured condensed milk while its farm products subsidiary delivered fluid milk. In some cases, such as with their Belvidere plant, Borden shifted from condensed milk to fluid milk to fulfill demand and maximize profitability. In other instances, it deemed the competition with cities for milk unprofitable. It closed condensing factories in Huntley, Illinois, as well as Salem and Burlington in Wisconsin, all in late 1923 or early 1924. Condensers, cheesemakers, and others saw the only remedy as a further move to areas far from large urban populations. Dairy concerns sprung up in Minnesota, Iowa, and Nebraska. But each of those processed milk places incurred extensive transportation costs. Indigenous midwestern populations were already served by the remaining condenseries such as Dixon, Lake Geneva, and others. Starkville was potentially different. There were no big cities within a hundred miles. No local or nearby condensery served the southern United States. Labor unrest was a rare occurrence; wages were low. Placing a condensery in a region that used considerable condensed milk would be a profitable masterstroke.[24]

Neither the Chamber nor Starkville's citizens generally expected the drama of a new condensery to play out for this long. They were finally notified that the Starkville milk condensed in Dixon passed all tests, even the six-month test. Their joy was replaced by frustration and a sense of foreboding when Borden sent yet another veterinarian to town. Dr. C. H. Taylor's stay was to be indefinite. His mission was in part to confirm what Starkville had told Borden about dairying in Oktibbeha County. He would visit each and every farm and talk to each and every farmer within ten miles of Starkville. His charge included determining "just how many cows they are keeping and how much milk they are securing from them." He would also undertake "a thorough study of pastures, of feedstuffs grown and used, of housing conditions for cattle, of the labor problems related to dairying, and all other kindred subjects." He was also to determine if a condensery were indeed possible. He was directed by Borden to ascertain "those interested in and who will patronize" the condensery.

Borden was adamant that Taylor talk to every farmer, Black and white. Golson applauded that approach. He thought the Black dairymen were "already maintaining herds and handling them economically and at a profit." They had demonstrated that "with fair backing and some instruction," and "proper encouragement" they could "make the business a success, thereby making [themselves] good and useful citizens."[25]

The Chamber did not let Taylor flail about the countryside. As secretary of the Chamber, Ben Hilbun, who had recently graduated from Mississippi A&M, accompanied him every step of the way. In the course of their travels, Hilbun learned as much about Borden methods as Taylor learned of Oktibbeha dairying. He tried to explain the company's condensery approach in several articles in local newspapers. He also urged his fellow citizens to remain calm and to help Taylor at every turn. Hilbun announced that one of Borden's innovations was "to have the product produced in sections demanding the finished product." Rather than centralize production, Borden's policy was to decentralize its operations, which reduced manufacturing and shipping costs. It also placed the corporation in an intimate relationship with the community in which its factory resided. Put another way, Hilbun explained that Waters's words were from Borden's corporate heart. If Borden were to come to Starkville, both the corporation and its officers as well as the city and its citizens would be partners, with relations far deeper that running a factory.

Hilbun maintained that "nothing is overlooked" in Borden's investigations. That was as it ought to be. "A highly efficient business organization must run according to the best-run business principles or it will ultimately fail." All of their investigations "are orderly and well organized. They know exactly what they are about and how to proceed in order to obtain desired information." They move slowly but their thorough methods mean no "regret by either Borden officials or local citizens. The cards are on the table and both parties are looking them over." He ended his discussion by stating that he did not know if Borden would in fact locate in Starkville. He was sure, however, that whatever the company decided would be fair, its analysis complete.[26]

After five weeks, Taylor had the material he needed and left Starkville. Beattie sent copies of Hilbun's articles to Lobeck, who responded a short while later. Lobeck reported that Taylor was quite smitten with Starkville and the area and that his investigation suggested there were cattle enough in the area for a "small-unit operation." He also told the mayor that Borden still had much to consider before Lobeck would put the Starkville dossier and project before his board of directors.[27] About a month later, Borden sent in Waters and its chief construction engineer to suss out a location and potential costs for a condensery, should the company choose to place such a facility in Starkville.[28]

While Starkville waited nervously for Borden to complete the process and make its decision, the town continued the projects that had long consumed it. Just before Aberdeen and other Mississippi cities opened their grand hotels, Starkville began to negotiate for one of its own. It first contracted with a Jackson developer and entertainment impresario, A. H. Alvis, who had been involved in grand hotels in Jackson, Huntsville, Baton Rouge, and Albany, Georgia, but those plans fell through. This "business necessity," "civic improvement," "absolutely safe investment" failed to secure the class of bids for construction it sought when put out the first time so the Chamber had to readvertise. When a Memphis company submitted an acceptable bid, work went quickly. By October, the site had been graded and the foundation almost completed. Its anticipated opening was mid-February. Other established local endeavors continued apace. Starkville citizens met to contemplate establishing their own egg hatchery to capitalize on the growth of the county's poultry industry. County residents continued cow testing, bull clubs, and county dairy days. The city worked with two sources to get high voltage hydroelectric power transmitted to the municipality.[29]

In early November, almost a year after the railroad car to Dixon test, Waters returned to Starkville and announced that the Borden board had authorized funding to build a condensery in Starkville, and he was there to scout out potential sites. That was not the end of the matter, however. The board's action was contingent on several particulars. It refused to release the approximately $300,000 in funding without an agreement with the railroads on freight rates for Borden products. If Starkville were to serve as the central manufacturing, distribution, and storage facility for the entire region, it meant that products Borden sold but were not made in Mississippi would be stored in and distributed from Starkville. Borden did not want to have to pay two sets of rates—the first for bringing finished products, such as malted milk or chocolate milk, from other factories to Starkville, and the second for their distribution in the South after their storage at Starkville. Second, the company needed clarification of the terms of corporate law in Mississippi, which had long had an archaic provision that kept outside corporations from owning more than one million dollars' worth of property located in Mississippi. Implications were clear. Borden could not expand significantly in Mississippi. It would be virtually prohibited from purchasing additional milk plants or other enterprises in the state.

While these sundry issues might take time, Waters expressed optimism that they could be worked out to the company's satisfaction. The corporate law question was resolved rather quickly, when Waters learned that the legislature had recently repealed the one million dollar provision. Corporations could own any amount of property in Mississippi. A third and new concern was more delicate. It had nothing to do with Starkville per se. It involved Oktibbeha County farmers. The company did not like taking risks. And it was somewhat wary after its Fort Scott condensery developed as slowly as it had. Borden wanted to guarantee a sufficient quantity of milk available when—and if—the factory started up, and to predict an actual developmental rate as the anticipated facility moved to reach premium capacity. Although it had not worked very well, the company modified its Fort Scott questionnaire. It wanted each dairy farmer in the area who hoped to work with Borden to fill in and sign the following pledge:

> Providing The Borden Company locates a factory in Starkville, Miss., and provides a market where whole sweet fluid milk will be purchased from dairymen and delivered to said factory when the same is ready for

operation and will deliver milk from (Fill in the blank) cows, twice, daily, morning and evening, sweet and in good condition, It is my intention to increase my dairy until it consists of (fill in the blank) cows.

(Signature)

Golson got to the heart of the situation. He noted that the company had authorized money for the facility if and only if "farmers and dairymen will produce enough milk to guarantee the operation of the plant and increase their number of milk cows." He told his readers: "Let us all get behind this proposition and work for its successful conclusion."[30]

Borden's reluctance placed the Chamber in a tight spot. An anticipated cold winter had created a increased demand for dairy feed. The Chamber feared that the dairymen and women would do what they have done since time immemorial. They would send their cows to slaughter to avoid having to feed them, and use the revenue thus generated for other farm activities. The Chamber understood that the practice might skew the survey's statistics results; Borden might find milk production in Starkville and its environs not measuring up to a condensery's needs and might then terminate the venture. The Chamber took the rare action of printing a front page letter to address dairymen directly. It urged them not to engage in this practice in great numbers, and if they did feel forced down this path, to retain their best milk animals. As Jarnagin put it, "KEEP OUR GOOD COWS."[31]

While the Chamber dealt with one aspect of Borden's questionnaire, farmers had many questions about others. Borden required "whole sweet fluid milk" twice daily and dictated that it be delivered to the plant. When farmers would receive their checks also caused concern. Apparently Hilbun let Waters know of the potential dissatisfaction with the company's demands and Waters sent Hilbun a letter to share with Oktibbeha dairymen to diminish discontent. It was clear but unyielding, precise, and detailed. It was the encapsulated Borden corporate ethos. Waters argued that the way the company maintained quality was to place a dairy inspector near every condensery. He moved from farm to farm, inspected the animals, the equipment, and the surroundings. Stables and milk houses had to be clean and screened to keep out flies and other insects. The inspector also answered any questions involved with dairying. He worked to ensure a good water supply on the farm to cool the milk and to keep it at a sufficiently low temperature on the way to the condensery. Waters then shifted to what the dairymen needed do on their own. Each dairyman purchased the 10-gallon cans and marked them with his name or initials. Morning delivery was 7 A.M. to noon, while evening drop off was 6 P.M. to 9 P.M. Waters suggested that dairymen could deliver their milk individually or collectively. They could take turns delivering the fluid, split up weeks, or find some other accommodation. Borden washed the cans after use and returned them to their owners. Payment was provided on the fifteenth of the month that followed delivery. Waters closed by asking any farmers needing to know "special information" to "kindly let us know." The company "will try and furnish" the requested answers.

Waters's letter appeared in mid-December. Ryder had made his first visit to Starkville eighteen months earlier. The wait for a final decision would continue for Starkville, but some observers acted as if it were a fait accompli and waxed philosophic about its significance. In several instances, these included ruminations as to just what prosperity meant. Commentators saw modern life as more than just getting by. What the Borden plant would unleash for Starkville was a potent indication of the marvels of modern, rural, small-town American life. It was a union of a large corporation and a rural area, of a manufacturing plant and the town in which it resided, of the town and the countryside that nurtured and benefited from it. As the wait continued, Starkvillians and others speculated about the relationship between small towns and their neighboring farms, and about what the modern world demanded from cities and farmers. Wages—income—was one part, of course, but it was now the beginning, not the end. An editor of the *Commercial Appeal* consciously summed up what Borden's entry into Starkville meant. He reminded his readers that Borden's canned milk was the food on which babies—the future—were raised. Starkville had long had excellent rail connections, thick pastures, good soil, and fine weather. It had raised and milked cattle and resided next to a superb agricultural school. Now it had Borden and that made all the difference. "There had been a decay in country life all over America. . . . When Borden comes to Starkville, you will see something very different, something transformed. You will see, proverbially, a forest where you had formerly only had trees; you will see richly tapestried families and a community where only desperate people had been. You will see herds of cows on hillsides covered by lush grass. Up the hill you will see a barn and a silo. . . . A silo may be a beautiful thing," the author continued, with "young men giving attention to cows and . . . young girls at home helping their moms," preparing dinner for their brothers and other farm workers, who would have spent the day toiling with the dairy animals. The writer goes on, describing how trucks would go to town on good roads, loaded with milk. Their drivers would return with Borden money, which would then become clothes and a means to lessen indebtedness. This farm could now boast "a musical instrument, a phonograph, a radio, some good newspapers and magazines." With these things, with this financial and spiritual prosperity, the old farm could become attractive, with indoor plumbing and central heating. Because of Borden, this ideal farm "more than meets the demands of the family unit and the family is happy and content." Joy, happiness, fulfillment "come out of a can of condensed milk, which Borden will pack at Starkville in Mississippi."[32]

Appreciative of the success of Starkville's Chamber of Commerce and its dogged pursuit of Borden, the *Times's* William Ward chose to highlight just how essential they were in securing Borden for the city. His strategy was to defend forthrightly that critical class of a community of members nationwide. Writers often ridicule their organizations, he noted, and claim that their "superficial" members stand as "self appointed guardians of culture." He vehemently disagreed. Identifying oneself with a place, making it barely distinguishable from yourself, is an "American characteristic" and has "a very definite and valuable place in the upbuilding of a better country." He encouraged his readers to think of what it means "to have thousands of small cities scattered throughout the width and breadth of the land all 'Boosting' to build themselves up industrially, commercially, and intellectually." Prosperity begets culture, maintained Ward. "Before a nation can set about the task of improving itself mentally, its citizens must first" be free from want. That was Borden's benediction to Starkville.

A letter writer identified only as "Free Lance" argued that "prosperity and the dairy cow are synonymous terms in the agricultural life of any people." In "every community, in every county, in every state, and in every country where the dairy industry has been developed . . . prosperity has followed as sure as night follows the day." The Borden condensery was the embodiment of that sentiment. "Here's to the dairy cow, the farmer's rainbow of promise." It held the potential for a full life.[33]

Area newspapers claimed that Borden put "Starkville on the map." The new plant focused "national attention" on northern Mississippi. "The Bordens are a big corporation. They just don't locate plants in a section just as a matter of favor." The company recognized something in Oktibbeha, something other than the production of milk, something it felt it could be part of. Oktibbeha was an investment, to be sure, but it was more. It was a place to live, a place fit for life and living. Borden will "supplement in a big way the already consuming and manufacturing facilities" in place. "We are entering upon a new era of progress and development. The Borden plant is blazing the way." To paraphrase Voltaire, with great opportunity came great responsibility. "Our advantage and our possibilities ought to weigh heavily on the conscience of our citizenship," the newspapers continued. "Nothing will be left undone to press on in the forward movement." Put simply, developing and maintaining community took hard work, work as intensive as the actual act of dairying. Borden gave Oktibbeha the opportunity to undertake that effort.

Golson remembered that everyone in the county pitched in to bring Borden and the prosperity it carried with it to northeast central Mississippi. "The people of Starkville and Oktibbeha County have every reason to put on a 'cheeky front' and feel good," reported Golson. They worked together "in every way," participated "in every effort." "To their cooperation is due the success" of the venture. He went further. He wanted to single out the "interest manifested by the negro dairymen." This group "aided in every way they could"; they proved a vital cog in the Oktibbeha community. Without Black farmers, these "enthusiastic boosters," the area never would have secured the plant. "Good people of Starkville and Oktibbeha County," he continued, "a new era is dawning upon us—the beautiful Sun of Prosperity is already rising above the Hilltops!" He urged his fellow citizens to "be fully awake to the many advantages and possibilities" the condensery will bring. So long as we "cooperate and pull together, our future is bright."[34]

C. H. Markham, still Illinois Central president, generalized from the Oktibbeha County experience. Echoing a dichotomy drawn in Abraham Lincoln's "A House Divided" speech, he argued that "this country cannot live half prosperous and half poverty-ridden. We cannot have a true measure of prosperity for all kinds of business and all classes of the population unless every kind of business and every class shares in it." Those were the material aspects, he noted. Prosperity had another, greater benison. "We are united by spiritual bonds that are far stronger than material bonds." Those bonds of humanhood, "interrelationships" bordering on kinship, were the ones of "supreme importance." Material prosperity may have been a necessary precursor but interrelationships were the ones that made live worth living.

Throughout the entire Borden-Starkville process, emotions peaked and waned. Euphoria, followed by icy silences, and sudden visits then hurried requests for further information became the norm. It should have been no surprise then that the industrial committee soon recognized it was coming face to face with a deadline suggested by Borden. The issue at hand was the pledge that the company had required of all dairymen before proceeding. The Chamber committee had received only about one hundred in early January, a far cry from what the company needed. The committee blamed the disappointing return on the poor winter weather and the holidays, and assured its fellow citizens that it indicated "no lack of interest among farmers and dairymen." The industrial committee tried to assuage dairymen's concerns over the operative statements in the Borden pledge form by arguing that the pledges were not in fact milk delivery contracts but only a promise. The document, moreover, did not specify duration. A dairyman who found delivery to Borden inconvenient could quit at any time. To answer individual questions and to get the pledges signed, the committee agreed to go to each farm in the next week and bring back the forms.[35]

T. C. Richardson, editor of *Farm and Ranch,* a very large Dallas, Texas, publication, came to Starkville to examine "the Starkville miracle" just as the industrial committee was visiting farms and getting signatures. He heard the stories of Montgomery, the deliberate cautiousness upon which Borden acted, and more. All that was a fine backdrop to the story that Richardson chose to tell. He was quite interested in the Black farmers as dairymen. Moore told him that the percentage of white and Black dairymen bringing in first-rate cream was identical; Black farmers proved as competent as their white compatriots. Landlords of Black tenant farmers found themselves "highly pleased" with the way the tenants managed the herds. But Richardson also was interested in Starkville's uniqueness as the South's first dairy center. He found it in the nature of the Starkville community. It was not the land, the cows, or any other physical attribute. Several southern places offered similar inducements. Condenseries are to be built in the South "whenever and wherever a community will come about making a field for them as has Starkville." It was not about "handsomely printed literature" or "the manifold advantages of a section." It was about the people.

If other southern places wanted to attract a condensery, these "southern communities [must] set this goal and work systematically towards it." Bringing in a company like Borden had to be a community endeavor.[36]

The community of Starkville had a deadline to meet and it systematically compiled the pledges in due time. Farmers had promised over six thousand dairy cows. Ward congratulated the Chamber and the farmers for working together to complete this essential project. "When people band themselves together," he wrote, "they can accomplish anything." Starkville had averted that crisis, but another brouhaha soon ensued. Beattie had accepted and the aldermen approved a bid from the Mississippi Power Company for the city's electrical power. Citizens complained about the agreement's terms. Plaintiffs then went to court to block the sale. A judge ordered a stay. While campaigning for public support, Beattie apparently argued that if the sale did not go through, it might jeopardize the city's attempt to secure the condensery. Waters "resented the efforts to bring his company into the light plant controversy" by Beattie, stating the company would not locate here unless Mississippi Power provided the plant's electricity. Beattie had "misrepresented the company's attitude." The mayor's comments provoked "distrust" and could "drive off the Borden plant."[37]

As the scandal erupted, the Chamber embarked on another Borden-mandated challenge. A special committee went to Memphis to lobby representatives of the Illinois Central and M&O railroads about granting Borden's request for a special "stored in transit" rate. Borden wanted to use Starkville as a storage facility for its noncondensed milk products. It did not want to pay two shipping charges—one for sending the material to Starkville and the second for shipping the material to its final destination. A single direct freight charge from its place of production to place of consumption was far cheaper. The august Memphis-bound body included almost all of Starkville's heavy hitters: R. C. Jarnagin, H. A. Beattie, A. W. Reynolds, F. L. Wier, J. S. Moore, G. Odie Daniel, William Ward, and M. A. Saunders. The committee argued that the plant would expand the northern Mississippi dairy industry and, by extension, benefit the entire South. The railroad representatives pronounced themselves convinced by the arguments and promised to bring the matter to the March 17 meeting of the Southeastern Traffic Association, which had the final say.

Waters attended the Memphis meeting. He offered the committee good news but with the usual caveat. He planned to visit Starkville the next week to secure options on factory sites and to lease contracts for boring wells. Final action would be held in abeyance, however, until after the traffic association met and ruled upon Borden's request for storage in transit.[38]

The committee returned immediately from Memphis and was greeted in Starkville by an unlikely but impressive delegation. Not linked to the Borden Company per se, the group was visiting Oktibbeha expressly because Borden appeared certain to erect its condensery there. These men were Wisconsin dairymen and they came to the county to possibly establish dairy farms. Such an initiative would resolve one of the burning issues that the Chamber felt incomplete. Northeast Mississippi required white dairymen immigrants. Wisconsin farmers more than fit the bill. Steeped in the findings and traditions of the Old Northwest, these immigrants would bring northern farming methods to the Jersey County of the South. Some thirty years earlier, Wisconsin governor William D. Hoard, editor of *Hoard's Dairyman,* toured Mississippi. He noted that Mississippi had numerous dairy advantages and none of Wisconsin's pitfalls. He boldly predicted that someday Mississippi would assume the mantle of the nation's leading dairy state. That Oktibbeha could attract investors from America's dairyland marked a coming of age for the place. Many Starkville dairymen agreed with Hoard's long-ago prediction and envisioned their section becoming the Wisconsin or Illinois of the South, a place where dairying and what it brought were inseparable. Wisconsin meant money, pride, nicely appointed farmsteads, and progressive traditions. Investors from that region could not help but assist Starkville to achieve the dream. Wisconsin farmers were but one of many groups inquiring about purchasing Oktibbeha farmland. Those inquiring held a vision and principles already accepted by local Mississippians. As Ward put it, Starkville businessmen and Oktibbeha farmers had "one great interest in common—namely, to build up a more prosperous and thriving city and a better agricultural community and to make life richer, happier, and more pleasant and comfortable for all." They had to "work hand in hand, know each other, and like each other." "Cooperation" was the key, because their interests were mutual.[39]

In anticipation of the railroad association's decision on storage in transit and Borden's likely construction of its condensery, Starkville's Chamber of Commerce was deluged by personal visits, "letters, telegrams and long distance telephone calls." The "stimulus created by the outside world learning of the Borden plant to be located" in Starkville sparked inquiries about the county's immigration possibilities. Individuals asked about the price of land, which sections of pastures were naturally well watered, the availability of small tracts for dairying, and nearby truck farming markets. In addition to economic questions, they sought information about Starkville schools, churches, and other institutions upon which the community was built. While different in specifics from the Wisconsin group, these potential new immigrants wanted more than economic success from any relocation to Mississippi. They hoped to become part of a well-integrated social entity—though not in the racial sense—with the accoutrements and institutions of the modern era.[40]

As March 17 approached, Waters and the special Chamber of Commerce committee hopped a southbound train to participate in the Southeastern Traffic Association's New Orleans meeting. Opposition to Borden's request was stiff. Several of the southern railways represented in the organization appeared worried of the precedent that would set by granting the waiver. But F. B. Bowes, vice-president of the Illinois Central Railroad, made an impassioned plea to look at the bigger picture. He recognized the Borden factory as the first of its kind in the South, and a harbinger not simply of future dairying efforts but of the development of the South generally. It would be the first step in "solving . . . the Industrial and financial status of our section." After further deliberations, the group approved Borden's request. Waters immediately notified the Chamber that the company would indeed build the condensery in Starkville. The relief that the area felt was embodied in the first paragraph of the announcement in Golson's paper." It went:

> That the South, Mississippi, Oktibbeha County, and Starkville, the Jersey center of the South, is coming into their own heritage, made possible principally through the hard and cooperative efforts of the general citizenship, the activities of the Oktibbeha Chamber of Commerce, local Business Clubs and the active and energetic efforts of the railway men of this section who have shown themselves so wide awake to the developmental program and that they have not been slow in helping plan and lay, is now an assured fact.

Ward was more celebratory. "Watch Starkville Grow! The Borden Plant is Ours. Jarnagan [*sic*] and Party Brought Back the Bacon," his headlines screamed. Today "will go down in the history of our town and community as the biggest day, when . . . everlasting energy, wit, and perseverance was not weakened and led their efforts to victory."[41]

Ward certainly did not overstate the importance of the plant to the area. Its significance was felt as far away as Allentown, Pennsylvania, and Dayton, Ohio. Newspapers carried short stories hailing the event.[42] In Starkville proper, two other momentous events shared the front page with the condensery. Both were likely beneficiaries of the long, hard trail to get the milk plant here.

March 18 marked the opening of Starkville's grand hotel. It was filled to three-quarters occupancy that first night. Formerly named Hotel Alvis after the last name of the impresario who was to operate it, Starkville changed the building's name to Hotel Chester, after Alvis's son. Alvis had walked away from the venture when funding was unsure but the Chamber, the banks, and individual Starkville residents had chosen to finance the hotel as part of their investment in the town. They continued their dialogue with him, since he oversaw numerous grand hotels in larger southern cities, until he capitulated. To a great degree, investment in the wake of a Borden factory was and should have been obvious. The investors' futures were tied to Starkville and Oktibbeha County. They owned businesses, farms, dairies, and more. The potential location of the Borden plant in town guaranteed a swift business for a fancy hotel, and they furnished the funding for the place. The investors hired noted Jackson, Mississippi, architect, N. W. Overstreet, a graduate of the local agricultural college, to design the facility. Overstreet and Alvis had worked together on several projects both inside and outside the state.

The hotel stood three stories tall, on top of a slight rise in the central business district so as to appear even taller. Perched there like a beacon, it shone its light on Oktibbeha County as the county bathed Mississippi in its glow. Hotel Chester had all the modern amenities. A cigar and newspaper stand took up part of the lobby, leaving room for a telegraph office, several phones, and a series of fully equipped writing desks. The kitchen and coffee room had the newest, most modern sanitary counters and appliances. The guest rooms were fully appointed, decorated in Early English décor. Every aspect of the hotel smacked of prosperity, even opulence, but always business. The hotel set aside two rooms for traveling men, endeavoring to make them as much like home as was possible. To some, the hotel was almost something of a relief. Its absence had been a blot on Starkville's commercial fortunes. But others adopted a more positive outlook, suggesting that the hotel heralded better ways and better days for the county. It signified "the materialization of individual, civic, and commercial bodies in organization." Its $95,000 cost was "fostered and financed by Starkville citizens with the Chamber of Commerce as central figure in the effort." More than a structure, it celebrated partnership, successful partnership.[43]

The Mississippi Power Association's purchase of the City of Starkville electric company became the third epic event to celebrate on March 18. The judge lifted the stay and the company sweetened the pot by providing Starkville free street lighting for twelve months. It also agreed to pay the town to operate the plant for one year. Mississippi Power offered the prospect of lower rates as the company, in conjunction with its sister company, Alabama Power Company, promised to dam up parts of the Tennessee River in order to deliver hydroelectric power at a pittance. In the 1920s, electric power had long supplanted other types of power as an ideal and was a window through which prosperity could be seen and achieved. Borden would welcome cheap power, and the power company indicated it might begin to electrify rural Oktibbeha County once the dams were built, the generators up and running, and the power lines strung. In that scenario, area farmers would have all the comforts of many small towns and cities.[44]

The promise of hydroelectric power and the impressive new hotel, coupled with the new milk plant, became visual representations of the modern ethos embraced by both city and county. The area's passion for all the modern mechanical and social contrivances may well have been a critical factor in Borden's decision to work so diligently with Starkville. It saw a forward-thinking place with which it could partner, a place that shared at least some of the vision that Borden Co. held. Magruder summed it up in a sentence. Borden placing its plant in Starkville "means that the great Borden corporation believes in and has faith in the future of Northeast Mississippi." By the time Borden encountered Starkville, it was not the flailing small town it had been just years earlier. It had a Chamber of Commerce that knew its mind. There were several Jersey associations and kindred institutions. And that was important. Providing monuments to signify what a place or a people had become—not to create a newer reality but to reflect the new reality—often generated efforts to create what that place or people yet wanted to be. Success could well breed success, as victory in a particular direction promised not simply consolidation, but progress.

Such was the case among Starkville's citizens. While within a month, the city water tower boasted "Starkville, Home of Borden Milk Plant and the Jersey Cow Center of the South." "This is big time stuff, folks," Ward reminded a town that needed no reminding. He continued, saying that Starkville was "the biggest little town on earth." Starkville was inundated by "many outsiders." They could not "help but see the sign and read . . . the few words that mean so much to the future" of Starkville and Oktibbeha County. Within this ethos, construction of good roads, both for economic advantages and social ones, emerged as more than a crusade. Good roads seemed to be a modern area's lifeblood. The place was in demand—it was at the center of the action, a vital facet of a great new socioeconomic and cultural center—and its residents demanded that paved, well-conceived roads lead to and from a place. Starkville wanted to connect to everywhere and everywhere wanted to connect with Starkville. A major new highway linking Columbus in the east to Greenville on the Mississippi River now made a detour to go through Starkville. Lack of money, the bane of earlier Oktibbeha roadbuilding, suddenly became much more available. Starkville was transformed. It had become someplace from which to go and some-place to come. In a small, rural sense, it had become cosmopolitan.[45]

Being cosmopolitan required ties to other like-minded groups, and the decision of some Starkvillians to seek a Rotary club charter a few months earlier reflected that. Both Memphis and Columbus, the latter four times the size of Starkville, helped foster the institution. Almost from its inception, Starkville emerged as a hub in what was known as the InterCity Rotary group. Comprised of Rotary clubs from the far larger cities of Columbus, Aberdeen, and West Point as well as Kosciusko, the group welcomed Starkville's participation soon after Borden settled its plant there. Within a year it hosted a grand program attended by over four hundred visiting Rotarians and their guests.[46] Its members recognized that cosmopolitan venues needed further amenities, and Starkvillians desperately sought them. Just before Borden agreed to put the plant in Starkville, the city's Presbyterians decided to build themselves a fine new church. As the Presbyterian church made preparations to celebrate its new building's scheduled completion, the Methodists announced plans to create their own new house of worship. They were not to be outdone. The religious home of many of the most wealthy Starkville citizens and members of the Chamber, the Methodist church was to sit atop the highest rise near downtown. The gargantuan edifice was said to cost more than the mighty Hotel Chester, which had opened just a few months before. There can be no doubt that the church was positioned to lord itself and its parishioners over the community. It aimed to be first among the city's nongovernmental institutions. The city's Black Methodists soon followed their fellow white co-religionists' lead. They received a permit a few months later to build their own new church. Putting their anticipated condensery money to good use, the new Black Methodist church building was capitalized at $20,000.[47]

Within two months of Borden giving the go-ahead to build the new plant, Starkville residents identified as essential several institutions around which to fashion a community few had thought possible twenty years earlier. V. C. Curtis, the pastor of the august new Methodist Church, proposed the creation of a "community hospital." He sought a facility with about a dozen beds, some emergency services, and a small operating theater. His reason for urging a hospital's creation in Starkville's midst was about family, about community. A community hospital, he concluded, will enable us to "have our sick ones right here at home where we can be with them." To Golson, wanting a hospital was almost as good as getting a hospital. That was because of what city residents had come to be seen as having become. "One outstanding trait as a people of Starkville is that they usually get things they go after." What was needed to get the hospital in the city was, he maintained, "cooperation. Let's get together and build one." Ward concurred. "If every one takes hold as they should[,] a hospital for Starkville will be as certain as the Borden plant."[48]

A public library also became a Starkville agenda item. A public library was many things. Its manifold virtues touched every facet of the community and community life. Its utility for childhood and adult education were nonpareil. It also housed technical information and manuals for "all persons upon whose work depend the intellectual, moral sanitary and political welfare and advancement of people." It offered "thousands the highest and purest entertainment." It lessened "crime and disorder." Libraries made "a city a more desirable place of residence, and thus retain . . . the best citizens and attracts others of the same character." The library constituted social betterment. It was "a living organism." It elevated "the general standard of intelligence throughout the great body of the community upon which its material prosperity, as well as its moral and political well-being, must depend."[49]

A complete system of public schools also made the list of institutions Starkville residents now coveted. Its backers claimed that "Starkville's greatest industry" was not the Borden plant or any other such material business. Its highest enterprise was "making good citizens." That required education. "Our public schools" stand as the "greatest force" to produce good citizens. Rather than modern, sleek institutions for the effective, efficient provision of knowledge, the city's schools were a jumbled mess. One school building accommodated 275 pupils, 5 teachers and 5 distinct high school vocational tracks. Another served primary schoolchildren. A mill school with one teacher taught all the children working there and whose parents worked there. Black children, almost as numerous as their white counterparts, were consolidated into a single, woefully inadequate schoolhouse. Proponents of the public schools argued that creating and then configuring space promised to resolve the educational morass. By making separate classrooms and work spaces for each age group and vocational interest, each would become the sole focus. The weight of effort would press toward that discrete end. In addition to these specialized spaces, schools were communities. They needed shared spaces. Libraries, auditoriums, cafeterias, and study halls were places where students from across the curricula met and interacted. All this rationalization of space took money. It required new facilities designed and structured to house this new education. Without significant opposition, Starkville residents recognized the public school's centrality to their community building efforts and appropriated over $100,000 to design and open an up-to-date physical plant.[50]

While Starkville carved out new or revamped community-fostering institutions—including a community pool—Borden worked heavily on its new facility. After some considerable discussion as to where to set up the plant, Waters settled on an area not far from downtown. The parcel of land included Wallace Maxwell's family home. Beattie lived nearby. Blueprints show that the facility was to be 266 feet long—almost the length of a football field—and 56 feet wide—roughly a third as wide as a football field. An addition 96 feet in length was to be constructed separately. Brick was the primary component. The Illinois Central ran on one side of the proposed condensery and the M&O on the other. The same Memphis firm that built the Hotel Chester received the Borden contract. G. A. Page, Borden's general supervisor of construction, and M. J. Smith, superintendent at a Borden New York condensery, came to ride herd on the building's construction.[51]

Before the first shovel load of dirt hit the ground, the Borden Co. had one final task. It needed to indemnify itself and protect its officers by creating a wholly-owned subsidiary with expansive powers and authority. Borden's creation of subsidiary corporations—the Borden Farm Products Company and the Borden Farm Products Company of Illinois—had a speckled past. Disgruntled stockholders in Borden Co. had accused the company of establishing subsidiaries simply to enrich the Borden Co. officers and board of directors at the expense of Borden Co. stockholders. Rather than pool resources of the several corporations under the Borden Co. and then pay stockholders dividends, several New York stockholders maintained that the subsidiaries used moneys that should have been considered profits to pay premium stipends to the board and officers.[52]

Borden had an even more immediate reason to incorporate the Starkville operation separately. To attract capital to the state and to entice firms to set up facilities in Mississippi, the legislature passed an act exempting them from state, county, and local taxes for a specified period, providing the new enterprise incorporated as a Mississippi body. To exploit that provision, Borden Co. filed a charter on August 8, 1925, to form a Mississippi corporation, the Borden Southern Company. It listed as its incorporators Page and Smith and then five local citizens. Each of these Oktibbeha people were highly regarded in the city and county. They included W. H. Sudduth; W. W. Magruder; H. A. Beattie; Ben Hilbun; and F. L. Hogan, former president of the Starkville Public Schools and of the Oktibbeha Livestock Association, prominent wheat farmer and a staunch backer of the creamery. The charter listed Starkville as its home—it identified all seven persons who filed the incorporation documents as Starkville residents—but stated that the new corporation could have several offices both inside and outside Mississippi. Meetings of the stockholders, directors, and committees could be held anywhere. The board of directors were nine in number but they did not need to be stockholders or incorporators, although the charter's signatories would serve as the board until their first meeting.

Almost all the stipulations provided the corporate office in New York great latitude. So too did the corporation's purpose. It could "manufacture, purchase, sell, and otherwise deal in condensed, preserved, evaporated, malted, desiccated, vaporized, and all other manufactured forms of milk." It could also "manufacture, purchase, sell, and otherwise deal with ice

cream and ices of any and all forms, confectionery, and all food products."
Furthermore, the Borden Southern Company could "raise, purchase, sell,
and otherwise deal in all garden, farm, and dairy products." It could "raise,
purchase, sell, and otherwise deal in cattle or other live stock" or "manufacture, lease, purchase, and sell all machinery, tools, implements and other
articles" related to those activities. It could also transport any of the above
items, export them or import things that assisted in their manufacture or
sale. The charter further enabled the corporation to deal the above materials at wholesale or retail rates and carry on a "general manufacturing and
mercantile business."

The corporation also gained some banking powers. It secured the authority to "act as agent for individual, firm, association, or corporation"
entities. It could behave like a general commission agent. "It could advance
money, obtain credit, "either on its own endorsement or otherwise," for
any manufacturer or producer who made or sold a "product which is dealt
in by the company." Buying and selling land, water rights, the ability to
dam rivers for mills, and a whole slew of more highly articulated privileges
found expression in the charter.

The charter gave the corporation the right to offer $300,000 in capital
stock, valued initially at $100/share.[53] With that out of the way, construc-
tion began. Most building went smoothly except for sinking the well and
laying the various piping to bring water to several parts of the condensery.
Repeated breaks and difficulties in drilling slowed matters, but not dramatically. By the end of November, the roof was almost complete. When that
task was accomplished, the company took great care to set up its extensive
and sophisticated machinery. The cream-colored smokestack, composed
of fire bricks, with the word Borden featured on its side, could be seen
from afar. Construction moved rapidly and followed its anticipated course.
Waters predicted that the factory would accept its first milk shipment in
March or April.[54]

Meanwhile, Borden Co. was not sitting idle. In the course of a bit more
than a year starting in March 1925, the company doubled its capitalization
to over $50 million. Clearly, the corporation was planning dramatic new
moves and it needed the financial flexibility to implement its agenda.[55]

EVERYBODY LOVES STARKVILLE

The Chamber of Commerce, the Starkville Miracle, and
Economic Security for Mississippi Small Towns

Starkville realized just how impressive it had become. It had attracted the nation's largest milk producer–distributor-dealer to the county. It would house the first milk plant—the first condensery—in the American South and thus open dairying to the entire region. Securing the condensery for Oktibbeha was a tremendous achievement and one that citizens thought ought to be widely shared. When Waters made his estimation that the plant would begin receiving milk shipments in March or April, Starkville decided to shout it from the rooftops. It began to think about planning a massive celebration to commemorate an event of almost unfathomable scope and importance to small town rural America. The *Clarion-Ledger* said it simply. Starkville was making plans "to jollify," to "hold a big jollification celebration" to dedicate the marvel in its midst.

The Starkville Rotary Club proposed the idea of organizing the event around "Home Coming Week" and wanted to bring many former Oktibbehans back for the event. It took the idea to the Chamber with the notion that that body organize all civic organizations to work together. It also composed a potential list of invitees. Borden officials, officers of the Illinois Central and of the M&O and the Mississippi governor were suggested. Waters's return from a quick New York trip helped set the date. He reported to the Chamber that his bosses wanted guests to be able to inspect and walk through the plant before it went into operation so they opted for March 10 and 11 for the formal opening. Making the event a two-day affair had an express purpose. The first day celebration was for white folk, while the second day was reserved for Blacks. Clearly, the separation of the celebrations by race reflected the Mississippi status quo. But the fact that there was a day reserved for Black people to mark their special accomplishment was a critical reminder that the whole program of securing the condensery depended heavily on Black sharecroppers and tenant farmers. Without their active support and hard work, the Borden project would have collapsed. Borden was able to satisfy itself that Starkville's fluid milk production was more than sufficient to provide for the condensery because of the partnership, while racially unequal, of Blacks and whites. To finalize the agenda, the Chamber then decided to schedule a meeting on Saturday for its industrial committee to meet "the presidents of the several civic organizations in the city."[1]

That statement—several civic organizations in the city—signified what Starkville had become. Ten years ago, it could not sustain a single civic organization. Several had been established, and each had failed in a heartbeat. The Chamber had emerged as Starkville's first sustainable civic organization and it required emendation just to survive. Now in 1926 there were many standing organizations: Rotary, Lions, Parent Teacher Association, Oktibbeha Federated Club, Daughters of the American Revolution, Sorosis Club, and Neo Cycle Club as well as the Chamber. Shared success in attracting the Borden plant had created an environment for successful sharing; success had bred success. Collectivism—working together toward a common purpose—became the town's way of the present and the way into the future.

All these organizations' presidents met with the Chamber's industrial committee as did any number of representatives from the college—faculty from the dairy, extension, and agriculture department, the experiment station, and the county agent. Beattie chaired the effort. The group declared itself a steering committee and divided the work of the celebration into six committees: finance, refreshments, arrangements, entertainment, and publicity/invitations. Golson headed the steering committee. It decided to invite roughly the same group that the Chamber had favored earlier. There was one notable exception. They wanted to have Wallace Maxwell as a guest of honor because he "first conceived the idea of a Borden plant in Starkville."

The steering committee's initial act was to address "the People of the Community." Heralding the plant as the "biggest event that has ever happened in the history of Starkville," it quickly moved to heap praise on the company that would run it. Borden erected a half-million-dollar facility in Starkville. "Other cities in the South would have gladly given a hundred thousand dollars or more to secure this great industry." Borden never asked Starkville "for a penny, but gave [the town] the plant because [Borden] was convinced this was the most suitable location. It is a magnificent gift." The committee called on fellow citizens to attend the celebration, reminding them that they would "reap the benefit of the great prosperity" that will come to Oktibbeha "from the location of this huge enterprise in our midst."[2]

The various celebration committees undertook their work in earnest. The Fox Film Company scheduled a visit during the celebration to feature the event in its newsreels. The Illinois Central also prepared to send a motion picture crew. Borden directed its southern salesmen to attend the Starkville event. The college band practiced for the festivities. Estimates of thousands of guests attending with more than five hundred from out of state required plans to house and feed the guests. The city's merchants agreed to close all their stores and join the event at eleven o'clock in the morning. Public schools and the college canceled classes for that day. To ensure that no one missed the significance of the event, signs reading "You are now Entering Starkville, the Home of the First Milk Condensery of the South. The Borden Company Extends a Cordial Invitation to Visit Their Plant" were set at every road leading to the town. Beattie declared the week before the event as "Clean-Up Week," told everyone to clean their premises and to place garbage for convenient removal.

Two singular events were to mark the occasion. Any number of influential speakers would provide the early focus by addressing the solemnity of the event and its importance to Starkville and all who assisted in securing the plant. A covered temporary stage was to be constructed for those speakers. In that way the throng could fill the streets in every direction and hear the pearls of wisdom near and far. The commemoration was then supposed to give way to a carefully choreographed parade. The Boy Scouts, deputized for the day by Mayor Beattie, directed traffic. A series of floats, each of which depicted a crucial event in Starkville's history and was designed by someone with a personal or intellectual tie to that event, were placed early in the march. Later, other floats representing community organizations or Starkville enterprises would work their way past a reviewing stand where the floats were judged. Winners in various categories would receive monetary prizes. A picnic-style lunch of "sandwiches, pies, cakes, ice cream, coffee" was to be served "cafeteria style."

Entertainment was also to mark the occasion. Boxing, public speaking, band and Charleston contests were scheduled. So too were a glee club and three vaudeville acts.

The city's newspapers covered preparations for the second day, the day of the celebration for Black Oktibbehans, less thoroughly. E. W. Hayes, the Black farm demonstration agent, took charge. Like white children on their day, Black children would have no school. Hayes contacted several notable Black people, asking them to come and address the group. He reported that the county's Black farmers were as excited about the celebration as their white counterparts and that a large crowd would surely attend their event.[3]

As the city and county prepared to celebrate, Borden set out again what its suppliers should do in preparation for the factory's opening. The specificity of Borden's outline, the details that it articulated, and the care the company took to have its dairy farmers get it right, all struck a chord with the way the risk-averse company deliberately selected Starkville. Its spokesman, M. J. Smith, even suggested what fair rate transportation costs ought to be per mile and hundredweight of milk. And as always, the company sought to head off problems rather than resolve them after the fact. It stood ready to answer and assist any issue a supplier had. Oktibbeha County agent, R. M. Lancaster, followed up Borden's directive with a series of dairy meetings in various county locales to answer questions and solidify plans.[4]

While Borden planned and Starkville planned to celebrate, many area residents were working to capitalize on the enthusiasm generated by the opening of the Borden plant. Borden's benediction—locating in Starkville—meant something. The struggling cooperative creamery found itself in high cotton as soon as Borden agreed to build in Oktibbeha. Local dairymen expanded their herds in preparation for the event. The creamery and the farmers raked in the profits. It paid farmers over $200,000 in the year before the plant opened, a nearly eightfold increase in a few short years. A dairy feed store opened to cater to the anticipated herds of milk cows supplying quality milk to the new condensery. A new bakery took root. A federal post office building was in the offing. A special training school for Black people was in the process of being built next to the factory. Mississippi Power promised to have its hydroelectric power to the factory in time for its opening. The school board considered how to divvy up the $100,000 building fund. The only matter that failed was a bold half-million-dollar bond issue to build "a county-wide system of good roads." Many outside the city saw the costs prohibitive and questioned why the proposed roads bypassed their struggling towns.[5] Prominent Chamber members—Beattie, Wier, and Jarnagin—joined with B. M. Walker Jr., a local lawyer and son of the college president, and longtime alderman and dinnerware merchant, J. L. Martin, to form a vegetable packing corporation in Starkville. Both white and Black farmers held its stock.[6]

Constructing and staffing a modern hospital was perhaps the most significant community initiative. The Chamber of Commerce, Lions Club, and Rotary Club worked together to form a corporate entity to construct and operate the hospital, and sold its stock to Starkvillians. Pastor Curtis chaired the effort. At the meeting, the group chose the hospital's location and hammered out its finances. Profit governed the project. Curtis included the rationale for investing in the venture in his church's weekly bulletin. He reminded his congregants that "it is the duty of the church people to heal the sick." He pointed to Catholics, who gained considerable good will by running hospitals and maintained that "Protestants can well profit from their example." He assured the Methodists that he was not asking the congregation to fund the hospital. It was to be individual investors, many of whom he hoped would be from his church. Curtis saw the hospital as a sound deal. It was for-profit—charitable organizations needed to pay for charity cases receiving hospital care—and he expected it to declare a dividend yearly. Investors would be "assisting in taking care of the sick" and "helping yourself while you are well." He ended his plea for investors on a more somber note. "You don't know who will be the first to be carried" to the hospital. In a half page public announcement in the *Starkville News*, the hospital committee hit similar points but a bit more crassly. Oktibbeha County residents send $30,000 for hospital services yearly out of county. If a medical facility were there, "would not every business man profit from it?" A "good hospital is the best advertising agency a town can have." Many places that "are prominent today would not be known, were it not for their hospitals." A hospital made good sense for many reasons, the committee noted. It could provide emergency care and save lives. It would reduce individual travel expense to go and stay in a hospital town. Patients and families would not be separated. Finally, a hospital in Starkville meant that "we will have competent surgeons and nurses at our door." The ad ended with "you or some member of your family may be the first to go to this hospital" in large bold type.[7]

At the end of February, the *Starkville News* announced that on March 5 it would produce a special Borden edition of the paper. It planned to highlight both the plant and Oktibbeha County. Borden Co. asked for 10,000 extra issues to be printed so that it could have them "distributed all over the South." The Chamber asked that each visitor attending the celebration receive a complimentary copy, which necessitated printing at least 5,000 more.

Clearly this special edition of the paper dwarfed anything ever attempted by the *Starkville News*. The ambitious edition could not be a catch-as-catch-can enterprise. It was the biggest press run in the the paper's history. Golson, who was now vice-president of the Chamber as well as editor of the paper, had an awesome responsibility and opportunity. This issue would set out exactly what the Starkville entrepreneurial and progressive class wanted to set out. What many would know about Starkville throughout the South and elsewhere would be what was presented in this special edition. What posterity would remember was what was printed there.

The responsibility was magnified by the fact that the *News* and *Times* had just merged and therefore the *News* was Starkville's sole public voice. Its stock was now owned by the city's mercantile elite, and Golson remained at the helm of the redrafted venture.[8] He did not shirk his civic duty as Starkville's chronicler at its most auspicious moment. The special section of the twenty-four-page paper began with a story, the story of how a small town and a large corporation found mutual interest and formed a partnership that produced the condensery. Told in loving detail and likely derived from several accounts of Starkville citizens and Borden employees, the multipage piece laid out many of the particulars of Borden's dalliance with Starkville. In some cases, letters were included in their entirety. In others, confessions of losing hope along the way were revealed. It very much captured the uncertainty that characterized the nearly two-year relationship that preceded Borden's decision to begin construction.[9]

Other sections were nearly as thorough and introspective. Hilbun's section, "The Hand of Progress," discussed how it touched "the gentle slope of landmarks" to produce "a structure of cement, brick, stone, and steel so placed together that modern efficiency and medieval beauty are interwoven into the creation." With a poetic lyricism, a hint of nostalgia, and hard-headed realism, he described the shiny behemoths that were the boilers, condensers, evaporating pans, and the like that went into the industrial production of condensed milk. He conveyed both the scope of the machines and the flow of the factory as he described how milk wound its way from machine to machine, throughout the facility. Hilbun found himself almost overcome by the elegance of the plant's inner workings. "Nothing is wasted. Everything is used," he marveled, as he described the closed system where exhaust steam heated the boiler to produce more steam, which then became water. Like the continuous loop of steam and water, Hilbun's mind went from "the factory to the farms where the milk necessary to the life of the industry is produced." Interdependence—partnerships—characterized the facility's industrial design and the nexus of the Borden milk plant and Oktibbeha dairying.[10]

J. D. Ray's essay titled the "Borden Plant Itself" told how the facility was located on prime residential land. Pastor of the Starkville Baptist Church, Ray reflected on how the plant had replaced several stately antebellum homes and commanded the eye as any train approached the city. Its more than 100 foot tall smokestack with Borden on its side could be seen from every direction. Two wells, one 1,000 feet deep, the other 1,300 feet, served the condensery. He paid special attention to the filler, a device that filled twelve—and only twelve—cans at a time. If there is one short, it will not fill any. If there is not enough milk loaded to fill twelve full cans, it will not start. Each is filled to the same one one-thousandth of an ounce. Ray was astonished by the machine's ability to think; he called it "as near human as a machine can be." Summing up, he talked of what the plant symbolized to him and the South. "We have thought in terms of cotton." Now we are thinking "in terms of cows and condensed milk." Our land, Ray prophesized, "veritably shall not only flow with milk but money too."[11]

Markham wrote how in just a few short years dairying had become the leading branch of agriculture in Mississippi. He recounted the Illinois Central's participation in that transformation—its purebred stud program, its farm experts and trains, its butter makers, its war on the cattle tick. "Prosperity follows the dairy cow," Markham reminded readers. It is the "source of wealth" that enables farmers to "build up their land, improve their homes, educate their children, and generally improve their standard of living." James H. Collins, who had recently published *The Story of Canned Foods*, wrote about Gale Borden's discovery of the condensing process and its development both prior to the Civil War and after.[12]

Higgins, still the college's dairy specialist, offered a much more forward-looking contribution as he outlined the dairy opportunities in Oktibbeha

County and the adjacent territory. He surveyed grasses, silage crops, feed corn, the cooperative creamery, and the Borden plant in a no-nonsense look at what possibilities the area offered farmers interested in immigrating. L. P. Sweatt, general manager of Mississippi Power company, told how cheap electric power would make many tasks a breeze and others possible. Mississippians "stand awakened." They want "to share in the good things of life. They want progress and prosperity. They realize that these things can be had, and they intend to have them." Moore returned to an historical bent as he told about the cooperative creamery and its influence on the establishment of the local dairy industry, "where very little progress ... was made until a little more than a decade ago." The "real progress in dairying for this section and in fact for the State, began with the establishment of [the college] creamery," he argued unabashedly.[13]

Many local businesses and services took out ads in the special issue. Most were small, less than a quarter page. Only two groups purchased full page ads. One was Borden. Its ad spoke about the company and condensed milk but was especially interested in reminding the Oktibehha community what the Borden plant meant to them. "From this day on," prophesized the ad, "the Borden Company will play an important part in the life of the town." Because of the plant, Starkville's influence "will extend throughout the South." This almost biblical injunction concluded with the company promising that it would "take an interest in worthy local undertakings and boost the community in every way."[14]

Borden was not simply here to stay. It was anxious to further its new home, to make it prosperous in every intellectual, cultural, social, and economic way. The second full-page ad came from the Chamber of Commerce. It identified fourteen principles that the group cleaved to. This manifesto claimed the Chamber to be "the voice of the city and county," "reflect the ideals of the community," and give "direction to the aims of the citizenship." The Chamber would bring together individuals who felt powerless alone, plead for the voiceless, and fuse "unorganized elements to an organized unit." It would defend the good name of the city and fight slanderers. It would focus on worthy initiatives and be the "center of worth-while [sic]enterprise." It would draw "the outside world" to Starkville, serve as a "clearing house for civic pride," and relentlessly be "a power house of progress." Its last principle incorporated the rest. The Chamber was "a composite picture of a city or county as its citizenship would have it."[15]

The special issue encapsulated the city's story, both its past and its future. It solemnly drew a path for where Starkville had come and envisioned prospects for where it was going that had been unthinkable a decade earlier. At the same time, it sketched a similar portrait for Borden. Its past lay in the origins of the condensing process and the initial steps to make it a going concern. Its present was heroic, at least in the South where huge yet graceful machinery produced condensed milk and profit for itself and its local partners. Its future was in the small towns of the rural South and it was the company's intention that Starkville would be the gateway.

Nothing remained but to hold the celebration the following week. That did not go as neatly as planned. A torrential downpour washed out any possibility of a parade on the first day. The speeches and dedication were moved indoors to the new plant's storage room. An estimated five thousand attendees packed the room. The A&M Cadet Band played as the throng filed in. Magruder hosted the dedication, which was covered by Turner Catledge, a *Memphis Commercial Appeal* reporter. (A Mississippi A&M graduate, Catledge later moved to the *New York Times* where he became managing editor.) For the Starkville dedication, he was very much in his element. "It was a great day for Mississippi," he intoned. The storeroom was filled with people—"farmers, merchants, railroad men, educators, newspapermen, and representatives of practically every walk of life," all to welcome Borden to the South. Catledge did not miss the significance of a diverse throng. He termed the grouping "the greatest visible expression of cooperation . . . that this part of the country has ever seen." Many former Starkville residents returned "to pay with their presence" compliments to their former home. Celebratory speakers included representatives from Mississippi Power, the M&O, Illinois Central, the railroad commission, the *Commercial Appeal*, and the *Progressive Farmer*. Each congratulated Starkville and Borden, forecasted great prosperity for both, and then talked of the future of the South and Mississippi.

The final speaker was W. D. Strack, a Borden vice-president. His dedication was far from traditional but certainly squarely in line with the philosophy that Borden had espoused since its initial dalliance with Starkville nearly three years earlier. Catledge maintained that the dedication blossomed from "the soul of the Borden company." Strack's speech was extremely brief. "We are glad we're here," Strack told those who came to witness this momentous occurrence. He then repeated what had become a Borden corporate vow to Starkville. "We've come to be part of you. We want to enjoy with you your industrial and commercial prosperity. We want to share with you your trials and problems. We have adopted you as our people and your city as our city."

Strack talked of union, even communion, with Starkville, "an expression of feeling [the company had] in opening the magnificent plant in Starkville."[16] While based on milk, it went far beyond milk. It was portrayed as almost a sacred trust, as Starkville was becoming the latest member of the Borden family. Certainly it was self-serving. And it was not a compact between two equals. The weaker partner knew quite well what it had bartered for. It was nothing less than survival, prosperity, and freedom from want. It was choice. With the plant in Starkville, the place had options. It need not run in panic after any prospect. It could think, analyze, and decide. As significant, it was fame. Starkville was the first, the pioneer. The town's activities had opened an entire new avenue for small towns in the southern United States.

All that was worth celebrating, and that is just what Starkville did. Its March 11 parade was spectacular. Another newsreel crew, from Pathé News, a concern with an extensive distribution network in Europe, joined with the Fox film company and the Illinois Central to provide three separate film records of the proceedings; Starkville would be featured in movie theaters in America and Europe. Led by a herd of Jerseys, the parade commenced with members marching down the town's main thoroughfare and passing by a large reviewing stand filled with dignitaries. A field marshal with two aides on mounts, a drum major, and two different A&M College Cadet bands took the lead, to be immediately followed by the parade's pièces de résistance—the floats.

The first eight floats told the story of Starkville's history that its program committee wanted the assembled to know. It set as its baseline a 1626 small Choctaw village under the Spanish. That initial float was followed by another that remembered the French control of the Mississippi territory and then another celebrating the first English settler's cabin. After those preliminary floats came the representation of the 1820 founding of the Mayhew Mission, the first permanent white settlement in the area, to "civilize" the Choctaw. The next float commemorated the 1833 creation of Oktibbeha County. Its formation followed the Choctaw's ceding the land to the United States in the Treaty of Dancing Rabbit, and the subsequent

Trail of Tears—the forced march of the Choctaw to the Oklahoma territory. With "civilization" firmly entrenched, the sixth float, entitled "Before the '60's," depicted a log cabin and a schoolhouse, signs of progress. The Civil War and its aftermath were omitted from the celebration. The seventh float, "1875. Coming of the Jersey. Introduced by Col. W. B. Montgomery" was the penultimate historical float. It was related to the final float in this series. Titled "1926," the float was composed of a cow and a replica of the Borden plant with an outrageously large door. On the cow's back was an equally large key for the lock in the door. On the key in big letters was written: "Prosperity." Oktibbeha County and the Borden Co. fit together like key and lock, hand and glove.

Civic then commercial floats touting Starkville followed. Observers found them "resplendent in color and beauty, touching in sentiment." After the final float, Hayes, who also taught agriculture in the town's Black schools, led a march of several hundred Black children. Hilbun, who wrote the story on the parade, told readers that Black farmers "contributed a great deal to the cause" of getting Borden to Starkville. Hilbun took the opportunity to thank Hayes "and his people." For their assistance, "the people of Starkville and Oktibbeha County are truly grateful."[17]

The Black celebration followed the parade. Held at the Borden plant, it demonstrated its revelers' "complete devotion to the state and section." O. R. Sanders, a member of the faculty at Alcorn College, the state's Black agricultural school, declared Mississippi "the best place on earth." Its beauty was such that he was sure that the psalmist must have had a similar place in mind when he wrote: "The heavens declare the glory of God and the firmament showeth his handiwork." According to Catledge, the Black audience "went into uproarious applause." Sanders then segued into home- and land-ownership. When you own land, he continued, "you gain the confidence of the white man" as a stakeholder in the community "that would otherwise be impossible." S. A. Scott, of Port Gibson, Mississippi, also addressed the crowd. Heralding "the fast age," he urged his audience to "progress with civilization." Blacks need "concerted effort." "We must work for our own welfare and not depend on the white man to do it for us." He urged patience. Blacks have been free for only sixty years. "It takes God 100 years to build a great oak tree."

Following the speeches, the Black contingent held "a real oldtime [*sic*] southern negro dance" at the plant. They invited white folk to join them and an impressive number did. The highlight of the evening was a Charleston contest. A young slender Black man with slicked back hair won first prize.[18]

Festivities at an end, Starkville paused to catch its collective breath as it waited for the condensery to begin accepting milk. National agricultural journalists wrote about "the Oktibbeha miracle" and its implications. Cully Cobb's *Southern Ruralist* pronounced it a new day for northeastern Mississippi. Cotton had given way and its replacement promised "a prosperity quite unlike anything before." Cobb identified Montgomery—because of the Jerseys—and Moore for the creamery as heroes for transforming this "one time plantation community" into one of the leading dairy counties in America. The Borden condensery fit "splendidly into the general scheme of things." What has been done in Oktibbeha can be done elsewhere, Cobb maintained, but there must be men of vision "to take the lead, men of courage and unselfishness" who can withstand "ridicule, who won't quit." That constituted the key to the county's successful union with Borden and why "we today offer our hearty congratulations."[19]

Collingwood predicted that the Borden plant heralded a tremendous shift in dairy production from the Midwest to the South. Years ago, if someone offered that opinion he would be call "an impractical dreamer or treated as an insane man." Collingwood recounted the limestone croppings of the area, the ubiquitous grasses that cotton farmers relentlessly attacked, and the introduction of Jersey cattle. The transformation from cotton to dairy culture took place out in the open but few noticed the changes. Only when Borden decided to lower distribution costs by planting a condensery in an area were its goods were sold did the secret get out. That decision took off the blinders. New, active dairy sections in the South were being discovered. "The success of this condensery at Starkville" changed the nature of dairying. "The revolution is sure to go on," he concluded, as facilities migrate to wherever dairying occurs."[20]

John Stanton, editor of the *Milk Reporter*, focused on the work of the Oktibbeha Chamber of Commerce. Located in Sussex, New Jersey, the *Milk Reporter* covered New York-based firms. It recognized the significance of Borden's foray into the deep South. The condensery was "one of the largest joint agricultural and industrial development in the South." But what really attracted his attention was "the co-operative efforts of citizens, the activities of the Oktibbeha Chamber of Commerce" and its industrial committee to make the Borden condensery "now a reality."[21]

James Speed, editor of the Nashville-located *Southern Agriculturist* asked how did a significant dairyland develop that could attract a large condensery owned by the largest American milk firm. He reported how persistence, geography, and opportunity joined with hard work, first to pique Borden's interest and then to convince the company of the area's virtues. The rest was history. The qualities exhibited in Oktibbeha County far exceeded the several other possibilities the Borden Co. examined. Now that the plant was complete, Borden reaffirmed its view. It pronounced itself "highly pleased" with how its Starkville operation unfolded.[22]

Words of praise and encouragement proved endearing. A few days before the plant was scheduled to accept its first milk shipments, Golson reminded dairy farmers that "the success of the Borden plant depends upon the dairymen of this section" and he urged them to make the condensery triumphant. When the plant actually opened on April 1, Oktibbeha produced. Its morning shipment came on huge trucks "loaded to the guards with milk cans" as well as any number of automobiles and wagons. Exceeding Borden's expectation for the first day, 133 farmers sent 11,179 pounds of milk. The money generated for Borden and for Oktibbeha dairymen and women was even better. A letter from Arthur W. Milburn, Borden Co. president, arrived at about the same time that the first fluid milk shipment arrived at the facility. It thanked Oktibbeha residents for the "many acts of courtesy and helpfulness" during the investigative and building processes and predicted that that sort of spirit would make it "surprising if Starkville is not eventually classed with our most prosperous condensaries." A single week after his letter, Milburn seemed prophetic. The quantity of milk per day nearly tripled. The experience of Fort Scott, where the Kansas farmers struggled to meet expectations, was not replicating itself in Oktibbeha. Within two weeks, the plant produced enough condensed milk to send a full freight car to New Orleans. It left Starkville with "First Milk Condensed in the South" on one side of the car and "Made in Starkville, Miss.–the Borden Southern" on the other. To further convince the Louisianians that it was truly from cows in the South, Borden temporarily branded the milk "Magnolia Condensed Milk." Before the end of the month, dairymen were delivering more than 53,000 pounds of milk per day. By mid-May, the number jumped to 68,000 pounds.[23]

Starkville so far beat expectations that Borden sent Waters down to celebrate the first payday. He noted that the plant outshone any other condensery Borden had ever opened. By the end of May, the amount of milk brought to the condensery daily was significantly larger than the Borden refrigeration capacity, so the company rushed in additional units to keep up with demand. Local farmers took in nearly $52,000 for the month of May. The creamery, which received the excess cream that Borden separated off from butterfat-rich Jersey cows, took that cream and also gobbled up the surplus whole milk, providing Oktibbeha farmers an additional $25,000.[24]

For a single month, $77,000 was an extraordinary amount for a city as small and as struggling as Starkville to add to its economy. April's pay had been $45,000 for the condensery and creamery combined. If sustained, it was nothing short of life altering. The town was secure. Farmers could pay off debt. Mercantile establishments blossomed with the newest goods. The money permitted those cotton farmers to continue their boom-or-bust agriculture, while also enabling dairy farmers to go full bore. Part of the key was that the demand for Oktibbeha milk was apparently insatiable. Borden seemed to welcome as much as dairy farmers brought to their facility.

Placing the condensery in Starkville made people across rural America sit up and take notice. Watching the money roll in as predicted proved even more compelling. Even the smallest, three-cow farm reaped a profit after expenses of $50. In the state of Mississippi, several entities tried to capitalize on the Oktibbeha-Borden model. But that consensus proved illusionary. The sole factor they held in common was the attraction of the additional funding brought in by dairying. For example, the Jackson-based Mississippi State Board of Development, a merger of the state Chamber of Commerce and a similar, competing organization, saw the condensery as the expression of a successful cattle tick campaign. Once farmers outside of north central Mississippi rid their cows of ticks, they needed "to start repairing their dairy barns," get as many good cattle as they could afford and prepare for the state to replace Wisconsin as America's dairyland. A Holly Springs state legislator, Hugh K. Mahon Jr., argued that the grasslands of Mississippi and mild winters simply meant that the land would naturally support dairying without any intervention. The state only needed to acquaint "the investors and industrial moguls of the North" to these facts, show them the excellent climate and "surplus labor" and a dairy-revealed prosperity would sweep the state. Lieutenant Governor Dennis Murphree argued that for dairying, Mississippi was one of the most favored spots in the world. That is what led the state to produce "more creamery products than all the other southern states combined." This good fortune also enabled Starkville to exceed Borden's two-year estimates in just thirty days. At their annual meeting in Jackson, Mississippi, newspaper editors recognized in the immediate expansion of Borden's capacity a "gratifying indication" that numerous other milk plants will open throughout the state. A short piece in the *Winona Times* noted that for the first time Mississippians were drinking Mississippi-produced condensed milk, which "is superior to any." In Mississippi, dairying was charmed. "Only the cattle tick is vile."[25]

The Oktibbeha County Chamber of Commerce was not content to let others tell its story: it wanted to control the narrative. It created a pamphlet titled *Fact Concerning the Borden Plant at Starkville, Miss.* This bulletin gives a brief summary of the first two months of operation. Its stated purpose was to have "educational value that reaches in a beneficial way various classes of people in different localities and different sections." The back of the trifold piece had a picture of three full milk trucks waiting to upload their wares at the south side of the Borden plant. The address label page contained two sayings. A quote from a Borden executive stating that of the 36 condenseries built by the company, "this is the best beginning we ever had at any plant" graced the left side of the page. Underneath the space for the address was found, "A visit to Starkville Will Interest You. Come to See Us." Inside it told briefly of Borden's arrival in Starkville, the natural advantages of Oktibbeha County, and the success the city and county had achieved, including the factory's generous payouts as well as those at the creamery. Its goal was to encourage reticent county dairy farmers to join in the prosperity and to bring new dairymen to Oktibbeha. Its closing line was simple but apt. It read: "When you have read, please hand or mail a friend."

The Chamber printed up several thousand pamphlets and sent them to newspapers throughout the region and to anyone seeking further information about Starkville and Oktibbbeha County. Demand quickly outstripped supply. Alabama Power Company wanted 250 more. Mississippi Power Company sought an additional 500 "as a starter" with more to come later. Although their enterprise did not come to Starkville, representative of the Frisco line, the rail line that served Fort Scott, expressed interest and wanted additional copies. The Memphis business community asked for some. The Illinois Central's Schwietert asked for a thousand "for his office." Stuart Peabody, the new Borden advertising manager, asked for 500 for his operation. Birmingham businesses asked for 300 more. Railroads that received the pamphlet sent surveyors to explore the area.[26]

The pamphlet was such a hit that the group published a second pamphlet a few months later. This one had a broader agenda. A photo of a large Jersey cow—billed as a "typical Oktibbeha Jersey"—appeared on its cover. It too highlighted the plant and the excellent financial benefits dairymen reaped, but this more comprehensive pamphlet also pointed to the wide variety of suitable agricultural pursuits available in the county. Its purpose was to entice businesses of all kinds to the area. Together, both pamphlets showcased what Oktibbeha had to offer. The campaign to promote the area gained traction in some quarters. Starkville became a destination for meetings of merchants, bankers, and others not directly associated with the milk industry. Where there was money there was opportunity, and these groups hoped to gain a foothold there. Within the city and county things began to happen. Starkville formally established a fire company to protect the buildings and goods in this revitalized place. A $200,000 Good Roads levy for the county passed. Street paving contracts were let in the city, to expand downtown and enable more merchants to locate there. The subsequent building boom suggested that the paving initiative succeeded. During this expansive growth, Borden's Smith wrote a lengthy letter to the citizenry of Oktibbeha to remind the group not to forget upon what this activity was based. There existed a fundamental interconnectedness between the condensery and everything that the county cherished. "If the dairyman is prosperous the community is prosperous." It becomes "a drawing card for better dairy herds, better roads, and better living conditions." These enhanced conditions, Smith reported, "attract the better class of people who are looking for a place to relocate."[27]

While the pamphlets followed up Oktibbeha's triumph and extended the county's reach, the Chamber had one more major project. To complete the county's narrative, it published longer articles on aspects of the histories of city and county. Able to delve into details that did not fit the first two pamphlets, the group claimed that in each of the anticipated nine articles, "the truth is told and not exaggerated in the least." The series hit the standard themes—the county's administrative history, the coming of the Borden plant, the geological peculiarities of the place, and the A&M. college. That was not surprising, because that is what the region had to sell. Despite its sheltering of Borden's facility, the area still wanted more. It did not recognize new businesses or farmers as a threat to the status quo. It embraced them. It acted as if prospects were nearly infinite, as if it were just brushing the surface of what Oktibbeha could be. Borden opened the possibilities. Starkville residents embraced the opportunity as a challenge to become a most modern and prosperous place.[28]

Embedded in the hoopla that the area generated was an inevitable spawning of imitators. Starkville did not care. It was proud of what it had become and impervious to any challenges to that station. In fact, the city labored in such a way that it did everything it could to recreate the Starkville miracle throughout Mississippi. Other cities and counties were attuned to such prospects. County banks lent money at reduced rates for farmers willing to purchase prime, purebred dairy stock. Borden also seemed aware that its success was likely to encourage other dairy industry members to come to the South and set up facilities. After all, that is exactly what happened in Fort Scott. As soon as Borden demonstrated that dairying was possible and profitable in wheat and corn country, other condenseries descended on the area. And so it was in Mississippi. But Mississippi was an extraordinary case. For years rumors suggested that southern heat made a dairy industry impossible. The heat both affected the cows and the milk. Borden had shown that was nonsense. Furthermore, the alacrity with which the milk plant expanded indicated that the land was not simply acceptable for dairying but fecund. With only a few moments of hesitation after Borden's proof of southern dairy farming, northern milk companies began to investigate the South for large-scale dairy industry development. Like Borden, they no doubt recognized the savings in transportation costs of developing production facilities near significant markets. And with Starkville's meteoric rise noted throughout America and even Europe, they realized that Mississippi offered almost limitless potential.

Carnation became the first major condensing company to act. In December 1925, Stanley McNees, Superintendent of the Carnation Milk Products Company, came to northeast Mississippi to surreptitiously scout it out for suitable places to establish a condensery. He went to Tupelo in Lee County and found it miserable. There were no pastures, and the town was not "devoting enough time and money" to dairying. He also visited tiny Macon, a city of about two thousand some twenty miles from Starkville, just at the edge of its milkshed.[29] With a clear acknowledgment of the benefits that Borden brought to Starkville, both Macon and Houston, Mississippi—

an even smaller town fifty miles north of Starkville—worked to convince Carnation to put its plant there. Carnation also looked at other condensery sites.

Macon was an interesting case. A contemporary of W. B. Montgomery, Matthias Mahorner, had been the area's largest landowner. Like his friend, he became infatuated with Jersey cows. Mahorner joined several Montgomery initiatives. An avid trader and seller of pure Jersey stock—he got his initial Jerseys from the Isle through New Orleans—he sometimes traveled with Montgomery to secure even better animals. Mahorner provided some of the funding for the agricultural college to ensure its location near Starkville, served as the longtime secretary of the Mississippi Livestock Breeders' Association, was president of the Noxubee Loan and Trust Company, and proselytized for Jerseys and grasses. He remained content to let Montgomery hold the bully pulpits and command public attention.[30]

Because of Mahorner's foresight, the Macon area had cows and grasslands. However, it lacked significant infrastructure. The town had been twice destroyed by fires that occurred some years apart. In both instances, citizens spent their limited capital on rebuilding the town. They could not afford to enhance roads or other infrastructural amenities. Tupelo had the opposite situation. It had fine roads and good city services but lacked cows. Even without dairy animals, Tupelo became interested in a condensery. A city about double the size of Starkville, the town was blind to McNees's assessment that it was miserable. Tupelo envied Starkville's success. The editor of the *Tupelo News* attended the Starkville celebration and pronounced the plant "undoubtedly the biggest thing in the history of Starkville." Area dairymen "will be assured hereafter of a ready market for an unlimited supply of milk and cream at profitable prices."[31] At a meeting of the Tupelo Chamber of Commerce, R. E. Kurtz, traveling industrial agent for the Frisco Railroad, pledged to help the city snap out of its economic doldrums. He too surely knew of the success of Starkville and the role that the Illinois Central played in Borden's decision. Kurtz went directly to Oconomowoc, Wisconsin, to talk to the Carnation people about Tupelo as a suitable condensery site. But McNees's report had soured them on the town, and they failed to be swayed. Kurtz time and again petitioned the company on behalf of Tupelo. His persistence finally paid off. Carnation subsequently sent representatives to Tupelo. By now Starkville's huge paydays, always reported in the state's newspapers, had Tupelo and Lee counties firmly committed to the idea of a condensery. As it examined Tupelo, Carnation found itself impressed by a surprising fact. For several years the Lee County Bankers Association had employed, at the then-princely sum of $4,200 annually, a dairy agent, Sam B. Durham, to develop dairying in the area. That showed Carnation commitment and financial backing. The company also noticed Tupelo's hard paved roads running to and from the city, making it simple to bring milk to the plant in any season. But when Carnation people came to survey the site they found the grasslands infested with bitterweed, a grass that soured the milk to taste and rendered it unsuitable for condensing. It also sucked soil moisture and crowded out and killed clover.

While Kurtz talked to the company, Durham engaged area dairymen. In his periodic *Tupelo Journal* column, "News of Interest to Dairymen," he repeatedly bemoaned bitterweed, arguing that if "it was not for this bitterweed the building of a great whole milk plant would be going on today." The plant, which he estimated would cost $300,000, would be a "revelation to our section." He figured there were less than 150 condens-eries nationwide and noted that they "made the country wealthy where they have gone." He urged area farmers to make "a desperate fight on this pest . . . to cut this pest and rake and burn it." "It would be better," he con-cluded, "to lose the rest of this year's cotton crop than to let the bitterweed go to seed." The greatest handicap to the future welfare . . . is bitterweed in the pasture."[32]

Newton, Mississippi, learned of Carnation's investigations into suitable condensery sites and made its pitch for the plant. After talking about its fine farmland and its location near the center of the state, Nar McArthur Cunningham, editor of the *Newton Record*, acknowledged that dairying had not yet been developed there, but that could easily be remedied. Some banks in the state lent farmers interested in dairying money at 5 percent to buy at least four purebred dairy cows, and that could and would certainly happen in Newton. Then came the crux of the matter. "What the Borden plant is doing for Starkville and vicinity, the Carnation plant could do for Newton and Newton County." "We want to do whatever is possible in get-ting" the plant here. Area businessmen were on board. They were "no less interested in their county than those of other counties." Always "by co-operation great things can and are accomplished."[33]

While Carnation looked for a suitable site, the Mississippi State Devel-opment Board (MSDB) got involved. Although it built from the Borden model, it decided to go in a slightly different direction. The board's general manager, L. J. Folse, contacted Wisconsin dairy interests to explore establishing a network of cheese factories in the state. He was convinced that many Wisconsinites had moved to Mississippi to pursue dairying opportunities in the past few years. They could trade on their connections to their old homes to spearhead a movement in Mississippi. "This is a natural dairying state," Folse continued.[34]

The MSDB acted in other ways, establishing an office in Tupelo and dividing the state into several districts. Each district had its own board-determined agenda but each county and city in a unit was to engage in "co-ordinated work." Tupelo and the several surrounding counties were placed in District #1. That district targeted "eradication of bitter weed" as "of the highest importance" because it hindered milk quality.[35]

As the campaign against the noxious weed commenced, Carnation made its decision. It counted on the campaign to be successful and chose to place its condensery in Tupelo. All the details that had delayed Borden's decision were glossed over. Some were resolved by the operation of the Borden plant. Carnation could use those precedents. And the plant would rest at a strategic fork made by the Frisco Railroad in Tupelo. But other issues had to be worked out on the fly. There were expectations for the factory—it was to open by May 1—but there had been no cow census, discussion with dairymen, or tour of farms. Carnation had opened a condensery in the Missouri Ozarks three years earlier. It based its Tupelo projections on that model, much as Borden did on Fort Scott.[36]

Carnation's decision was announced a few days after the New Year. Hilbun took the New Year as an opportunity to see what having a condensery had done for Oktibbeha County in eight brief months. His musings also appeared in the same *Tupelo Journal* edition as the Carnation announcement. Oktibbeha, he said, "is without a doubt a land of MILK and Money." The dairy cow has "the Midas touch." In Oktibbeha, cotton was no longer king. Money generated at the condensery and creamery more than doubled revenue from cotton. Hilbun also noted that cow dung used as fertilizer enabled the county to produce the same amount of cotton on far fewer acres. But that was only half the matter. He also contended that the security of monthly dairy checks allowed farmers to expand to raise poultry, maintain beef cattle, and move into sheep. As a consequence, claimed Hilbun, agriculture in Oktibbeha had become "a well rounded program that almost defies seasonal uncertainties."[37]

Following Carnation's excellent news, once Lee County residents had caught their breath, they engaged in a cow census, the initial results of which found three thousand cows in the area, far beneath the threshold Carnation required to justify its condensery. In a panic, "banks, business men, chamber of commerce [*sic*] and the press" called a mass meeting to take place three days hence. Within a day, thirty-five thousand circulars were printed and distributed in Lee and neighboring counties, inviting anyone interested in the welfare of the area to attend. At the meeting, the business organizations impressed upon the assembled the importance of the Carnation plant to themselves and posterity, and urged each farmer present to pledge how many cows they would purchase to feed the condensery. That number topped ten thousand, which proved much more to the company's liking. Given a chance to reflect on the situation, Frank Kilcannon, editor of the *Tupelo Journal,* reminded his readers just what the plant meant to each of them. The condensery "means more to the people of this section than anything that could have been brought here." "Within the reach of every family [is] the opportunity to better their condition." Children could receive an education and not be forced into the field to pick cotton. The family could "get the milk check" and go "to town and let them buy what they want." You will never again "have to ask for credit." Kilcannon noted that each town he had heard from in Mississippi wanted a milk condensery. He understood that not everyone would get one, "but those who get them will never regret the day." The "benefits will spread over the country like the dew."[38]

In preparation for the condensery's opening, the *Tupelo Journal* published a special celebratory issue. It was less historical or philosophical than its Starkville counterpart. The issue served as a beginner's manual for a part of the state just entering dairy farming. There was one exception. Kilcannon took the opportunity to thank everyone involved in securing the condensery for Lee County, but he saved his more telling remarks for Carnation. He thanked the Carnation people for demonstrating "their faith in us by placing one of the condenseries in our midst." Carnation's faith "gives us faith in ourselves." Carnation pointed out "to us our possibilities which we have heretofore overlooked and neglected." "We are proud of the fact that a company that stands so high in the business world is willing to come here and become a part of us."[39]

Unlike the rain-plagued Starkville celebrations, the Tupelo celebration went off as anticipated. It was more clearly an event of Lee County than just the city. Each small town within the county was represented with at least one float. Tupelo was engaging in creating a milkshed where there had not been a very large one before. It needed help. Area farmers needed to adopt and adapt to dairy farming. In that sense, it held more in common with Fort Scott than Starkville, which sat in the middle of a highly extended dairy enterprise.[40]

At the time the Tupelo facility was being built, Macon stepped up its game and contacted Borden. Unlike Starkville and then Tupelo, the town did not have to convince the large northern company that its milkshed was great enough to host a condensery. Starkville's success had demonstrated that. What concerned the company was the lack of development of the town as a whole. Macon recognized its deficiencies and provided a series of financial inducements to get Borden to place its plant there. These enticements to locate in Macon were not monetary but rather internal improvements—an adequate water supply, graveled roads, suitable land for a condensery site. In effect, Macon simply raised its offer to match other more developed places. Cows were not the problem, the town's physical plant was, and when Macon improved the site according to specifications, Borden Co. placed its condensery there.[41]

Even before Tupelo opened, while Macon was in the process of formulating its successful offer, and as Starkville farmers were racking up big profits, other localities in the state started to clamor for their own condenseries. They did not necessarily know what a condensery was, but they knew what it made. It made area farmers and towns less poor, and that influx of money changed the fortunes and reputations of places. In a very real sense, few cared to differentiate among kinds of for-market dairying. It was the establishment of a dairy-based profit center in a central place that mattered. It enriched the environs and the people residing there. Edgar S. Wilson, a columnist writing on agricultural and other matters, surveyed 132 Mississippi newspapers and found dairying and roadbuilding as the predominant editorial and feature stories. Rarely did a newspaper editor or writer acknowledge that both standing condenseries resided in the Mississippi prairie. They looked at almost any Mississippi venue as a potential dairy site. Lee County provided newspapermen a useful model: It was in the process of becoming a sustainable dairy region. Carnation committed to the area because of pledges, not actual dairy cattle, as well as the Tupelo bankers' longtime financial support of a county dairy expert. Nor was Carnation the only large northern milk firm to seize on Borden's success and move South. As it had in Kansas, Pet Milk Company began eyeing the area almost from the moment that the Borden gambit was underway.

Mississippi towns and counties often tried to examine why Starkville and much less frequently why Tupelo received condenseries. Oktibbeha County was a dairy hotspot. Lee County was not. What made both attractive to northern industrialists as they sought to bring dairying southward? Invariably, those discussions focused on "the cooperative spirit," the notion of "local jealousies" put aside when "promoting community of interests." Engagement, manifested in a local institutional structure, such as a vibrant Chamber of Commerce, or in public enterprise, such as a successful good roads campaign, seemed to figure prominently. It was not enough for a community to want a condensery. That desire had to have tangible manifestations.[42]

Private enterprise sometimes joined in the inevitable march of northern capital to the dairy South. A consortium of Kansas farmers purchased several large tracts of land near Greenville, on the Mississippi River. They planned to bring large herds of Guernsey cattle to the area, grow grasses and fodder crops, and create a dairy industry empire right there. These Kansas dairy entrepreneurs proved the exception rather than the rule. Multimillion-dollar northern dairy companies did nothing simply as a lark. Every single initiative they took was preceded by intensely careful investigation, thought, and planning. Pet's procedures were ostensibly different than Carnation's and Borden's but were really very much of a piece. Unlike those two corporations, Pet did not hold its plans in confidence. It leaked them and then had interested cities and towns state their cases. For example, several members of the Chamber of Commerce at Vaiden, a town of about 600 in Carroll County in west central Mississippi, went to Starkville to talk to its Chamber about what it might learn to help them recruit a condensery. From these discussions, the Vaiden Chamber composed a dossier to show that while the area presently grew corn and cotton, it could easily be adapted to growing grasses and hay. There was already a small but vibrant dairy industry. Its animals were largely purebred and its farmers produced butter for sale. Vaiden was not alone. Houston, Grenada, Maben, and Mathison all were interested in being the site of Pet's first Mississippi condensery.[43]

Data—the dossier—was a key element in the initial evaluation of a place as a suitable milk plant site. It stated in hard dollars and cents whether the proposed plant would fly in that area. Feasibility of the environs, actual cow population, and dairymen pledges, were the first steps, but assessments of the residents was also crucial. Had there been a tradition of interest in dairying? What entity could ride herd on reluctant or reticent farmers? Did community organization dictate at least a modicum of a chance of success? Answers to these questions were often intuitive. It is the reason why northern firms sent their trusted and experienced men into communities to talk with the locals. These men evaluated whether the populace and its institutions could support prime dairy industry sites. Reports of these visitors greatly mattered. Sometimes second, third, and even fourth sets of eyes were sent to provide confirmation. Half-million dollar or more investments were never undertaken lightly.

As Vaiden and other places waited, Louisville, Mississippi, decided to try to curry Pet's favor. A series of visitors from the nearby city of Starkville talked up the condensery and peaked the Louisville Rotary Club's interest. When it heard rumors that Pet was interested in a Mississippi location, Rotary canvassed territory around Louisville to determine the number of dairy cows and how many more it could garner in pledges. Gathering that data went slowly. After nearly four months, the Rotary reported over eight thousand cows and cow pledges, easily enough for a condensery. This assessment did not cheer the group, however. It feared that the area's lack of good roads would be "the greatest hinderance [*sic*]" to receiving a condensery. It prepared residents for the worst.[44]

Winona proved far more optimistic. A town of Starkville's size sixty miles to the west, it had long corresponded with Pet. Its Exchange Club, a branch of the national service organization that served in Winona as a Chamber-like organization, even had sent a representative to Pet's headquarters in St. Louis, Missouri, to make the city's case, which included the fact that the town had excellent transportation connections. It sat at the intersection of two railroads and a system of highways. Winona businessmen had boosted dairying for a decade, and the town already sheltered a prosperous creamery. Pet asked for a dairy cattle census and Winonans raised $500 to hire men to undertake it. While Winona conducted its census, Pet pledged not to make a final decision without formally considering that city. Walker Wood, secretary of state for Mississippi and owner-editor of the *Winona Times,* lent a heavy hand to the condensery quest, writing letters to Pet and pushing the case in his newspaper. A month later, a Pet representative came for a short visit. He arrived when the town was closed, mourning the sudden passing of Governor Henry Lewis Whitfield, whose funeral train was just then at the Winona depot. He waited for the train to leave and asked to speak to the county agent. The agent was out of state selling dairy sires. The investigator then headed back to corporate head-quarters without the information he had been seeking. With the visit a de-bacle, Wood reminded his fellow Winonans that placing a condensery was "a hard boiled, business proposition," not based on superficiality. He urged them to not try to press the case outside of formal channels. Trying to influ-ence a company or using "cajolery" would fail. He implored his town to not send further delegations to St. Louis unless requested. "Facts are what they want" for this $500,000 decision, and the city had provided all it could.[45]

An officer of the Pet Company did come to examine Winona again. When he left, he assured the group that their city was still in the running, and that the previous visit had not removed it from consideration. Still another Pet representative returned a month later. Greeted by eight bankers, the group discussed specifics of building and locating a condensery in Winona.[46]

As the flirtation with Winona heated up, Pet also became interested in Kosciusko, and Kosciusko in Pet. Kosciusko's interest was new. About thirty-five miles south of Winona and slightly smaller than Starkville, Kos-ciusko had had its sights set on securing a major cheese factory. It lost that battle to Durant, which became the home to Mississippi's initial Kraft cheese plant. A large Chicago concern, Kraft brought cheese making to Mississippi as "an experiment in de-centralization and extending business." The company planned to establish several small factories in different sec-tions of the state and then "encourage dairying in the surrounding districts" to ensure a year-round milk supply. Kraft's decision to locate first in Durant rested on a stipulation: area businessmen had to hire an agent to develop dairying in the territory, a demand that Durant immediately accepted. When the Chicago company announced its cheese decision at the end of June, disappointed Kosciusko scrambled after the Pet condensery and was "making a desperate fight to win." C. P. Barrett, formerly Oktibbeha County agent and now Attilla County agent, used his familiarity with the process to help repackage Kosciusko's Kraft application to bear on the Pet condensery. The material interested Pet and they sent down representatives in early

July. Kosciusko was ready. It organized a grand show of support for a condensery. It held a huge rally in town and then it took the Pet men to three neighboring places—Carthage, Thomastown, and Dossville, the first two in adjacent Leake county—where similar rallies in support of Kosciusko and the condensery were held. At Carthage, the visitors met separately with the city's bankers. That town's businessmen expressed their desire to be thought of, not individually, but one dynamic entity. They had formed a compact with each other, which they called "The Community Circle." The group declared that "the spirit of working with and for one another— cooperation—is the Vital Force in the Development of any community." It pledged "its whole hearted co-operation." At the meeting with the Pet people, promises were made and money may have changed hands. Within a few short days, Pet announced it had selected Kosciusko. At almost the same time, Kraft announced that it had awarded Louisville a cheese factory, the second in the state. Kraft took that action after the Mississippi State Development Board promised to host several meetings in Winston County to "stimulate even greater interest in dairying." Winona, which had scheduled a big last push for the condensery, learned of Pet's decision the day before the scheduled meeting. The city received nothing.[47]

The *Star Herald,* Kosciusko's major paper, told its readers just what getting the Pet condensery meant. While acknowledging the great benefits to the town, it was the "farming interests" that "will take on new life." That new life will be "better farms, better homes, with a larger measure of home comforts." The condensery in town will provide money to put "flowers in the yards, nice furniture in the homes, running water in the kitchen, [and] carpets on the floor." Without hyperbole but with great satisfaction, the *Star Herald* maintained that "we have won a great fight and we are proud of it."[48]

Cutthroat competition for these jewels of modern industry reaffirmed just how revolutionary small towns realized them to be. Towns lusted after them. But if they did not, their newspapers hinted that something was drastically wrong with the place's business community. That sentiment was especially intense right after a facility was awarded to another municipality. Clarksdale's City Hound columnist urged town businessmen to attract a condensery by setting goals "and then CONSTANTLY work[ing] to secure them." Guy P. Clark, editor of the *Clarksdale Press Register,* argued that "Clarksdale should put forth effort, continuous, cumulative effort." None of these places was more favored by nature than Clarksdale. "The answer to Clarksdale's dream is COWS." Six months later, Clarksdale tried again. It called a mass meeting of the entire county "for adopting the cow as a factor in prosperity building." Identifying the cow as central to development efforts gave Clarksdale no particular traction. A similar lack of effort seemed to afflict Union, a small town of about a thousand that was seventy-five miles south of Starkville. S. P. Stribling, *Union Appeal* editor, complained that "it behooves our business men to get busy." Union has "the milk cows for a milk condensery and should have one here." "If our Chamber of Commerce ever had a chance to do something for Union, the chance is here right now."

A town's business elite was not always culpable. Sometimes they faced recalcitrant farmers. Such was the case with Charleston, which came a bit late to the condensery quest. In July 1927, it created a comprehensive survey for farmers to fill out. Only one in fifty completed the document. The Charleston Chamber followed up a week later by publishing a letter in the *Sun-Sentinel* explaining why they needed the data to make a condensery case. Six weeks later few surveys had been returned. The Chamber then called a countywide meeting at which it dissolved itself and reformed as a countywide unit with each municipality represented. The new group agreed among its first acts to attend the celebration marking the opening of the Kraft facility in Durant. That did not seem to create the esprit de corps that its proponents desired so at the end of October it tried again. This time the Chamber created a one-thousand-dollar revolving fund to help possible dairy farmers purchase prime stock.[49]

By December—if not before—the Chamber had come to the hard realization that it was neither going to get the survey results it needed nor significant claimants for the revolving fund. It shifted gears and brought in poultry experts. It also became somewhat snippy. It discussed what was happening in distant McComb to provide "an example of what wide-awake people citizens accomplish." The Chamber tried yet another approach. It sought to convince area residents that locating industries in big cities was an "old idea." Now "many smaller factories [were] located in cities about the size of Charleston." Companies appreciated the lower labor costs, markets near manufactories, cheap electricity, and raw materials near factories. In places like Charleston, "where dairy farming is not well developed," farmers could find seasonal employment in factories "located in nearby towns." Work could be had there in winter months and provide agriculturists wages when they most drastically needed them. Charleston might want to set its sights there.[50]

With that proposition, Charleston's Chamber had effectively thrown in the towel. Even without that town's participation in the condensery quest, competition for milk plants remained so intense and rewards seemingly so great that the battle generated a considerable dairy cow black market. Pledges to engage in dairy farming fueled the market. Companies committed to building many condenseries and cheese plants because of pledges of cows in particular areas, not the actual presence of those beasts. Chambers of commerce gathered those pledges, often through face to face conversations, from sometimes wary or hesitant dairymen. In a goodly number of cases, guarded farmers with dairy cattle said one thing and did another. Often they found it more certain or profitable to sell their animals now than wait for the condensery or cheese plant to be built and receive money from milk later. Aspiring dairymen bought the stock but that failed to increase dairy cattle numbers. It simply just rearranged them. Nor did it necessarily keep them in the same milkshed—or even in state—since these black market dairymen sold their animals to the highest bidders. That act also raised cow costs for farmers seeking to hew to their pledges, which could lead them to change their mind and spark a second wave of selling. Chambers of commerce found the practice troublesome. Unless checked, it could mean that pledges in one place unexpectedly failed to meet expectations, imperiling a plant's functioning once it had been built.[51]

Chambers of commerce had only a bully pulpit from which to address what they saw as personal greed, a failure of public spirit. Having greater authority, then-governor Dennis Murphree took his public utterances in another direction. He adopted the dairy industry, which had skyrocketed under his watch, as a major campaign theme. He took personal pride in those milk plants already in the state and pushed for many more. He hailed the condenseries in every stump speech and maintained that the prosperity brought to some dairy farmers could be extended much further. The dairy industry "that is being builded *in* Mississippi needs to be encouraged," his ads noted. Advocating exemption from taxation for a period for five years for each head of dairy cattle added to a herd, he decried those who claimed he was playing politics. His measure was "not politics; it was good business." Calling his stand "practical government," he celebrated the condenseries as "the first to be located south of Mason and Dixon's line," and championed the cheese factories with equal vigor. He concluded his plea simply. "If you believe that encouragement to Dairying, Farming and Industry is best for Mississippi—then vote for Dennis Murphree." His rival, Theodore Bilbo, refused to leaving dairying entirely to Murphree. If elected, he promised to go to Denmark to study dairying and to bring his insights from that leading dairy country back for the Magnolia state's dairymen.[52]

The dairy industry was the way to success. But the manner by which the large corporations dispensed condenseries and cheese plants fostered competition. Borden, Pet, Carnation, and others were not eleemosynary institutions, after all, and they expected to make money on these ventures. "Almost every community in Mississippi [was] now entering spiritedly into campaigns for condenseries, cheese factories, creameries, etc.," wrote Helen Goodwin Yerger, a weekly columnist for the state's department of agriculture. Anything that might grant a town an advantage became fair game. Lives of communities were at stake. Chambers of commerce scanned newspapers looking for tips, and editors published an extraordinary amount of material to celebrate triumphs, material that could provide the keys to the condensery kingdom. These keen contests also produced a new type of expert. Attracting a dairy facility to a town created a great demand for those who had successfully led such efforts; other places wished to establish similar structures. Towns and cities asked successful applicants to come to them to speak or, even better, to work.[53] Far more common were de facto pilgrimages by farmers or businessmen. They took the trip to Starkville, and later to Tupelo—but to a significantly lesser extent—to get it straight from the cow's mouth. They toured the plants, talked to the Borden and Carnation people, met with the Chamber of Commerce and bankers and often went to see some successful dairies. Almost invariably they arranged their trips to include payday. Payday was the clincher. Watching milk seemingly be turned into money, watching a condensery give out $100,000 in a single month, turned heads.

No one did payday like Starkville. A trip by a contingent from Louisville to the Borden plant in Starkville in mid-1927 was indicative of these visits, which had been ongoing almost since the condensery's opening. Led by Will Hight, editor of the *Winston County Journal*, the group arranged its trip to see the "great milk boom . . . now sweeping Mississippi" and to experience payday. They came to the "revolutionized city"—Starkville—and "found it absolutely swamped with people." Cars with license plates from a handful of states made the streets almost impassable. Black and white citizens waited to receive their paychecks. Hight recognized a large delegation of Alabamans headed by that state's former governor. Nearby were "several hundred enthusiastic citizens" from Blytheville, Arkansas. The editor talked to "several hundred from the northern borders of Mississippi and Alabama." They, like the Louisville contingent, came to learn what Borden had wrought. Ward, the former editor of the *East Mississippi Times,* met the Louisvillians and took them through the condensery. He told them that the place had already exceeded its five-year projections and was nearing capacity. To handle the overflow from Oktibbeha County, the company planned to build a larger facility in Macon. The group then ventured to the bank to see "satisfied people" cash or deposit a "huge number of checks." Hight marveled that most of these people earned their checks from land that had been left to "grow up in weeds and bushes" until the last few years. The Louisville contingent ate lunch at the Rotary Club, where Magruder talked about the ins and outs of dairying and recounted the story of Starkville's history with Borden. He then took them to what they considered a model dairy farm nearly halfway between Starkville and Louisville. Looking back at the experience, Hight found the one thing that characterized Starkville's success: commitment. Each man—whether farmer, banker, or factory worker—was "thoroughly embued with the idea [of committing] and put their whole thought into it." He wanted every farmer from Winston County to develop similar passion, persistence, and competence. They must "visit the Borden Condensery at Starkville . . . and wake up and get in the game."[54]

Hight's Starkville experience was transformative. What he indeed found was a "revolutionized" city. He did not mean that it was wealthier, although it was. Nor did he mean to suggest that prosperity changed the city's character, although it likely did. What he found compelling was the abundance of joy that he found almost everywhere, the embrace of one's task and one's role in what was a collective enterprise. The condensery flourished because of its partisans unparalleled desire to make it successful for themselves and their fellow participants. They "earned" their joy by the notoriety that their city and its condensery had achieved. They earned their joy by being part of something magical.

Hight encountered hundreds of fellow spectators from Mississippi, Alabama, and Arkansas during his visit to Starkville. The Illinois Central and other railroads had numerous special trains and several day excursions to "see the 'Great Borden Condensery'" and, if on the fifteenth of a month, to watch the dairymen "as they receive their milk checks from the past month's supply." They and the other tens of thousands like them were each there for a similar purpose. They needed to know what a condensery could do for their place and what they could learn about how to get it for their environs. Even the staid *Wall Street Journal* acknowledged Starkville as the progenitor of the Mississippi dairy industry. And Hight's experience at Starkville was not remotely abnormal. While guests—invited and otherwise—regularly came to the plant from the entire South, the number of visitors always peaked around payday. Newspaper headlines shouted the latest monthly or yearly total to bear witness to the modern miracle.[55] Payday humanized and personalized condensing. As Hilbun and Ray noted, the actual act of condensing milk was awesome. Glorious machines manufactured and canned milk. But it was the milk producers that truly mattered. A consequence of a condensery in a locale was the senses of freedom and success that it unveiled. People were liberated, their shackles removed, even triumphant. Their questionable futures now restored or secured. Optimism, possibilities, and confidence took hold.

H. Rey Bonney, McComb's *Semi-Weekly Journal* editor, was less ethereal but just as passionate when he attended a Starkville payday about six months later. He noticed hundreds of out-of-state visitors who came for "the purpose of witnessing the sight of this pay-day." As if one they pronounced themselves "amazed" at the spectacle. "From early morning until late at night the streets of Starkville were thronged with people." "The banks were taxed to their limit cashing checks [and] receiving payments on notes." "Every business house in the city was congested with traders." He realized that dairy-borne prosperity brought prosperity "to every other industry." He left the city committed to bringing a condensery to McComb.[56]

Starkville embodied the condensery experience in a way that Tupelo and later places could not. As the first condensery in the South, its story was the creation story. It was the place from which all other dairy industry sites metaphorically had sprung. It was the Zeus from whose head dairy Athena emerged. Virtually every article written about Mississippi dairying celebrated Starkville as the place of origin. Starkville also benefited from the fact that it was a small town that had altered its course. The condensery added the then-fantastic sum of nearly $2 million dollars yearly to the wallets of county residents a mere two years after it had opened. Starkville had immediately and immensely blossomed. The amount of money generated by the condensery so far exceeded expectations that it attracted notice from almost everywhere. That three news organizations documented the condensery's birth was extraordinary. That its performance blew away unrealistic expectations contributed to its powerful mythology.[57]

In the latter half of 1927 and the first few months of 1928, the Mississippi dairy industry continued to explode. The Illinois Central sanctified the prodigious expansion by declaring "Mississippi as a Dairy State" in a slick, four-page essay in the railroad's magazine.[58] Vaiden sought and obtained a Pet whole milk plant as the giant company tried to establish dairy service in central Mississippi. Pet increased it capitalization in Mississippi to $5 million as it ramped up for further expansion. Borden Co. raised the Borden Southern Company's capitalization to $3 million, in part to finance construction of its new Macon condensery. Chicago's Swift & Co. established a dual factory in West Point, half of which would produce cheese, and the other half would raise hens and eggs. Armour and Co. established an ice cream manufactory in Vicksburg. Kraft upped the number of cheese plants it had in the state from two to six, adding Houston, Water Valley, Newton, and (blessedly) Winona.[59] Philadelphia and Corinth each secured a cheese factory. Members of the Chamber of Commerce of Yazoo City pooled their resources and created a cheese-making plant in their town. After a productive trip to the Starkville Borden plant and the agricultural college, X. A. Kramer, a McComb entrepreneur who made his money in ice manufacture and icehouse storage, put together a consortium of investors to establish dairy plants. His group sent a representative to Wisconsin to purchase cheese-making equipment, and pledged to open new cheese factories in McComb, Magnolia, Liberty, Osyka, and Tylertown. Kramer was able to establish these facilities because cheese factories required fewer, less costly machines than condenseries, and could operate profitably with milk from many fewer cows.[60] Senatobia got a Swift cheese plant, while Artesia went with Kraft. Local investors financed the Montrose cheese plant. Standing back from this proliferation of milk-based facilities, Murphree boldly predicted that the time is near "when there will be a cheese factory, a creamery, or a condensery in every town in the state."[61]

Murphree was being just a bit hyperbolic. Some of the state's largest cities proved reticent to pursue dairying. Greenwood, the cotton capital of the Mississippi Delta, never seriously contemplated the dairy industry, although its newspapers followed the story in the small towns around the state. Cotton was king in Greenwood, the source of the city's great wealth, and emblematically remained so.[62] Jackson, Mississippi's largest city and state capital, paid rapt attention to the emergence of the dairy industry. It waited for well over a year before it undertook a several month-long investigation to see if dairying ought to become a Jackson staple. It narrowly decided against that course.[63] Columbus, a town that had conveniently dismissed all places within fifty miles as "The Radius" in classic metropolis-hinterland fashion, finally declared "the Radius the dairy empire of the Mid-South" and tried virtually every other possibility before relenting and chasing a cheese factory. It initially attempted to interest Wisconsin dairy men to come to rural Lowndes County and establish two experimental farms. One would have Holstein cattle, the other Guernsey. The goal was to see which type of animal proved more suitable to Mississippi dairying. Then the Columbians would raise that breed and repopulate the entire state with those cows. Jerseys were not included in this contest. Since they dominated northeastern Mississippi, there was no money unless they were replaced. Columbus then went after a railroad, hoping to get the Frisco to pass through the city. When that failed, it sought a paper mill. After a few other failed gambits, including a bid to capture the Pet condensery that went to Kosciusko and nicknaming the town "Cow-lumbus," cheese came into focus.[64]

Pursuit of dairying throughout the state had an additional benefit. Its profitability led those farmers in areas still plagued by the cattle tick—mostly the southwest and southeast—to urge state government to wage an effective war to rid the state of the pest. For the first time, Mississippians throughout the state expressed overwhelming support for cattle tick eradication. Trips to the Borden plant furthered the anti-tick crusade. A 215-person contingent from McComb who had taken a special train to see the Starkville plant were so moved by the extraordinary prosperity they saw there that they memorialized the legislature on the train ride home, demanding that Mississippi enforce its tick eradication legislation.[65]

Folse, surveying the situation from his perches in Jackson and Tupelo, offered a very different consequence of the Mississippi dairy explosion. He claimed that dairying in Mississippi "to the negro race [*sic*] alone means more to their welfare and future progress than the Emancipation Procla-

mation." He took the experience of the place he knew well—Starkville—
and worked from there. Of the 1,200 farmers serving the condensery, he
identified 501 as Black. Black tenant farmers and sharecroppers generally
received half the price of the product at market. If the condensery paid out
$2 million, that meant that each Black farmer would receive on average
well over $500 per year. After expenses, that might be reduced to some-
thing over $300. On these farms, cotton production had not dropped but
cotton acreage had. That meant that the dairy wage was in addition to the
cotton stipend. Folse saw this as a benison to the social order. Blacks were
by no means the sole beneficiaries of the dairy industry. He prophesized
that "the complete economic liberation of the negro [*sic*] and the so-called
poor white farmer of the South is coming rapidly through the dairy cow
and hydropower." Condenseries, cheese factories, whole milk plants—the
dairy industry generally—were revolutionary. In Folse's world, it would reduce the dependence of Blacks on whites (and poor whites on other whites)
and allow them to chart out a consistent, positive future for "the race."
While dairying did little if anything to encourage social equality, Folse saw
it as assisting Blacks in developing those traits and habits he assumed
whites (but not poor whites) had from birth—dependability, responsibility,
pride, and initiative. To Folse, the inculcation of those attributes among
Black Mississippians furthered the situations of both Blacks and whites.
Dairying did not reaffirm the status quo. It held in Folse's estimation the
ability to take an ideal and to translate it into reality. Dairying would replace social tension with social satisfaction.[66]

7 | WHAT HATH STARKVILLE WROUGHT?
Spreading the Starkville Story, and Conquering
Tennessee and Alabama

Mississippi Representative John Rankin took to the floor of the US House of Representatives to argue that Lindbergh's transatlantic flight was no more revolutionary "in execution or effect" than the proliferation of condenseries and cheese plants in Mississippi in the previous few years. The monthly paycheck, readily available free fertilizer, demise of the one-crop system, and the availability of ready markets for raw milk had changed the nature of the state's fortunes. Farmers now approached their work "with hope for and confidence in a lasting, permanent prosperity." The South had never experienced anything like that. It all came about when "the Borden people went to Oktibbeha County" and established the first condensery in the South. The company had hoped that area farmers would deliver 40,000 pounds of milk daily within a year or so. Instead, they daily brought 160,000 pounds, a mere eighteen months after the facility opened. The plant had to expand twice during that period to handle the tremendous milk flow. That seemingly miraculous outpouring of public support for a condensery was unprecedented in Borden annals. Oktibbeha dairy farmers had triggered a dairy mania as northern capitalists established condensery after condensery then cheese plant after cheese plant in Mississippi small town after Mississippi small town. Everywhere in northeast Mississippi, the dairy industry continued its insatiable spread. To Rankin, the future was certain. Soon "practically every farmer" in the region "will be on a milk route, thus bringing the market right to his door and putting him on the monthly payroll." No wonder, he concluded, that the area was "attracting nation-wide attention."[1]

It surely attracted the *Boston Herald*. Every day in Mississippi a "town is celebrating the establishment of a new cheese factory," and another nearby "town is campaigning to persuade one of the largest cheese companies to locate in its midst." "Once dreaded and feared by the rural dwellers," large national corporations fueled this dairy hysteria. "These strange creatures of modern business" established milk plants in Mississippi, and Chambers of Commerce and dairy farmers swarmed to them. Small towns and their surrounding farms realized that a corporate behemoth was not "a big, fierce animal that lurks behind a tree waiting to pounce on [them.]" These industrial giants proved much more benevolent, although much more insidious. Corporations brought the techniques of modern business with them—efficiency, sustainable profitability, and permanence—and indirectly gave rise to a manufacturer-supplier partnership. Embedded in milk plant–dependent dairy agriculture, these principles and precedents permeated the dairy farms, both changing them and the activities there, and undercutting the boom-or-bust model so prevalent in cotton agriculture.[2]

Sid Noble narrated a different story. Assistant editor of *Better Crops With Plant Food*, he wove a romantic web of a new dairy South, "a story of dreams come true," a story about a "county that cows built." Montgomery was one of Noble's heroes. Through pluck, persistence, and a vision that looked forward a half century, he literally planted the seeds that took down the old cotton South and converted Starkville and Oktibbeha County into dairy territory. Gail Borden—who created a process to preserve milk and was rewarded by the "sweet taste of success"—was the other hero in Noble's saga. "The far reaching influence of those two benefactors of the human race have converged in the first southern milk condensery" at Starkville. It was this most precious gift that the two benefactors gave the modern world.

The growth of the Borden condensery in Starkville proved nothing short of astounding and an allegorical tale for the American South. In 1928 Noble predicted the milk plant would handle nearly a quarter million pounds of milk daily. Local dairymen were awash in money. Noble noted that the county's "annual receipts from dairying are about six times the value of its cotton crop." Because of this huge influx of cash and the stability it brought, the city and county had undergone a total transformation. Now Starkville's roads are paved, its farmers' notes paid. "All Oktibbeha is green with his grasses; and the milk of Oktibbeha cows is in the marketplace of the world. [Montgomery's] people have found the land flowing with milk and honey."[3]

Mississippi, long "the most backward of southern states," no longer wore that mantle. The *Ashville Citizen* cited several business sectors and events to support making that claim. Among the most significant was the dairy explosion. The *Citizen* focused heavily on Starkville and the Borden plant. Borden had doubted it could secure 40,000 pounds of milk a day, but within several months was forced to double plant capacity. The *Citizen* continued, pointing out that people who were thinking of the Mississippi of five years ago or "even in terms of three years ago, need to wake up." Mississippi "has learned more in the past decade than almost any other State." More importantly, Mississippi has "turned its knowledge to eminently practical account."[4]

"Dairy gold is pouring out of the green pasture lands of north Mississippi," wrote the *Manufacturers' Record*'s Craddock Goins. The imagery continued. "A vast number of southern communities have renounced King Cotton and taken out new allegiance to the dairy cow, queen of prosperity." It all began in Starkville. "The first milk condensery in Mississippi was established" there, he noted, and "it was been a tremendous success from the start." Condenseries and cheese plants were all over the northern part of the state. Goins predicted that "many more milk condenseries are in prospect. Scores of Mississippi towns and cities are waging aggressive fights. Many will win these fights." Out-of-state dairy industries were as anxious to locate in Mississippi as Mississippians were to have them. What happened in Mississippi was a tremendous story. "Right now the story and its lessons are spreading far and wide." "People from many states are visiting . . . and seeing for themselves just what people in the South can do."[5]

The *Memphis Commercial Appeal* reduced the Mississippi story to a single sentence: "When [the Starkville] plant made money from the very beginning, Mississippi's reputation as a dairy state was secure." It was the story behind the story that was the true story. It was not the success of the plant that astounded, it was that Borden's extensive experience and preparation did not forecast it. Borden had been scrupulously thorough in its investigation of Starkville. It had recorded the number of dairies, cows, white and Black dairymen, barns, milksheds, kinds of grasses and clovers, water supply, water temperature, number and kinds of roads, yearly rainfall, yearly average temperature, and "most important of all the attitude of the people toward dairying." It was that last category where Borden so clearly underestimated the town. The company failed to anticipate the extraordinary commitment to the project by the people of Starkville and Oktibbeha County.[6]

National news stories certainly recognized that Mississippi had undergone a profound change. They agreed that Starkville was central to the transformation and that its activities led other small towns to try for similar coups. They also apportioned part of the credit for a new Mississippi to the corporate invasion of the South. The invasion funded an industry that freed farmers from an almost total dependence on other kinds of agriculture, especially monoculture. Whether each part of these stories was accurate is not the point here. What is useful is that those three parts of the story—Mississippi, Starkville, and Borden—could be fashioned in any number of ways. They provided the main characters but each author wrote its own details. They provided context around which to wrap a story that highlighted what each author wished to highlight.

This was especially important because it meant that the Mississippi-Starkville-Borden story became the southern story, with each locus having its own perturbations, morals, and consequences. That triad provided the appearance of coherence to a phenomenon that lacked more than cursory coherence. Part of the explanation for that almost absence of coherence is that the Mississippi story was an amalgamation of all the Mississippi stories. Put another way, each Mississippi rural place had its own story that intersected with part of the Mississippi story and was familiar with other aspects. But each place had its own unique story, one that it cherished as its own and one that resonated with what a place and persons in that place did and did not do. Put yet another way, each local story did not start with Starkville or Borden, although virtually all claimed to have begun there. These men and women encountered Borden and Starkville through their own eyes and with their own traditions. In that sense, they did not encounter them at all. They used them to resolve the issues that constituted their personal histories and situations.

Looking at the history of the coming and growth of the dairy industry in other southern states points to the same phenomenon. Commonality remains the frame and the mechanism to achieve a desired end but not the end itself, not the guts. Each place worked to survive and if successful to thrive. Each had significant problems and issues that predated 1926. Each gravitated to the Mississippi-Starkville-Borden trope because it held power. It was a parable of success for that day and could be employed to document whatever premise its chronicler intended. It was the smell of survival for a besieged town.

That aside, the reality of dairying in Mississippi had changed markedly in the several years after Borden came to Starkville. Before Starkville, virtually all the twenty-odd creameries in the state were cooperative or owned by local investors or governments. There were no condenderies or cheese factories. There were a couple of ice cream manufactories. By late 1929, there were roughly four hundred condenseries, cheesemaking facilities, ice cream manufactories, and creameries. There also were dried buttermilk plants, dried skim milk facilities, wholesale milk shipping centers to New Orleans, Birmingham, and Memphis, and several retail milk outlets within the state. A nascent industry had developed into a dairy powerhouse, and the towns and cities that served it had changed in a myriad of ways.[7]

Tennessee's dairy transformation occurred roughly at the same time as Starkville's. As a consequence, of all of the southern states, it pointed the least to Starkville. Borden spent considerable time in 1923 considering Tennessee sites before finally deciding to go with Starkville. The choice was not easy. Dairying in middle Tennessee had developed before that time. Mississippi had a slightly larger dairying population and purebred herds, but Tennessee moved to keep pace. It too invested heavily in Jerseys, especially in middle Tennessee where almost all the early dairy industry resided. That area grew pasture grasses well as deposits of ocean limestone sweetened the soil. University of Tennessee, like the Mississippi Agricultural College, worked to expand dairying.[8] Like Mississippi, it had a state Jersey breeders association and a state creamery group. The biggest difference between the two dairy states was that Tennessee was not as dependent on agriculture as Mississippi. It contained three major cities—Memphis, which stood as the commercial, industrial and cultural metropolis for both the Arkansas and Mississippi Deltas; Chattanooga, an old river city and commercial hub; and Nashville, the young but growing manufacturing city. These places competed with agriculture for public attention.[9]

As was always the case, Borden conducted its initial investigations in Tennessee somewhat clandestinely. It visited different areas, talked to business people, and checked out farms almost sub rosa. When it examined middle Tennessee, it had several recent precedents. Borden had been the first major dairy manufacturer in virgin territory at least twice before, in Fort Scott, Kansas, and Starkville, Mississippi. In Fort Scott, Borden na-

ively envisioned creating a huge dairy industry from dross and then capitalizing on it by erecting satellite institutions to create a complete dairy
complex. Borden scrapped that latter notion when the area's cattle farmers did not expand their herds as rapidly as was anticipated. In contrast,
Starkville was already primed as a dairy site. Wary not to repeat the Fort
Scott experience, Borden moved slowly, checking every step along the way
before placing the Starkville condensery. When that endeavor far exceeded
expectations, the company had another model to work with. Instead of
trying to make a dairy industry out of wheat fields, it proved much more
profitable to place condenseries in already-developed dairy areas away
from major cities.

That accounted for the company's interest in middle Tennessee, sometimes referred to as a "dairyman's paradise," and it found willing partners
there. Citing Starkville as their model, the Columbia and Shelbyville business communities during July 1926 tried to entice Borden to visit their
areas. The Pulaski Chamber of Commerce went one better. It wrote both
to Borden and its rival, Carnation, inviting them to the area to see what
a jewel Pulaski was. Borden accepted and sent four men the next week.
In preparation for the visitors, the Chamber embarked on a cow census.
While Borden and Carnation were content to investigate the area within
a few counties of Nashville—the densest dairy counties in the state—Pet
began to explore further east, in a serious consideration of that region for
a Pet condensery.[10]

Contemporaneous with these investigations was a State of Mississippi
public relations campaign. Entitled "Know Mississippi Better," the campaign
incorporated a train that went throughout the upper South, and placed numerous ads in local and city newspapers along the route, which included
middle Tennessee. In every ad, Borden and Starkville were featured. The
amazing story of Oktibbeha farmers providing daily the quantity of milk
within a month that the company had estimated would take a year to reach
became a tag line to show just how fecund Northeast Mississippi was.[11]

Carnation devoted considerable attention to Murfreesboro rather than
Pulaski. Its bankers invited the firm, and the county agent undertook a
cow census to prepare for the visit. As Carnation looked at Murfreesboro,
Borden announced a bombshell it had kept to itself for some time. It would
establish a large condensery in Lewisburg and surround it with smaller
facilities—branch receiving stations and the manufactories for other Bor-

den products—at Shelbyville, Columbia, Petersburg, Fayetteville, Murfreesboro, and Pulaski. Patterned after the Fort Scott initial plan, Borden no doubt hoped to grab the huge middle Tennessee milkshed all for itself.

Borden had contemplated this gambit for several months. All the tributary communities had fine rail or paved road connections to Lewisburg, which was close to the Alabama border. Two counties within that milkshed were certified as bovine tuberculosis–free, the only two counties so designated in Tennessee. Dairy censuses by Borden employees showed the area ripe for the milk complex. Within twelve miles of Lewisburg, censuses found 13,000 cows, including 9,000 heifers. They estimated those numbers would be doubled in a scant two years. Borden representatives had checked more than twenty communities in the area and arrived at these five counties and seven towns as prime Borden territory.

The company noted that its other southern condensing operation, Starkville, rested "in the center of the dairy section . . . in the prairie belt of North Mississippi." Given the scope of the venture and how much of the area's milk output the company had hoped to use, local newspapers felt obligated to point again to Starkville. This time they sought to assuage farmers who feared that Borden would put the local creamery out of business. Just the opposite had occurred. The Oktibbeha creamery expanded considerably when the condensery opened. Jersey cow milk content was so high in butterfat that their milk could support the manufacture of both condensed milk and butter, providing farmers two paychecks rather than one.[12]

Within days the edges of the plan started to fray. The exact communities Borden had hoped to add as subsidiary plants apparently had more grandiose ambitions. They continued to talk to Carnation. The Borden plan itself seemed solid, but just which other cities would join Lewisburg in the complex remained up in the air.[13]

No matter the outcome, James Finney, editor of the *Tennessean*, declared success for the area. "Borden company is an intensely practical concern," he wrote. "Its investments are not made until careful investigation and painstaking research have demonstrated that they should be made and that they will be profitable." That spoke volumes about the future of middle Tennessee. It would become "one of the foremost dairy centers of America." The dairy industry would bring an "ever increasing flood of wealth into the county." A stable market would exist less than a dozen miles from the condensery's dairymen.[14]

Construction of the Lewisburg facility began almost immediately, and Borden anticipated the entire complex to be completed by March 1927. In preparation, the company purchased all the creameries and cream stations in that five-county area, and sketched out the cost of the soon-to-be-built subunits. Each was estimated to cost $100,000 and contain significant cold storage and house machinery to manufacture evaporated or powdered milk.[15]

For the next two months, Borden, Carnation, and several commercial groups from smaller middle Tennessee towns jockeyed for position. Which towns would host which enterprises remained in doubt. Some towns took the pilgrimage to Starkville to see what they could learn there to clinch a milk plant for their town. Others referred to the outstanding success of Starkville, including exceeding milk estimates in thirty days, and recognized that Mississippi's triumph had led to Borden's interest in middle Tennessee. But they also argued that "what Starkville has done any good town in Tennessee can do better." Not to be outdone, the town of Lewisburg hoped to reap the same reputational success as Starkville, and appropriated a considerable sum to publicize the place and the condensery in its midst.[16]

Before the end of October, Carnation had settled on Murfreesboro for its large condensing plant. Murfreesboro had been among the possibilities that Borden announced when it revealed its condensery complex. Rather than settle for a secondary site, the place had continued lobbying the Wisconsin company as part of a milkshed of Rutherford, Wilson, and Sumner counties. That three-county group included the extreme northern part of Borden's anticipated five-complex area. Murfreesboro's reticence to assume secondary status led Borden to drop the site from its complex formulation well before Carnation's announcement. Carnation had held off making its decision public until it could confirm cows enough in the area to make the condensery successful. Beyond that, the company asked for a farmers' meeting where dairymen ritually promised to expand their herds to ensure the condensery's future success. Yet another promise was made. Carnation would only place the plant in Murfreesboro if the town of Murfreesboro and the county of Rutherford picked up the nearly $50,000 cost of an already extant property. Several in the town volunteered to cover Murfreesboro's obligation and the county commitment went almost as smoothly. It required a meeting of county residents and after some squabbling, the group unanimously acceded to Carnation's demands. When the farmers and town announced that they had accomplished those tasks, the company simply said, "We are here to stay." Jesse C. Beesley Jr., editor of Murfreesboro's *Daily-News Journal,* was almost as eloquent in his brevity. The condensery will provide "stability and a forward look to agriculture and life happiness on the farm." Enthusiasm and fealty were essential. Both sides were bound to each other. Finney celebrated Murfreesboro's pluck. The amount of money that the city and county had to pay was simply the cost of doing business. If one hoped to get a jewel in one's midst, a jewel attractive to many competitors, one expected to pay a premium. "It takes push, energy, and a willingness to make some sacrifices in the common cause" to win the condensery, Finney noted. It also showed the "efficacy of advertising," which had attracted the attention of Carnation and Borden to the area and therefore made the condenseries conceivable.[17]

Local leaders had told of Starkville's success with its Jerseys to encourage dairymen around Murfreesboro to back a condensery. The Jersey milk was high in butterfat content and could support two facilities in Starkville—the condensery and the cooperative creamery—providing farmers two checks monthly. When all the signing was done, Carnation did not choose to adopt that practice. The company disliked Jersey cows, the backbone of the region's milk supply. It found the butterfat content too high, and that necessitated skimming, a waste of time and money for the company. To that end, it shipped several cars of excellent Holstein breeding stock to the area for purchase. Holstein had sufficient butterfat for condensed and evaporated milk and did not requiring major skimming. Carnation aimed to replace the Jerseys with the Holsteins, even if it took some years. That was not necessarily a benison for dairymen. Condensery patrons with Holstein cattle would receive only one check—the check for the milk—on the fifteenth of the month. There would be no creamery check.[18]

Well before the plant actually opened, the Jerseys of Rutherford County were setting records almost every month at the local creamery. A rather unusual situation was taking shape with Carnation's introduction of Holsteins. The condensery would take milk from Holsteins and the creamery would cater to Jerseys. You would have, in effect, dual dairying herds and farmers who specialized in one type of cow and not the other. Creamery members increased by over sixty in a single week after Carnation's announcement. Jesse Beesley, editor of Murfreesboro's *Daily New-Journal,* recognized a silver lining in this dualism. He argued that it would lead dairy farmers to adopt modern sets of business principles and practices as they tailored their production to different markets. But even if that had not been the case, Beesley remained a champion of dairy farming. "Contented cows mean contented farmers," he noted.[19]

While Tennessee commentators certainly appreciated Carnation's size and business acumen, they heaped a different kind of praise on Borden Co. Borden was the gold standard for modern agricultural cooperation. A venture of the size proposed for Tennessee depended on Borden resources, judgment, and experience, and therefore had as much chance of failing as "the United States Treasury." Citing Starkville, Borden relied on "essential co-operation" with farmers, working "side by side," the "type of co-ordination now so desired in the business world." Its complex organization changed dairying forever, situating Lewisburg at the center and satellites at Columbia, Pulaski, Shelbyville, and Fayetteville, which now housed a powdered milk facility. It converted middle Tennessee into a modern industrial plant. Borden's on-site experts trained and taught dairy farmers. "With good fellowship" they urged farmers to take the most modern methods, employ sanitary procedures, cull inefficient cows, measure the values of different kinds of fodders versus costs, and much more. Behind that notion rested a simple premise: dairymen's success was the sole way for Borden to profit. Borden's coming to middle Tennessee was "considered by thinking people as one of the greatest progressive steps taken in a half century," one observer claimed. Another stated that the move was extraordinary as it created an "epochal relationship" between producers and industrialists.[20]

As a sophisticated industrial machine, Borden understood that its Tennessee works markedly increased the quantity of condensed, powdered, and evaporated milk it produced. In the modern parlance, that sort of act necessitated market generation: Borden needed to create demand. As it had since A. H. Deute originally signed on as head of advertising sales with the company, Borden took advertising deadly seriously. To provide for the increased output, "the Borden sales and advertising campaigns for 1927 . . . [were] more comprehensive than ever before in the history of the company." Expansion of production was bound to continue. As Borden pursued that expansion, they claimed that the resulting "Borden prosperity will be reflected in the prosperity of the communities where its activities are carried on." Their foremost middle Tennessee ad hit that sentiment squarely. Under the provocative title, "The Borden Southern Company is now at home in Middle Tennessee," the company highlighted modernity at every step—newest machines, most up-to-date practices, sanitary and chemical safeguards—and ended with these lines: "We want you to know us and our products better. We urge you to visit our plants—try our products—get acquainted as new neighbors should. We appreciate the hospitality that Middle Tennessee has extended us. We want to return it. Come and see us soon!"[21]

As in Mississippi, the towns fortunate or skilled enough to receive milk plants recognized that such an opportunity must not be missed. That was no less critical in eastern Tennessee as in the middle of the state. Soil-depleting tobacco ruled the roost there. Pet had initially searched middle Tennessee for suitable sites but Borden and Murfreesboro had a bulldog like grip on the area. It next went to the easternmost part of the state and found numerous supplicants there. It looked at or corresponded with Bristol, Jefferson City, Knoxville, Athens, Rockwood, and Sweetwater, all of which desperately sought a condensery.[22]

So too did Greeneville. Located not far from the North Carolina, Virginia, and Kentucky borders, Greeneville's commercial elite had always relied on its major commercial tobacco exchange. With tobacco prices falling, they now investigated dairying and worked with the Southern Railway to encourage each of three "major" condensers—Carnation, Pet, and Van Camp, truly a bit player in the milk business—to place a milk plant in that area. Greeneville's audacity proved almost legendary. Virtually no commercial dairying took place in east Tennessee and few farmers even owned cows. None of the condensers initially showed even the most cursory interest. The Greeneville Rotarians then wrote Starkville, which responded with stories of fabulous payouts and lives changed because of condensery and creamery checks. That further whetted their and farmer's appetites and the Chamber of Commerce pursued a condensery in earnest. It knew it had to make its case so it designed a brief form from which to take a cow census. The form began: "Farmers, Attention! Your salvation is at hand." The form continued that a major firm has "practically assured" the Chamber it would come if milk enough was found or fostered in the area.

When silence from corporate offices ensued, Gregory W. Humphrey, agricultural agent and dairy expert for the Southern Railroad, continued to push Greeneville. He finally got Pet's representatives to visit the area, which lay 175 miles east of the site that had attracted the firm a year or so earlier. Borden and Carnation's aggressive condensery colonization of middle Tennessee had effectively frozen Pet out of that market. While many places in that region still yearned for milk plants, competition for dairymen against the established interests there made any milk facility problematic.

In Greeneville, Pet found a radically different situation. The area had no entrenched dairy interest. It had almost no dairying. But Pet representatives saw many of the ingredients necessary for a condensery. They found themselves impressed with the near unanimous support a condensery had gathered in the city of Greeneville and the fact that red clover seemed to grow everywhere. To their mind, excellent pasture was in abundance in the area and could feed enough animals to provide milk for a new plant. They also noted that processed milk from that city could reach over 45 percent of the country's population within a day's rail ride, thereby reducing transportation costs from Pet's primarily central and western American business. But in Greeneville, some doubts lingered about farmer support for a condensery. Tobacco, not cotton, dominated the area. There was precious little precedent of inducing tobacco farmers to develop dairying even as a sideline. To make a compelling case to Pet, they conceptualized a five-county milkshed—forty miles in every direction from Greeneville—an unusually large area from which to pull milk, and gathered pledges from residents promising to buy cows and to convert a portion of their operation to dairying IF a condensery were located in Greeneville. To further entice Pet, the Chamber took out options on several places it considered prime condensery real estate—near rail lines and water sources.[23]

Greeneville's commitment to getting a deal done moved Pet. Perhaps as significant, it had recently established two small milk plants in Kentucky. It now had familiarity with a tobacco-milk nexus and did not see the challenges that Greeneville posed as insurmountable. After an intensive two-week period of negotiations with the president of the local Citizens' Bank, and after the mayor and aldermen acceded to all the company's demands, Pet announced the Greeneville condensery on May 19, 1927, with a simple message. It urged the area to go out now and build their herds so that they would be ready to deliver milk when the plant opened. Pet was in the community for the long haul, not today or tomorrow but for "twenty-five years from now."[24]

The stipulation of the Citizens' Bank on the purchase of prime bulls was different than in other places. Its terms aimed to speed dairy development in the area. The bank purchased the animals and held the note until such time as the novice dairymen paid off their debt. A payment schedule commenced only after the plant began to furnish a market for the milk. Payment was taken out of each milk check.

The bank's generous terms—essentially an interest-free loan until dairymen received money from Pet—signaled just how novel dairying was to Greeneville. It also demonstrated to what lengths the city's businessmen were willing to go in order to entice Pet to the area. Pet had never placed a condensery in a region with so few cows and dairymen. The Borden and Carnation facilities in the state exacerbated the situation as the few Greeneville-area milk producers sold off stock at premium prices to middle Tennessee dairymen. The city's bankers warned against that practice. As the company made preparation to build its plant and engaged in its construction, a series of local and other leaders and extension agents, including the Southern's Humphrey, labored to make dairymen out of tobacco farmers. Fashioning themselves as the "Greeneville Dairy Boosters" and operating under the direction of the Chamber-dominated Greene County dairy committee, they announced for November an "East Tennessee Dairy Week" to draw eyes to their project. The boosters also went from county to county putting on special programs in school auditoriums for county farmers. Over fifty meetings were planned. At these meetings and on many other occasions, they tried to convince farmers of the virtues of prime stock, cooperative purchasing of purebred bulls, growing their own ensilage and fodder, harvesting the manure, sanitary practices and other activities associated with dairy farming. They relentlessly promoted the benefits of dairying. Dairying was liberating. It freed farmers from the vagaries of tobacco. It ended mortgages, loans, and other forms of debt. It was stable and dependable. Unlike condenseries in regions where dairying was an established fact, the economic rather than the cerebral and spiritual implications of dairy farming carried virtually the entire weight.[25]

Pet also lent a hand. It tried to entice farmers in the five-county milkshed area that substations in their vicinities would be opened if there was sufficient milk to merit that decision. Kraft reduced the likelihood of that becoming actualized as it opened a cheese factory in Bristol a few days before the Pet condensery was scheduled to start receiving milk. It capitalized on the message Pet and Greeneville had been preaching, hoping to siphon dairymen off from the as yet functioning Pat condensery. Perhaps to more completely control the milkshed through personal contact, Pet employed its milk trucks and milk haulers to work the distant parts of the five-county area. Each day the trucks and men would go off and bring in the milk. Individual dairymen would not have to cart their milk to the factory but have it collected by a familiar face. They paid the company from their checks. By late summer 1928, the plant was processing 50,000 pounds of milk a day. At that point, the company started to consider substations, beginning construction before the end of the year.[26]

In many ways, the Pet Greeneville project proved similar to precedents set in Tennessee and Mississippi. It took its time selecting a venue, encouraged local leaders to convince the company of the area's prospects, built an impressive up-to-date modern condensery, and worked to mine the milkshed in which each was located. But Pet was more insular than Borden or Carnation in any number of ways. Even the event to signify the opening of the plant was considerably different than the others. It was less a celebration of the place and area than a sober marking of a new business venture. Like those of Mississippi and Tennessee, huge crowds were predicted, impressive politicians, businessmen, Pet officials, and others gave inspiring speeches, and condensery tours were undertaken. The Modern Woodmen of America band played. But there were no students, no community leaders other than those giving speeches, no entertainment, no dance, and especially no parade.[27] Up to that point, every condensery had a parade—the one in Fayetteville was said to be two miles long. Not to be outdone, Murfreesboro's was reportedly five miles long. Lewisburg's "gigantic parade" included planes "zooming overhead [and] giant firecrackers booming." In his dedication, Strack called on Lewisburg to emulate Starkville's example of explosive production—with floats, historical and otherwise.[28] The way the company and the city pressed the idea that dairymen would receive a significant payday also was different. Rather than cite Starkville, the press and speakers used Pet sources from Wisconsin or the new Kentucky facilities. Having their own vehicles and haulers—it provided drivers Christmas dinner—also increased the sense that cotton mills, not milk plants, provided the model for this enterprise. The company president and his brother repeatedly visited the area, often arguing that they did not care what kind of cows the dairymen owned. Pet only cared about the sweet milk from those cows. They did acknowledge that cows that yielded more on the same amount of feed were more profitable and they also noted that

Holsteins were premier dairy cattle but that was only in the sense of executives surveying their facilities. Even the types and number of visitors to the site were diminished. Neither Pet nor Greeneville discouraged them. But very few were reported to have come, perhaps because of the condensery's distance from traditional dairyland.[29]

A legion of other Tennessee towns pursued condenseries and cheese plants in the wake of Borden's, Carnation's, and later Pet's success. After Greeneville, none of these supplicants considered geography a limitation. Rossville, Saulsbury, Dyersburg, Huntington, and Martin in western Tennessee lobbied for milk plants. Memphis also began some preliminary investigations before deciding against the venture.[30] Carthage, Gallatin, Franklin, and Watertown in dairy-rich middle Tennessee wanted a facility[31] as did Sweetwater, Clarksville, Bristol, and Knoxville in the east.[32] In fact, Pet and other milk companies asked "virtually all east Tennessee counties" to conduct cow censuses so as to enable the companies to plan their operations better.[33]

Within a few short years, the dairying mania that had afflicted Tennessee had touched off a renaissance equal to that of Mississippi. It seemed that everywhere there were milk plants, and where there were none, they were wanted. Small towns in Tennessee had wholeheartedly embraced the dairy industry and the cash that it provided. Tobacco and cotton no longer strangled Tennessee agriculture. The sincere revamping of farming and small town life led some in Tennessee to recall and reexamine Starkville. They did not dispute its inspiration and influence in creating the initial dairy wave. But they became prickly and chauvinistic that it continued to serve as the touchstone for the dairy industry's emergence. George H. Armistead, editor of the *Nashville Banner*, chaffed at the idea that Starkville still dominated discussion. He found the Starkville story "outstanding," but complained that it now should be superseded by Tennessee examples. Many local communities "have experienced benefits equally convincing." The time was ripe for change as "the process of profitable expansion as yet has barely begun."[34]

The situation was different in Alabama. As he had in Tennessee, Borden's Ryder had examined several places in the state as potential condensery sites before the company had finally selected Starkville. Alabamians remembered Borden's interest, and when it shipped the railroad car of raw milk from Starkville to Dixon, Illinois, in November 1923, Alabama's major newspapers covered the event. In his editorial on Starkville's Borden triumph, William T. Sheehan, editor of the capital city's *Montgomery Advertiser*, saluted Starkville, the self-proclaimed "premier county of the south," for its dairy prowess. He also reminded readers that for several years Montgomery County dairy products had been greater in value than its cotton, and predicted that in a few short years "Montgomery will be the outstanding dairy county of the South."

Sheehan's portrait of Montgomery was misleading. Montgomery had ready markets for all the milk it did produce. It daily went as fluid milk to nearby Birmingham and to Pensacola, Florida, with which the city had direct rail connections. From there it was distributed throughout Florida. The town also had a small ice cream plant. Montgomery cows were rarely purebred or culled, and produced milk at one-third the rate of most dairy sections. Poor performance by the cows was matched by their owners. Few provided fodder or other winter feed crops for their animals, preferring them graze as long as possible and then to supplement that diet with feed purchased elsewhere.

Dallas County also engaged in dairying, although not nearly as extensively as Montgomery. Located on a similar type of geological formation as the area around Starkville, Dallas County, which included the city of Selma, had plenty of pasture land. Its dairy industry was not highly developed. It lacked the obvious markets that fueled Montgomery's potential expansion. Ryder had visited the area on his 1923 trip and spent two days there. After visiting the Farm Bureau and Chamber of Commerce as well as several dairymen, Ryder concluded that the concentration of cows in a twelve-mile area around Selma was much too thin to satisfy the corporate policy of hauling milk no more than twelve miles prior to processing to ensure freshness. Before he left, he told his hosts that they would need to intensify efforts if they hoped to secure a milk plant.[35]

Apparently they did, because in summer 1924, Ryder returned to Selma. Two other groups accompanied him, presumably to take a de facto cow census and to determine the tenor of the populace. They met extensively with the Chamber, which cautioned newspapers not to publicize the meetings. The *Montgomery Advertiser* did not heed the advice and published an article proclaiming that Borden intended to put a milk plant in Selma. That report was erroneous, however. A little more than a week later and after the Borden men had left, Selma's Chamber received a note from Borden headquarters alerting the city that they would not be going forward with milk plant plans.[36]

After Borden's rejection, Selma decided to confine its dairy industry to the two significant creameries there. Other locals in Alabama reached out to Borden, especially in the wake of the announcement of the Starkville condensery. As that Mississippi plant was being built, Montgomery announced that Southern Dairies—a concern in Washington, DC, that catered to the whole milk, ice cream, and butter needs of major southern cities—was going to establish such a multipurpose facility in Montgomery, a city of about 50,00 people. Birmingham, with roughly 200,000 people, and Selma, with a bit less than 20,000, already had Southern Dairies plants. The presence of Southern Dairies created a situation somewhat different than in Mississippi or Tennessee, one that had more in common with the North. A fluid milk company served the needs of a populated area, such as East Coast and midwestern cities. Southern Dairies, especially the Selma plant, also furnished the fluid milk needs of Florida.[37]

Alabama, then, had a dairy industry that aimed primarily at serving the needs of its bigger cities. Farmers near these populous places had familiarity with dairying, and ready markets for their products. The large national condenseries from the North shied away from such places. Much of the anticipated demand was saturated by the cities they served.

Southern Dairies's strategy of basing their business model on the major city in which it was located meant that much of Alabama was untapped. The western part of the state remained outside that company's sway. Southern Dairies further confined its plants to areas that were either Black Belt or limestone lands, lands excellent for pasture and grasses. Aside from a few fertile strips, much of the rest of Alabama was coastal plain or Appalachian (piedmont) plateau, soils not nearly as well suited for dairying. Few in those areas had experience dairying; they remained first and foremost cotton farmers. They possessed little reason to learn dairying. No easy markets existed for whatever milk they would produce. The Chamber of Commerce of Atmore, Alabama, near the Florida border, put the situation this way: "Right now," it wrote, "if we had as few as 2,500 dairy cows in the area, we could get Borden Company . . . to establish a factory in Atmore. . . . Pensacola is begging for milk and so is Mobile and Birmingham. Florida is a great potential market." Lack of dairying in the area stemmed from two factors. First, grasses did not grow profusely there. Second, dairying required "a matter of personal inclination and liking for this kind of work." Third, starting dairy farming from scratch was capital intensive. It depended on fine, high-producing cows, nutritious food, pristine barns, stalls and milking floors, transportation, simple access to markets, and milking and separating machinery. Those were potent barriers to dairying in the eyes of reluctant farmers asked to convert to this new liquid crop.[38]

That view often put farmers in direct, persistent conflict with the Chambers of Commerce and other businessmen's organizations in small town and cities. Yes, these commercial groups argued that dairying provided stability as well as a safety net to farmers otherwise engaged in single crop agriculture. That was true, but it also was besides the point. What these small town and city merchants truly wanted was stability for their towns, their businesses, their lives. Rarely could they achieve that unaided. In the case of dairying, it usually required northern capital and a huge, forceful campaign to convince independent farmers to relinquish their senses of autonomy to adopt new practices for a promise of enhanced future autonomy. The devil you knew often was better than the one that you did not. City fathers and mothers tried to recruit them to this difficult bargain and farmers rejected it many times. In a real sense, the Chamber and other town groups wanted to dictate to farmers what to farm and how to farm. Farmers would presumably benefit with an improved and/or stabilized lot but the real beneficiary would be the town. When the condensery came in and sunk over a quarter million dollars into the economy, it was loathe to fail. So too were the city fathers, each of whom struggled to get their cities and small towns—and businesses—to survive. Virtually the only way to achieve that goal was on the backs of farmers, and that required these reputed yeomen to shun their old practices and traditions in order to hitch their stars to a potentially ephemeral industry. Even for these commercial giants, that was not an easy sell.

Starkville's successful two-year courtship of Borden provided hope to small towns and cities. It demonstrated that hard work, perseverance, and fortitude could win the day. Starkville's commercial elite spent considerable effort to woo Borden and the area's dairy farmers, even though they had been dairying for years. And still Borden and the farmers were not sure. For the condensery to be successful the vast majority of dairymen had to change to comply to the condensery's dictates. Civic and familial responsibility became twin cudgels to speed and cement the transformation.

Within a few days of the condensery's opening, the *Florence Times-News* applauded Starkville's business community for its diligence and argued it provided a model for other places. Starkville had put on "a gallant and determined fight for city and county development." Its businessmen had "refused to be halted by many serious obstacles." Their efforts "should serve as an inspiration . . . to carry on undismayed at the difficulties which must be faced in community endeavors." Addressing the Florence business community, the editor put it bluntly: Are we "willing to put forth the same effort as the Starkville citizens?" If so, he ended, then we will "be certain of the reward."[39]

In no Alabama place did these sentiments resonate more genuinely than in Tuscaloosa. Home of the University of Alabama, Tuscaloosa stood as a town of about 15,000 almost midway geographically between Columbus, Mississippi, and Birmingham. Dairying in that area had been minimal. Coastal and flood plains marked the region, not particularly good for pastures. The Chamber there had acted in fits and starts to put the place on more stable footing. It pursued a branch of the Frisco Railroad and supported a statewide good roads program. It rarely was successful.

W. C. McClure helped change that. A longtime resident of Demopolis, a small Alabama Black Belt town, McClure held several positions in the years immediately preceding his 1923 move to Tuscaloosa. A salesman by trade, McClure worked as a general agent for several insurance agents, sold real estate, and was the southern representative of the *Chicago Journal of Commerce and Daily Financial Times*. One of his life insurance ads encapsulated his approach to his product. He reminded readers to "always remember" that purchasing a life insurance policy embodied "Unselfishness, Independence, Thrift, Determination, Character, Credit, and Peace of Mind." McClure was both plain spoken and outspoken. Whenever he talked at a public gathering or wrote one of his innumerable letters to editors all over the state of Alabama, newspapermen and others identified as him as "well known in this section." The newspaper greeted him upon his move to Tuscaloosa by calling him "a new citizen who is able to express his ideas forcefully." McClure had opinions on many things. He favored good roads throughout the state and wanted Alabama to finance them directly. As a juror, he once gave a speech at the conclusion of a trial thanking the judge for his impartiality. He thought the Black Belt was wasting a precious opportunity. Instead of relying on Black tenant farmers and sharecroppers to work "the best land for a combination of general farming and livestock on earth," he argued that the area should keep "the good ones now there," get rid of the rest, and bring in whites from the hill regions to replace them. Hill folk had children "not ashamed to chop and pick cotton" and a "wife not only willing, but one with a vision of the future and gifted in the art of selling hens . . . before breakfast." These hypothetical new Black Belt farmers would "look upon grass as a blessing . . . rather than a curse." McClure felt compelled to write this letter, he contended, because "he who helps his country helps all things and all things helped will bless him." McClure praised his new residence, Tuscaloosa, for making a newcomer feel at home. That was part of the town's culture. It also had not "forgotten the bedrock upon which all growth and prosperity are built—agriculture."[40]

McClure took it as his solemn duty to involve himself in community efforts. He found a home in pushing a Tuscaloosa condensery. Starkville and Tuscaloosa were only one hundred miles apart. They played each other in athletic events. Yet during the six months the Borden condensery was being built, the Tuscaloosa press rarely mentioned it. Perhaps absence of condenseries in the South explained the oversight. Whole milk–ice cream–butter establishments in Selma, Montgomery, and Birmingham obscured just how revolutionary the Starkville plant was. That metaphorical blind spot persisted through the condensery's opening celebration and for more than first six months thereafter.[41]

The situation changed in the fall of that year. On September 4 McClure took it upon himself to contact several northern milk producers about Tuscaloosa's prospects for housing a condensery. His letter to Libby, McNeill & Libby, a large canning company but a small participant in evaporated or condensed milk, was bold in its inception and naïve in its characterization. It was representative of the letters that McClure sent the others. The unsolicited letter asked the company "whether you would be interested to locate somewhere in the central south a milk condensery, or concentration plant, similar to the plant of the Borden company located in Starkville, Miss." If the company had planned this strategy, "Tuscaloosa would indeed be glad to lay before you its location and advantage for such an enterprise." He chose "not at this time to go into details" but he hoped he would get "an opportunity to become active, with others, in placing our claims before you." Libby's, like the other milk firms written by McClure, was appropriately noncommittal. McClure had been struck by Borden's announcement that the future of its condensery business lay in the South and that the Starkville plant exceeded all other Borden openings. He became further interested when he learned that in the month of August alone, Oktibbeha farmers received over $85,000. He compared that rate of return to lumbering and figured that sales of that magnitude required an entire stand of trees to be clear cut per month. In dairying, a similar amount of product was available month after month and year after year. He felt sure that Tuscaloosa-area farmers would welcome such a plant.

In November McClure decided to let the Chamber of Commerce know of his correspondence with the various milk firms. The Chamber thanked him for his initiative, consigned his report to its industrial committee and pledged to go forward if a large milk company expressed interest. The Chamber's lack of initiative and enthusiasm may well have sprung from several things. It may have objected to McClure's contacting various industrialists at Tuscaloosa's stead. The Chamber may have had, in fact, little interest in dairying as few dairy animals surrounded the town. In any case, McClure would not go quietly into that good night. He followed up his first salvo with a letter to the editor of the Tuscaloosa daily newspaper. He took on the claim that the "people of Tuscaloosa and west Alabama [were not] dairy people" as irrelevant. The land around Tuscaloosa could produce milk. That was the crux of the matter. As cotton farmers, "we are all stuck fast in the mud and the thing to do is get out." Dairying provides a "prosperity more permanent, a prosperity which nature says we are entitled to have." With the goad of McClure at their heels, the Chamber's secretary went to New York to talk to Borden. Unfortunately, the individual he hoped to talk with was not in town. The secretary then reported that the Chamber was beginning a milk survey of Tuscaloosa but had found that the little milk from the area all went as fluid milk to serve Birmingham.[42]

While the Chamber dithered, some Tuscaloosans and others throughout Alabama heeded McClure's message and looked to Starkville for what might be. Invariably, they found that town and Oktibbeha County transformed. To the *Montgomery Advertiser*, it was the "land of milk and money" and the "ideal place" to hold cattlemen's and dairy conventions. The *Tuscaloosa News* reported that 570 land transfers had occurred in Starkville during the nine months the condensery had been in operation. Moreover, it noticed a steep dropoff in the number of Oktibbeha County–held mortgages as farmers paid off their notes with alacrity. Both events signified a real rise in the county's economic fortunes. McClure commented on these reports, of course. He noted that one young girl earned over one hundred dollars with her lone cow in six months. A farmer with one or one hundred cows could profit. He noted that Borden was not content to rest on its Starkville plant but had begun to build a huge complex around Lewisburg, Tennessee. McClure admitted that Tuscaloosa presently had far too few cows to sustain a condensery but felt confident that those cows could be secured expeditiously. The city could surely benefit from "$50,000 to $75,000 per month liberated" by dairy farming. Tuscaloosa was surrounded by potential dairy land, even if it was at least 35 miles distant. He maintained that if only a condensery would come to Tuscaloosa, the animals to milk would follow almost immediately. The condensery issue must "be pushed, talked, investigated, understood and appreciated and put over before there's any let up." "Lessons of the past, demands of the future and opportunities of the present all argue" for Tuscaloosa to relentlessly pursue a condensery. He reminded readers that "farmers are all smiling at and around Starkville."[43]

The Chamber was less enthusiastic about McClure's most recent idea. He claimed that industries moving into the South would encounter many unanticipated expenses, costs that might prohibit relocation. He therefore suggested that such businesses pay no tax for ten years as compensation. Tax rolls would not be unaffected, he continued. Higher land values would generate compensatory tax income. Chamber members hit back at that proposal. They did not favor a large northern corporation coming to their town but sought a local operation, something on the order of the Selma creameries that served Birmingham. Even that modest effort required additional dairy cows and farmers, but the Chamber had a plan there, too. More advertising of Tuscaloosa would produce a migration of dairymen into the area. Two specific proposals were offered. One dealt with placing signposts touting Tuscaloosa's prowess at every road leading into the city. The other asked for the Civic Club to bring in Roger Babson, prominent entrepreneur-economist, to help publicize the place.[44]

As the Chamber mulled over these pathetic recommendations, other places acted. Pet came to visit Huntsville, in north central Alabama on the Tennessee border, and Dothan, a town about the size of Tuscaloosa in southeast corner of Alabama. It found the cows near Dothan barely able to furnish that place's milk needs, which ruled out a condensery there.

Huntsville bordered the middle Tennessee milkshed and thus that region could easily serve as a tributary to any new Huntsville plant. After several visits, Pet decided that "due principally" to the farmers' lack of interest in dairying, the company was discontinuing interest in Huntsville.[45]

For several months McClure failed to move the Chamber. He continued to write letters to the editor hammering at the same theme in slightly different ways. He was indefatigable, so much so that the Chamber after a period of months finally gave him a title, chairman of the condensery committee. That title helped constrain and channel McClure. He was now part of the establishment. It would be much harder to go off on his own and disregard his colleagues. On the other hand, he now became officially central to all Chamber condensery dealings. In late May 1927, a Libby's representative, A. R. Hansen, paid a visit to Tuscaloosa. Hansen had been given the task by the company to identify a prime place in North America to put a condensery. He first went to Canada but he decided the Midwest and South offered better opportunity. In his search, Hansen visited sites in Missouri, Kansas, Arkansas, Tennessee, Mississippi, South Carolina, and Alabama. While he was in Tuscaloosa, McClure spent the entire time at Hansen's side as an unofficial tour guide, driving around the rural environs near Tuscaloosa. Despite his persistence, McClure was unable to convince his travel mate Hansen that there were nearly enough cows to sustain a condensery. Hansen also noticed that these cows were neither in herds nor purebreds. Each farmstead had a couple, which were used primarily for family consumption. Tuscaloosa bankers pledged to help upgrade the area cattle with loans at favorable rates. The Chamber also promised to indemnify the project, pledging that there would be a specific amount of milk brought to the facility or the Chamber would pay a penalty.[46]

Tuscaloosa did not have to wait long to hear back about the condensery. A second visitor came to confirm his predecessor's impressions of Tuscaloosa dairying. At the same time, two communities over 25 miles distant, Gordo and Reform, took steps to interest their farmers in a Tuscaloosa condensery. Reform asked for Tuscaloosa to send speakers. Gordo's Chamber guaranteed that a Tuscaloosa milk plant could count on Gordo to provide milk from 500 cows. At the Libby visitor's urging, the Tuscaloosa Chamber began a cow census of the county. Final results later that month reported many more cows than anticipated. The Chamber happily sent these results to the major condensers.[47]

The Tuscaloosa Chamber had a sense of what having a large factory in its midst would mean to city merchants and others. It was less certain as to how farmers might accept a condensery. To that end, it scheduled a trip to Starkville to learn "the value of a condensery to farmers." Learning was only part of the equation. The apparent antipathy of Tuscaloosa farmers toward dairying made it unlikely to attract a condensery to Tuscaloosa. The Chamber hoped that seeing the success of Oktibbeha County and its resident dairymen would serve as a goad to Tuscaloosa farmers. It would get them to adopt dairying in numbers that would entice a condenser to establish a half-million-dollar plant in the town. As one of the junketeers maintained "what we want to find out is just how good it is to the farmer" producing milk for a condensery. "We want to show his side of the story as well as that of the town of Starkville and the condensary." As Aaron Miller, editor of the *Tuscaloosa News,* indicated, the trip would give "a very good idea as to whether or not" Tuscaloosa and its surrounding farmers would want a condensery. Borden had chosen its southern condensery sites where "men's faces looked to the future," where "progressive farmers . . . realize[d] that King Cotton was soon to lose his throne and that a new ruler, Milk, was to bring a reign of prosperity." Tuscaloosa had natural advantages consistent with a milk plant. What it lacked was a "wide-awake community willing to cooperate."[48]

The Starkville trip, then, was to show Tuscaloosa businessmen compelling reasons why farmers should cooperate in a condensery and how that cooperation would alter their lives. One of the things the Alabamians took back to Tuscaloosa was how pivotal good dairy cows were to a farmer's fortunes. Good cows meant efficient production and that increased profitability. If Tuscaloosa wanted farmers to cooperate in a condensery venture successfully, creating dairy herds of prime milking cattle was essential. It dictated profitability. The entire touring group concluded that Tuscaloosa must have a condensery and pledged to do whatever it took to make that happen. The group would labor "to enthuse others" with condensery zeal and work to see "no opportunity be lost." Several Kiwanians were among the tourists and brought the matter to the organization's next meeting. Their report produced unanimous agreement to make a condensery a Kiwanis project.[49]

McClure now had the solid backing of the Tuscaloosa businessmen. He then turned his attention to writing letters "of special interest and importance to our farmers." In a piece titled, "cows, condensery, cream, cheese, cotton, and cash," McClure told farmers that Tuscaloosa County had many more dairy cows than previous expected, and that it could comfortably increase herd size several times. The county lacked only a "ready cash market for the milk we can produce." A milk plant would provide that market, a seemingly insatiable market. To farmer readers he said, "All you [need to] do is deliver sweet milk." He tempered that a bit. In order for Tuscaloosa to receive a condensery, farmers needed to respond "with a strong desire for this great thing for us all" and guarantee that they "will patronize it." That was no small distinction. He concluded the letter by asking farmers to "look over the situation around you and decide what you are going to do about it." In a letter he issued two days later he kept the same theme but set a more somber tone. "We are not an outstanding cotton county and are no longer timber country," he explained. "What better route have we to go then to enthrone Queen Cow alongside of King Cotton? We have "but to make the right . . . decision, and stick to it, and we could not keep the condensery . . . away from here if we tried."[50]

McClure and the Chamber's secretary, R. J. Gulmyer, took a quick trip to Wisconsin to meet with five large milk firms and Kraft Cheese. He reported their findings at a meeting of the Tuscaloosa Farm Bureau. Gulmyer learned in Wisconsin that Borden paid Starkville farmers the same price as Wisconsin dairymen, even though northern dairying was considerably more expensive. But whenever the two men broached the Tuscaloosa condensery question in Wisconsin, they were asked "do the farmers of your vicinity want us down there." Implicitly, McClure thought yes but he understood that confirmation was required. He proposed a mass farm meeting, followed by a survey of what these farmers planned to do with their acreage in the near future. Several attendees balked at the idea of a condensery. One farmer cited figures stating that farmers rarely made money from dairying. He argued that the only reason Starkville seemed profitable was because "idle labor" was "put to work in the supplying of milk" to the condensery. The community gained money but the farmer got nothing. Gulmyer tried to save the day by reminding the assembled that "the cooperation of Tuscaloosa county farmers in making it a success was asked," not compelled, and he hoped that the group would embrace the condensery project.[51]

McClure and the Chamber had much work to do to convince Tuscaloosa farmers to embrace the condensery scheme. McClure now published his farmer-directed letters under the headline, "The Chamber of Commerce Says," giving them extra heft. Sometimes he went folksy. His "For the Farmers" columns were also signed Chamber of Commerce but they included subtitles like "Cow-Operation." Some Chamber members proposed alternative solutions to the dilemma posed by farmers wary of dairying. One suggested dropping the condensery quest and focusing on a cheese plant, which required considerably less milk per day. Others went in the opposite direction. They sought to develop a whole-milk demand in Tuscaloosa and Birmingham to encourage reticent farmers to embrace dairying. Once that demand had been established, Tuscaloosa could go after a condensery. To get new ideas, a committee of the Chamber, including McClure, ventured to Mississippi to tour the new Durant cheese plant and the anticipated Kosciusko condensery, stopping at Starkville on the way home. They learned techniques for attracting northern suitors at the first two places and marveled at the hustle and bustle of huge crowds in Starkville as groups from all over the South had come to see next day's payday. Starkville "completely sold" them on a milk plant for Tuscaloosa. McClure got the Rotary to invite more than twenty farm leaders from the county to one of its meetings, where he recounted his Wisconsin trip and told of the concern about farmer engagement. He told the assemblage about his visits to Starkville and other Mississippi venues, where he found dairymen "universally prosperous"; he maintained that dairying was "by far the most profitable endeavor."[52] McClure enlisted the county's agent, R. C. Lett, to bring together a similar group of leaders at the meeting of the Civitan Club, where he preached the same sermon.

McClure used the Civitan and Rotary meetings to convince farm leaders to bring their fellow farmers to a series of grand meetings to discuss a condensery. For their education and edification, he worked to attract a Starkville "farmer-speaker" to talk about the condensery and what it did for Starkville, and "a widow who has educated her children and cared for her family by selling milk to the Starkville condensery." Both were unavailable for the grand meetings. Despite the absence of these powerful speakers, the enthusiasm generated at these events paralleled that of several small-town businessmen's meetings in the Tuscaloosa region. The business communities of these towns championed a condensery and gave their unwavering support to locate that condensery in Tuscaloosa. To further the attempt to gain a condensery for the area and the benefits it would bring their merchants, these businessmen proved willing to cede any claim to have the facility in their towns. When condensery representatives visited, these neighboring places could announce their full throated backing of a Tuscaloosa plant, signaling the community's cooperative spirit.[53] To prepare itself for the meeting with farmers, the Tuscaloosa Chamber undertook several acts. It designed a statement, far more draconian than other places, to be signed by farmers "setting forth the number of milk cows the farmer possesses and the number he will add to his herd for the purpose of the proposed plant." When these documents were signed and collected, they would "warrant a guarantee . . . to a condensery or cheese plant [of] a definite minimum quantity of milk." This ham-handed attempt to demonstrate farmer interest in a milk plant was joined by an equally questionable effort to delineate the routes milk trucks would take for a proposed condensery. The reason for that was twofold. It demonstrated to farmers that they could be part of the expected prosperity if they chose to convert to or add dairying, and it surreptitiously enabled Tuscaloosa to draw its anticipated milkshed significantly further from the city than other places. In addition to partnering with farmers, the Chamber worried about the lack of knowledge of dairy farming among area agriculturists as well as the timing for any dairying development. It began preparations to find if it could ship Tuscaloosa County–generated milk to another site while the town of Tuscaloosa waited to seduce a condensery or watched it being built. Chamber members stressed as they had for over a month that the time to act was now, and they again maintained that consistent effort would see the matter through.[54]

The meetings continued and McClure pushed farmers to fill out their cow promissory notes. Then a new threat emerged. Kraft Cheese purchased the Selma site from Southern Diaries and another cheese manufacturer set up a facility in Columbus, Mississippi, just across the border. A Kraft representative visited Tuscaloosa but nothing resulted. Farmers in the area seemed to be selling the dairy cows they had to neighboring places that were expanding their herds to cater to their new enterprises. Frustration began to appear. "Why not West Alabama," one newspaper asked.[55] When things looked the bleakest, McClure received word that two different condensery groups planned to visit Tuscaloosa in about a week. In addition to stressing the importance of completing the cow census, his "For the Farmer" piece explained what was expected of them. The coming Tuesday was reserved for farmers to demonstrate their support of a condensery. McClure put together a banquet and wanted "a great mass meeting of farmers of this and adjoining counties." This was "vitally important." The dairymen of the Tuscaloosa milkshed "must show these parties our real genuine and strong desire" for them to build a plant here by pledging to them, "in unmistakable fashion, our promise and purpose of such cooperation as only Tuscaloosa . . . is capable of doing." He told area farmers to lay aside all personal business to attend this event, maintaining that "nothing else within the range of possibility compares with the condensery." A few days later, he reiterated his stance. "Whether or not Tuscaloosa gets a condensery," argued McClure, "will depend largely upon the good attendance at the mass meeting here Tuesday."[56]

While both dairy firms praised the enthusiasm, neither placed a milk plant in Tuscaloosa. McClure expressed his frustration brusquely, saying, "If anyone tells you there is not milk enough in this section now to operate a condensery, tell them there was never any tonnage for a railroad until the road was built and ready to receive freight." In mid-November, another company scheduled a visit for the end of the month and the cycle began again. The Chamber, area dairymen, and McClure all geared up for the late November visit. This time things appeared more promising. The visitors, representatives of Libby, McNeill & Libby, pronounced themselves convinced that Tuscaloosa area farmers would produce sufficient milk to support a condensery. But the firm also noted that if the company decided to place the plant in Tuscaloosa it would have to hire a full-time dairy agent to help farmers select animals, purchase equipment, and undertake dairying at the most progressive level. Buoyed by the conversations, the Chamber agreed not to negotiate with any other company for two weeks while Libby's headquarters mulled over Tuscaloosa as a possible condensery site. In the meantime, the Chamber sent McClure to Chicago to talk condensery matters with several firms with offices there.[57]

McClure, who sometimes joked that the C in his name stood for "Condensery, Cows, and Cash," talked to Libby and the other firms. He also returned to Tuscaloosa with the outline of a condensery agreement between Libby and the Tuscaloosa Chamber as well as a caveat. The firm would approve the document as written but needed Tuscaloosa to agree to a series of specific terms. McClure thought the entire deal far from done. In fact, he wondered out loud about "whether or not the Chamber of Commerce and the people of Tuscaloosa can and will meet the terms of the tentative agreement." Apparently, one aspect of the agreement tied the potential Tuscaloosa plant to the kind of explosive growth that marked the Starkville plant. The company expected Tuscaloosa to start modestly and then to ramp up to high gear relatively quickly. That could not sit well with the Chamber, who had taken it upon themselves to guarantee the farmers' promissory notes. The document also set the condensery's payout price to farmers as the average prices offered at the Starkville, Macon, and Tupelo facilities. The Chamber endorsed "the principles set forth in the proposed contract" and got "down to work on the details." The issue of guarantees and a few other specifics required further negotiations, and the Chamber sent Mc-Clure and two others to continue discussions in Chicago. The discussions went well as the company's counterproposal straightened out most matters. The Chamber felt so confident that before the document was finalized, they launched two distinct campaigns to increase the county's dairy cattle. The first sought to increase the gross number of milch cows and consisted of a marketing campaign to get farmers in a five-county area to purchase any kind of dairy cows without respect to their lineage. Bankers promised liberal terms to assist prospective dairymen. The second aimed to add at least 2,000 more purebred dairy cattle to the milkshed. The proposed method of funding this latter proposition proved novel. Merchants, not the banks, would purchase these registered bulls and heifers and lend them to farmers in the surrounding area. It was not clear if this plan was another form of sharecropping or if the merchants hoped to make their investment back solely on increased trade in Tuscaloosa. Libby, McNeill & Libby asked the Chamber for some further changes, which it discussed and acceded to. The main area of compromise was that the Chamber would underwrite the new condensery's growth for two years, but at a rate far lower than the expansion at Starkville. The company pronounced itself satisfied. The Tuscaloosa property was to be Libby's first southern effort and it hoped to have its other canning divisions tap the region once it became familiar with the region.[58]

The dairy marriage between Libby and Tuscaloosa was curious. Libby had no southern experience. It also had no experience operating a condensery in a place that lacked a thriving dairy industry. More than most other places, Tuscaloosa saw the way to a condensery through hard work, not a viable dairy industry. It beseeched farmers to buy into dairying, but it did precious little until about the time the agreement was signed to take action to assist them in that transition. There was a certain fragility to all this.

Libby recognized the challenge and the danger. It sent its general field agent, John Glidden, to access the situation. For several days Glidden moved among the farms outside of communities in the distant parts of the milkshed, promising if they produced milk enough he would ensure that Libby provided trucks to take their milk to the condensery. He also familiarized himself with tenant farming and decided that Libby should hire a Black woman as its agent, to convince tenant farmers' wives to adopt dairying and to teach them how to undertake that chore. Glidden met with owners of large properties and encouraged them to shift some of the activity on their land from cotton to milk. He went to ad hoc gatherings of farmers to introduce himself and Libby, and worked with some of these small-town banks to ensure that they would lend farmers money to purchase prime dairy stock. He also encouraged Tuscaloosa bankers to loosen loan terms to get more dairy cattle in the area.[59]

Glidden's trip exposed some of the fragility in Tuscaloosa's approach. He reported to his superiors that he lacked confidence in whether the area could produce enough milk to sustain a condensery any time soon. Libby took this information and wanted the Tuscaloosa Chamber to change the terms of its guarantees. It demanded a third year guaranteed but phased in the targets at lower levels. It required 25,000 pounds of milk daily at the end of the first two months and escalated to 150,000 pounds by the end of year three. As McClure wryly admitted, "the company does not want damages. It wants milk." The company also wanted the title to the condensery site land free and clear, delivered by March 1. In return, it promised to spend about $250,000 on the condensery building and equipment. After considerable discussion, including whether the group might be better served waiting for another condensery to locate in Tuscaloosa and rejecting the changes, the Chamber sent two representatives to hammer out the difficulties. When they returned, it agreed to the emendations, thereby creating "the greatest opportunity which has been open to an Alabama county" and "the greatest opportunity ever afforded any set of people."[60]

For their part, small towns in the expansive Tuscaloosa milkshed understood their opportunity to benefit from the condensery. They held farmers' meetings to convince agriculturists that dairying would be profitable. Pickens County had much to recommend it geographically. It was located considerably closer to the cheese factory at Columbus and the condensery at Macon than it would be to the Tuscaloosa facility. A representative of the Columbus plant was featured at the Pickens meeting, along with Mc-Clure, who represented both the Libby plant and the Borden Macon plant. Pickens County took other steps to mine these now invaluable resources. Its county agent had aggressively worked to start a Jersey breeders club as well as a Jersey calves club for young boys and girls. He also established a dairy development association to teach interested farmers the ins and outs of dairying.[61]

Tuscaloosa did some of this, including establishing a meeting every Saturday morning where farmers could talk to other farmers about dairy-ing and the condensery.[62] To oversee the attempt to make sure farmers met the Chamber's guarantees, the Chamber hired McClure as their spe-cial agent, to guide and organize the campaign to secure the minimum promised amounts. McClure wasted no time. His first plan was unveiled at the grand public meeting announcing the condensery. McClure declared that in the next few weeks and months the Chamber would be sponsoring tours of the various condenseries and cheese plants in the South and the farmers who patronized them. Open to all in the milkshed and led by the Tuscaloosa Chamber, the region would learn dairying and dairy farming by reaching out and visiting others who had successfully managed the transi-tion. Starkville on payday was the first place they toured[63].

Starkville understood the role that it played in the creation of a south-ern dairy industry. Paydays were legendary. Crowds fed off each other as they watched the unforced revelry of satisfaction and success. Thousands and thousands of people came to share the joy and excitement of the milk earners on the fifteenth of each month. That was the most compelling exhibit for anyone hoping to establish a dairy business. But while that was the pièce de résistance, it was only part of the experience. Almost without exception, most of the heroes of the Starkville miracle played roles in the condensery production. They greeted groups by train and car. They pro-vided tours of the factory. Visitors went to the agricultural college and met Moore. They heard the story of how it all unfolded, from the proverbial cow's mouth. Perpetuating the Starkville story became their de facto oc-cupations. Certainly the town and its merchants benefited. The glorious Hotel Chester was perpetually booked. Town restaurants made a killing. Tourism may well have approached the amount of money generated by the condensery itself. Farmsteads with smiling children and happy wives received visitations. Stories of the before time and triumph were shared. A vital and viable consulting industry emerged as town after town and farm after farm wanted to learn the whereabouts of the holy grail of dairying. What did Starkville know? "What could we bring back to our town to cause such an awesome change in fortunes?" Sometimes what they brought back were Starkvillians, who not only shared their story with those who sought them out but also with those who did not yet believe. It was a particularly well-done piece of theater, one that brought credit to the place and kept it relevant no matter what else occurred.

In the case of the trip on February 15, 1928, fifty-five Tuscaloosans went to Starkville. They were greeted by F. L. Hogan, one of the signatories of the Borden Southern Company charter, and H. O. Jones, secretary of the Chamber of Commerce. They then went to the Chamber auditorium where they stood to hear bankers, businessmen, and "practical dairymen" recount their experience and share their financial sheets with the assembled. Hogan told the group that his tenants share the profits equally but he also allowed them to have as their own property half the cows born under their watch. Sudduth, who was also one of the "magnificent seven" to sign the Borden Southern charter and a partner with Hogan in many livestock ventures, told of Oktibbeha County, a place where "there was no further need for land loans." Land prices had skyrocketed, more than doubled in two years. Within ten miles of Starkville, 80 percent of the cotton was grown by dairy farmers. "It was free of debt when it is ginned and there are no credit stores in Starkville." Black farmers in Starkville, according to the Tuscaloosans, were "enthusiastic" about milk production. These producers said that payday "was equal to Christmas" and virtually no Black farmer did not keep at least a handful of dairy cattle. Moore was the last speaker before the group left to see nearby dairy farms. He gave "a rousing talk" crediting "the dairy cow with the upbuilding of Starkville." The visitors stopped at several "extremely interesting" farms where homes were "most modern." Half of them returned to idyllic Starkville and took the train back to Tuscaloosa. Those who had come by motor car stayed a day or two longer to visit Tupelo.[64]

Planning a large condensery meeting for farmers to consider how to apply the Starkville miracle to Tuscaloosa was one of the most significant outcomes from the trip. McClure and the others thought so much of and were persuaded by Hogan, Jones, and Sudduth that he booked each of them for the March 29 meeting. McClure asked them to "bring facts and figures of the success of the dairy industry and condensery" in Starkville. They were to be the only speakers. It was their job to do in Tuscaloosa what they did in Starkville: convey the drama, satisfaction, good feeling, and taste of success that Borden's facility brought throughout Oktibbeha County. More specifically, they were to convince farmers to become dairymen. It was not so much about how to be a dairyman. It was about creating a desire to be a dairyman. That was a first step but it was the most important step in ensuring that the Tuscaloosa plant would succeed.[65]

For the next several months, McClure continued to orchestrate the education of the farmer in dairying. A nonstop program of farmers' institutes, lectures, meetings, and bull-buying blanketed the counties around Tuscaloosa.[66] A huge crowd had turned out for the Starkvillians and it had been a tremendous success,[67] so much so that McClure scheduled another Starkville tour for mid-April. Farmers from the Tuscaloosa milkshed filled eight railroad cars and several motor cars to see for themselves what Borden had wrought. Like the first visit two months earlier, the visitors hailed the trip as a tremendous success.[68] McClure booked another expedition to Tupelo for June. That journey had 269 eager participants.[69] In August Starkville notables came again to Tuscaloosa County to tell the story of the first southern condensery and its spectacular growth.[70]

On a sojourn to Starkville, McClure learned an interesting tidbit. Montgomery and Mahorner had an Alabama compatriot, Thomas Jefferson Patton, who lived about ten miles from Tuscaloosa. McClure decided to investigate that relationship. He uncovered a trip to Mobile, Alabama, about fifty years prior that those three men had taken to buy stock from the Isle of Jersey. These animals purchased by these three men were from the same lines. It was from these animals that the Jerseys around Alabama and presumably Starkville and Macon stemmed. Never nearly as numerous as the Mississippi cows and surely no longer by any means as preblooded, McClure's yarn tied Tuscaloosa to Starkville in yet another way. Both had forefathers present at the creation of what was becoming the southern dairy industry.[71]

The massive dairy farmer–manufacturing effort and its relationship to Black farmers was a different tale. McClure failed to include them until July. There had been one exception. When the Starkvillians made their first appearance in Tuscaloosa at the end of March, Black farmers "were privileged to attend." The spellbinding story of Starkville cut across color lines; Starkville condensery proponents had always been clear that they would never have secured the condensery without the avid assistance and participation of Black sharecroppers and tenant farmers. Efforts to educate Black farmers in the Tuscaloosan region occurred only after groups of them said they were "interested and desired to know more about the condensery." Ironically one of the farmers requesting additional information had cows from the "Patton . . . strain of Jerseys." Black churches held these ad hoc condensery meetings.

McClure and the other Tuscaloosans notified the churches of a meeting only a day or two before it occurred. It remained the churches' obligation to spread the word through their membership. The actual meeting programs seemed to differ little from the standard condensery agenda. Dairy's ability to stabilize agriculture and to fill the pockets of dairy farmers were featured. Libby had sent a motion picture outlining the workings of a condensery and that became standard fare at all meetings. Personnel who would guide the work of the new plants answered questions and talked up the project. Meetings stressed getting farmers on board, not explaining exactly what that required. Not until September did the format change and then only to stress safe milk handling and condensery regulations.[72]

As McClure worked to entice farmers to adopt and advocate dairying and as Libby workers labored to finish the plant, groups from Alabama and the Carolinas started to agitate for cheese plants or condenseries in their locales. Quite often they went to see what a condensery could do for a city and its surrounding agricultural area. Starkville remained the unequaled and unsurpassed destination but sometimes Tuscaloosa welcomed dairy-interested visitors, too.[73] To Tuscaloosa, visitors hoping to learn about the condensery were a double-edged sword. Agitation for a community's own milk plant might draw from the now 40 miles in every direction area that Tuscaloosa now claimed as its own. It menaced the condensery and the Chamber's guarantees. The Chamber worked to combat this existential threat by convincing these places that they were indeed vital parts of the Tuscaloosa milkshed. Redrafting the dairy routes to tap these quite distant places became a strategy to ensure these neighboring regions that they would have easy, efficient routes to get their milk to the condensery. Initially, McClure thought 6 routes would be sufficient. The number was raised to 10–20 a bit later. That was replaced by a new proposal of 32 routes even before the plant was opened. The problem was there was just not enough milk in a 10- or even 20-mile radius to feed the milkshed. And as you drew out that radius further and further, the area between old routes widened considerably. For example, a milkshed of 10 miles in every direction encompassed about 315 square miles of area. A milkshed with a 40-mile radius was about 5,040 square miles to cover with milk routes. Tuscaloosa needed to try to reach that far just to secure milk in quantities large enough to support the condensery at a less than minimal rate.[74]

McClure understood the problem the condensery and Chamber faced. In the weeks and months after the milk plant opened, he did not let up. He arranged informational meetings almost as rapidly as he had in the past, working to convince more farmers to embrace dairying. As he always had, McClure attended the vast majority of these meetings. His "For the Farmer" columns became even more frequent.[75] Perhaps his masterstroke was the scheduling of the condensery's opening celebration. Rather than a single day, it was announced as a week-long gala. That grandiose event was misleading. Merchants primarily occupied five of those days. They stocked up on extra gear and claimed to offer seasonally low prices. Libby's sent "three advertising men" to Tuscaloosa to "decorat[e] local windows" with Libby paraphernalia, hyping the company's products and the condensery. The new Ritz Theater opened to play several Movietone and Vitaphone "talkies." Two parades highlighted the week. Held on Monday, the American Legion's Armistice Day parade marked a celebration of military life generally and included veterans of the Confederacy as well as the Spanish-American War and World War I. This event brought a large number of people into Tuscaloosa, where they could learn about its new initiatives. Wednesday was reserved for purely condensery-related events. It included a large afternoon purebred cattle show and sale, a means to get farmers to learn about dairying and to advocate for higher-producing animals. Speeches—McClure was the only Tuscaloosan tapped to talk—and a glorious parade were scheduled for earlier that morning. The day that McClure chose to hold the parade and the talks was not the condensery's actual opening. The facility had opened nearly a month earlier. The parade, which was led by a large Libby's float and would be filmed by Pathé News, and the celebration coincided with the condensery's first payday. Drawing again on the Starkville experience, McClure hoped to recreate the joy and magic of a Starkville payday in front of a throng of visitors and revelers. He hoped that the smiling and content faces of condensery dairymen would inspire others in the audience and around town to catch condensery fever. Newspapermen—McClure invited all the newspapers in the region as well as the papers in Birmingham, Mobile, and Montgomery—would share the excitement with their readers, spreading the "dairying pays" message throughout the milkshed.[76]

McClure was not yet done with this cabaret. His speech at the event claimed that the condensery was "the greatest agency for the development of West Alabama." He expected it to rid "uncertainty and want" for the lives of area farmers. He hoped that in some future date the number of milk trucks delivering their contents to the city "will equal the number of cars in today's parade." He then called for all the milk checks for the month and handed them out one at a time while he read the names of these "first patrons of the condensery" and maintained that they would "go down in history."[77]

On December 23, McClure announced that the farmers of the Tuscaloosa region had failed to meet the first guarantee of 25,000 pounds of milk daily. In fact, they achieved less than half that rate. After two months of operation, the number of condensery milk routes had been reduced by nearly half. Drivers for the milk routes made their wages through hauling and recruiting additional customers—Libby called them its field men. With many fewer farmers supporting the condensery than anticipated, many drivers could not sustain themselves on those terms and, when they quit, they were not replaced. In terms of daily milk delivered to the condensery, the first guarantee was by far the lowest target. Subsequent guarantees would escalate until they reached 150,000 in year three. Chances of achieving that stipulation looked bleak. The Chamber was responsible for the requisite penalties and looked to a far less optimistic future. The condensery was beginning to look like McClure's Folly.[78]

8 | SEE FOR YOURSELF

Starkville's Sway in Louisiana, Texas, and throughout the South

In 1925 H. C. Fondren, the Southern Pacific's Louisiana agricultural and colonization agent, met with a group of thirty-three Wisconsinites looking for a place where they could put down roots. The Wisconsin dairymen had grandiose aims. They wanted to create an improved Wisconsin, a dairyland free of the cold and where land was plentiful and cheap. They would breed and milk a great herd of dairy cows and build a large milk plant to serve the American South. Fondren lacked "the heart and nerve" to suggest Louisiana, certainly not Calcasieu Parish. Although that parish held the largest number of cattle in the state, he knew that it could not sustain the type of enterprise his Wisconsin visionaries sought. Fondren felt sure that if the Wisconsinites set up shop there "they would be certain to lose their cows" to the "Texas fever tick," which still ravaged the state's livestock regions. He did nothing and the Wisconsin dairymen chose tick-free Mississippi as their home base.

Calcasieu lost out on several grounds. It lost "industrious immigrants." It lost a facility to process milk that would have run in the hundreds of thousands of dollars. Area farmers lost the security this milk plant surely would have provided. Its establishment would have given farmers "a milk market for all they could now and hereafter produce, for all time to come." Calcasieu, Fondren concluded, "will never have a dairying industry to amount to anything as long as the fever tick is with us."[1]

The Calcasieu tragedy was repeated many times in the Louisiana of the late 1920s. Louisiana had never been a large dairy state. Its primarily scrub cattle wandered through fields and into bogs and swamps where they encountered the deadly tick. What milk that was produced was used in

215

the home. If not cooled and pasteurized very quickly, the milk turned bad. Louisiana, perhaps more than any other single state, depended heavily on condensed milk, brought to the state from the North.

Louisiana cattle had long had that sort of existence. Farmers thought of them as an essentially free resource. They wandered free through fields at virtually no cost to the farmer but yielded meat and some milk. Why go to the expense of penning or fencing them? That required farmers to feed them, either on pasture or with feed. Pasture and fodder necessitated farmers to reserve some of their acreage for these purposes. It took land out of market cultivation; it did not produce cotton, rice, sugar, or vegetables. A strong economic disincentive dissuaded farmers from dipping these cattle to remove the cattle tick. Dipping was costly to the farmer with little apparent return. It brought agents of the state and the federal government into what most farmers considered private space. Just as significant, tax assessors had difficulty pinpointing who owned which free-roaming cattle and therefore farmers generally kept these animals tax free. For scrub cattle, dipping was nonsensical. Their wandering habits in a terrain marked by swamps and lowlands—as was much of Louisiana—meant that freed cattle would invariably reinfect themselves over and over during their sojourns.

Farmers fought anything that added cost to raising scrub cattle. Their rebellions included dynamiting dipping vats.[2] Scrub cattle provided farmers an almost free benefit. Yet small towns and larger cities in the state often called for an end to free range cattle and demanded cattle be tick free. To these men and women, cattle were a potential engine of economic development for their town or city. Towns could prosper through the sale of the animals and their productions, and the revenue that commerce brought would boost merchants. Cities disliked paying premiums for milk and meat produced out of state and would benefit from becoming a cattle or dairy hub. The Louisiana State Legislature, like most state legislatures, provided rural peoples a disproportionate share of power. Farmers controlled the legislature. They, therefore, controlled the regulation of cattle.[3]

To small town Louisianans, farmers were the problem. Their refusal to adjust their ways and methods to cater to the desires of the commercial elite in these places stymied parish and town development. "Tick Eradication is fundamental," wrote H. N. Shesbusne, a resident of Plaquemine, a city of about four thousand in southeastern Louisiana. "Louisiana is not going to reach its rightful place in agriculture until we have the courage to face the tick." The tick, he continued, is "the greatest economic curse Louisiana and the South ever had." That "did not reflect good business sense." Having an open range made it impossible to rid a place of ticks. It also led to what Shesbusne thought was an inevitable chain of events: "Cattle, Ticks, Poor People, Poor Cattle, Sick Babies." He asked the newspapers of the state to take up this challenge and to work to pass laws prohibiting the open range and compelling tick eradication.[4]

When Louisiana newspaper editors looked toward the tick problem, they saw Starkville, Borden, and payday. Those optics began within a week of the Mississippi condensery's dedication. "If an operation of a condensing plant this size proves profitable, it will encourage establishment of other plants" throughout the South, noted Marshall Ballard, editor of the *New Orleans Item-Tribune.* Farmers in Oktibbeha County had rid the pest from their environs and now stood poised to reap tremendous rewards. Starkville could be "a convincing example" for how any quarantined place should act to prosper. These places simply needed to "get together, enforce dipping, and banish the tick." Referring to Borden's decision to place the condensery in Starkville, the *New Orleans Times-Picayune* encapsulated the opportunity that was missed in a single phrase: "It might have been."[5]

Embedded in the newspaper editors' and merchants' longing look at Starkville's condensery was a way of conceiving of cattle that was fundamentally at odds with the way that farmers understood these animals. To farmers, the animals were profit, with almost no upkeep or overhead. Although sometimes ticks killed the animals and always hampered them from achieving optimum weight, farmers accrued no loss. There had been no investment. Small farmers were more than happy the way things were. Scrub cattle provided meat and milk at no cost. Scrub cattle were security in troubled times.

That status quo thinking proved an abomination to small towns and cities. Opportunities to solidify banks and merchants went begging. To be sure, the denizens of rural towns saw advantages to farmers that tick-free cows offered. Cattle without ticks could be the basis of breeding, feeding, and dairying industries, each of which was a hedge against monoculture, helped fertilize fields, and could increase farmer comfort. What remained to be done was to convince the farmer. Arguments that "when the tick leaves, farm profits soar" were never as simple as small town proponents wanted them to be. That only proved the case if area farmers adopted some dairying or cattle breeding. Without moving in either of those directions, farmers lost, not gained, from tick eradication. Their free beef and milk would be no more.[6]

Two rumors quickly started circulating. Both rested on Starkville's prominence to serve their ends. A whispering campaign found its way into the newspapers that the Borden people truly favored locating the condensery in Louisiana. The company was all set to pick a site when it determined that the presence of the cattle tick made the state too risky for a large investment. It settled instead on Starkville and brought to Mississippi the glory and money that could have been Louisiana's. The other rumor had Pet Milk looking at the area near Lafayette, Louisiana, to establish one of six new condenseries. The land around the town looked like "a mighty good location" but the area lacked dairy farms, the direct consequence of the dreaded tick. Pet scuttled thoughts of investing a great deal of money in such a problematic region.[7]

By mid-1926 what Louisiana "progressives" had was a potent example of the fruits of success in a tick-free place, Starkville and Oktibbeha County. In June they used it to hammer at the Louisiana legislature's firm refusal not to repeal the "no fence" law. Cries of "free range cattle means prosperity to the small farmer" drowned out their dairy development argument.[8] In August, these small town entrepreneurs stepped up the cause. Thinking that seeing was believing, they initiated field trips to Starkville. Taking convoys of farmers there to view what dairying could produce would open the eyes of visitors and lead them to dairying. Visitors to Starkville would bring their recollections back to their fellow farmers and share what they had witnessed. The result would be first a fence law and eradication campaign and then a vibrant dairying industry to replace the uncertainty of single crop agriculture.

The initial group of Louisiana pilgrims went to Starkville courtesy of the Ruston Chamber of Commerce. It sponsored a nine-car caravan—about forty people—to take Lincoln Parish farmers to Starkville and the surrounding area to see the glories of the new condensery and the charmingly modern farms it created. The purpose was clear. The men would be seduced by the joy and prosperity of their counterparts that the new milk plant produced. It was to be a transformative experience. These farmers would return to their homes, tell their neighbors, and the no fence–no eradication crowd would be one step nearer to obscurity. At that point, then, Lincoln Parish farmers could build dairy herds and "become the center of a dairy section equal to the Starkville section." They were not alone. Shreveport sent members of the Chamber of Commerce, two county agents, and about twenty-five farmers to Starkville later that month. When they returned, the county agents rounded up farmers interested in dairying and took them to a special Chamber meeting to hear about the trip. The report of results was dramatic. "Many farmers who have not heretofore done so will begin at once to develop small herds of dairy cattle." Nor was that all. About a month later some of the Starkville visitors held a meeting at a farm to discuss dairy agriculture as they prepared to develop their section.[9]

Over the next two years, the question of tick eradication remained in the forefront.[10] Starkville was often the answer. Many of Louisiana's small towns and rural parishes made junkets to Oktibbeha County. In 1927 and 1928, Starkville junketeers hailed from the Rapides, Catahoula, St. Landry, Arcadia, Jeff Davis, Vermillion, Avoyelles, La Salle, and Grant parishes. Small towns represented included Tallulah, Lafayette, Arcadia, Opelousas, Eunice, Pinville, Sunset, Port Barre, Crowley, Ebenezer, Branch, Egan, Rayne, Church Point, Ellis, Iota, Washington, Cheneyville, and New Iberia. A group of Black farmers from Homer also made the trek to Starkville. The superintendent of "the colored training school" hosted them rather than the usual welcoming party. Some Louisiana places sent several groups at successive times. The Starkville sojourns were so routine for Louisiana small towns that it was not usual for there to be three or more Louisiana contingents in Starkville at the same time. Farmers comprised the bulk of the visitors but county agents and prominent businessmen often went along. Cost of the trips were usually borne by banks, Chambers of Commerce, or merchants.[11]

Most visitors reported on their trip to their sponsors, farmers, and often newspapers. Accounts had several common characteristics. All commented on the hustle and bustle of payday, the retail stores overflowing with people, banks with deposits at all-time highs, and the absence of credit.[12] Starkville's economy was cash and carry, no borrowing or paying over time. It needed not be anything else. Sometimes they pointed to the gross numbers that dairymen were paid a month at the condensery and creamery. Numbers like $140,000 in one month or $1.5 million for the year turned heads more effectively than did individual farmers' receipts.

Hardheaded analyses of dairy farming also framed many reports. A convincing metric offered to entice reluctant farmers to take up dairying was just how profitable dairy agriculture was in the South. How many cows did a dairyman own? What was his yearly feed cost and what did these animals generate after expenses? Starkvillians were especially adept at answering visitors' questions, and provided detailed explanations of what kinds of expenses dairying entailed. Sometimes they even shared their books with the questioners, providing yet another demonstration of how neighborly Starkville's residents approached the continual influx of visitors from throughout the south. It was easy for visitors to conceive how Starkville practice could translate into Louisiana profits.

Starkville was always careful to lay out the mechanics of dairying. They noted the split among tenant farmers and sharecroppers—always 50–50—and landowners. Persons who presented this evidence expressed their pride in Black farmers, making sure to mention that dairying in Oktibbeha County relied on nearly as many Black dairymen as whites. Visitors often talked to Black dairymen as they toured the area. When they reported their conversations, they frequently remarked how ably the Black dairymen carried out their work and how the profitability of dairying had rendered King Cotton in an entirely new way. Put more straightforwardly, dairying regularly covered more than the expenses of running the farm, feeding the family, and buying goods. It in itself was profitable. That meant that whatever the Black farmer gained through cotton production was gravy, simply profit.

During these visits, Starkville-area farmers talked openly about the problems of Louisiana dairying. Time and again, they remarked on how dairying there could never be profitable until the cattle tick was defeated. They expressed their belief that to try to raise a dairy herd under those conditions was foolhardy and that no northern dairy industry firm would think of gracing that land with a condensery. Northern dairy industrialists made profits, nothing more, nothing less. In that fashion, residents counseled their visitors that even if the cattle tick was vanquished, Louisiana would need to build up its dairy herds before any major company might be willing to invest there.[13]

Those sobering words went home to Louisiana. Many found them a more compelling reason to rid the state of the tick immediately. The tick cut off Louisiana from the future. It consigned the state to poverty and boom-and-bust agriculture. These battles for the future found expression in many of the state's newspapers. In almost every case, the tick was the villain, robbing Louisiana and its citizens of what was rightly theirs. Tourists to Starkville returned home "'sold' on the possibilities of dairy development." What had sold them was Starkville. The dramatic difference between Oktibbeha County and their homes proved irresistible. There existed a better way and it resided in Mississippi. "Business was rushing at the three banks and throughout the city," noted F. V. Mouton, secretary of the Lafayette Chamber of commerce. "Figures show that on that one day $68,000 was paid by the condensery." Adding that to the $46,000 paid by the creamery, the total single day payout was a remarkable $114,000. Clyde C. Tanner, a resident of Rapides Parish, wanted all no-fence proponents to "take a trip over to Mississippi and see for themselves." He argued that the parish would be far better off if it had Starkville's payday, "a payroll of one hundred forty thousand dollars per month year round, the money going to thousands of people." Joseph E. Ransdell, US Senator from Louisiana, argued that Louisiana's future was to emulate Mississippi's milk industry. That state aimed "to place every farmer on a milk route which is another way of putting him on a monthly payroll."[14]

W. J. Savage, who owned a large farm in Forest Hills, not far from Lake Charles, also spoke of payday but in very different terms. He had been impressed with "the care-free expressions on the faces of merchants and farmers." These expressions bespoke "volumes" to all "who experienced financial struggle for livelihood." There was no look on Starkville faces of a "chance of a complete failure in crops or uncertainty" of where the necessities for "loved ones were to come." This sense of peacefulness could only come from "permanent prosperity," Savage contended. It also manifested itself in "the harmony which seems to pervade all departments of the work and business" of dairying in Starkville. It results in "nice, well-kept homes and the hospitality extended us from all sides." Savage maintained that while in Starkville he never met a single real estate agent. There was no "long list of property for sale." He then moved to the crushing aspect of his report. He found his area vastly geographically superior to Starkville. But "after viewing all the favorable and unfavorable points," he was "thoroughly convinced that we cannot succeed" in dairying "unless we can have tick-free cows." Tick-free cows could never be had with "open range." Without fences, infected animals will be "spreading a new crop of ticks every few weeks."

Savage had recognized a critical aspect of the Starkville experience. It was not money per se. It was freedom, freedom of choice, freedom from want, freedom from worry. It was "permanent prosperity," a recognition that your labor had been successful and rewarded appropriately. It was independence, self-reliance, happiness, those things that farming was intended to provide and those things embodied in the myth of the yeoman farmer that dated at least as far back as Crèvecoeur.[15]

In 1927 and 1928, numerous attacks on the cattle tick referred to dairying as the solution and Starkville as the proof that the solution would work. Farmers increasingly voiced support for cattle dipping and fences. The legislature even passed such a measure in 1928 but then Governor Huey Long vetoed it. In 1920 Louisiana had 1,267,734 head of cattle. In 1929 the assessment rolls counted only 363,011. Mississippi built a fence along its shared border with Louisiana to keep cattle and the tick out. In 1930, an investigation by a *Times-Picayune* reporter found that the state spent over $30 million each year buying out-of-state dairy products. One-third of all the federally quarantined land was in the state of Louisiana. There was almost no talk of a national firm establishing Louisiana condenseries or cheese factories except in some far distant time, after the eradication of the cattle tick.[16]

Nonetheless, Starkville had a dramatic impact on the state. It galvanized the anti-tick movement. It helped fuel fence laws. It emerged as the touchstone to what Louisiana could become if only it acted. It became a most potent force in the battle to eradicate the tick.

Ironically, the state after which Texas Fever was named had a mixed history with the pest. It passed mandatory eradication laws starting around 1910, although lawsuits sometimes undercut them. The state was so vast that the tick eradication campaign was done in three sections. Some sections came close to stamping out the tick, while other areas remained thickly infested. The state's established beef cattle industry, the nation's largest, certainly contributed to tick eradication—and tick persistence. So too did fluid milk operations in Texas. The state had five cities with populations of more than 100,000 in 1930, each of which required considerable coordination to secure and deliver milk. Beyond that, Texas's vast size encompassed a wide variety of ecosystems. There were many different kinds of agriculture practiced in Texas as soil, rain, and wind took their toll.

Industrial dairying in some of those contexts would seem natural; in others, ludicrous. Some dairies supplying the state's large cities tried to dry or condense their milk to ease the strain of daily delivery or to establish a secondary market. Occasionally, they dabbled in butter and established creameries but most Texas butter was made on farms for immediate needs.

Beginning in 1925, citizens around Austin, Fort Worth, and Bryan began to discuss creating efficiencies in their dairying operations. Purebreds became the order of the day, and trades and purchases of Jerseys and Holsteins increased. Importation of butter and cream from neighboring states seemed an unnecessary expense, and these dairymen hoped to streamline their operations to meet the untapped demand.[17]

Only after news of Borden's Starkville initiative did Texas locales begin to consider industrial dairying. Even then reports were few. Ryder had visited the Lone Star state when he was searching for the first southern condensery but it apparently did not engage residents. It remained until just before the Starkville facility was to open for Sweetwater citizens to suggest a broad collection of milk over a wide territory and a plant to process it. Right after the Mississippi condensery opened, Roy Mullins, Borden's sales representative for Fort Worth, suggested that it would now be appropriate for Borden to come back to where its founder, Gail Borden, started—in Texas.[18]

Mullins knew whereof he spoke. Most Texans did not. Texans used terms like milk plant, creamery, condensery, and fluid milk manufactory almost interchangeably in the later 1920s. Nor were they as wedded to bringing in major northern milk companies as other states. Located in Harrison County near the Louisiana border, Marshall, Texas was among the earliest, most strident communities interested in a milk plant, and also among the most thorough. A far eastern Texas city of about 15,000, Marshall had its earliest inklings in industrial milk because it helped supply the fluid milk needs of Shreveport, about forty miles away. With a ready market to absorb at least 500 gallons of milk daily, farmers began to expand their herds. J. L. Lancaster, president of the Texas & Pacific Railroad, raised the bar at the Harrison County–hosted Central East Texas fair. He opined that area dairymen should shoot for providing Shreveport at least 2,000 gallons daily. If that occurred, Lancaster continued, then "the establishment of a condensing plant such as is operated at Starkville, Mississippi, by the Borden interests is one of the possibilities of the future." He concluded that it was the support of Oktibbeha's dairymen and their willingness to cooperate with each other and Borden "that made it possible for the plant to be established there."[19]

Area farmers formed the Harrison County Dairymen's Cooperative Association soon after Lancaster's speech. Like most cooperative associations, it sought to boost common buying and selling to create economies of scale. But A. W. Kinnard, the Harrison County agent, saw a grander future. Cooperation was but a first step in securing a condensery. He reminded the assembled that just a few years ago, Borden's Ryder had come to the area to examine Marshall as the nation's first condensery south of the Mason Dixon line. The company rejected it as its dairy industry was not adequately developed. Area farmers needed to work to overcome that deficiency and a condensery would result. The town's Chamber of Commerce took up the cause and the two groups worked jointly. Understanding that a new facility required a minimum of 25,000 gallons of milk daily and that at least one condenser—Carnation—had shown an interest in Marshall, the Chamber claimed that the plant necessitated "everyone pulling one way," to seize "the opportunity of a lifetime" and conduct a postal census of area cows. "Progress is entirely possible without an oil boom," wrote W. A. Adair, editor of the *Marshall Messenger*. "We in Marshall are striving for a steady, permanent growth." A condensery would deliver security.[20]

Marshall farmers remained unsure of just how lucrative a condensery would be, so to assuage their concerns, the Chamber sent a delegation to Starkville and Tupelo to talk to farmers there, and then through Missouri north to Minneapolis to examine condensery machinery. As the delegation wound its way through the heartland, an emissary of Borden came to address a mass meeting of Marshallites. He suggested that the company was interested in considering the town for a condensery if the particulars were in order. As the town mulled over the proposition, the touring group returned to tell the Chamber and the co-op that expenses seemed far greater in Mississippi, Missouri, and Minnesota, yet farmers in those places claimed dairying was reliably profitable. They recommended that the group go ahead and vigorously pursue a condensery. The Kiwanis Club and the Rotarians added their support as did Adair, who published a full-page piece about the large checks Oktibbeha dairymen cashed every payday.[21]

The touring group offered one caveat. The milk output of Marshall farmers was too low to justify a national firm investing in a facility in town. After some urging, Harrison County dairymen pledged to expand their herds and up their output. To demonstrate their seriousness and to gather requisite facts, Chamber members themselves decided to conduct a 48-

hour, house-to-house canvass of the number of dairy cows there presently, and what development farmers could anticipate. The Merchants Association endorsed the plan and the condensery and assisted in canvassing. Black and white farmers were visited and asked a series of questions about their present arrangements and future plans. Included was the question, "What is your attitude towards the proposed milk plant?"[22]

The survey revealed a potential 15,000 cows in the county but "the visible supply of raw milk" was far below what was necessary to satisfy suitors. Dairying would have to be "cultivated and developed" before it could regularly "feed a factory." Nonetheless, the Chamber sent the report to Chicago for Borden's and Carnation's scrutiny. Both companies took a hard pass. The Chamber licked its wounds but refused to concede, and it investigated other ways of establishing a milk plant on a smaller scale.[23]

Sherman, Texas, a northeastern city of 15,000 abutting the Oklahoma border, proved an apt model. Rather than try to bring in a northern condensing company, it decided to go local. Investors in the Interstate Oil Cotton Refining Company—makers of Mrs. Tucker's Shortening—put up $50,000 to create the Meadowlake Milk Products Company to manufacture ice cream, butter, powdered milk, condensed milk, and "other milk products." Opened just a few months before Marshall's potential deal fell through, it needed only the milk from 5,000 cows to make a profit. Local dairymen pledged to raise their herds to that amount.[24]

Marshall's Chamber began the process of founding a milk plant by first determining what it wanted and what it could support. Neither had been an issue with the outside condensers, who had their own templates and agendas. The Chamber decided that a powdered milk plant was most versatile—powdered milk was frequently the base for ice cream—and that the county had all the ingredients to make the factory go. Several large dairy farms then carrying fluid milk to Shreveport promised if a milk plant was built to send their milk to the new facility rather than the Louisiana city. The Chamber then looked for someone experienced in plant construction and found a Chicago firm, Douthitt Engineering, that had built forty-five plants in the North and in Canada. The firm agreed to partner with Marshall for 50 percent of the plant's proceeds. The Chamber was left to raise $75,000 in stock. Its members contributed $30,000 almost immediately, but the remainder took nearly two months. Not until July 21, 1928, did the new facility, the Texas Milk Products plant, open. A pageant depicting the marriage of King Cotton to Queen Dairy Cow highlighted the event. Joining the King were his sons, "Bobbie Boll Weevil, Jimmy Leaf Spot, Too Dry, Too Much Rain, Bunnie Cotton Tail, Mack Rusty Boll, Johnnie Root Rot, and Willie Flea Hopper." Attending the Queen were her daughters, "Rosa Corn, Flora Pasture, Sarah Sorghum, Beulah Bermuda, Lottie Cotton Seed Meal, Gretchen Clover, Susie Sudan, Flossie Velvet Bean, Sallie Soy Bean, and Annie Cowpeas." The pageant featured the daughters killing the sons in the name of diversification.[25]

Adair celebrated the opening the way a booster should. He proclaimed that the Chamber "offered a plan of farm relief superior" to anything coming out of Washington or national politics. The Chamber offered farmers "a market and a payday every two weeks." It provided them "an opportunity to succeed in a way that has brought prosperity to every community in America that has had like opportunity." To local naysayers, he chastised their "prophesy [of] failure," but reminded county farmers that only they could "determine whether this new industry will succeed." He argued that "Marshall can do no more." It had "done its part. It cannot force the farmers into the dairy business." To farmers, the plant opens the possibility of "industrial freedom." Embrace it and gain "independency and relief from the hell of debt."[26]

Other parts of Texas took a more circuitous path to dairying. Farmers in the counties surrounding Waco, in east central Texas, actively looked for an alternative to exclusive cotton production. The handwriting was on the wall. The industry was moving south and west and these farmers feared they could not compete. Dairying seemed a promising alternative, so the farmers of Bosque County met with the Chamber of Commerce of Waco in October 1926. Would the Waco Chamber build a creamery to take the milk that these prospective dairymen hoped to produce? The Chamber agreed to consider the matter as well as a request to provide interest-free loans for dairy cattle, and asked its "Home Industry and Factory Committee" to provide a recommendation. The Committee reported favorably, and the Chamber made arrangements with two local parties to present their milk plant visions to the group. As the Chamber mulled over the proposals, the Waco business community called a several-days-long conference of central Texas businessmen to reorganize the section's agriculture and to promote dairying. As the group saw it, cotton and foodstuffs were unprofitable in that region, and farmers needed to turn to dairying. For that to occur, they needed a "systematized market": a dependable place to sell their milk. Conference attendees agreed that a creamery was the answer, and established a group to survey an area within a radius of fifty miles to see what size milk plant was necessary.[27]

Out of that conference came a new organization to redirect and revitalize Waco-area agriculture. Named the Agricultural Development Association, it was privately funded by Waco business interests to oversee the complex transformation from cotton to dairy culture. This was no small matter. The powerful and wealthy in central Texas made a measured assessment that the present course was economic suicide. Without radical refocus, their establishments and hence the seven-county area around Waco was doomed. The slow and steady grip of impoverishment and bankruptcies loomed as their future.

With potential economic ruin staring them in their face, the new Agricultural Development Association acted immediately. It joined with the general agent for the Trinity and Brazos Valley Railway (T&BV) to agree to the creamery plan and undertake the survey. But before the poll's completion, a Dallas dairy merchant swooped in and established a cream collection station for daily shipment back to his facility. About ten days later, a Houston entrepreneur opened a second cream collection depot. The two new creameries did not undermine the need for a survey or for dramatic economic change, and it was delivered about two weeks later. Investigators concluded that the fifty-mile region around Waco could easily accommodate at least 5,000 additional cows, just to service the area's present and anticipated milk needs. Sending milk products out of Waco would necessitate many thousand more dairy cows. When broken down into cohorts, the figures were more striking. The association found less than half of the section's tenant farmers kept dairy cattle and that about a fifth of the landowners raised over 55 percent of the milch cows. These figures told the group that area farmers had barely embraced dairying and the association felt confident that it could institute measures to dramatically expand the area's milk supply.[28]

Before the association unfolded a plan, a Waco dairyman established his own creamery in town. Where less than two months ago there had been none, now there were three Waco creameries or collection stations. These three cream-related facilities established a concrete demand for Waco milk. Some county schools embraced the opportunity to further dairying and taught agriculture classes in the evenings to prepare farmers as dairymen. The City of Waco followed suit with a similar program. Perhaps due to these evening classes, receipts at the creameries climbed. Waco's Agricultural Development Association took the enhanced creamery numbers as indication of an increase of dairymen and cows. The rise in dairying had been sufficiently painless that the group looked to dairying's future more optimistically. The group now set its eyes on the big prize, something far grander than a creamery. It wanted a condensery.[29]

In mid-August, the group reported on yet another survey that indicated that 3 to 4 million pounds of cream yearly were sent from Waco's fifty-mile milkshed to Dallas, Houston, and even Kansas City. That was an extraordinary amount that left the region but it suggested that on the outskirts of the Waco milkshed dairying was blooming. Statistics indicated that farmers held only 1,000 cows within a twenty-mile radius of the city. The committee's calculations revealed that at least 1,500 more cows were necessary in that smaller region to support a condensery, so they asked dairymen if they planned to expand herd size with a condensery in town. It also asked another telling question: Would you prefer a whole-milk market or the present cream-only market? That mattered. A cream-only market required farmers to own and use separators to skim the cream from milk and then have another outlet—generally pigs—for the skimmed milk. The whole-milk group had no skimmed milk for animal feed—they probably did not raise pigs—but it did not require investment in skimmers. The latter group was generally poorer or more cotton-dependent than the former.

The superintendent of the county schools provided an able assist to the committee when he directed the system's seventy-five teachers to require students to ask their parents how many cows they might add if Waco had a condensery. To fortify the condensery case, the *Waco News-Tribune* published a major story reporting on the Starkville miracle and payday. It took care to note that both white and Black dairymen shared in the bounty and that the rewards were far in excess of what might have been anticipated. The reason for that was clear. In Starkville, "milk checks so charm folks, both white and colored, that the close supervision necessary for sharecropping is not necessary" for dairying.[30]

In the wake of the Starkville story, the Waco business community reconvened and modified the development association by making it a permanent institution and funding it from their own pockets. They also changed its immediate mission. Realizing that a condensery would at least double cotton income in the area, the businessmen "sidetracked" all the association's other initiatives until the county secured at least two thousand more cows, the number the association now figured was necessary to attract a condensery. Within days, the association highlighted Starkville again. It marveled that Borden Southern's capitalization had increased tenfold almost instantaneously, and that the Starkville facility was not the only dairy plant in Mississippi. The group also cited Tupelo to show what a community was willing to do to achieve a milk plant. It had hired a county dairy agent, provided generous loans to farmers wanting to purchase dairy cows, and achieved "a certain amount of enthusiasm among the farmers." This latter stipulation indicated to Carnation that the quantity of milk would likely soon increase. The association sent postcards to 5,300 farmers in the Waco area with the slogan, "More Live Stock or Bust," embossed on the cards. It asked them directly whether they would want more cows or not if Waco captured a condensery. Not only did the area need at least 2,000 more cows but it also needed to show "'some enthusiasm' on the part of farmers" for the venture.[31]

The Agricultural Development Association did yet other calculations. It figured that a condensery would add $5 million to county farmers' pocketbooks annually. How it came up with that outlandish figure stemmed from what H. M. Madison, farm agent for the Southern Pacific, relayed to the group about Starkville's success. He maintained that before Borden came, Oktibbeha had only about 7,000 dairy cows. He had recently learned that over 40,000 dairy animals now populated the county. The group determined that Waco would experience a similar fivefold increase with similarly commensurate profits. Starkville's dairy explosion, coupled with its huge paydays, wowed the association when it plugged in Waco's numbers. Madison pushed Waco to a condensery in another way. He was aware of Borden's dalliance with Marshall; he knew of the company's interest in Texas. With his strong urging, the association authorized a representative, E. C. Barrett, who doubled as Chamber vice-president, to travel with Madison to discuss a Waco condensery with Borden in New York at their earliest convenience. The banks and newspapers did their part to ensure fertile ground for consideration. Bankers announced that farmers seeking loans to buy dairy cow would be "liberally treated." Newspapers reported how cotton land was rapidly going to pasture.[32]

As the delegation planned its Borden trip, the association secretary preempted them by writing Borden to ask it to place a condensery in the area by next spring. Borden recently had passed on the Marshall plant and it responded about the South's dairy fitness rather than the Waco proposition. The company recounted how Starkville had "backed up [the company's] growing belief" that the "great future of dairy farming lay in the South." It therefore planned to erect condenseries throughout the region. The company saw its plants "as a new business activity in the South, one that bids fair in time to rival the cotton and tobacco industries, if not ultimately surpass them." Dairy farming, it noted, "not only brings prosperity but stability." For dairy farmers and the company, Borden's Starkville and Tennessee plants "mark the beginning of an era of unexampled prosperity" in the South.[33]

The personal touch drew a more favorable response and after their New York trip, the delegation returned with news that Borden had promised to send a representative to Waco shortly. C. D. Pearce, head of Borden's Bureau of Dairy Development and its chief veterinarian, toured the area with the county agent as he had in Starkville years earlier, talked to dairy farmers, checked out the condition of the herds, and noted the geophysical conditions. He returned to New York to deliver his report.

Borden Co. spent considerable time on its due diligence before it committed to a next step. Waco interests took that opportunity to strengthen their case. They created societies to purchase purebred heifers and to share purebred bulls. They began a cow-testing group to cull the poorest milk producers from their herds. These organizations did not work alone. They agreed to join with the Chamber as a unified front. In the same manner, the development association agreed for negotiation purposes to fold itself into the Chamber so that Borden would have but one entity with which to barter.[34]

That precaution proved wise because Borden's Pearce came back to Waco at the end of May and asked for a quick but thorough survey of then-current dairies and dairy conditions. The Chamber enlisted 200 workers to visit every one of the estimated 6,000 farmers in the county, the total at the last census. The survey asked how many cows the farmer was presently milking, how many cows were dry, the number of heifers, and the number of heifer calves. It questioned the type of bull used, whether the farmer would join a bull circle to improve his breed, and the volume of milk, sweet and sour cream, or butter sold. It also asked if the farmer would buy additional cows if there was a market for their milk, whether he had hogs or chickens, and how much land did he devote to the following grain crops: sorghum, corn, oats, clover, alfalfa, native grass, and "garden stuff." The group reminded everyone that "establishment of a large milk plant here is of such paramount importance that nothing will be allowed to stand in the way of gathering all the information desired." Farmers were "to give the information asked promptly and fully." Persons asked to be census takers were "to respond willingly." Gaining the condensery was "the key to agricultural prosperity upon which the city's prosperity must rest."

This dire warning and strict instructions demonstrated just how desperate the matter seemed. Waco was at the crossroads. It needed to match Borden's template or the cause was lost. Among the unexpected items was the discovery that twice as many farmers owned cows as had seventeen months earlier. The total cow population surpassed 8,000. Two-thirds of the cow owners estimated they would double their herd size if a condensery came. The sole disappointment was that only 5 percent were purebred animals capable of high milk output.[35]

Armed with this knowledge, the Chamber sent a special committee to Starkville to see the situation there for itself. These men did not focus on farmers; they concentrated on merchants and bankers. Without exception, these Starkvillians hailed the condensery as creating "a prosperity which had not been dreamed of before." Everything was on a cash basis. Tenant farmers were buying radios, phonographs, and their own farms. Mortgages were paid off in a year's time. That report of the Starkville merchants' and bankers' experiences hit home, and the Chamber became further convinced that the condensery was its magnificent opportunity to cement its members' and the region's future. Their enthusiasm was boundless, so much so that the Chamber took three unprecedented steps. It appointed a committee to get farmers in the milkshed to sign "definite commitments" to the number of cows they would milk if the condensery were in Waco. If the signed statements promised milk enough for Borden to select Waco, the Chamber would provide the site for the condensery and prepare it for Borden at the Chamber's cost. If farmers guaranteed cows enough for the condensery but Borden and the Chamber were unable to conclude negotiations successfully, the Chamber would assume the financial "responsibility of providing a reliable market by some other means."[36]

Each of these acts was extraordinary, and placed the Chamber's members in a position of great financial risk. It needed to mobilize area farmers to the condensery cause and it appropriately charged a military man, Colonel R. B. Albaugh—who owned a moving and storage company and had chaired the committee that visited Starkville—to get farmers to sign their pledges. When the Chamber president appointed Albaugh, he talked of the "phenomenal prosperity which followed the condensed milk factory into Starkville, Mississippi" and acknowledged that Albaugh was the right man to get farmers on board. Albaugh and this committee met the next day with a representative group of farmers and offered them a Chamber-paid trip to Starkville to see the miracle for themselves. They demurred, arguing that time was of the essence and that they were so committed to the program that they immediately gave it their total support. They promised to work with the committee to get the requisite pledges.[37]

Newspapers, the Chamber, the farmers' group, and Albaugh brought their collective force to bear on the pledge question. Over 400 people were actively engaged in getting farmers to buy a proverbial pig in a poke. They would expand herds if a condensery came. The condensery would come if they expanded herds. Intense pressure was applied and Albaugh's visitors returned with signed pledges for over 15,000 additional cows. The Chamber then sketched on a county map the quantity each farmer committed to, and possible milk collection routes for a Waco condensery. It finally sent the map to Borden as a graphic demonstration of Waco's possibilities.[38]

The city heard nothing. In mid-August, the Chamber remained so invested in the condensery that it could not do nothing. It sent another delegation to corporate headquarters to see what it might do further to get the condensery to Waco. Later that month, Pearce made a third trip to Waco, this time with another Borden official. The two New Yorkers "suggested" certain things the company would like to see before it made a final determination. These included purchasing enough purebred cows to make the Waco facility succeed with money contributed by members of the Waco business community—farmers could pay this back over time. It also recommended that the Waco businessmen establish a $50,000 guarantee for construction of good roads along prospective milk routes. Almost instantaneously, Waco business complied. In late October, again after a considerable delay, Walter Page, who had been involved in the establishment of Borden's Starkville plant, came to Waco. He spent three days examining the area and the Chamber's dairy plans for the future. On the third day he met with the Chamber milk people and told them that if the New York people approved of the plan, he would return in mid-November. He did and on November 19, the Chamber signed the contract. Included were all the terms discussed previously. Newspapers heralded the event and wrote stories about the negotiations, the Borden company, Gail Borden, and the need for purebred dairy cows. Two other stories were prominently featured. The first was "the Romantic Story of Progress" of Mississippi. The second was more direct. It was headlined "Borden Plant at Starkville, Miss., Money-Dispenser."[39]

A county bond issue to establish a network of good roads throughout the county—to comply with the business community's promise—had been put on the ballot before the agreement was codified, and the election was set for December 18. All cast the measure as an adjunct to the milk plant, as the mechanism necessary for farmers to tap into the prosperity that the condensery promised. To make sure they redeemed their pledges, newspapers published the names of farmers who promised to expand their dairy herds. They also reminded farmers to purchase purebred animals and to make use of the interest-free loans backed by Waco businesses.[40]

These initiatives met with success. The bond issue passed by a margin of seven to one. Cattle purchasing, especially of purebred cattle, picked up markedly. The building of the plant went smoothly and the facility opened on July 10, 1929. Waco businessmen's gamble had been covered by the area's farmers.[41]

Waco then had a situation where its business and farm interests saw their futures as common enough to work together. Businessmen risked money. Farmers adopted a kind of farming with which they were unfamiliar. Both acted as if they lacked choice; their backs were against the wall. Borden recognized Waco's situation as a key opportunity but made sure that local Wacoans recognized that the New York firm was a definite part of this fascinating new kind of partnership. Speaking for Borden at the formal celebration marking the signing, Page maintained that he "had never witnessed such an aggressive spirit of progress" as he saw among Waco businessmen and farmers. He urged them to bathe in the light yielded by "the romance of accomplishment" where all parties pledged their efforts for mutual gain. He told how when he first saw the cotton monoculture of central Texas "it almost brought tears to his eyes." From that moment on, he knew that "these people must have help." "When one of our plants go into a community," continued Page, "we become part of that community, because the community's interests are our interests and when I say 'we' and 'us' I mean exactly that." Page then shifted to what he considered an essential ingredient to success. "The only way to go after this proposition is with enthusiasm, or courage on fire. Success follows the dairy cow." Translation: Embrace the endeavor fully and your future is assured.

Page's rousing comments were significantly more extensive and enthusiastic than the comments made by Strack at Starkville two-and-a-half years earlier. Yet they were of the same piece. The company portrayed itself as a partner with the area, as an actor in a play where all must do their parts. Borden could certainly survive the failure of one or more condenseries. But many small towns and farmers could not. Their economic and familial destinies were tied to that venture. It was in each of these partner's best interests for the partnership to run smoothly and profitably. Borden understood that, and took every opportunity (once it had invested in a community) to let the other partners know that the large northern corporation understood just what was at stake for all parties. But saying it did not make it so, and while it may have been a trope it certainly indicated that the company was well aware of what was on the line for its partners.[42]

As Borden built in Waco—the facility would open in July[43]—Carnation was looking in Texas. In what must have been corporate policy, Carnation followed Borden to Kansas, Mississippi, Tennessee, and now Texas. "Seeking an uncongested district where pasturage will be assured for many years," a place that had "the modern advantages," and one located on a railroad line, Carnation concentrated on southeastern Texas. Their advertising manager proclaimed the company would be "a factor in the dairy development of Texas." While the company was committed to establishing a plant in the region, it recognized that "much work remains . . . in educating farmers to keep better cows, to have adequate pasture and feed and to manage a dairy farm." Schulenburg, midway between Austin and Houston, was the town in which Carnation would erect the condensery, but it did not engage in the classic sort of one-on-one negotiation to select that venue. Carnation went from place to place in southeastern Texas and checked numerous towns in Fayette, Colorado, and Lavaca counties as condensery sites. A handful of towns in the region expressed interest and made pitches for the condensery. Carnation went back to each several times, in hopes of their sweetening the deal. Finally, the group of towns and Carnation created a "steering committee" to help the Wisconsin company decide the matter. Each town had a representative on the committee, and all pledged allegiance to the town that received the condensery. Primarily, the group served as a clearinghouse to ensure that measurements and metrics were standardized among the supplicants. The company announced its choice at a steering committee luncheon in Schulenburg. When told of Carnation's decision, the Schulenburg representative left the meeting to sound the fire alarm, literally. More than 300 citizens and school children rushed into the street to see what the hoopla was about and to engage in "enthusiastic demonstrations."

The terms of the Schulenburg-Carnation agreement were particularistic but not unprecedented. Carnation would pay no city taxes for five years. The town would pave the street leading to the factory, and for a spur of the Southern Pacific railroad to abut the plant. Carnation promised the plant would employ no less than a hundred men. When asked what set Schulenburg apart from its fellow suitors, an officer in the Wisconsin home office pointed to "the friendliness and hearty co-operation of the community and the courtesy and helpfulness of the Chamber of Commerce."[44]

Even before the openings of the Borden and Carnation facilities, Texas cities and small towns clamored for milk, cream, or cheese plants. The stories from the east, especially from Starkville,[45] created a lust for industrial milk manufacture. It was not the consumer product that mattered. It was what the facility and dairying meant to the region—a decline in monoculture, better fertilization, higher profit ratios, increased economic stability. Those economic benefits came with psychic trappings. They reaffirmed the idea of country living as virtuous living. There people almost always received what they earned and therefore deserved. They took pride in their job and they took further pride in doing it well. It provided a sense of well-being and confidence, the confidence that something they had labored their whole life for would not blow away like grass in the wind. Families had been there for generations. Dairying seemed capable of keeping them on that land for several more. The *Austin Statesman* celebrated milk plants in the South generally, but Texas in particular. "From these beginnings will grow a better and happier farm life, a sturdier economic independence." Milk plants were "of importance to every owner of land, every business man, and every citizen."[46]

These notions were not restricted to Mississippi, Tennessee, Texas, and Louisiana. Once the genie was unleashed, it was virtually unstoppable. A broad spectrum of states and people saw dairying as a panacea to the problems that had plagued the region for decades. It not only promised to stop rural decline, it offered to remake southern small towns so that they would surpass their former glory. That northern dairy interests fueled and financed these ventures was far less objectionable to small town southerners than the introduction of cotton mills had been decades earlier. Farmers often proved reluctant to shed the old ways for something that seemed speculative, but small town merchants and leaders rarely had that difficulty. They were not being asked to risk home and hearth in the way middling cotton and tobacco farmers were. Their economic surety depended on dairies as much as farmers but they did not have to retrain, retool, and reinvest. It was a much easier transition.

In this panoply of wants and desires, Starkville stood preeminent. It had accomplished the impossible, thereby rendering the impossible possible. It was first, which in the history of a developing world meant it was foremost, the progenitor of the rest. Any aspect of its story could be chosen to justify change. It simply depended upon what changes those who employed it wanted to make. The *Daily Oklahoman*, for example, found two lessons from Starkville. Its story encouraged every county to consider "latent and undiscovered possibilities." It also showed that "time and patience are required to develop prosperity." In North Carolina, Governor Angus McLean looked at "the Starkville miracle" and used it to push dairying in North Carolina. Taking the dubious philosophical position that east Carolina land was as good as any land in the South, he argued therefore that "dairy herds can be made as profitable in this state as in Mississippi." He then cited a litany of Starkville paydays to demonstrate what his constituencies were missing. South Carolina also noted Starkville's "great success" and called on its fellow citizens to participate in the "great future of dairy farming by working with northern firms to create condenseries in the state. Starkville was also on Georgia's mind. The *Atlanta Constitution* attended the opening of the Starkville plant. It predicted that "many new plants will be placed by [Borden] and other large concerns in different sections of the South." "As a consequence of the marked success of this plant," dairying "is expected to become an even more important factor in the South's development." To the *Constitution*, Starkville's condensery was analogous to the coming of the textile industry decades earlier. It made the South "the great textile section of the world." It was "inevitable" that Starkville would provide "tremendous impetus."[47]

Arkansas, which had thousands of citizens visiting Starkville, underwent a statewide campaign to make its farmers "dairy-minded." Discussion of this campaign, it was reported in the *Arkansas Gazette,* "comes at once to Starkville, that town of 5,000 . . . which always gets into the conversation when southern dairying is discussed." It was "the most celebrated dairying center in the South, and held up as a model for other communities." Starkvillians, the paper continued, "are thinking of dairying, talking of dairying, and practicing dairying." Such was the case among "large as well as small landowners, independent Negro farmers, and share-crop tenants." After the recitation of the various figures from payday, the *Gazette* called on "counties in Arkansas" to "follow the example of Oktibbeha County." Visitation was essential. No place in the entire South better demonstrated dairying's virtues than Starkville, argued J. W. Sargent, the county agent for Pulaski, Arkansas. People "see with their own eyes how dairy cattle have re-made a whole county, and talk with farmers, business men, bankers, and farm technicians who have worked together to bring about the change." If Arkansans could not make it to Starkville, then Starkville came to them. To recount the Starkville miracle, the Southern Arkansas Chamber of Commerce convention brought in W. H. Sudduth to serve as "headliner." He told his tale and the group maintained that if it followed the Starkville template its constituent communities would "blossom like the Roses of Sharon." The *Clarion-Ledger* reported on the response to a Starkville payday by a particularly large group of Arkansas and Louisiana travelers. In a phrase that evoked Caesar, it wrote "still they come, they see, and they are convinced."[48]

9 | THE NEW STATUS QUO
Starkville at the Crossroads and Small-Town Modernity

In 1906 Chicago hosted the first National Dairy Exposition. Dairymen, creamery operators, and cheesemakers gathered to talk cows and their products. For the next twenty-one years, the association met yearly, always in the North. Memphis and Atlanta both made concerted efforts to get the meeting in the South, presumably to their cities. In 1927 Memphis finally received "the honor of entertaining the convention, probably . . . on account of the rapid dairy development" in Starkville and Tupelo. The South has "wonderful opportunities for dairy development," observed S. H. Anderson, secretary and general manager of the sponsoring organization and a Chicago resident. All "hard-headed business men of all sections look to the South for the future development of the nation."[1]

The South had arrived. Its rapid development in the wake of Borden's Starkville condensery and the nationwide recounting of the Starkville miracle story raised the South's dairy status far beyond what it had merited in early 1927. Editor Cobb said it best several months later: "There are few communities in the United States that do not know about the development of Starkville." In the South, "the prosperity growing out of dairying and prevailing in the Starkville section" has caused unprecedented excitement for the dairy industry. Because of the example of Starkville and the elation accompanying the founding of condenseries in Tupelo and throughout Tennessee, the South was on the verge of developing a major new industrial sector. Dairying had made exciting progress and possessed almost inconceivable possibilities. That the southern dairy industry had not achieved its final form did not stop the recognition and accolades that were heaped upon the region. Placing the National Dairy Exposition in Memphis was of "great service" to the South, a tremendous indication of future success and a powerful opportunity to move one step closer to becoming a preeminent dairying section.[2]

The South as a region understood the good fortune that a national dairy show in Memphis offered. In most things the South's economy lagged behind the nation. Cotton, once its most successful economic sector, had become plagued by foreign competitors and was less vital each year. Calls to abandon cotton farming or at least to diversify southern agriculture did not go unheeded, but the proposals that accompanied them seemed unable to restore the South's luster. Dairying did not hold the stigma or problems that cotton did. Milk was a renewable resource. Dairying was generally not susceptible to climatic changes. In the South, it did not need the heavy insulated buildings so closely associated with northern dairying. Pasture was abundant and fodder crops simply took planning and care.

What was happening in Mississippi and about to happen in Tennessee promised to establish the dairy as a prominent characteristic of southern agriculture. In a world attuned to marketing and advertising, where demand could be constructed and then expanded, the several dairying states of the South opted to pursue the National Dairy Exposition collectively. To highlight the ascendancy of their section, they chose to argue for the South's rise rather than for individual states of the South, and put together a huge exhibit in which each of fourteen southern states shared. Dairy specialists from each state's agricultural college designed this showcase, titled "Dairying in Dixieland." It featured discussions of how to conduct a dairy, and the natural advantages of southern dairying. A large electric map of Dixie lit up the appropriate state whenever consideration turned to that state. A talking cow, a full-sized mechanical Jersey, told the facts about her breed and explained her manifold virtues if treated appropriately during her lifetime.[3]

Each state had its own exhibit in addition to the collective showcase. Starkville went further. With six contiguous counties with soil conditions similar to that of Oktibbeha, it formed the Prairie Lime Belt Association. The organization encompassed Macon, Tupelo, and Columbus among other cities and had but one purpose: to design a single exhibit at the national dairy show with one message in the literature puffing the region's dairy proficiency and possibilities. The Starkville Chamber of Commerce's previous success with its advertising pamphlets inspired the new group to adopt the same approach. It also enlisted the aid of the three major railroads that served the seven counties—the Illinois Central, the Frisco Railway, and the Mobile & Ohio—to advertise the area as a dairyland and to help disseminate the material. As it prepared for the meeting, the new association's members agreed to advertise the lime belt, rather than a single county. Within that general framework, each county provided the material it wanted to emphasize. Together, these seven contributions were bound as one document to be distributed at the convention. Extras—if any—would be used by the railroads to further the area's prospects.[4]

The group had initially printed 20,000 copies of this two-color, twelve-page document, but anticipated subsequent printings. Each county retained the right to press its own case either in the state exhibit or in an individual booth at the fair. Starkville, of course, seized that opportunity. It put together an Oktibbeha County–specific document and brought 5,000 copies to the convention. Its Chamber also wanted to make the county's mark at the meeting in another way. Maintaining that placing the meeting south of the Mason Dixon line was "a distinct compliment to the South, and an admission on the part of the dairy industry that the South is the coming dairy center of the world," the Starkville Chamber campaigned to have at least 500 and perhaps as many as a thousand Oktibbehans attend the Memphis meeting. It hoped to have more from that county at the gathering than persons from any other single destination. The visibility that these Mississippi dairymen would bring to Oktibbeha through their convention attendance ensured that Starkville and its feats would be impossible to ignore. Among the Starkville Chamber's techniques to generate excitement for the gathering was a highly advertised contest to distribute nine free trips to the fair. It wanted winners (and the county's contingent) to truly represent Starkville dairying so the Chamber, with financial assistance from Borden and the college, distributed the awards according to a discrete formula that would appropriately represent Oktibbeha County. Four trips went to white farmers, three to Black dairymen, and two to milk truck drivers.[5]

Over 275,000 people attended the Memphis meeting, the largest turnout ever for a National Dairy Exposition. Thirty thousand of those people were Mississippians. From coast to coast, participants saw American dairying. They had known about Wisconsin and Washington. They learned about the South and Mississippi. In fact, Mississippi Day—Wednesday—had the largest single-day attendance. The Exposition proved so expansive and the response so overwhelming that the group in charge voted to return to Memphis for its annual meeting the next year.[6]

In a handful of years, the South had become a significant factor in the American dairy industry. Many farmers understood the basics of dairying—purebred animals, culling the worst milkers from the herd, forage crops, pasture grasses, tick eradication, haying, and the like. They had been subjected to an unprecedented assault as the region's leading lights and others had labored to diversify cotton and tobacco monoculture and therefore set southern agriculture on a less insecure footing. Few anticipated the profound change that accompanied the northern invasion of dairy capital. What had promised to mitigate the woeful peaks and valleys single crop market farming now seemed to yield what had been inconceivable riches just a few years earlier. Borden and Starkville were at the epicenter of that event. Together they smashed barriers thought to inhibit dairy agriculture in the region. Their impact was so dramatic that by the late 1920s, there was a shortage of purebred dairy cattle in the United States, and the Wisconsin dairy industry began to teeter. Its output was smaller during the last years of the decade than it had been a few scant years earlier. Dairy cattle had begun to move southward.

Would the South truly become America's dairyland? It was hard to guess in 1929. As southerner after southerner noted, the South had ecological advantages over the North and the Midwest. Mild southern winters and long spring and fall seasons meant pasturing could function as a dairy cattle food sources for at least nine months of the year. The absence of severe winters reduced the cost of barns and other shelters, so pricey in the North.

The new corporate policy of decentralization argued against true southern dominance. Corporations located milk plants to reduce transportation, storage, and other costs, such as labor, strikes, the high cost of power, and the like. Having a condensery in Tupelo ship its milk to New York City did not make significantly more sense that having a New York City condensery ship it to Tupelo. The entire centralization ethos of the late nineteenth and early twentieth centuries unraveled when marketing and distribution joined the calculus. Economies of scale produced their own waste when finished products required transportation to areas near where similar products could be manufactured. In an article about Borden's Starkville condensery, Herbert W. Collingwood noticed that "modern business" has

LAND OF MILK AND MONEY

changed in the past few years. The old plan "was to concentrate in some particular locality or section, manufacture on a large scale, and ship the finished product" for distribution. The new plan, he argued, followed what he saw as biological laws. "Large manufacturing enterprises apparently reach full size, and after that grow by establishing branches in various parts of the country." That often permitted corporations to lower production costs because land and raw materials were often cheaper outside of major metropolitan areas. Plus, this usually tended to reduce shipping and delivery costs. Despite the concrete expansion of American dairying to include the South, the bugaboo that had afflicted America after World War I—collapse of the export market—mattered little. The dramatic advertising and health campaigns of Borden and other milk product manufacturers—as well as by city, state and federal governments—coupled with increasing urban populations, created a surging domestic market that American-produced milk could not satisfy as late as 1929. America had become a milk-importing nation.[7]

Collingwood's decentralization postulates found expression in the Borden Co. corporate strategy in the last half of the 1920s. Maintaining its corporate headquarters in New York City and continuing its fluid milk delivery business in that city, Borden branched out to seed condenseries in the West and Canada, where it long had a presence. It also moved full bore to create condenseries in the South. Borden's corporate strategy did not rest only with Collingwood's parameters, however. It was far more aggressive and more dynastic. It already led the nation, and perhaps the world, in fluid milk delivery and in condensed milk manufacturing. As a modern corporation, its officers understood it was not a milk company per se but a profit company. Whatever would enable the company to manufacture high, stable profits was what the company made. Cornering the condensery market and taking over fluid milk deliveries in more and more cities had inevitable flaws. Governments might pass unfavorable legislation to regulate the milk trade, or farmer resistance to company-determined prices could restrict the milk supply. Federal antitrust action might be triggered if regulators determined that Borden had a far too great footprint in the industry. Just as significant, Borden was reaching unprofitable or less profitable limits in each endeavor. Shipping fluid milk further and further from its source to deliver it daily had led Borden to terminate condenseries in the New York and Chicago milksheds as noncompetitive with its fluid milk trade.

Condensed milk would eventually saturate the market, although that did not appear likely any time soon. In any case, condensed milk, evaporated milk, and powdered milk were just plain limited. A modern corporation appreciated the stability of the two trades and their profitability. Borden managers saw more. Already they had a creative team writing copy that helped expand fluid and condensed milk consumption in the United States. Its market research arm was the company's sales force. It was necessarily embedded in communities to consciously pursue consumer input. They relayed consumer concerns and thoughts to the main office where they became advertisements and revamped manufacturing processes. New York took advantage of its already widely disseminated sales force when it embarked on it largest and most significant new initiative. It stood poised to market an expanded product line.

What it meant to expand a product line and how that might be conceived was the heart of the advertising strategy that Borden's Stuart Peabody outlined for the company's 1927 campaign—just before Borden inaugurated its mania for mergers and acquisitions. Borden enhanced demand and saved on advertising by creating brand identification and then cross-advertising. The company chose to inaugurate five separate ad campaigns for its product line—condensed milk for coffee, condensed milk for cooking, Eagle Brand for infant feeding, an evaporated milk campaign, and a malted milk campaign. Peabody justified the utility of five campaigns this way: The purpose of five separate campaigns was to show consumers that Borden was "the only company offering an assortment of milk products sufficient for every need. . . . The woman who is sold on Eagle Brand, for instance, is in a receptive mood towards other Borden products." All one needed to do was "tell her about evaporated milk, and malted milk, and their special uses and chances are she'll stock up with the complete line." That means, he added concisely, "three sales and three profits where one grew before!"[8]

Borden was risk averse. Creating new products and seeing if they would meet public expectation—was the taste right, was the price point too high, was the container appealing—was time-consuming and expensive. Worse, it could fail. Money and time would be wasted and profits missed. Borden acted to avoid that morass. It opted to add new product lines not by starting from scratch but by acquiring and merging with many smaller, local companies that already produced and marketed the products that Borden now chose to invest in.

Starting slowly in about 1925 and accelerating in 1927, Borden gobbled up hundreds of companies involved in fluid milk– or condensed milk–adjacent products. That they were adjacent was critical. Brand identification and cross-advertising within the same general food area reduced advertising expenses while boosting advertising efficiency. That practice enabled Borden to stick to what they knew while at the same time fattening the corporation's bottom line. Among the product lines they acquired, several were quite substantial. Some purchases involved patented processes or trademarked goods. The purchase of Walker-Gordon Laboratories gave Borden the rights to acidophilus and other cultured milks. In other instances, the company gained patents for loaf cheese and a myriad of ice cream confections. It even entered the milk-dependent chemical field when it purchased the company that had patented a casein-based, water-soluble adhesive. Borden acquisitions and mergers involved securing new product lines, buying processes that could produce new product lines, eliminating competitors to new product lines, or acquiring established facilities to improve industrial capacity—all to produce the products that had long been produced in those facilities. Rather than necessarily build a functioning plant from the beginning, Borden simply adapted the standing factory to its similar purpose. Arthur W. Milburn, President of Borden Co., explained the corporation's acquisitions/mergers principles this way: Every company Borden had acquired has been "in the interest of an improvement of existing business; entrance into new territory having marked potentialities; or a further product diversification, all within the dairy industry." The company did more than determine whether the product fit within the scope of those statements, however. It evaluated each target for its "efficient and high class management as well as recognition of the pronounced potentialities in each business." Because of the metric by which it chose companies to absorb and because excellence in management was dear, Borden favored having "individuals largely responsible for the development of these businesses, together with their respective efficient staffs," be retained to "actively" oversee subsequent growth. Retention of these "men of character and ability," Milburn continued, "will bring much needed strength to the Borden organization."[9]

The *Wall Street Journal* wholeheartedly endorsed the Borden philosophy. "Geographical and product diversification, together with the character of its general businesses," the *Journal* wrote, "combine to make Borden a well-integrated organization practically exempt from the ups and downs of ordinary business cycles." To risk-averse Borden, that must have been music to its ears. As an example of how that worked in the company's favor, the *Journal* focused on milk and ice cream. "Borden's business, especially its fresh milk department, is seasonal, with peak demand in the winter," it noted. "Ice cream companies do their largest business in the summer when Borden has excess supplies. As a consolidated company, [they] should be able to do a larger gross business without increasing plant investment. Consolidation would also permit savings in overhead, insurance, personnel, and purchasing costs." That policy improved Borden bottom line significantly. Percentage of profitability on sales soared by 20 percent in a three-year period. At the same time Borden became one of the largest corporations in the United States. In 1926, its sales registered about $125 million yearly. By 1929 that figure had become $328 million.[10]

Borden absorbed these companies primarily through stock swaps. It used some of the cash the corporation had on hand—and it had a significant amount—to retire bonds and preferred stock the companies had issued prior to merger. If it incurred debt, it removed it as soon as possible. Significant funds on hand enabled the company to build new condenseries in the South to dominant that area, while at the same time gobbling up manufactories and companies throughout America. Cheese plants in Columbus, Mississippi, became a Borden acquisition, placing the company in a dominant position in northeast Mississippi comparable to its central Tennessee properties. The company even started an extension division to assist milkshed dairymen to reduce costs and increase output.[11] While it had a tight, integrated corporate strategy that favored decentralization as well as a closely knit association among manufacturing, sales, consumer research, and advertising, Borden operations were less important in that regard than what they fostered. Creating the Borden plant in Starkville and the various plants in Tennessee (and even Kansas earlier) led others to ride on its coattails and to create numerous milk manipulating plants in literally hundreds of small towns and cities in areas where there had been no such meaningful facilities before. Borden inspired many times more milk plants in small towns than it ever built.

In almost every case, outside capital, usually from the north, paid for all or part of these facilities. In rural America, however, the entrance of large corporations was a complicated lot, which scholars sometimes cast collectively as decentralization. But decentralization meant different things to different groups. Movement of much of the steel industry from Michigan to Birmingham decentralized steel manufacture but it also spawned industries in Alabama that fed off that industry.[12] In the later 1920s, New England shoe factories went west and textile mills south. The Atlantic region's towns despaired at the movement. Places like Toledo and Muncie were devastated by the specter of decentralization. Their Chambers of Commerce bemoaned that industries chose factory sites "without sentiment" and "opened plants throughout the country in order to be near sales centers." As far as they were concerned, as factory after factory left those two cities, "the decentralization of industry" was "an ill wind that blows nobody good."[13]

The general analysis of 1920s decentralization favors industrial and corporate perspectives. To carry this approach further, the rhetoric has corporations "targeting" new, distant places. They were making choices of industrial design and profitability.[14] Small towns, especially small towns in the South and Midwest, had very different stakes. The stakes were immediate and dire. Their very survival frequently depended upon supplementing or stabilizing their inhabitants' incomes through commerce or industry. Rarely could they rely on direct proceeds from the agriculture they had been practicing. For those whose industry was monocultural agriculture, economies gyrated wildly. Diversification mitigated those perturbations but they did little to smooth over the violence done by insect pests, funguses, floods, or droughts. The normal condition for most small towns and cities was to linger on the edge of an economic precipice, facing abandonment in the wake of cataclysmic events or even long-term economic dislocation or depression. That was equally true for the clearcutting lumbering communities of northern Wisconsin, which craved the dollars that hardwoods brought, or the farmers of Enterprise, Alabama, who made the boll weevil a virtual native son because of their insistence that its devastation caused them to find a more stable future. In a few cases, relocation of large industries to rural areas was a benison to farmers and the small towns served by them. New plants were new markets that came to them; the locals served these new ambitious ventures and the people that accompanied them.[15]

That was a drop in the bucket. Almost all rural places had to find a different course. State government or agencies sometimes helped as did land-grant and other schools. Being a county seat offered some stability as the functions of government took place there. Railroads were especially active in offering opportunity but almost always near towns and cities served by their lines. Rural places generally had low overhead costs so that rarely served to discriminate among them. A good portion also paved roads and made deals for electric power to charm industrial suitors. Serendipity and whimsy saved some places but the vast number of small towns and cities were left to their own devices.[16]

Chambers of commerce and other businessmen's groups often worked to secure their and the areas' future. They— not the democratically elected local government—served as the economic engine for their places. The locus of action was rarely contiguous with the boundaries of a rural municipality. Things frequently depended on the surrounding countryside and the people residing there. How aggressively these businessmen's collectives pursued opportunity mattered. Fortuna did also. The single characteristic that marked all these business groups, however, was desperation. Places were pitted against one another as each advertised their availability and desirability, through newspaper ads, glossy brochures, and unsolicited letters to corporations. Sometimes the greatest bribe won the day. In fairness, bribes—in the form of roads, tax breaks, and land—often helped a venture succeed. These business communities' anguished concern regularly led them to try each and every opportunity, no matter how outlandish, in the hope of landing any single one. Their anxiety resulted in promises they could not hope to deliver, promises so far afield from a small town or city's strengths and advantages, that such an economic marriage was imperiled from the start. This scattershot approach had yet another consequence. It tied the place to the corporation or capitalist that first positively responded—if any did so—and then to a destiny that depended on the economic engine that it had reeled in. Systematic planning—targeting just one possible savior or field of endeavor—was infrequently attempted.[17] Seizing the moment, learning from the success of another community, most frequently was the course that these small towns and cities took. In that sense, imitation was the sincerest form of small town economic development.

Such was the case with Starkville. It was both the narrative and the visual of paydays marked by joyous men with money seemingly to burn that proved so relentlessly compelling. It was why, within a three- or four-year period, tens of thousands of visitors came to see with their own eyes what salvation looked like. Starkville's residents certainly played into that. The town stood front and center. Rather than hide or disguise the parameters that enabled it to become legendary, even apocryphal, Starkville's citizenry welcomed strangers and even put together special itineraries for each group. It was a most extraordinary thing. The town's elite functioned as tour guides and docents. They also whipped up special talks at a moment's notice. But it was not just the elite that participated in this constant barrage of visitors. It was the prosperous and not so prosperous farmers, tenant farmers, and sharecroppers—both Black and white—plus bankers, lawyers, merchants, and Borden officials operating and supervising the condensery. Often the agricultural college was part of the mix as were the county agents and various professors. Moore, from the college dairy division and creamery, and Sudduth, president of one bank and vice-president of another, and owner of one of the largest dairy combinations in the county, were on almost every visitor's agenda.

Large gatherings almost always stayed at individual Starkvillians homes. The Chester had only about forty rooms and those filled rather quickly. The Chamber secretary, H. O. Jones, a longtime dairyman, called for more hotels in town. There were four restaurants to choose from, not enough when an average payday brought county dairymen and at least 500 visitors to the town. Merchants expanded their lines and kept more stock on hand to satiate the groups that arrived with money to spend.

Many group visits to Starkville began when the Chamber of Commerce of the prospective place wrote to schedule a trip. Whoever received the letter passed it on to Jones, who responded for the Chamber. That organization's letterhead stationary had all of the following slogans embossed at the top: "Oktibbeha County, the Dairy Center of the South"; "Southern Pioneers in Dairying and Condensing"; "Home of the Borden Southern, the First Milk Condensery in the South"; and "Starkville, the Dairy Capital of the Mid-South." In the small space left for writing, Jones welcomed the inquiry by telling the group that Starkville has had many visitors from that state or area in the past. After that grace note, Jones asked the letter writer to please provide more details of what they hoped to learn at Starkville so "that they might see for themselves." He asked this question so he could fashion a schedule to help visitors get their "time and money learning many phases of dairying and dairy manufacturing" while in Starkville. He told the letter writer that the Chamber "will be glad to furnish gratis, guides and well-informed college professors, dairymen, and businessmen to give lectures" and otherwise engage the visitors.[18]

The highly solicitous nature of the Starkville response suggested that Starkville saw economic benefits to the steady stream of visitors cascading through the city. Hotels and boarding houses, restaurants, and merchants all benefited. Stores and restaurants remained open well into the night. The Chamber proudly recognized that "Oktibbeha has certainly received more publicity than almost any county in the South." While some might call it "free publicity," Jones vehemently disagreed. It "represents talent, system, diligent study, and hard work." Why should not Oktibbeha garner "a great amount of publicity?" What Starkville and Borden had done was monumental, "worthy of countrywide discourses." Starting in 1926 the Chamber, Jones confessed, contemplated how it might employ its remarkable union with Borden to get more people to reside in Oktibbeha County. It decided that goal could best be achieved "through visiting delegations, and especially delegations interested in dairying." Starkville worked hard to tell people about Borden, its condensery, and Oktibbeha County. "Today we see wonderful results from our efforts." He noted that "many throngs have visited here—some individuals as many as two, three, and four times in a single year." Each time they "learned something of Oktibbeha, her plants, schools, soils, cows, and about other opportunities." One consequence was a thriving dairy cattle trade. "We have choice cows for sale by the thousands." That "had been universally broadcasted." It resulted in a constant significant stream of sales, even "to our fartherest [*sic*] away states."

Jones acknowledged that Starkville received kudos for its policy of promoting its dairying success and welcoming visitors into its midst. F. A. Callis, who ran a Kentucky advertising agency, found Starkville's public relations campaign "surpasses any one in efficiency that he had ever seen." Another commentator claimed that "Oktibbeha has received more publicity in the daily press and scientific journals" than it could have "purchased through an advertising agency for the combined capital of the three banks of Starkville." The Chamber was about to add to its program. As the three-year anniversary of the dedication of the Borden condensery approached, the Chamber decided to recount the miraculous story of Starkville and Borden and to document the transformative events and occurrences that had taken place in three scant years.[19]

To the Chamber, immigration was publicity's most critical and most tangible benefit. Believing that seeing was believing, Starkville hoped that its willingness to have visitors flood the area would bring upstanding citizens into the county to dairy farm and into the city to help further its development. That most of the letters came from businessmen's organizations and that most of the guests were businessmen or farmers indicated that the visitors had the passion, the experience and even the capital to fit seamlessly into the fabric of Starkville life. Having them witness the luster and opportunity of Starkville, the Chamber thought, would prove an almost irresistible lure.

And then there was payday. Guests marveled "at the smiling countenances of the farmers as they return to their homes with a good big wad [of cash] struck down their jeans." One visitors' group went to each of the city's three banks to watch what occurred after dairymen received their checks. The voyage down the streets between banks proved problematic as "the crowd of white and black dairymen at times were so dense that it took a few minutes to wedge [the tourists] through." Each Starkville bank employed additional tellers to dispense cash after deposits. Observers noted that the cashiers operated at the speed "equal to an adding machine." Notes were paid off and mortgages lifted. In almost every case, farmers deposited at least a portion of the milk money. As a Starkvillian noted, payday was "an amazing sight" to guests. They always "gazed in awe" at the joyous celebration of the fruits of dairying.[20]

Oktibbeha County wanted immigrants but payday overwhelmingly worked to reaffirm the reason the Chambers and other groups throughout the South chose to visit Starkville. It convinced many small towns to seek a milk plant. Craddock Goins, publicity director of the Mississippi State Board of Development, summed up why towns wanted dairy facilities. These institutions mean "the difference between failure and successful farming; between rundown roads and good roads, poor schools and good schools, prosperous towns and one-horse towns."[21] Starkville's payday signified precisely what the visitors hoped, a freedom from want, a prosperity that seemed continual, and an appreciation of the style of life they held dear. By and large, small towns and their business communities wanted small town rural life, albeit with the amenities, conveniences, and stability that their children often sought in big cities. There were two distinct issues. There was town survival and there was town thriving. The Starkville miracle embodied both.

The opening of the Borden condensery solidified Starkville's financial future. How did Starkville and Oktibbeha County seek to take advantage of that blessing? How did they capitalize on a situation that was relatively rare in the late 1920s and into 1930? What did they deem critical? In the process of sorting through this unusual condition, Starkvillians worked out for themselves what characterized successful small-town southern life. In that sense, Starkville was symptomatic of how rural small-town men and women negotiated what they desired their towns to be. What institutions did they choose to build? What did they consider essential? What would they not do? How did economic security play out in real time, in a real place, with real people?

From reports of payday, Starkville's success showed on the faces of its dairymen. Group after group of visitors pointed to the boundlessness that the county's farm men and women expressed simply on their faces and then with how they divvied up their paychecks. For those with loans, some went to the bank, some went to pay bills, and some usually went to savings. What about Starkville per se? With the final announcement that Borden had decided on the city came a swift investment in many institutions— grander houses of worship, a community hospital, a magnificent hotel, a new school building, and a vegetable canning plant. Other things mentioned were a public library, a complete system of schools, a community pool, and more paved roads.

Those were spur-of-the-moment thoughts. One thing that Starkville could not shake—nor did it want to—was its fame. It was a place with an identity, a place people knew. When a Starkville Chamber committee took an August 1928 trip to Huntsville to inspect cotton mills there, the *New York Daily News* and the major papers from Memphis, Jackson, and New Orleans all covered the story. Chamber secretary Jones considered it "interesting publicity" as numerous textile companies wrote to learn if the county was interested in becoming a mill site. The *Manufacturers Record*—the Baltimore-based weekly touting the newest industrial, railroad, and financial undertakings in the South—asked the Starkville Chamber to regularly keep it apprised of what it had just undertaken or was about to undertake.[22]

No doubt the idea of the preeminent dairyland of the South investigating an industrial pursuit seemed ironic to some, but two things factored into the Chamber's thinking. First, it realized that only a percentage of the community engaged in dairying or felt the immediate effects of dairying. Second, years of uncertainly with cotton monoculture had led the Chamber to understand that a many-sided economic engine was preferable to a single-source economy. They wanted Starkvillians to earn paychecks from more places than the condensery and creamery. Failure of the vegetable cannery compounded the concern. It was reorganized at a trustee's sale one short year after its founding. None of the original principals continued in the corporation, which now accepted selling canned products of others on consignment. Within a year the machinery of this revamped factory was sold at auction and the factory closed.[23]

Even as it considered how to broaden the county's economic base, the Chamber devoted most attention to Oktibbeha farmers. It tried to maximize each farm's productivity as a means of increasing money within the area. The Chamber always remembered that the city of Starkville first and foremost depended on its farmers for its success. Some effort went towards the significant but seasonal turkey trade, and there were a few attempts to start a hen and egg industry, but overwhelmingly it was dairy farmers who garnered the bulk of the Chamber's attention. A surprising number of dairies operated within city limits. On just one half-mile stretch of a city road, seven separate families kept herds of between five and thirty dairy cows. Article after article in the newspaper reminded dairymen and women how best to maintain and expand their operations. Some highlighted cow testing to enable farmers to cull low producers from their herds. Foremost among these advisories was the notion that provision of feed for dairy cows was not a haphazard act but took careful planning and that careful planning, coupled with most modern practice, could wring additional profit from dairy herds. The Chamber had an additional stipulation. It adamantly opposed purchasing feed for dairy animals. Nothing destroyed profits from the dairy trade more than spending considerable funds to feed animals through winter. Dairymen needed to grow feed in spring for the dead of winter. Pastures throughout the year required care, mowing, and occasional reseeding. The Chamber knew this simple truth: Maintaining the profitability of dairying was the surest way to maintain the milk supply for the condensery and creamery and to keep them operating at full throttle. It was the most important single practice to keep payday joyous and merchants happy. Borden, with its veterinarians sprinkled throughout the United States, weighed in as a good partner should. It pressed for Oktibbeha farmers to raise the relatively new crop, soybeans, to winter their cows. High in digestible fiber, soybeans provided cows with the protein necessary to produce milk and grow properly.[24]

Both the Chamber and the college abhorred the idea that dairy farmers would purchase feed. That reduced dairy profit margins but it also sent money out of Mississippi. Both were antithetical to the notion of a well-regulated enterprise. The situation was far more egregious than it initially appeared. Dairymen routinely sold off their male animals and a certain proportion of their female animals as either breeding stock or for meat. These animals too needed to eat in the winter until marketed. Even then the amount of return depended on the weight of the animal, and well fed animals weighed more. Reminding their compatriots that "the Lord helps those who help themselves," the Chamber urged them to "Plan as well as pray—It takes more labor to kill grass than to make more hay." Pithy statements like "Full barns this year help lots," "Plant food crops enuf so there'll be plenty, if it's too dry," and "Sow your pasture land with future fertilizer free," each addressed the Chamber's worries about county farmers in an approachable way. One tagline used by the Chamber summed up the ultimate goal of these country-flavored aphorisms—"One of the Greatest Prizes in Life is INDEPENDENCE." Growing one's own animal feed made that objective one step closer.[25]

As a fairly well-to-do place, Starkvillians demanded that the city proper become well appointed. A building boom included not only the new hospital, which soon was expanded, but also a "great white way." The rationale was simple. "Many of the progressive towns in this section have installed white ways and . . . Starkville should not fall behind in so an important a civic matter." Running for about a mile and a half from the college entrance to downtown Starkville and ending at the new hilltop Methodist Church, the highly illuminated thoroughfare would physically join the city and the college, symbolizing the closer connection between these two entities after the condensery's opening. Yelling "Forward for Starkville" and "Come and join us," the city's mayor pushed for modernizing—paving—other roads and having homeowners tap into the new sewer system as he had city hall renovated.[26]

The long-sought public library came to fruition. Women's groups argued that a public library was akin to a public school and ought to be financed through taxes, rather than subscriptions or beneficence. Mrs. M. J. Smith, affectionately known as Borden Smith because her husband superintended the condensery, led the charge. Whitman Davis, the librarian at the agricultural college and chair of the Chamber's civic affairs committee, extended the justification for a public facility. "If it is the duty of the State to teach boys and girls to read," he argued, "it is the State's duty to assist these same boys and girls in getting access to books to read after they left school." Noting that only about 25 percent of school children would attend past sixth grade, he urged the county supervisors to appropriate funds to erect a library for the good of all Oktibbehans. Such an act would certainly bolster the county's appeal to potential immigrants. A public library, Davis concluded with hyperbole, would "do more to advertise the county to persons living in the north, east, and west" than any other conceivable project.[27]

Immediately following the library's creation according to Davis's terms, the Carnegie Foundation for Peace began to send the library books. It soon had enough reading material to inaugurate its first program, a story hour for children. It proved a great success. A new institution, the Community Council, a joint venture of city leaders and agricultural college professors interested in civic well-being, reached out to young boys and young girls. Its board of directors included representatives of the Chamber, Lion's Club, Rotary, American Legion, and the Ministerial Union of Starkville. Two representatives of the Parent Teacher Association and the Mayor of Starkville filled out the last three posts. The college had no standing on the board, probably because the organization's charge was children far younger than college age. The Community Council established a chapter of the Boy Scouts of America and of the Girls Reserves, a program of the Young Women's Christian Association that featured religious messages, good works, singing, and poetry. The council also supervised "Play-ground Activities" for younger children as it sought to foster structure and responsibility for all Starkville youth.[28]

An assortment of modern conveniences and entertainments came Starkville's way. Its November 1927 opening of a Piggly Wiggly, a self-serve grocery store with prices marked on the items and cashier-staffed checkout aisles, drew a crowd of over 3,000 people. The "Pig" was joined by a Jitney Jungle a few months later. The Jungle's policy of not offering credit for groceries eliminated carrying bad debt and enabled it to charge prices lower than its competitor. An ice cream manufacturing plant settled in Starkville as it capitalized on the extensive dairying that marked the county. A furniture store purchased an ambulance and donated it to the city. The Hotel Chester was consistently booked. For a two week span it averaged a waiting list of nearly 30 people per night. Starkville reduced the hotel room shortage when a new, modest twenty-room hotel opened, but it did not stop the plea for further hotel space. Starkville was a destination. It needed the rooms. A series of small cafes opened and did a brisk business. To further provide Starkville with the trappings of modern civilization, city aldermen let out a contract to deliver natural gas to the city via pipeline. A series of circuses included Starkville on their tours. The Rex, the town's movie theater, began to show talkies. "His Captive Woman" was its first offering. Education also got its due. In 1928 the city's schools received the prestigious Grade A-1 designation, the highest honor offered by the Southern Association of Colleges and Secondary Schools. Not coincidentally, 42 out of 45 graduates of Starkville High School attended college that fall.[29]

The Chamber backed a citizen-proposed measure to open an airport in Starkville, to train A&M students in all matters of aviation. The plan fell apart when Charles Lindbergh, fresh from his solo trip to Europe, would not reschedule his tour to christen the new Starkville facility. Even though the airport scheme fell through, Starkville remained an attractive business proposition. A large general contracting firm established itself in town. No longer would Starkville need to rely on general construction firms from Memphis and other major cities. As another inducement to build large facilities in Starkville, a major Jackson-based building and loan operation set up an office. A consortium of large banks to handle the financing of large projects, Jackson was betting that Starkville's anticipated expansion would soon be seeking that assistance.[30]

The *Commercial Dispatch* gushed at Starkville/Oktibbeha's transformation. It saw "better farms and luxuries that were not enjoyed before are possible now." That was not the most impressive facet of the changed town and county. "Best of all, the standard of living has been raised." If that were not enough, Starkville now had "better schools and churches." "Every day, in dairy way," the *Dispatch* concluded in a piece of doggerel—the town and county "are getting butter and butter."[31]

Starkville concentrated on furnishing its citizens with services and amenities that were coming to define modern life. In that sense, the city was unexceptional. Provision of services and amenities reflected what citizens with agency and voice wanted out of life, what they thought was important, what they deemed would bring them and their county acclaim. Certainly these measures and actions were new to small southern towns and cities in the 1920s but not to America generally. Sociologists, psychologists, and others had been writing about rural dissatisfaction for decades; providing rural people the amenities that their urban counterparts treasured became an apparently easy fix. Much of Starkville and Oktibbeha's efforts were of a slightly different piece. The Borden condensery had provided latitude that few small towns had. A substantial segment of the community possessed a dependable income, one free from the usual market forces that characterized many agricultural commodities. Starkville's Chamber and many of its other business organizations understood their good fortune and proved determined to capitalize on it. They sought to take advantage of the relative economic quietude provide by Borden to decide what the future of the county should hold. They seized on the moment to formulate plans for Starkville and Oktibbeha's economic destiny.

It took nearly two years for the Chamber to come to the realization that it held such an awesome power. The Chamber had always catered to emergencies; it acted on whatever matters came before it. In a series of ad hoc moves, it supported building subdivisions to serve the many individuals moving to the city and county; it also welcomed a major new employer, a Coca-Cola bottling company. A Pennsylvania oil exploration firm established a Starkville office and toured the countryside looking for possible targets to drill. Borden kept expanding its plant, which not only produced condensed milk but because of its transit agreement also became a major warehouse for the South.[32]

That had been business as usual. Until early 1927, Starkvillians acted according to the premise that a good town was defined as a good place to live, "a good locale for children, a sturdy defense for the moral influences that govern human living." Graham Golson, editor of the *Starkville News,* wrote about the importance of not losing sight of the great purposes of community life." A "bigger more prosperous Starkville" was desirable but that "ambition for greatness" must be accompanied by "a determination for right living." What "a progressive city requires" was "opportunity for every living soul." A town's impetus to be great came from "with in the breasts of its people, it is consciousness that they have a good town, the ambition to make it better." He argued further that "cooperation spells success." Any town "can grow and prosper if the people who live in it get together, stay together, and work to a common goal."[33]

That consensus began to crack later that year. Increasingly, persons of modest means refused to sanction initiatives that the economic elite decided were essential to furthering Oktibbeha County. The Chamber's commissioning of a survey of raw materials in Oktibbeha County that might be exploited as engines of economic progress was an early indication. Flushed with the success of the condensery, which took advantage of a local natural resource, it tried to apply the same principle to fuel other industries. The Chamber chose to see just what industries the mineral properties of the county might yield. To that end, it contracted with the Mississippi State Chemist, William F. Hand, to undertake a geological/chemical survey of Oktibbeha County. In particular, the Chamber wanted to know about the extent of the limestone croppings in the county and what industries could be sustained by them.[34]

Undertaking a meticulous geological survey was a time-consuming process. It took well over a year. Before the Chamber received the results, it began to fret about the behavior of many dairymen in the area. They failed to strive for bigger, better dairy herds. Rather than continually seek more and better cows, they appeared satisfied with their lot. They had money enough to care for their needs and more. The lives of these farmers had been on the edge prior to the condensery. Within a year or so of its opening, they had devolved into a complacency that set the whole economic calculus of Starkville at risk. Although Oktibbeha dairymen owned more cattle per capita than any other Mississippi county in 1928, their 3.2 cows per farmer were far fewer than Wisconsin's 10 or Minnesota's 7.5.[35] If Oktibbeha were to challenge those places and grow the economy as the Chamber had hoped, it needed to step up its dairying. That was not happening. The amount of money generated by the condensery and creamery each month remained rather constant. Merchants who immigrated to the city looking forward to a fine, dependable payday, now found themselves competing for a share of what was a consistent, not growing, economic pie. Economic stagnation rendered the purchase of dairy feed an anathema. It hurt the dairymen but it also hurt the town. Feed shipped Oktibbeha money elsewhere. It was not put into the local economy where it could be circulated and compounded many times.

The alleged complacency of Starkville's dairymen may have enhanced their joy—after all, they were doing what they wanted when they wanted as they wanted—but it made the revenue generated by agricultural tourism a must. Visitors provided funding for merchants, hoteliers, restaurateurs, and a whole slew of others. While Starkville no longer faced doom, it had not actually achieved the state of economic bliss its advertising presented. The Starkville miracle was indeed miraculous in that it helped save the town from the fate of so many small towns in America—dissolution and abandonment. But miracles only go so far. Prosperity often yielded complacency, which created and exposed tensions in what had seemed a united community during the condensery crusade.

The city government's July 1928 contract for a natural gas pipeline provided Starkville a copious supply of that propellent. Partially subsidized by Mississippi and other southern states, this new energy source, coupled with the city's hydroelectric power lines, highlighted the question of complacency versus development. It granted Starkville options, options it did not have just a few years earlier. It also exposed the tear in the community's fabric. The *Commercial Dispatch* expected the pipeline to "stimulate the industrial progress and development of Starkville and all the communities which it touches." Oktibbeha would now have "a steady and progressive industrial development." That prospect accentuated the very real question of what did "small town America" mean. Was it the survival and the quiescence that had sustained those kinds of places over a century or was it hauling the place into the rat race of the twentieth century, a place marked by modern marvels and means? What served its citizenry and perpetuated the essence its champions so very effusively hailed?

The Chamber knew on which horn of this dilemma it stood. If the dairymen remained complacent, so be it. The Chamber understood that dairymen's intransience should never be permitted to control the county. Aware of the general notion that "no community . . . ever became fully prosperous through agriculture alone," it needed to investigate other means to achieve its modernist ends and to shake what it recognized as citywide lethargy. Declaring that "dependable fuel is one of the greatest assets that a city can have," it noted that ceramics manufacturing had adopted natural gas for most of its processes. Oktibbeha's many clay beds could sustain a ceramics industry for "many hundreds of years." The pipeline made contemplation of that prospect conceivable. Its limestone belts could spawn cement and other industries. "It is now time," the Chamber concluded, to "think of the possibilities offered to new industries" by the natural gas pipeline. The area must decide which new industries are best "and then open our doors for a greater Starkville and Oktibbeha County."[36]

The *News* echoed those sentiments. Starkville was "well supplied with business houses, newspapers, professional men and other business institutions." Critical to the county's well-being were "more payrolls and a brand of salesmanship that will sell our city and county to our home people." "Hard work and clean living will bring prosperity and happiness. Then, and not until then, will prosperity and happiness smile upon us." The *News* was referring to more than simple economic success, of course. Its use of prosperity was meant to include a sense of pride, satisfaction, and joy, not dissimilar to the reports in other newspapers of the rewards expressed on the faces of Oktibbeha dairymen on Borden's payday.[37]

That sense of bliss was purposefully nostalgic. It was a goal, not a means. Starkvillians seventy-five years prior had reputedly achieved that state by owning farms and plantations and living off the land. It was that mawkish sensibility that the Chamber hoped to restore or recreate, through introduction of new modern industries and methods. To those men and women, that is what made small-town life worth living.

Within this tangled milieu, the aforementioned trip to Huntsville proved catalytic. Jones returned impressed, and recognized the city's hydroelectric power as an untapped resource that could add payrolls to the area. He argued that Oktibbeha needed "big manufacturing plants" to foster prosperity, and so conceived of an Oktibbeha County awash with cotton mills. Set outside the city limits, near Sturgis to the west and Sessums to the east, these mills would require extensions of power lines to run machinery. With these lines running through the county, it would be simple to connect the entire county to the grid. Rural residents, he argued, "need power and light on their dairy farms." Such a move would enable the county "to balance our economic conditions." There must be "a commonly recognized interdependence between farm and factory." Starkville and Oktibbeha County could not afford to stand still, to let events from outside the area dictate the direction of the place. The only way to capitalize on Oktibbeha's dairy success was to see it as a road map to the future. The Borden plant demonstrated that "Oktibbeha had showed her capacity to lead." It was not only dairying that the Chamber saw from the Borden plant. It was community action, common cause, the "spirit of co-operation," and "efficiency in team work and leadership." Oktibbeha County needed to identify agreed-upon targets and then go after them with the persistence and patience that won the Borden fight. Borden claimed that it had placed the condensery in Starkville because of the cooperation of its citizens both in the town and in the country. Oktibbehans achieved everything the northern company asked for, and they did so in a way that impressed the New York corporation. Jones wanted a return to that Borden-securing spirit, and that required a new consensus. The area needed to plan objectives. It needed to come together to determine not what it could get but what it wanted to target. Experience had shown that community action carried the day. The Chamber continued to take that as an article of faith and worked to develop a common scheme for its economic future. In this framework, common cause would produce impressive results.[38]

Golson likened the process to an architect building a structure. Visualization of the structure was but the first step. The real danger was in the application of materials. Inappropriate materials caused weakness that could cause the entire physical entity to collapse. He implored his fellow citizens to put aside pettiness and to not do the "little, mean, and sordid thing." We need to remember the "marvelous development of the last decade." The "passing of prejudice and the entry of understanding" reminded him that "all men in a community are there to earn a livelihood." He urged all the people of Oktibbeha County to remember that fact and work together to achieve this goal.[39]

Golson's comments on backbiting aimed directly at the new merchants who had immigrated to the city. With the county population increasing more modestly than the exploding merchant population, competition, rather than cooperation, reigned. Merchants increased stock in hopes of proving more attractive than their competitors. Trade, once the property of one or two friendly rivals, now became cutthroat as each of these suddenly redundant merchants fought for their commercial lives. This new reality alarmed the Rotarians, who decided to dedicate their educational programming for the year to "community building." They did not intend to have the various merchants do more than act professionally with one another, and perhaps discuss ways of ensuring that they could each make a proper living. To the Rotarians, community necessitated the expansion of the pie at which all feasted. Creating new payrolls in Starkville provided the organizational answer. Enticing new, different industries to settle in Oktibbeha County was the means.

That these economic issues threatened the prosperity so hard won with Borden—and then extended by the area's massive public relations campaign—alarmed the Rotarians. It also worried others in the town. To restore those lost virtues, "community" and "community-building" became the new watchwords for Starkville's newspaper as well as for the Chamber and other civic organizations, as they looked backwards to recapture what they remembered as the spirit that gained the condensery. That the entire "progressive" coalition used a similar verbiage ought not to surprise. Starkville's elite had proven themselves and their institutions more than adept at tailoring a message and disseminating it in the fashion they desired. Experts in defining what they wanted and then persuading others to claim it as their own, Starkville's business community encouraged acceptance of their new agenda. It was tried and true, familiar and desirable, even as it was used in a new context as the group moved into new vistas.

Sudduth, who at that point chaired the Rotarians' Public Relations Committee, crystallized the matter when he sponsored a session to discuss the premise "More Stores Versus More Factories." It featured a talk by Raymond Goodman, scion of a family dry goods store, movie theater owner, Rotary charter member, and Peoples Bank director. Goodman maintained that the town had been so adept at puffing itself and attracting newcomers that Starkville now had "a highly competitive market with a great unnecessary duplication of stocks of merchandise," volume enough "to take care of three times the retail trade." Each additional store meant "little to the general welfare" but it increased pressure on all stores of that type to succeed. More factories meant the converse. Each factory brought money into the community. It either converted raw materials into money or handed out pay checks, which would go to support Oktibbeha merchants and the public efforts that so characterized the county. Goodman noted that new factories increased the city's tax rolls, enabling it to pursue an even more aggressive community-building and improvement agenda.[40]

Goodman came down heavily on the side of factories. The Chamber worked two different manufacturing angles. First, it sponsored a more extensive trip to Huntsville to investigate the cotton mill option. Second, it engaged in community-building with its neighboring communities. It invited the leaders of the other significant towns in Oktibbeha County—Maben and Sturgis—to come to Starkville and embark on an Oktibbeha strategy to cement "into a cooperative body of work for the upbuilding and benefit of Oktibbeha County as a whole." Starkville would need the assistance—or at least not the active opposition—of the other county municipalities for either its cotton mill or limestone dreams to come to fruition.

Certainly neither of those sorts of facilities would be built within Starkville city limits. Yet it did not want the other local communities to impinge on its initiatives. The meeting gave Starkville what it sought. The Chamber declared this conclave "the greatest meeting yet held" by the group, the "outcome of which will be far-reaching and of untold benefit to Oktibbeha County." The other Oktibbeha towns assured the Starkville Chamber of their fealty to its efforts. "We are one community, one people and brothers" stressed J. A. McReynolds, president of the Sturgis Chamber of Commerce. To make the county "blossom" only "requires the cooperation of every community in the county." He proclaimed that "a new day has dawned for Oktibbeha County and greater things can be accomplished by cooperating and pulling together." He then described Sturgis as developmentally "the Child" and urged the Starkville Chamber, in the interests of the whole, to take charge of group projects. Walter Sanders, Maben Chamber president, reiterated McReynolds's thoughts. Maben was anxious to cooperate because "only by pulling together the greatest good could be accomplished." He then invoked the precious memory of the condensery. He reminded his colleagues that it took "the cooperation of all the communities of Oktibbeha County to secure the establishment of the great Borden" milk plant. "Had it not been for the spirit of cooperation shown by the people outside the city all efforts would have been in vain." Starkville Chamber president, M. H. Moore, business manager of the nearby agricultural college, updated the others on Starkville's limestone survey and dalliance with Huntsville, and pledged that they could count on Starkville's cooperation. "With all communities in the county pulling together," closed Moore, "great things could be accomplished."

McReynolds unveiled plans to investigate a pulp mill and a cabinet factory, leveraging the heavily wooded areas around Starkville. He also disclosed a survey that found extensive bauxite deposits in the county and wondered what opportunities it might present. McReynolds's revelations seemed to open potential new vistas. They did not seem to encroach upon anything already underway in Oktibbeha County. Golson even argued that they would be a benison to dairying or other farms. More people with paychecks in the area would "create a greater demand for milk and farm products." New factories situated in the county required new and extended electrical lines. That meant the possibility of "light and power on the dairy farms." Electricity "would make the lands of our county more attractive and inviting to homeseekers as well as our own people." Electricity would keep farmers farming and entice town dwellers to adopt the practice.[41]

Shortly after the meeting of Oktibbeha towns, a significant Starkville contingent, with their automobile back panels proclaiming that "We are from Oktibbeha. The County Cows Built," toured the Huntsville area. They met members of the local Chamber, toured cotton mills, and ventured into the countryside. The lesson they learned was surprising. Huntsville had turned its attention to farm-related activity. Its representatives acknowledged that Huntsville made a mistake. Its industrial capacity so far outpaced its farming sector that it dominated the region. The grass was not metaphorically greener in Huntsville. Factory paychecks and wealth that came to the city and the surrounding county had not brought contentment. Farming seemed left out of the new Huntsville, a factor that inhibited whatever notion of cohesiveness the Chamber sought. It proved to be a sobering moment. The Oktibbehans recognized the need for balance. For months they had been arguing that Starkville needed a manufacturing complement to its dairying.[42] But after viewing Huntsville in detail, their ardor for extensive cotton mill manufacture dwindled. Even as they pointed out how Oktibbeha held all the natural advantages that the Huntsville area had, the Chamber turned its attention back to industries it had already contemplated.

Part of the Chamber's disillusionment with attracting new cotton mills stemmed from the fact that Alabama and other southern states had captured the largest and most prominent firms. Oktibbeha lagged far behind, in part because until recently Mississippi laws precluded out-of-state corporations from owning more than a small amount of property within the state. That had been the rationale behind the Borden Southern Company's creation. It enabled Borden Co. to circumvent Mississippi's anti-carpetbagger statutes. Alabama's and Georgia's early hydroelectric power feeds had also provided Borden the opportunity to develop first. The cotton mill building boom was ending and it passed Mississippi by.[43]

Woodworking factories—cabinet, furniture, and similar manufactories—seemed natural Oktibbeha industries. Targeted by Sturgis months earlier, these indigenous activities utilized local products and employed local people. Embedded in the Chamber's championing of woodworking was a principle it apparently had lost sight of—the principle of building and growing from within. The organization went on record as promising to "concede equally as much, or more, benefits and privileges to home institutions than is now being offered to proposed manufacturers" to establish facilities in the county and to relocate there. Jones put it simply. The "plants are here. We know them and understand their business methods. They are operated by our people." The community needed to nurture that investment in Oktibbeha County. "To us their success means progress," continued Jones. "Their failure would mean disaster."[44]

This inward turn—as a directive, striving to develop Oktibbeha to its fullest potential before seeking the pot of gold at the end of the rainbow—marked a new chapter in the "progressivism" of Starkville and Oktibbeha. Here, community-building was not anti-industrial. It was pro-Oktibbeha. The now frequently used phrase, "Dairying and Progress," better expressed the new message. Progress meant many more things than industry but it certainly did not exclude factories and other manufacturing facilities. It included revisiting dairymen to urge them to grow feed for their cows. It meant creating a vital hen and egg culture. It meant reengaging with the Prairie Lime Belt group to establish a joint advertising policy for the section. Starkville also invited every other place in northeast Mississippi with a milk plant to payday, and after the festivities the Chamber and the college held a joint meeting on how to encourage dairymen to increase their herds and their profitability. The inward turn also led to a much more strenuous effort to ensure that the county's Black farmers and dairymen squeezed every bit of profitability out of their tenancy or farms. Regular columns titled, "For Colored Farmers and Dairymen," written by the E. W. Hayes, agricultural instructor of the Oktibbeha Country Training School for the Colored, targeted Black farmers and dairymen and provided step by step direction in virtually all farm activities.[45]

Internal improvements received new immediacy. Starkville prioritized paving residential city streets and highways running through the county. Starkvillians constructed overhead railway bridges to eliminate blockages when trains passed through town. These overpasses also reduced pedestrian and vehicular accidents. Starkville modernized its downtown. Underground telephone lines replaced poles as the downtown moved to a common battery telephonic system. The city even declared a community-wide playground "a municipal utility." Starkville considered this community park—complete with a swimming pool and a wading area for young children as well as more conventional playground apparatus—as much an essential part of town as the telephone, natural gas, and electric companies.

A community pool required water, and Starkville began construction of a new well almost immediately. The rise in population had taxed the old well system to its limit. Two other civic institutions deserve special mention. In 1928 the Community Council considered creating a Salvation Army unit in Starkville to aid the indigent or troubled. When that initiative finally failed, it convened a meeting of citizens and created a community chest. Overseen by the Council and limited to $1,500, the group used some funds for the Boy Scouts, Girls Reserve, and playground but set aside the rest for relief. The chest was managed by a Council board member, who served as "charity officer." The officer had discretionary use of the chest to resolve immediate issues but needed directors' permission to expend large amounts over time.[46] A few months later, another proposition came up for public discussion. The same organizational coalition favoring the community chest, joined by all Starkville physicians, pushed for a full-time county health unit. Starkville was not the first place to agitate for a community health unit in Mississippi. Twenty-nine other counties had such units. Comprised of a doctor and a nurse, the unit took the entire county as its locus. Its task was disease prevention, not treatment. It stopped epidemics through vaccination, noting disturbing situations and reporting incipient outbreaks to the state health authorities. Its more immediate concerns would be preventive measures to ensure individual health. Relief rolls swelled when illness made it impossible to work. Businesses suffered as they had to find and train replacements or simply do without, which often meant lost opportunity. A similar situation occurred in schools. Absenteeism for medical reasons placed sick children behind the others. Attendance while sick was even a bigger curse. Disease was likely to spread throughout the class and perhaps the school, leaving lessons unlearned. A full-time county health unit provided prenatal care, midwife training, annual examinations to public school children, and inspected the sanitary condition of grocery stores, hotels, cafes, and dairies.

Advocates offered a two-pronged justification for the Oktibbeha County board of supervisors to establish such a unit. First, the state paid half the freight and for all the requisite medications. That meant the county would be responsible for only half the estimated $5,000 yearly tab. That cost was sliced further as Starkville proper agreed to pay its share of the county's annual bill. Time lost from work and school far exceeded the annual cost. The second was impassioned focus on children. "Every right thinking citizen of Oktibbeha County," wrote Grady Imes, who took over the *Starkville News* just a few weeks before, supported this measure that "means so much to the health of our future citizens." He demanded that the supervisors "GRANT THIS MOST URGENT APPEAL for humanity's sake."[47]

While Starkville worked on social services it continued its decade-long campaign to attract new residents to the area. The town welcomed groups to watch payday, sometimes scheduling more than 600 visitors in one weekend all through 1929. Potential immigrants were impressed by what they saw and heard, and contacted the Chamber requesting further information in impressive numbers. In the first two months of 1929, 116 people wrote. With this volume of interest in perhaps relocating to Starkville, the lack of good, relatively inexpensive housing plagued the city, even after it created several housing subdivisions. Citing high property taxes in the city, builders refused to build additional stock. "Carpenters, bricklayers, laborers, plumbers" and others involved in construction found little work. To stimulate building and to make the housing market more appealing, the mayor and board of aldermen enacted a measure that they anticipated would lower residential housing costs. Any residence completed in the next eighteen months was tax exempt for five years. In effect, the council gave its builders, construction workers, and property owners the kind of breaks it might well have employed to attract outside industry to Starkville. Borden had received that benefit when it came to Starkville. The *News* reported that the five-year tax-exempt measure met with "popular approval."[48]

The new principle of helping Oktibbeha industries at least as much as those from distant areas got a major test in early 1929. Sanders, owner of the city's sole cotton mill, wanted to rebuild and expand his structure. Created at the turn-of-the-century as a teaching facility for the A&M college, J. W. Sanders had owned the facility since 1922. During that time he acquired a series of mills across Mississippi and Alabama. He gave the city an ultimatum. The mill had become antiquated as had some of his other properties. He wanted to increase efficiencies by closing some of his mills and expanding others with up-to-date equipment. He would rebuild and modernize his Starkville mill and double or triple its size and its payroll but with one stipulation. He did not want his operation to be subject to

Starkville's laws. Here the matter was less about taxes than about regulations. Mills were essentially plantations, self-contained economic units each constructed to pursue a single purpose. Each were corporations with distinct sets of operational regulations and requirements. If the aldermen did not grant Sanders his request, he planned to shutter the Starkville operation and build the new facility in Kosciusko.

Starkville did not want to lose the mill. It provided paychecks for an estimated 500 workers and their families. Losing those jobs would have proven catastrophic to area merchants and others. Sanders' offer was far sweeter than maintaining the status quo, however. He promised to at least double the number of factory positions and hence the number of people dependent on the mill. In small town Starkville, adding 500 citizens was huge. The town's 1929 population was roughly 3,500. Additional millworkers and their families would swell that number considerably.

The mill matter came to the aldermen immediately after they had voted to pave the streets in a planned but not yet built residential subdivision. The notion that assisting a developer sell residential units by using public funds and power to enhance the value of the property was indirectly juxtaposed against Sanders' demand. As the aldermen adjourned for a month to consider such an important issue, the Chamber's industrial committee actively negotiated with Sanders and the aldermen to broker a desirable solution. The mill was too big to allow to get away. The Chamber fashioned a compromise to place the mill outside the city limits but kept the mill residences within it. When the aldermen reconvened to begin discussion, a large delegation of citizens, led by Chamber president M. H. Moore, came to explain why they favored the compromise. Keeping workers' housing within city limits required them to pay taxes, which generated more than enough to cover the expense of the separate public school for mill children. Sanders' mill rebuild and revamp would use local material and provide construction jobs. Building additional housing for 500 more people would keep construction in Starkville booming. Finally, they reminded the alderman that if that group failed to agree to the compromise measure, Sanders would leave. Starkville would lose 500 people almost instantaneously. Following these arguments, the aldermen approved the compromise and released the territory upon which Sanders wanted to build his expanded mill from city jurisdiction.[49]

Once the genie was out of the bottle it became impossible to control.

The very next matter before the aldermen that night was the cooperative creamery. It stood as the next claimant. The creamery too hoped to construct a new extensive facility located in what was then Starkville but only if it were not subject to Starkville regulation. The creamery sought the same sort of deal that the aldermen had just made with Sanders. Professor J. S. Moore, the cooperative creamery's president, led a delegation of creamery workers and others to press the case. Moore told the aldermen that the creamery's board of directors had met earlier that day and decided to overhaul the nearly twenty-year-old structure and modernize its equipment, with the proviso that the property on which the creamery wanted to build was removed from city authority. Having just granted Sanders's request, the aldermen quickly provided a similar deal for the new co-op building.

To his credit, Mayor Julian J. Gill, a druggist by trade, led the public defense of the aldermen's actions. He claimed that it was "a forward step industrially" simply because if the aldermen had turned the propositions down it "would have killed all possibility of future industrial development for at least another generation." He urged citizens to give the deals some time, to "just put a peg right here in your mind and see the status few years hence." Both the Chamber's M. H. Moore and the Creamery's J. S. Moore concurred. They termed it "a most important move in the right direction" for Starkville's industrial development.[50]

Golson celebrated the resolution with an editorial. "Things are looking mighty bright in the old burg at this time," smiled Golson. The aldermen had made it possible for the creamery "to expand its business to unlimited proportions." The cotton mill compromise signaled "more cash and better days ahead." Nor was that all. "Plenty of grass and clover" meant "larger returns" at the condensery and "smaller feed bills." Yes, argued Golson, "thinks are lookin' good—mighty bloomin' good for the people of Oktibbeha County."[51]

Golson's chipper assessment may have been an overstatement, but he had another initiative he had been pursuing and was about to unveil. For the past month and a half, the *News* had solicited and organized material for a special supplement to mark the third anniversary of Starkville's Borden condensery. Golson had lofty ambitions for the tabloid. He wanted to broadcast "to our own citizens and to the world the vast achievements of Oktibbeha County and the surrounding section in the past few years." Aiming "to parade our success for 'all to see and admire,'" he wanted "eminent experts" as well as county residents to contribute to this monumental work. He reminded his readers that the county "was blessed with law-abiding, Christian citizens, live civic organizations, modern churches, ideal living conditions, well conducted and well attended schools, well financed banks and . . . a fine road system." This "lasting record of the vast strides made in the past few years" would provide a road map for "the present and future of our county."[52]

Three years was an unusual amount of time to celebrate. That was clearly not the actual reason for the supplement. The savvy Golson used the occasion as a rallying point. The editor understood the benefits of publicity and advertising. This supplement would be cast widely—to every home in Oktibbeha County and throughout the United States, even to the "Hawaiian Islands." It would acquaint those unfamiliar with the Oktibbeha miracle and fortify the appreciation of the miracle among those who had been aware. Golson's ambitious goal was far larger. His real target was Oktibbehans themselves. He hoped to provide citizens of Starkville and Oktibbeha County a renewed sense of time past. The supplement was to stand as a living monument to the Starkville miracle for now and for posterity. Put simply, Golson tried to build a renewed sense of community among the populace that would enable them to again do great things and to truly appreciate what their collective effort had achieved. Pride in what was done would lead citizens to support what must be done.

Golson recognized that "one of the greatest assets that any community can have is a feeling of good will among inhabitants." In the past, that spirit was rampant within Starkville. But "the modern age of speed" finds "us rushing through life," without appreciating what we have. A community was like a chain, no "stronger than its weakest link." He wanted this publication to serve as "a manifestation of the spirit of pride and ambition that brought Starkville and Oktibbeha County to the fore front." To do so, something had to restore that joie de vivre. The supplement's construction was that mechanism. Neighboring towns and villages pitched in with their stories, pictures, and triumphs. The supplement was "one of the most constructive undertakings in our community," having only "one prime requisite, a complete participation by our entire citizenry." The *News* had received "scores of interesting contributions of pen and pictorial character" daily but Golson demanded more. Likening his community building effort to "a lusty infant and growing in scope each day," he assured contributors that the supplement will "show the outside world the spirit of commercial activity that is existent" in Oktibbeha. An act of community in creating the special issue would help restore a sense of pride in accomplishment generally and a sense of community particularly. On a practical level it would lead to "more milk production, and more farmers interested in raising dairy cattle and producing milk." Advertising "us to us"—"selling of our fair homeland to ourselves and acquainting ourselves with our possessions" (forcing Starkvillians to realize what they were, what they had, and what they had misplaced)—and to the world would generate "civic pride" and make "Oktibbeha County more of a business success than it is now."[53]

The Chamber was fully onboard with Golson's supplement. Its members even went to the Chambers of Sturgis and Maben to get them to back the effort and to solicit visual and written contributions from their citizenry. It was a total *county* community-building effort. When the supplement appeared at the end of April 1929, Mayor Gill introduced it by recounting Starkville's attributes. His discussion of racial matters was front and center as it was an accomplishment of which he was quite proud. He noted that the city was two-thirds white and that almost all the population growth it had experienced in recent years was of white people. Gill observed that Blacks and whites "dwell together in perfect accord." He saw no "race conflict or even 'race confusion'" during the twenty years he had lived in the city. Starkvillians accepted precise social relations between Black and white people. They did "not allow nor practice social equality, nor do I think our colored people aspires to such relation." Legal matters were something else. "Our state and municipal laws afford every one equality before their tribunals and we are living and growing each in our relationships in perfect harmony and satisfaction," Gill contended. After finishing ticking off Oktibbeha and Starkville firsts, he stated a case why out-of-area readers should settle in Starkville. Starkvillians "are sold on Starkville," Gill maintained. It was a place of opportunity, "a healthful and enjoyable climate where you can grow old happily" and enjoy "all the concomitants of life." Opportunity was "large; development and growth are here; cultural and educational advantages" abounded. Persons aspiring "to comfort and happiness for themselves and children" would find Starkville most appealing. He closed with a formal plea. "We cordially invite good citizenship of whatever creed or race and especially do we need those who can help us to a larger development."[54]

The supplement itself was primarily a recapitulation of the Starkville miracle with praise for the efforts of the Chamber of Commerce, especially its industrial committee. To be sure, it had many photographs and short pieces, but its essence was the Starkville/Oktibbeha/Borden story. Golson recapitulated the supplement's purpose: to use the tale of the past six or seven years "to bring out more vividly the present" and "to create a more abiding community pride." Yet he also expressed some disappointment with the issue. Idealism "reduced to cold type" loses "the warmth and beauty" that characterized Oktibbeha's people. Second, it failed to convey "the real and abiding sentiments" that "the good people of this section . . . hold its destiny in their hands."[55]

The special supplement was consistent with the course that Starkville and Oktibbeha County had been pursuing for months. With the help of the Illinois Central, the Chamber completed its lime and clay surveys and investigated the possibility of establishing a cement plant in the county. It continued to support Sturgis's interest in furniture and other wood manufactories. It negotiated with a half-hose manufacturer, the substance for which came from wood and other forms of cellulose, such as cotton, and that was a favorite of flappers. A garment plant with 100 machines and at least 110 employees considered coming to the town to manufacture goods from Starkville chambray—the primary product of Sanders's Starkville plant—and other fabrics. The building industries took off. Fueled by the aldermen's five-year tax avoidance, builders rushed to get houses constructed. At least twenty of Starkville's prominent citizens built new homes. The Catholic Church erected a fine new edifice. A great many merchants remodeled or built new stores. The cotton mill expansion and rebuild, coupled with the creamery, totaled over $200,000 in new construction.[56]

With these final initiatives, Starkville completed its multiyear voyage to identify what small town life meant in the United States in the late 1920s. To the best of its citizens' powers, it had constructed that life. Like virtually every other town in America, Starkville and Oktibbeha County were unique. Their history, people, and environment were variables different than other places. They lived the consequences of slavery, continued bigotry, and Jim Crow. Starkville and its county were hardly egalitarian in almost any sense. On top of that, Oktibbeha had Borden. It had a baseline stability that freed it from the most severe wants that most small towns and cities had. Just a few short miles away was a state college. Although the legislature investigated it and threatened to move it many times, that deliberative body never did. The college provided county folk with immediate access to farming expertise that most places lacked. The city of Starkville and its elites were unsurpassed in their ability to advertise the place, its accomplishments, and its promise. Most every small town in the South and Midwest puffed itself. Few were as remotely successful as Starkville. The city also garnered spectacular success with its agricultural tourism/agricultural voyeurism industry. It provided a steady, predictable, solid income for the town and its surroundings. Yet as Starkville's trip to Huntsville and other places to see an industrialized cotton mill valley demonstrated, agricultural/economic tourism was alive and well across the land in the 1920s. Starkville visited places that had proven successful, in hopes of learning from them how to achieve some sort of economic assuredness.

For all of Starkville's uniqueness, and even with its relative economic surety, it was very much like any other small town or city. First, it truly wanted to remain a small town or city. While it might hope to expand, it had no ambition to become the next Jackson, Memphis, or Birmingham. Like other places, Starkville looked longingly to an idealized past and used that sense of nostalgia to craft its future. It marveled at the modern age and the virtues that it brought while at the same time was repulsed by its sentiments and excesses. Small towns everywhere hoped to pick from the modern virtues to assure relevance. Happiness—traditional values of family, home, hearth, and labor—animated small towns and cities as they sought to stem the tide of young people leaving for presumably greener pastures and to attract a series of people who would join with them to work on a shared vision for the future. To those ends, they each built and refurbished institutions, erected glorious structures, and highlighted certain goals.

Starkville was remarkably typical in each of those endeavors. The condensery with its paychecks and the extensive agricultural tourism provided Starkville one specific freedom, a modicum of economic security. Neither Starkville nor Oktibbeha had to run pell-mell to find an industrial suitor to help the town survive. That freedom allowed Starkville to deliberately pick what its future might be. It need not be wedded to a bad industry or a corrupt or fickle owner or corporation to survive. Its choice of indigenous industries, patterned in part after its dairying coup, reflected that flexibility and ability. Starkville continued that thread through 1929. Just before Black Tuesday, the Chamber called a meeting of all county residents to determine what kinds of other industries and economic activities the citizenry would like the Chamber to pursue. In effect, it asked for an economic plebiscite to determine in which direction the county would next go in its development agenda. Without security, that sort of request would have been unthinkable.[57]

The city was lucky to be the site of the first condensery south of the Mason-Dixon line. But it proved exceptionally special in capitalizing on it and running a narrative that was most compelling and seemingly miraculous. The town, especially its Chamber, had real genius in getting everything the city did in print. It had connections and used them. It was anything but shy, willing to devote as much time and energy as was necessary to carry the story forward and to remind people again and again that a great miracle had happened there. In the course of doing all that, the Starkville story resounded in place after place. It enchanted literally hundreds, perhaps thousands, of small towns and cities. Most at least explored the possibility of creating such a miracle in their town. Many wrote to northern condensers and competed with nearby burgs to get some sort of milk plant located there. Relatively few got a major company to establish a condensery in their town. But a huge number wound up with a milk plant of some sort. Whether a condensery, creamery, powered milk plant, ice cream manufactory, cheese, or some other milk-manufacturing/manipulating facility, each tried to recapture the Starkville miracle. In Mississippi, for example, there were no milk plants in the state before 1912. Cities received fluid milk and farmers often made butter but there were no commercial milk establishments. In 1926, the year of Borden opening the Starkville facility, there were perhaps twelve, maybe fifteen, creameries offering butter for local sale. The number had actually declined in the early 1920s. But by early 1929 there were over 300 Mississippi milk plants. The Mississippi commissioner of agriculture called it "a veritable flood of 'white gold'" pouring over the state.[58]

That extraordinary growth resulted from the work of Starkvillians and the myth of the Oktibbeha County miracle. The beauty of the story and the miracle attached to it was that both were adaptable, flexible. Localities chose to focus on aspects that suited their needs and so tailored its lessons to their particular situations. Starkville pressed it at every opportunity; the town milked it for everything it was worth as did its recipients. Mississippi was not alone in the allure of the Starkville story. People came from far and wide and built a plethora of milk plants in Tennessee, Arkansas, Texas, Alabama, Louisiana, and other states to make the South a major dairy industry player. Not every small town or city prospered through dairying. But many did. They had managed to stave off the twin fears of small town America—abandonment and dissolution—and the psychic and economic devastation that accompanied them. Dairying enabled them to survive if not thrive, although some did both. They could keep going, to try yet again. In the case of the South, dairying had marked advantages over cotton, tobacco, and textiles. Everyone drank milk. The weather was rarely a factor. Oversupply seemed unlikely. A milk plant required regular, continual product to operate.

Borden, of course, backed Oktibbeha's advertising efforts all the way. There is no doubt that it provided the milk company incredibly favorable publicity, marked it as a daringly deliberate, innovative company and a fine partner. It eased the large corporation's ability to gobble up other smaller milk-related facilities and so grow its businesses well beyond condensed and fluid milk, with profits skyrocketing accordingly.

The other major milk condensing companies and then the large cheese firms all saw in the South opportunity and markets not previously imaginable. Borden's Starkville plant had proved a southern dairy industry possible, and when the story spread that the facility was not simply successful but spectacularly so, Borden competitors invaded the region with capital in hand and profits on their mind. In many instances, these major economic players established facilities where there had been no dairy tradition. How could there have been? There had been no place to market the milk, no one beyond local fluid milk drinkers. Starkville and Borden showed what was conceivable and then made sure that everyone knew about it.

APPENDIX
The Great Depression and Beyond

The dairy industry proved a huge bulwark for southern small towns during the Great Depression. Dairying acreage, dairy farms, and milk plants all increased in size and number. Cotton, corn, or other types of farming declined markedly. Mississippi boasted four hundred milk manufacturing facilities in 1931, an increase of about a hundred over its 1929 total. While milk production and prices did fall modestly during the 1930s, that commodity remained at a far higher plateau that other southern agricultural sectors. Dairying kept places and people afloat during some of the worst economic times faced by the nation. The region's dairy industry seemed such an imposing force that Wisconsin dairymen heatedly lobbied their state legislature in the 1930s for help to beat back the encroaching southern menace.[1]

Though at a reduced rate, visitors from across the South scheduled trips to Starkville through the early 1930s to witness condensery paydays. The allure of the Starkville–Oktibbeha miracle, combined with the hardheaded reality of milk's comparative prosperity, brought the dream to place after place. The city and the county itself continued down the path its Chamber laid out for it. Furniture making, clothing manufacture, and chicken raising were all indigenous activities that stood alongside dairying as Oktibbeha's foremost economic pursuits, although the Chamber—in the purported service of community—periodically urged that other industries be brought into the mix. In 1937 the *Starkville News* took stock of what had happened in the eleven years since the condensery. Citing "innumerable improvements," the paper proclaimed that what marked the past decade was that Starkville became "modern."[2]

Borden Company proved tremendously successful. The dairy juggernaut's profits exploded in the early 1930s. They slowed some in the middle of the decade but rebounded by its end. Its prospects again boomed as condensed and powdered milk again became war effort staples. Borden continued to expand into new areas and even created some of the most memorable iconography of the period. Few at mid-century did not know of the domesticity of the cow couple, Elsie and Elmer, she with her milk, he with his glue, and their bovine children as they lived and fostered the American dream. The company had become a highly profitable international behemoth.

But all things come to an end. The condensery persisted until 2005, when not enough area dairy farmers remained to provide sufficient milk to keep the plant open. Most local dairy farmers had long finalized their federal farm buyouts as government worked to reduce the nation's oversupply of milk. In fact, most milk processed in Starkville during the condensery's last decade was not locally produced but shipped from distant Sulphur Springs, Texas. Borden sold the sad, shuttered Starkville factory four years later, to a local developer who gutted and retrofitted the interior. A restaurant, bicycle shop, the developer's office, interior design concern, storage company, and trendy apartments now fill the space.

Borden underwent a similar fate. In the twenty-first century, the latest knowledge of nutrition questioned the virtue of regular milk drinking. In increasing numbers, mothers chose breastfeeding over condensed milk. Milk consumption plummeted by more than 25 percent during the fifteen years prior to 2018. The company clamored to diversify into other foods but the handwriting was on the wall. On January 5, 2020, Borden filed for bankruptcy.

NOTES

ABBREVIATIONS

Regional Publications

AC	*Atlanta Constitution*
BDR	*Belvidere Daily Republican*
BS	*Baltimore Sun*
FST-M	*Fort Scott Tribune-Monitor*
LSJ	*Lansing State Journal*
PC	*Pittsburgh Courier*
T-T	*Times Tribune (Scranton)*

Agricultural and Trade Publications

CCG	*Cultivator and Country Gentleman*
CMPM	*Creamery and Milk Plant Monthly*
FMB	*Farmers Mail and Breeze*
HD	*Hoard's Dairyman*
HW	*Harvester World*
ICM	*Illinois Central Magazine*
MD	*Milk Dealer*
MAR	*Manufacturers Record*
MR	*Milk Reporter*
NYPRAC	*New York Produce Review and American Creamery*
PF	*Prairie Farmer*
PFSG	*Progressive Farmer and Southern Farm Gazette*
PrF	*Progressive Farmer*
RNY	*Rural New-Yorker*
SA	*Southern Agriculturist*
SC	*Southern Cultivator*
SLJ	*Southern Livestock Journal*
SR	*Southern Ruralist*

Notes

National and New York Area

BDE	*Brooklyn Daily Eagle*
BG	*Boston Globe*
BSU	*Brooklyn Standard Union*
BTU	*Brooklyn Times Union*
CSM	*Christian Science Monitor*
CT	*Chicago Tribune*
EW	*Evening World*
HC	*Harford Courant*
LAT	*Los Angeles Times*
MC	*Morning Call (Paterson, NJ)*
NYT	*New York Times*
NYTR	*New York Tribune*
WP	*Washington Post*
WSJ	*Wall Street Journal*

Alabama

BN	*Birmingham News*
DT	*Demopolis Times*
EWO	*Eutaw Whig and Observer*
MA	*Montgomery Advertiser*
OMH	*Our Mountain Home*
PCH	*Pickens County Herald and West Alabamian*
STJ	*Selma Times Journal*
TN	*Tuscaloosa News*

Louisiana

AM	*Abbeville Meridonal*
AP	*Assumption Pioneer*
C-P	*Clarion-Progress*
CDS	*Crowley Daily Signal*
DA	*Daily Advertiser*
MNS	*Monroe News-Star*
NE	*New Era*
RB	*Richland Beacon*
RT	*Rayne Tribune*
SJ	*Shreveport Journal*
ST	*Shreveport Times*
TG	*Tensas Gazette*
TT	*Town Talk*

Mississippi

CD	Commercial Dispatch (Columbus)
CL	Clarion-Ledger
CP	Choctaw Plaindealer
CPR	Clarksdale Press Register
EMT	East Mississippi Times
GC	Greenwood Commonwealth
HCG	Hinds County Gazette
HN	Hattiesburg News
JDN	Jackson (MS) Daily News
KSL	Kosciusko Star Ledger
MB	Macon Beacon
MS-S	Mississippi Sun-Sentinel
ND	Neshoba Democrat
NR	Newton Record
SCE	Stone County Enterprise
SCN	Simpson County News
S-WJ	Semi-Weekly Journal
SN	Starkville News
TC	The Carthaginian
TJ	Tupelo Journal
UA	Union Appeal
WCJ	Winston County Journal
WPL	West Point Leader
WT	Winona Times
YCH	Yahoo City Herald

Tennessee

BH	Bristol Herald
CDT	Chattanooga Daily Times
CN	Chattanooga News
DD	Decatur Daily
DGM	Daily Gazette and Mail
DNJ	Daily News Journal
GDS	Greeneville Democrat-Sun
JCC	Johnson City Chronicle
JCSN	Johnson City Staff News
KJ	Knoxville Journal
KN-S	Knoxville News-Sentinel
LCN	Lincoln County News

| NB | *Nashville Banner* |
| NT | *Tennessean* |

Texas

AS	*Austin Statesman*
FWR	*Fort Worth Record*
FWST	*Fort Worth Star-Telegram*
MM	*Marshall Messenger*
MN	*Marshall News*
WNT	*Waco News-Tribune*
WS	*Whitewright Sun*

INTRODUCTION

1. *SCE*, 9/19/29:7; *WT*, 11/7/30:4; *MC*, 1/22/30:4.

2. *SN*, 11/25/29:1; *AS*, 1/20/30:4; *Wisconsin State Journal*, 12/4/29:16.

3. Hunziker, *Condensed Milk;* Bell, *A Portrait of Progress;* Fite, *Cotton Fields;* Giesen, *Boll Weevil Blues;* Olmstead and Rhode, "An Impossible Undertaking"; Strom, *Making Catfish Bait;* English, *A Common Thread.*

4. Several persons have examined the General Motors transformation. See Sloan Jr., *My Years.* Also see Hounshell, *From the American System to Mass Production,* and Marcus and Segal, *Technology in America.*

CHAPTER ONE

1. *HC*, 5/22/1899:6, 10/23/16:11; *WSJ*, 4/26/1899:2; *CT*, 4/25/1899:3.

2. *HD*, 1914:166 and 406.

3. *CT*, 2/4/13:3.

4. *CT*, 3/7/13:8, 3/8/13:3, 9/2/14:1, 9/3/14:5, and 9/16/14; *HD*, 1914:194; *NYPRAC*, 3/12/13:1.

5. *CT*, 9/16/14:1.

6. At the start of World War I there were roughly 240 condenseries in the United States. Half were in New York, Illinois, and Wisconsin. See *HD*, 1914:635. Elgin, Illinois, became a de facto condensing center. See *HD*, 1914:224–25, 247. For statistics of the prewar period, during the war and post-war export of condensed milk from America to Europe, see *CMPM*, 4/1922:54.

7. Hunziker, *Condensed Milk.*

8. See Marshall, *Elbridge A. Stuart,* and Bell, *Portrait of Progress.*

9. For some of the properties Borden purchased during the war, see *Chilliwack Progress,* 8/8/2004:4; *Logan Republican*, 2/22/12:1; *Modesto Morning Herald*, 8/25/16:1; "Commercial Notes," *Elgin Report*, 6/17/16:3; *Elgin Report*, 6/23/17:2.

10. *FST-M*, 5/15/14:2, 4/23/15:2, 11/9/15:6, 11/26/15:7, and 5/29/16:1; *Fort Scott Republican*, 5/31/16:6. Some of the dairymen around Kansas City sought to form a union, see *FST-M*, 7/30/15:4.

11. For Fort Scott, see, for example, *FST-M*, 10/14/15:8, 10/19/15:4, and 11/17/16:3.

12. *FST-M,* 8/25/16:4, 8/29/16:4, and 9/28/16:1.

13. *FST-M,* 11/11/16:1.

14. *FST-M,* 11/17/16:2.

15. *FST-M,* 12/5/16:2, 12/9/16:1, 12/14/16:1, and 3/14/18:9.

16. *FST-M,* 12/26/16:3, 2/2/17:2, and 4/17/17:6.

17. *FST-M,* 5/15/17:4, 9/18/17:1, and 4/18/18:1; *FMB,* 6/30/17:1; *Fort Scott Monitor,* 4/17/17:1.

18. *HD,* 1914:650, 837, 1222.

19. *CT,* 3/16/16:7, 3/19/16:12, 3/31/16:1, 4/1/16:17, 4/2/16:1, and 4/3/16:17; *LAT,* 4/2/16:L1, 4/3/16:4, and 4/4/16:1.

20. *CT,* 4/6/16:1, 4/8/16:1, and 4/10.16:17; *HC,* 4/7/16:10; *RNY,* 1916:721.

21. *CT,* 4/20/16:1, 4/21/16:17, 5/3/16:7, and 8/2/16:13; *NYT,* 10/1/16:1.

22. *CT,* 9/17/16:7.

23. *CSM,* 9/26/16:5; *NYT,* 12/14/15:7, 9/26/16:9, and 9/27/16:8.

24. *NYT,* 8/19/16:16, 8/26/16:10, and 8/31/16:3. See John J. Dillon, *Seven Decades of Milk;* Roswell D. Cooper, *Origin and Development of the Dairymen's League* (n.p., 1938); and *Fifty Year Battle.*

25. *NYT,* 9/30/16:5 and 10/1/16:1; *RNY,* 1916:1240.

26. *NYT,* 10/2/16;1, 10/2/16:3, 10/2/16:1, 10/3/16:5, 10/4/16:1, 10/4/16: 6, and 10/5/16:1; *Evening Statesman,* 10/5/16:1.

27. *BG,* 10/6/16:2 and 10/7/16:3; *NYT,* 10/6/16:1, 10/7/16:1, 10/8/16:1, and 10/9/16:22; *HC,* 10/7/16:17 and 10/8/16:16; *HD,* 1916:478, 550–51, 586–87; *LAT,* 10/7/16:I3; *RNY,* 1916:1313.

28. *NYT,* 10/11/16:7 and 10/12/16:14; *BG,* 10/12/16:13; *HC,* 10/12/16:8.

29. *NYT,* 10/13/16:1 and 10/15/16:17; *BSU,* 10/14/16:1; *BG,* 10/15/16:11.

30. *CT,* 10/20/16:1; *NYT,* 10/22/16:21; *CSM,* 10/19/16:1.

31. *CSM,* 11/17/16:5; *CT,* 11/16/16:20.

32. *Day Book* (Chicago), 12/9/16:4 9; *Cook County Herald,* 12/22/16:1; *Oklahoma Farmer,* 12/25/16:16.

33. *CSM,* 3/3/17:22; *CT,* 2/7/17:13, 2/23/17:2, and 3/15/17:11.

34. *CSM,* 6/30/17:4 and 9/28/17:10; *CT,* 9/5/17:15, 9/20/17:1, and 9/22/17:17; *BG,* 9/28/17:5; *HD,* 1917:441. For an overview of Hoover and the dairy industry during the world war, see Guth, "Herbert Hoover."

35. *CSM,* 9/28/17:10 and 10/19/17:7; *CT,* 4/18/19:11, 3/2/1918:15, 9/28/17:1, 2/6/18: 3, 2/8/18:7, 3/29/18:17, 7/19/23:9, 10/19/19:A8, and 10/31/19:1; *HD,* 1917: 504, 506; 1918: 929, 994.

36. *NYT,* 9/29/17:11, 9/30/17:14, 10/20/17:15, 10/22/17:11, 11/5/17:15, and 11/11/17:6; CT 11/1/17:3; *HD,* 1917:520.

37. *NYT,* 4/25/17:17 and 5/6/17:24; *WSJ,* 10/29/17:6; *RNY,* 1917:859.

38. *CT,* 12/22/18:A2; *WSJ,* 12/23/18:2; *CSM,* 1/13/19:7. For the impediments, see *HD,* 1918:1024–25.

39. "Profiteering," *Senate Document No. 248,* 65th Congress, 2nd Session, 2/27/18; *NYT,* 6/30/18:1,9: *New York Herald,* 6/30/18:1,6; *NYTR,* 6/30/18:1,10. For defenses of the indus-

tries, see, for example, Arthur Richmond Marsh, "The Report of the Federal Trade Commission on Profiteering," *Economic World*, 7/6/18:3–4; "Cost Finding and Keeping," *Business Digest*, July–December 1918:219–21.

40. *LSJ*, 10/15/19:1 and 10/17/19:2; *BDR*, 10/20/20:6; and *Anthony Republican*, 11/27/19:1.

41. *NYT*, 1/19/19:25, 8/27/19:15, 11/13/19:17, 11/ 24/19:17, 12/10/19:30, 12/26/19:2, 12/29/19:1, and 12/30/19:12; *CSM*, 1/10/19:11; *RNY*, 1919:49.

42. *EW*, 11/4/19:10, 11/5/19:5, 11/5/19:9, 11/6/19:3, 11/11/19:10, 11/13/19:18, 11/14/19:3, 11/14/19:22, and 11/18/19:3.

43. *HD*, 1918:870–72; *EW*, 11/17/19:3, 11/19/19:3, 11/24/19:3, and 11/28/19:17.

44. *NYT*, 11/15/19:18; *MD*, 1/20:36–38; *EW*, 11/21/19:9. For a rebuttal, see *EW*, 11/15/19:3,10. Some saw the plan as Borden's flagging interest in fluid milk as the condensed arena boomed. See, for example, *EW*, 8/26/19:10.

CHAPTER TWO

1. *WSJ*, 10/3/19:11, 15; *NYTR*, 8/27/19:6; *CT*, 10/3/19:25.

2. "Serving the Cause," advertisement, and "Gail Borden Pure Milk Code," advertisement, *Dixon Evening Telegraph* (Dixon, IL), 5/28/19:6 and 7/16/19:2; "Founded Upon An Ideal," advertisement *The Logan (UT) Journal*, 1/17/20:7; and "Since 1857," advertisement, *Springfield (NY) Journal*, 2/26/20:3.

3. "Balance of Trade of the United States in Dairy Products, 1913–1921," *CMPM*, 4/22:54. Also see *NYT*, 5/22/21:33; *Dairy Record*, 6/20:28; *MR*, 9/20:15.

4. *Convention Canner*, 1919:158–61; Eliot Jones, "The Webb-Pomerene Act," *Journal of Political Economy*, November1920:754–67. The milk section also discussed an industrywide campaign to drink condensed milk. In addition to the source above, see *Canner*, 5/8/20:47.

5. *Canner*, 7/17/20:40, 8/7/20:38, 9/11/20:50, and 4/9/21:42.

6. See, for example, *MD*, 8/20:56–58.

7. *Daily Republic (Rushville, IN)*, 6/7/20:7; *Buffalo Enquirer*, 6/7/20:5; *Women's Wear*, 6/7/20:5 and 30; *Associated Advertising*, 7/1919:103–105; *Printers Ink*, 1/1/20:17–20 and 1/15/20:138–142; *Burlington Free Press*, 5/24/29:22.

8. *Canner*, 11/15/19:38.

9. *NYT*, 8/6/20:7. Also see *Brooklyn Citizen*, 6/16/20:3.

10. *Buffalo Times*, 6/6/22:20.

11. *FWST*, 1/13/22:9; *Oklahoma City Times*, 3/29/22:10; *BN*, 4/17/23:11; *Tucson Citizen*, 5/22/23:12; *NB*, 6/12/23:2.

12. "The Cream Pitcher," *Tucson Citizen*, 4/6/23:8 and *CT*, 5/31/23:5.

13. *Spokane Chronicle*, 6/5/23:5.

14. *St. Louis Post Dispatch*, 4/25/23:13.

15. *Chehalis (WA) Bee Nugget*, 7/6/23:4; *Wisconsin State Journal*, 6/12/23:3; *Greensboro (NC) Daily News*, 10/8/22:21. For some examples of Borden's advertising in non-English languages, see "Ar Jusu Kudikis Miega Gerai," *Draugas* (Chicago, IL) 7/27/22:3; "Zamowcie Dzis To Mleko," *Dziennik Chicoski* (Chicago, IL), 11/23/22:7; "Por Que el Primer Ano de Su Nino es el Mas Importante," *La Prensa* (San Antonio, TX) 12/21/22:2.

16. *T-T,* 10/14/22:3, 11/22/22:18, 1/12/23:20, 3/12/23:15, and 3/20/23:23; *Scranton Times,* 11/9/22:18; *Scranton Republican,* 1/11/23:12; *Barron's* 6/25/23:13; *Bennington Evening Banner,* 7/6/23:2.

17. *T-T,* 11/29/22:3, 12/16/22:23, 1/18/23:12, and 1/25/23:16; *Poughkeepsie Eagle-News,* 7/6/23:11; *Scranton Republican,* 10/30/22:2; *Norwich (CT) Bulletin,* 9/4/22:6. For another city and another worker, see, for example, *KS,* 11/10/22:4, 12/11/22:9, and 12/19/22:16.

18. *MC* (Paterson, NJ), 3/19/23:7; *News-Journal (Lancaster, PA),* 3/15/23:1 and 3/16/23:5; *AC,* 2/5/22:6; *Spokane Chronicle,* 5/29/23:9 and 6/19/23:15; *BTU,* 11/13/23:2; *Oregon (Portland) Daily Journal,* 9/13/22:2.

19. For Barton's biography, see Fried, *The Man Everybody Knew.*

20. *NYT,* 3/15/20:7, 3/18/20:17, 3/25/20:32, 3/26/20:18, 3/29/20:17, 3/30/20:16, 4/2/20:10, 4/7/20:1, 4/12/20:2, 4/26/20:1, 5/20/20:1, 5/27/20:8, and 9/19/20:E1. *RNY,* 1918:561.

21. *CSM,* 6/9/20:5; *NYT,* 10/4/20:19; *Woodstock Daily Sentinel,* 12/13/22:1; Borden was not the only dealer recognizing dairymen–dealer partnerships. See *NYT,* 11/28/20:27.

22. John Le Feber, "Remarks by the President—Opening Session," *Proceedings of the Eleventh Annual Meeting of the International Milk Dealers' Association,* 1919:9–12; *CT,* 12/14/18:10.

23. *BSU,* 8/19/19:6; *NYT,* 8/26/19:13, 8/27/19:15, 4/5/20:10, 6/23/20:23, and 12/4/20:20; *CSM* 12/4/20:5; *MD,* 10(10/20):60 and 10(1/21):24–25; *HD,* 1918:734, 774; *MR,* 36(1921):1; *RNY,* 1918:795, 1885.

24. *NYT,* 11/20/20:1, 11/21/20:12, 11/29/20:5, and 12/3/20:14. For some co-op successes, see, for example, *NYT,* 1/29/22:29.

25. *WSJ,* 12/7/20:9.

26. *Canner,* 7/31/20:42; *CMPM,* 6/21:40; http://daytoninmanhattan.blogspot.com/2015/10/the-1924-roosevelt-hotel-madison-ave-at.html, accessed on 6/14/2020; "A Rendering of the Building at 350 Madison Avenue," https://teslauniverse.com/nikola-tesla/images/rendering-building-350-madison-ave-borden-building-where-tesla-once-had-office, accessed 4/14/2020; Marchand, *Advertising the American Dream.*

27. *Binghamton Press,* 4/11/21:14.

28. *NYT,* 1/23/21:10, 5/22/21:34, 6/1/21:15, 10/31/21:1, 11/8/21:1, 11/9/21:15, 11/11/21:13, 11/24/21:21, 11/26/21:14, 12/3/21:22, and 12/14/21:16; *MR,* 11/21:1; *LAT,* 11/9/21:I1; *Standard Union,* 1/5/22:1.

29. *Women's Wear,* 11/3/21:3. For the Hawthorne experiment and personal management implications, see Marcus, "'Would You Like Fries with That, Sir?'" and Baritz, *The Servants of Power.*

30. *NYT,* 2/10/22:3; *BDE,* 2/10/22:14 and 5/10/22:10; Borden's New York competitors quickly created systems similar to Borden for their operations. See, for instance, *NYT,* 2/11/22:8 and *Record* (Hackensack, NJ), 7/21/22:1,10.

31. *NYTR,* 2/15/22:8; *Coshocton (Ohio) Tribune,* 2/19/22:8; *Minneapolis Star,* 2/23/22:3.

32. *NYTR,* 11/17/22:6; *BSU,* 11/23/22:11; *BTU,* 11/24/22:6; *BDE,* 11/24/22:9; *Brooklyn Citizen,* 11/24/22:9.

33. *Collier's,* 10/6/22:6.

34. *Poughkeepsie Eagle-News*, 3/31/22:5; *Oneonta Star*, 5/1/22:6; *BSU*, 4/28/22:2; *NYT*, 5/7/22:39, 9/8/22:14, and 9/24/22:42. There were inklings that Borden was contemplating a new relationship with the co-op a few months earlier. See, for example, *NYT*, 3/31/22:6. A suit by a producer who claimed that the agreement hampered his ability to get a fair price for his milk was Frederic C. Barns v. Dairymen's League Co-operative Association and Borden Farm Product Company, Inc. Supreme Court Case on Appeal (1924). It appears that the decision was made in early March by the company's officers. See *HD*, 6/3/21:820–21 and *BSU*, 9/5/19:3.

35. *CT*, 8/10/21:1, 6/27/22:13, 6/30/22:15, 11/7/22:2, and 12/30/22:10.

36. *FST-M*, 4/5/18:2 and 4/30/18:2.

37. *FST-M*, 4/17/17:6 and 5/1/18:1.

38. *FST-M*, 9/26/18:8, 10/10/18:7, 4/10/19:3, 11/13/19:8, 11/20/19:7, and 11/29/19: 1.

39. *HD*, 1919:581; *FST-M*, 11/28/18:6, 12/18/18:1, 4/10/19:3, 6/26/19, 11/27/19:8, 12/22/21:8, and 8/17/22:8; *CMPM*, 11/19:22.

40. *FST-M*, 2/6/19:5 and 7/8/20:1.

41. *FST-M*, 8/5/20:1.

42. FST-M 10/9/19:5, 10/16/19:1–2, 11/17/19:1 and 11/20/19:1, 2, 5.

43. *FST-M*, 10/1/20:1, 4, and 12/1/20:1.

44. *FST-M*, 1/5/21:1.

45. *FST-M*, 1/11/21:6, 2/22/21:3, 6/16/21:4, 8/18/21:5, 8/30/21:1,5; 10/24/21:2, and 7/19/23:8; *Uniontown Cicerone and Redfield Ledger*, 1/19/22:2; *Bourbon News*, 7/5/23:1.

46. *FST-M*, 11/17/22:1, 3, 1/16/23:1, 5 and 4/12/23:7.

47. *FST-M*, 2/21/23:1–2; "From the Kansas City Star of July 29, 1923," *Peabody Gazette*, 8/9/23:5; *Wathena Times*, 6/22/23:2; *Alta Vista Journal*, 9/6/23:4; *Smith County Journal*, 8/9/23:6; *Olathe Register*, 8/29/23:9; *Salem Post and Democrat Bulletin*, 8/23/23:8.

48. *Fredonia Daily Herald*, 3/10/23:1; *Iola Daily Register*, 2/1/23:1 and 11/12/23:1; *Caney Daily Chronicle*, 7/31/23:1 and 12/13/23:1; *Neodesha Register*, 2/22/23:1 and 3/1/23:3; *Lyons Daily News*, 1/20/23:2; *Neodesha Daily Sun*, 2/9/23:2 and 4/6/23:3; *Girard Press*, 8/2/23:1; *Horton Headlight Commercial*, 7/5/23:1; *Jewell County Monitor*, 11/9/23:2; *Cawker City Ledger*, 11/15/23:1; *Washington Palladium*, 10/19/23:1; *Blue Rapid Times*, 10/18/23:3; *Greenleaf Sentinel*, 10/11/23:1. The Kansas condensery mania spilled over into Oklahoma. See, for example, *Craig County Gazette* (Vinita, OK), 3/8/23:1,4.

49. *FST-M*, 7/12/23:2; *Tiller and Toiler* (Larned, KS), 8/9/23:7.

50. The classic work on this subject is Reich, *Making of American Industrial Research*.

51. *Third Annual Report, The Borden Company and Subsidiary Companies for the Fiscal Year Ending December 31, 1921* (New York: Borden Company, 1922); *Fourth Annual Report, The Borden Company and Subsidiary Companies for the Fiscal Year Ending December 31, 1922* (New York: Borden Company, 1923); *Fifth Annual Report, The Borden Company and Subsidiary Companies for the Fiscal Year Ending December 31, 1923* (New York: Borden Company, 1924); *Sixth Annual Report, The Borden Company and Subsidiary Companies for the Fiscal Year Ending December 31, 1924* (New York: Borden Company, 1925); *WSJ*, 4/3/23:12 and 5/5/24:9; *NYT*, 5/4/24:S7.

CHAPTER THREE

1. Some of these efforts were extensive. See, for example, PFSG 3/15/13:1,16 and 3/29/13:14.

2. *CSM*, 1/7/16:20 and 2/19/19:6; *WP*, 1/3/15:E5; *WSJ*, 1/11/15:2; *NT* 2/9/15:12 and 8/30/15:9; *NB*, 11/26/16:C5.

3. *AS*, 3/29/19:1; *Nation's Business*, 12/20: 8, 12; *WP*, 11/ 8/20:5; *CSM*, 5/17/20:11; *WSJ*, 12/28/21:1.

4. See, for instance, *HW*, 5/12:22–23. For diversification in the south, see Fite, *Cotton Fields*. Also see Hurt, *Problems*.

5. *JDN*, 9/6/10:8; *KSL*, 9/16/10:2; *HW*, 4/12:3; *NT*, 12/4/10:31; *AC*, 10/24/10:1; *New Orleans Times Democrat*, 2/20/11:6. For a report on the southern demonstration farms, see *HW*, 6/11:18, 3/12:18–19, 12/13:10–11, and 1/15:20–21; *IHC Demonstration Farms of the South* (Chicago: International Harvester Agricultural Extension Department, 1917).

6. *Daily Times* (Davenport, IA, 11/16/12:5; *Muscatine Journal* (IA), 11/19/12:8; *Inter Ocean* (Chicago),11/24/12:2; *NYT*, 11/24/12:26; *HW*, 12/12:24–25 and 3/14:4–6. For International Harvester and agricultural industrialism, see Fitzgerald, *Every Farm A Factory*.

7. *State Sentinel* (Stigler, OK), 8/20/14:2; *Muskogee Times-Democrat*, 9/1/14:11; *MA*, 2/15/15:3 and 3/3/15:9; *SN*, 10/24/13:2.

8. George Howard Alford, *How to Prosper in Boll Weevil Territory* (Chicago: IH Agricultural Extension Department, 1914; A. E. Chamberlain, *The Farm: The Greatest Purchasing Power* (Chicago: IH Agricultural Extension Department, 1914); *Diversified Farming is Safe Farming* (Chicago: IH Agricultural Extension Department, 1917); *How to Vitalize the Teaching of Agriculture in the Rural Schools* (Chicago: IH Agricultural Extension Department, 1917); *The Liberty Book*, (Chicago: IH Agricultural Extension Department, 1918); and P. G. Holden and C. M. Carroll, *We Must Feed Ourselves*, (Chicago: IH Agricultural Extension Department, 1919).

9. C. M. Carroll, *Every Farm is a Factory: The Opportunity of the Town Lies in the Country* (Chicago: IH Agricultural Extension Department, 1915), p. 4; *Greensboro Daily News*, (NC) 10/9/15:4.

10. *MB*, 5/1/14:6; *HN*, 5/2/14:8; *NR*, 5/7/14:2; *CD*, 5/7/14:2.

11. *JDN*, 5/8/14:8; *Grenada Sentinel*, 5/8/14:1; *HN*, 5/9/14:8.

12. *GC*, 5/29/14:3; *JDN*, 5/23/14:5; *Vicksburg Evening Post*, 5/25/14:6; *Tallahatchie Herald*, 6/4/14:3. For railroads and industrial development in the twentieth century see Scott, *Railroad Development Programs*.

13. *Pascagoula Democrat Star*, 6/12/14:1 and 6/26/14:2; *Lexington Advertiser*, 6/26/14:4; *CD*, 6/28/14:2.

14. *Sea Coast Echo* (Bay Saint Louis, MS), 7/4/14:1; *HN*, 7/11/14:1; *JDN*, 9/20/14:1; *Natchez Democrat*, 9/29/14:7.

15. *Chronicle-Star*, 5/29/14:1–2; *JDN*, 5/27/14:1, 10/1/14:8, 10/4/14:11, and 10/23/14:8; *EMT*, 7/10/14:4; *Yazoo Herald*, 6/5/14:3; *Commonwealth*, 6/5/14:3; *Jones County News*, 11/5/14:1.

16. *MB*, 10/9/14:8; *JDN*, 10/26/14:52, 76.

17. *Times-Post* (Houston, MS), 7/23/15:1–2; *KSL*, 4/2/15:5; *JDN*, 6/10/15:5 and 6/21/15:2; *NR*, 6/17/15:1; *Vardaman's Weekly*, 6/17/15:24–25.

18. *JDN*, 7/23/15:2; *MB*, 7/16/15:5; *Lexington Advertiser*, 4/23/15:1.

19. *HN*, 8/16/15:3; *JDN*, 3/21/15:12; *WT*, 2/19/15:5; *Times-Post*, 10/15/15:5.

20. *HW*, April 1914:21–22; *JDN*, 3/22/15:7.

21. Carroll, *Every Farm*, 5–8; *HW*, 1/16:26–27; *Webster County Times*, (Eupora, MS) 10/28/15:1.

22. *SN*, 4/23/15:1; *JDN*, 5/24/15:5. For Chautauqua see Rieser, *The Chautauqua Moment*.

23. "An Act To Provide for Cooperative Agricultural Extension Work between the agricultural colleges in the several States receiving the benefits of an Act of Congress approved July second, eighteen hundred and sixty-two, and of Acts supplementary thereto, and the United States Department of Agriculture" Chapter 79 of the 63rd Congress; Approved on May 8, 1914; 38 Stat. 372, 7 U.S.C. 341 et seq.

24. True, *Agricultural Extension Work*; *SN*, 4/2/15:1.

25. *FWST*, 1/8/15:10; *MNS*, 9/6/17:6, 11/2/17:1, 11/28/17:1, 11/30/17:1, 8, 12/1/17:6, 12/2/17:1, 6, and 12/4/17:6.

26. *MNS*, 12/12/17:4, 1/22/18:6, 1/29/18:6, 1/31/18:6, and 2/7/18:2.

27. On wartime extension is Danbom, *Born in The Country*.

28. *RNY*, 1920:1642, 1921:15, 954, 998.

29. *University of Arkansas Bulletin. Annual Catalogue*, 1920–21:151–154.

30. *Clemson College Bulletin. Catalogue* 1918–19:175.

31. These are a few notable exceptions. *NT*, 12/12/22:A6; *Chicago Defender*, 4/8/22:3 and 9/30/22:9; *AS*, 10/3/23:2; *CSM*; 9/23/22:11.

32. *CT*, 4/23/23:14 and 9/12/23:13; *WSJ*, 5/5/23:11; *LAT*, 4/23/23:I2; *BS* 4/23/23:2, and 8/12/23:35; *AS*, 4/27/23:1 and 7/29/23:1; *WP*, 4/28/23:6; *NYT*, 4/23/23:4.

33. *CSM*, 8/1/23:1; *HC*, 5/3/23:14; *CT*, 9/17/23:17; *PC*, 10/27/23:1.

34. *CSM*, 2/14/23:1; *NYT*, 5/6/23:XX1; *WP*, 10/21/23:5.

35. *CSM*, 7/30/23:1; *PC*, 9/22/23:3; *NYT*, 12/16/23:XX4.

36. *CSM*, 8/4/23:1; *LAT*, 9/13/23:I4; *NYT*, 10/22/23:31 and 12/2/23:E7; *AS*, 4/29/23:6.

37. *AS*, 2/18/23:A8; *WSJ*, 9/19/23:8; *NYT*, 5/25/23:35; *NT*, 3/18/22:1.

38. *WSJ*, 1/2/22:8; NT, 12/4/22:1; *LAT*, 1/9/23:I1 WP, 10/9/23:9; *NYT*, 1/10/22:15 and 9/3/23:17.

39. *WSJ*, 1/7/22:6, 12/22/22:9, and 12/31/23:11; *NYT*, 4/2/22:93 and 10/5/22:39; *PF*, 9/23/22:8; *HC*, 4/14/22:20; *WP*, 9/4/22:2 and 11/4/23:2; *NT*, 12/18/22:5; *AS*, 6/29/22:10.

40. *NYT*, 5/8/22:31 and 12/3/22:132; *CSM*, 2/26/23:1; *NT*, 1/22/22:SM6; *WSJ*, 1/6/22:9.

41. *RNY*, 1923:594.

42. *RNY*, 1917:938, 1923:494, 750, 833, 880, 953, and 1924:930. For Collingwood, see "Herbert W. Collingwood," *NYT*, 10/22/27:17.

43. *RNY*, 1917:420, 858, 893, 1920:1769, 1921:933, 1922:1020, and 1923:941–42.

44. *RNY*, 1921:1446; *PFSG*, 11/18/11:2.

45. Duncan Stuart, "Southern Markets for Dairy Products"; George M. Whitaker, "The Milk Supply of Southern Cities"; B. H. Rawl, "Why Dairying is Undeveloped in the South," in the *Twenty-Fourth Annual Report of the Bureau of Animal Industry for the Year 1907* (Washington, DC: Government Printing Office, 1909): 308–317, 318–328, 329–339.

46. *NT,* 12/23/18, 1/13/19:10, 1/20/19:10, and 3/3/19:11.

47. MD 4/20:10, 12, 52–53.

48. *NT,* 5/29/C5; *MD,* 2/21:54; *NT,* 11/23/19:B1.

49. *NT,* 1/16/21:E1 and 2/22/20:A1; C. L. Goodrich, "Factors that Make for Success in Farming in the South," *USDA Farmers' Bulletin 1121* (Washington, DC: USDA, 1920).

50. *NT,* 2/27/21:A11, 4/10/21:A5, 4/17/21:B5, 4/24/21:A5, 10/23/21:A2, and 10/30/21:C8.

51. *BG,* 9/2/21:8; *WSJ,* 4/19/21:1 and 9/24/21:2; *NYT,* 3/26/21:11 and 9/22/21:5; *NT,* 10/9/21:B1.

52. The cattle tick did also. That nasty pest required farmers to dip their animals in a tank to kill the insects. The USDA mobilized to help rid the South of the plague. See Strom, *Making Catfish Bait.*

53. *SC,* 3/15/21:1,3 6/15/21:2, and 8/15/21:13.

CHAPTER FOUR

1. *STJ,* 1/29/23:3 and 2/20/23: 6.

2. Thomas Battle Carroll, *Historical Sketches of Oktibbeha County* (MS), edited and amended by Alfred Benjamin Butts, Alfred William Garner, and Frederic Davis Mellon (Starkville: Mississippi State Printing, 2006).

3. None of these newspapers had their entire run in Starkville. Ultimately, the larger cities of Memphis, Birmingham, and Atlanta would beckon. While they were in Starkville, the *Southern Livestock Journal* was edited by W. B. Montgomery and Edwin Montgomery. G. H. Alford edited the *Southern Farm Gazette;* worked for the IH Extension Department; served in the Mississippi legislature; was a county agent in Mississippi; led Maryland's state agents; served as a federal field agent for Maryland, Virginia, West Virginia, and Kentucky; managed the Texas Farm Bureau and headed the Magnolia Electric Association. Cully Cobb edited the *Southern Ruralist* in Starkville before taking it to Atlanta. Tait Butler, professor of zoology and veterinary science at Mississippi Agricultural College, edited the *Progressive Farmer* before moving it to Memphis. For southern agricultural journalism, see Osborn, "The Southern Agricultural Press."

4. *Fall River News,* 4/12/1875:1; *Huntsville Weekly Democrat,* 10/18/1876:4; *Southern Planter,* 3/1/1877:1; *Herd Register of the American Jersey Cattle Club* 2 (1872) (Newport, RI: American Cattle Club, 1873); *Index of Owners; Herd Register of the American Jersey Cattle Club* 4 (1876) (Newport, RI: American Cattle Club, 1877), p. 22; *SLJ,* 12/14/1882:6; *CD,* 10/3/26:8. Of interest is Matthew Carl Paoni, "'Dixie's Arms are Open:'The Promotion of Settlement in the Postbellum-Era South, 1870–1920," Johns Hopkins University Press Dissertation, 1910.

5. *Clarion,*7/31/1878:2, 12/18/1878:2, and 4/9/1879:3; *SLJ,* 12/9/1880:2. For Mississippi agriculture during Montgomery's heyday, see A. B. Hunt, *Mississippi: Its Climate, Soil, Productions and Agricultural Capabilities,* USDA Miscellaneous Special Report No. 8 (Washington, DC: Government Printing Office, 1883).

6. *Southern Plantation,* 12/7/1876:8; *SLJ,* 8/24/1882:4.

7. *SLJ,* 10/7/1880:1, 10/14/1880:3, 10/21/1880:2, 4/17/1881:3, 4/28/1881:2, and 12/21/1882:2.

8. *SLJ*, 7/7/1881:2, 7/14/1881:1, and 5/18/1882:2.

9. *SLJ*, 10/28/1880:2 and 7/14/1881:2; *Aberdeen Examiner*, 4/24/1884:2; *Clarion*, 7/24/1878:1; Useful is *Southern States*, 5/1895:93–98 and 6/1895:149–154; E. G. Wall, compiler, *Resources, Condition and Wants—Mississippi State Board of Immigration and Agriculture*, 1879:28–34; S. M. Tracy, "Grasses and Forage Plants," *Mississippi Agricultural Experiment Station Bulletin No. 20* (February 1892).

10. *SLJ*, 11/18/1880:1.

11. *Aberdeen Examiner*, 4/23/1884:2; *Grenada Sentinel*, 11/8/1884:4; *SLJ*, 9/2/1880:2; 9/23/1880:1; *SLJ*, 12/2/1880:3, 12/9/1880:3, 12/23/1880:2, 3/3/1881:2, 3/17/1881:2, 7/28/1881:1, 9/29/1881:2, 12/1/1881:6, and 6/23/1882:5.

12. *SLJ*, 1/4/1883:2, 2/21/1883:2, and 6/14/1888:603.

13. *SLJ*, 11/11/1880:2, 7/27/1882:2, 11/17/1882:135, 7/9/1885:3, and 11/24/1887:151.

14. *EWO*, 5/6/1878:4; *Comet*, 3/26/1881:4; *Clarion*, 11/8/1882:3 and 2/7/1883:7; *CCG*, 58(1893):29; *SLJ*, 9/2/1880:2, 9/30/1880:2, and 9/3/1889:738.

15. *SLJ*, 2/9/1882:6 and 3/9/1882:2.

16. *Southern Argus*, 4/11/1873:1; *Southern Plantation*, 3/1/1877:257–58 and 3/15/1877:3; *SLJ*, 2/24/1981:2, 3/24/1881:2, 5/18/1882:3, 11/23/1882:2, and 11/24/1887:150.

17. *MA*, 5/9/1882:1; *Mississippian*, 9/12/1882:4; *EWO*, 9/13/1887:1; *Weekly Democrat* (Greenville, MS), 9/29/1883:4; *Clarion*, 2/24/1878:4, 7/25/1877:2, and 12/2/1880:1; *Times-Picayune* (New Orleans), 2/8/1872:8.

18. *Times-Democrat* (New Orleans), 9/28/04:8; *SN*, 9/30/04:4.

19. *EMT*, 11/19/10:2; *SN*, 2/20/03:5, 5/13/04:5, 4/17/03:5, 7/8/1904:3, 7/24/1904:5, 4/21/05:6, 8/24/06:1, 8/31/06:2, and 5/31/07:6.

20. *SN*, 7/19/07:2; *EMT*, 1/24/08:7.

21. *SN*, 2/21/08:1, 3/27/08:2, and 4/10/08:2; *EMT*, 1/1/09:2 and 5/14/09:2.

22. *PFSG*, 5/10/10:1.

23. *EMT*, 8/27/09:1; *SN*, 9/10/09:2.

24. *EMT*, 1/7/10:1 and 1/28/10:5.

25. *PFSG*, 5/21/10:8 and 6/11/10:12, 13, 16; *EMT*, 5/20/10:1, 7/1/10:2, 7/15/10:2, and 7/29/10:2.

26. *PFSG*, 7/9/10:10.

27. *PFSG*, 12/9/11:1, 1/20/12:1, and 3/16/12:1; *SN*, 9/26/13:1.

28. *SN*, 3/4/10:3, 3/1/12:1, 4/19/12:4, 8/9/12:2, 2/23/13:1, and 11/21/13:4; *PFSG*, 5/28/10:8 and 7/9/10:1; *EMT*, 4/5/12:5.

29. *EMT*, 1/14/10:2 and 12/29/11:4; *PFSG*, 4/29/11:10, 5/14/10:12, 10/8/10:11, 4/29/11:1, and 4/13/12:1.

30. *PFSG*, 5/21/10:10.

31. *JDN*, 5/1/12:8; *CL*, 4/7/12:5; *CP*, 10/4/12:3.

32. *EMT*, 6/28/12:1 and 8/2/12:3; *SN*, 6/28/12:4.

33. *JDN*, 8/31/12:2; *SN*, 8/30/12:3.

34. *JDN*, 9/15/12:2.

35. *PFSG*, 9/14/12:1, 11/2/12:12, and 12/21/12:1.

36. *SN*, 8/30/12:2.

37. *SN*, 5/8/14:2, 7/24/14:1, and 10/29/15:1; *JDN*, 5/27/15:1; *EMT*, 9/5/13:4, 9/24/15:4, and 9/29/16:4.

38. *SN*, 4/30/15:2 and 6/30/16:1; *EMT*, 6/30/16:1.

39. *JDN*, 5/2/16:9, 5/19/16:7, and 8/29/16:6; *PrF*, 8/14/15:14.

40. *EMT*, 10/1/15:1 and 12/8/16:2; *SN*, 10/15/15:3.

41. *SN*, 10/24/19:4 and 11/28/19:6; *JDN*, 1/16/19:6 and 2/10/19:3; *Lexington Advertiser*, 3/5/20:4. During the war, the transformation of southern agriculture mimicked that of the dairy industry. See, for example, *KSL*, 3/7/19:3.

42. *CL*, 9/27/00:6, 6/24/01:2, and 6/25/01:8.

43. *SN*, 10/19/06:1; SN 11/2/06:1,4, 11/8/07:4, 8/23/07:8, and 3/31/11:1; *EMT*, 2/4/10:1.

44. *SN*, 7/14/05:6, 8/18/05:2, 12/14/06:2, and 10/18/07:1.

45. *SN*, 1/1/09:4, 2/12/09:4, and 6/11/09:1; *EMT*, 4/23/09:2; Tracy, *Grasses and Forage Plants;* and *CL*, 3/29/1888:1.

46. *EMT*, 5/10/12:1, 5/24/12:1, 7/12/12:1, 2/2/13:4, and 2/27/14:2. "Historical Statement," Official Proceedings at the First Session of the Southern Commercial Congress (Washington, DC, 1909), 3; and G. Grosvenor Dawe, "Introduction," "Proceedings Third Annual Convention Southern Commercial Conference (Atlanta, GA, 1912), iii–vi.

47. *EMT*, 2/25/16:4 and 4/14/16:1–2.

48. *SN*, 3/31/16:1, 4/7/16:1, and 5/26/16:1; *EMT*, 3/31/16:2, 4/7/16:1, and 4/21/16:2,3.

49. *SN*, 12/1/16:1, 1/12/17:1, and 4/6/17:2; EMT 12/1/16:4.

50. *SN*, 8/24/06:1,10/5/06:1,4/19/12:2, 10/10/13:1, and 8/18/16:1; *JDN*, 10/30/14:8: *EMT*, 9/25/14:2 and 8/4/16:1.

51. *EMT*, 3/9/17:1; *ICM*, 3/17:29–37.

52. *SN*, 3/8/12:1, 8/9/12:4, 7/4/13:3, 9/19/13:1, and 10/3/13:1; *EMT*, 1/10/13:3 and 8/1/13:4.

53. *EMT*, 5/3/12:1, 7/26/12:4, 6/20/13:1, 9/5/13:1, and 7/10/14:4; *SN*, 9/13/13:1; *PFSG*, 1/25/13:11.

54. *SN*, 2/6/20:1 and 2/27/20:2.

55. *SN*, 2/13/20:1, 2/27/20:1, and 4/9/20:1.

56. *SN*, 1/23/20:9; *JDN*, 2/12/20:5.

57. *ICM*, 9/20:32–39; *SN*, 8/13/20:1 and 8/27/20:8.

58. *SN*, 10/3/19:8 and 11/28/19:9–10.

59. *SN*, 1/23/20:1.

60. *SN*, 1/9/20:6 and 5/14/20:2.

61. *SN*, 4/23/20:1, 4/30/20:8, and 7/2/20:3.

62. *SN*, 9/24/20:1, 10/1/20:1, 10/8/20:1, 10/15/20:1, 10/29/20:1, 11/5/20:1, and 12/3/20:1; *JDN*, 11/8/20:7 and 10/14/20:37.

63. *SN*, 5/21/20:5.

64. *SN*, 10/1/20:1.

65. *EMT*, 6/24/21:1 and 8/5/21:4; *SN*, 6/18/20:6.

66. *SN*, 1/2/20:12 and 1/9/20:6.

67. *SN*, 3/5/20:11, 3/19/20:11, 4/2/20:11, 4/23/20:1,2, 4/30/20:16, and 5/7/20:1,4.

68. *SN*, 3/5/20:1 and 3/26/20:1.

69. *SN*, 3/26/20:1 and 4/30/20:10.

70. *SN,* 4/2/20:1,2 and 4/9/20:1.

71. *SN,* 4/16/20:1, 4/23/20:1, 4/30/20:1, 5/7/20:1, 5/14/20:1, and 5/21/20:1.

72. *SN,* 6/4/20:1; *EMT,* 2/4/21:2.

73. *SN,* 6/11/20:1–9,17, 6/11/20:17, 6/18/20:1,12, 6/25/20:1,2,16, and 9/10/20:1.

74. *SN,* 7/2/20:1, 7/23/20:1, and 9/10/20:5.

75. *SN,* 7/16/20:2, 7/30/20:1, 9/24/20:1, 10/8/20:1, 10/22/20:1,12, 10/29/20:1, 11/26/20:1, and 12/3/20:5.

76. SN, 7/16/20:6, 8/6/20:1, 8/20/20:1,6, 10/8/20:1,3, and 11/26/20:1.

77. *SN,* 11/26/20:4,8.

78. *SN,* 11/26/20:1 and 12/17/20:1.

79. *JDN,* 1/20/21:3 and 1/24/21:3; "Reprinted from the Commercial Appeal as John White, Cows Can Bring Relief," *UA,* 1/20/21:4.

80. *JDN,* 1/27/21:6 and 1/30/21:2; ND 2/3/21:3.

81. *JDN,* 2/10/21:6.

82. *SN,* 7/22/21:1.

83. *JDN,* 3/3/21:2; *EMT,* 3/4/21:8; *CP,* 3/4/21:1.

84. *JDN,* 3/3/21:2.

85. *JDN,* 8/1/21:3; *EMT,* 7/1/21:5 and 7/29/21:4,5; *ND,* 8/11/21:1; *SN,* 7/22/21:1, 8/12/21:1, and 8/19/21:1–2.

86. *Natchez Democrat,* 4/22/21:7; *WT,* 4/1/21:4; *BN,* 4/17/21:4; *Port Gibson Reveille,* 4/28/21:1; *MB,* 4/8/21:1; *SN,* 7/15/21:5.

87. *JDN,* 7/19/21:8.

88. *EMT,* 8/19/21:4.

89. *EMT,* 8/5/21:1; *SN,* 8/19/21:1–2; *JDN,* 9/12/21:2 and 9/17/21:2.

90. *JDN,* 11/24/21:5 and 12/18/21:4.

91. *SN,* 11/25/21:2.

92. *SN,* 9/21/21:1, 11/4/21:5, 11/18/21:2, and 12/2/21:8; *JDN,* 11/14/21:3.

93. *PrF,* 12/31/21:1; *RNY,* 1921:991; *SC,* 9/1/21:13.

94. *SN,* 12/8/21:1; *EMT,* 3/17/22:4, 7/7/22:5, 9/1/22:5, and 12/8/22:1; *CSM,* 4/10/22:13; Des Moines Register, 8/14/22:2; *CT,* 8/13/22:G24; *JDN,* 6/4/22:2; *ND,*10/26/22:6; *MB,* 12/21/21:3.

95. EMT 6/2/22:1, 4/14/22:1, and 7/7/22:1; JDN, 1/4/22:3, 1/28/22:6, 2/5/22:4, 3/26/22:5, 4/6/22:7, 4/20/22:5, 9/15/22:4, 9/23/22:2, and 11/14/22:7. *Creamery Journal,* 6/15/22:28.

96. *EMT,* 3/10/22:10 and 10/20/22:1; *JDN,* 10/24/22:6; *PrF,* 5/13/22:6.

97. *EMT,* 7/28/22:5 and 11/24/22:5; *JDN,* 9/27/22:4.

98. *EMT,* 5/19/22:4 and 12/1/22:2.

CHAPTER FIVE

1. *JDN,* 1/5/23:5; *CL,* 4/10/23:8; *EMT,* 1/12/23:2,3 and 3/23/23:2.

2. *Vicksburg Evening Post,* 2/24/23:2; *CP,* 3/2/23:1 and 3/9/23:1; *CL,* 2/24/23:5, 3/4/23:4, and 3/17/23:4; *WT,* 3/30/23:3; *EMT,* 4/6/23:2.

3. *JDN,* 2/1/23:7; *Birmingham Sun,* 3/25/23:1; *EMT,* 1/19/23:2.

4. *EMT,* 3/2/23:2

5. *EMT*, 3/30/23:1 and 4/6/23:3.

6. *EMT*, 4/13/23:2, 5/4/23:5, and 5/11/23:2.

7. *SN*, 8/18/11:1, 7/4/13:1, 6/19/14:3, 11/5/15:3, and 3/5/26:1; *JDN*, 3/16/17:5.

8. *Montclair Times*, (NJ) 7/25/08:5; *EMT*, 5/24/23:3.

9. *EMT*, 5/24/23:3.

10. *EMT*, 6/1/23:2 and 6/8/23:2; *HCG*, 6/15/23:2; *SN*, 10/23/25:4.

11. *EMT*, 6/8/23:1 and 6/22/23:2; "Corralling a Big Milk Condensery," *SN* (Special Borden Edition), 3/5/26:1.

12. Industrial Committee of the Chamber of Commerce, "Oktibbeha—the Jersey County of the South Why?" (Starkville News Print, 1923), found in the special collections department, Mitchell Memorial Library, Mississippi State University.

13. "The Borden Plant at Starkville, Miss.," typescript, F. L. Wier Collection (180–1933), housed in the special collections department, Mitchell Memorial Library, Mississippi State University.

14. *EMT*, 11/9/23:1; "Corralling A Big Milk Condensery," *SN* (Special Borden Edition), 3/5/26:1.

15. "Corralling A Big Milk Condensery," *SN* (Special Borden Edition), 3/5/26:1.

16. *CL*, 7/17/23:6; *NB*, 9/4/23:5 and 9/5/23:23; *NT*, 9/5/23:5 and 9/6/23:12.

17. "Corralling A Big Condensery," *SN* (Special Borden Edition), 3/5/26:1.

18. *EMT*, 9/21/23:1 and 11/23/23:1.

19. *TT*, 12/15/23:5.

20. *Daily Pantagraph* (Bloomington, IL), 11/26/23:11; *MA*, 11/25/23:4 and 12/2/23:4; *WCJ*, 11/30/23:2; *STJ*, 11/23/23:10; *TT*, 11/22/23:2; *Daily Times* (Davenport, IA), 11/23/23:29; *CL*, 11/23/23:7; *Huntsville Daily Times*, 11/23/23:7; *Battle Creek Enquirer*, 11/23/23:12; *CN*, 11/23/23:1; *CP*, 12/7/23:1; *HCG*, 12/7/23:1; *PrF*, 1/26/24:10; *NR*, 1/1/25:2.

21. *RNY*, 1923:1024.

22. *PrF*, 3/22/24:4.

23. *EMT*, 11/30/23:3. For a scrub bull trial, see Rosenberg, "No Scrubs.

24. *Burlington Free Press*, 1/17/24:1; *BDR*, 3/4/24:8, 3/6/24:3, 3/7/24:6, 3/17/24:5, 3/31/24:3, 10/16/24:4, 12/7/23:8, 12/10/24:2, 12/17/23:6, 12/19/23:4, and 12/20/23:8. The situation persisted. See, for example, *LSJ*, 5/28/26:32; *McHenry Plaindealer* (McHenry, IL), 4/29/26:1.

25. *SN*, 6/6/24:1; *CP*, 7/4/24:1; *EMT*, 1/18/24:1.

26. *EMT*, 7/11/24:1 and 7/18/24:1; *SN*, 7/25/24:1.

27. *SN*, 8/8/24:1.

28. *SN*, 9/12/24:1.

29. *EMT*, 1/18/24:1,2, and 3/21/24:1; *WT*, 6/20/24:8; *Winston County Signal*, 7/17/24:5; *CL*, 7/20/24:3; *HCG*, 8/22/24:4; *SCN*, 9/18/24:3; *CP*, 10/17/24:1; *SN*, 7/11/24:1, 7/18/24:1, 8/8/24:4, 10/17/24:1, 11/7/24:1, and 12/12/24:1.

30. *CL*, 7/7/25:2; *SN*, 11/28/24:1,4.

31. *SN*, 12/6/24:1.

32. Commercial Appeal, "What May be Behind a Can of Milk," *EMT*, 1/2/25:3.

33. *EMT*, 8/1/24:2 and 1/2/25:1.

34. *SN*, 1/9/25:4; *EMT*, 1/2/25:4; *WCJ*, 1/23/25:1; *WT*, 2/6/25:1.

35. *SN*, 1/9/25:1.

36. *EMT*, 1/23/25:1 and 3/6/25:1; *CL*, 4/29/25:8.

37. *EMT*, 1/23/25:1; 1/30/25:1,2,3; 2/20/25:1; and 2/28/25:1 (misdated: was February 27); *CP*, 3/20/25:1.

38. *SN*, 2/27/25:1 and 4/17/25:1; *EMT*, 2/27/25:2 and 2/28/25:1.

39. *SN*, 2/27/25:5; *EMT*, 1/23/25:2 and 2/27/25:1,2; *AM*, 3/14/25:6; *SCN*, 1/29/25:1.

40. *Weekly Democrat* (Natchez), 3/11/25:2.

41. *SN*, 3/20/25:1 and 5/7/25:2; *EMT*, 3/20/25:1.

42. *News and Observer* (Raleigh, NC), 4/18/25:4; *Dayton Daily News*, 4/27/25:20; *Charlotte Observer*, 4/29/25:12; *MC* (Allentown, PA), 4/28/25:22.

43. *EMT*, 3/20/25:1; *SN*, 1/1/25:3 and 3/3/25:1,3.

44. *SN*, 3/20/25:1.

45. *EMT*, 3/13/25:2 and 4/24/25:1; *WCJ*, 3/20/25:2; *SN*, 5/22/25:1, 5/29/25:1, and 10/14/25:2.

46. *SN*, 4/1/25:1; *CL*, 8/16/25:12; "Starkville Rotarians Receiver Charter," from the *EMT* dated 4/25/24 and reprinted in https://starkvillerotary.org/our-club/history/.

47. *WCJ*, 9/25/25:1; *EMT*, 4/24/25:1 and 5/1/25:1; *SCN*, 4/9/25:3; *CL*, 4/8/25:5 and 9/3/25:2; *WT*, 10/22/26:6. Methodists had purchased the site in 1923. See *MAR*, 11/22/23:95.

48. *SN*, 4/17/25:3 and 5/1/25:2; *EMT*, 2/24/25:1.

49. *SN*, 4/25/24:4, 5/1/25:5, and 8/14/25:4.

50. *EMT*, 7/3/25:1; *WCJ*, 9/25/25:1.

51. *CL*, 8/27/24:5; *SN*, 4/24/25:1, 8/14/25:1, and 9/25/25:1; *WCJ*, 8/21/25:1.

52. *Continental Securities Company and Clarence H. Venner vs. The Borden Company*, New York Supreme Court, Appellate Division, V01.3593.

53. *SN*, 8/14/24:1, 8/14/25:4, and 11/11/27:8; *WCJ*, 10/23/25:1; *Annual Report for the Fiscal Year Ended December 31, 1925* (New York: Borden Company, 1926).

54. *SN*, 4/3/25:1, 4/17/25:1, 6/26/25:1, 9/2/25:5, 9/11/25:1, 9/25/25:1, and 12/4/25:1; *EMT*, 4/24/25:1, 5/1/25:3, 5/8/25:1, and 7/3/25:1.

55. *WSJ*, 3/20/25:13, 4/7/26:13, 4/16/25:5, and 12/21/25:11; *NYT*, 3/20/25:28; *WSJ*, 4/22/26:11; *LAT*, 10/14/25:17.

CHAPTER SIX

1. *SN*, 2/12/26:1 and 12/18/25:1; *CL*, 1/2/26:6 and 3/9/26:7; *WT*, 2/19/26:2.

2. *SN*, 2/12/26:1.

3. *SN*, 2/12/26:2, 2/26/26:1, and 3/5/26:1; *WCJ*, 2/19/26:1.

4. *SN*, 1/22/26:1 and 2/19/26:1.

5. *SN*, 1/1/26:1, 1/22/26:1, 2/12/26:1, 2/26/26:1, and 3/5/26:1; *WT*, 1/8/26:7; *CD*, 10/20/27:12; *WCJ*, 1/29/26:4.

6. "Truck Crop Farming and Canning Factory," http://oktibbehaheritagemuseum.com/wordpress/2015/03/truck-crop-farming-and-canning-factory/; *CL*, 12/12/25:10; *Canner/Packer*, April–June/1926:39; *SN*, 11/23/25:1, 12/4/25:5, 1/28/26:1, and 2/12/26:2; *CL*, 3/30/26:1.

7. *SN*, 1/28/26:1, 2/12/26:1, 2/19/26:1, 2/26/26:1,5, 3/12/26:7, 3/26/26:1, and 4/2/26:7; *WT*, 3/19/26:1,4; *CL*, 3/24/26:12.

8. *SN*, 3/5/26:1, 3/12/26:2, 3/26/26:1, and 4/16/26:1; *WT*, 3/5/26:1 and 9/3/26:2.

9. "Corralling A Big Milk Condensery," *SN* (Special Borden Edition), 3/5/26:1.

10. Ben F. Hilbun, "The Hand of Progress," *SN*, 3/5/26, special:3.

11. Dr. J. D. Ray, "The Borden Plant Itself," *SN*, 3/5/26, special:2.

12. C. H. Markham, "Dairying Coming to the Fore" *SN*, 3/5/26, special:4; James H. Collins, "The Story of Condensed Milk," *SN*, 3/5/26, special:7, 8; special #2:2, 6–8.

13. L. A. Higgins, "Dairy Opportunities" *SN*, 3/5/26, special:6; J. S. Moore, "Dairy Progress," *SN*, 3/5/26, special #2:1; L. P. Sweatt, "Hydro Electric Power," *SN*, 3/5/26, special #2:4.

14. "On March 10th," *SN*, 3/5/26, special #2:3.

15. "Oktibbeha Chamber of Commerce," *SN*, 3/5/26, special #2:9.

16. *SN*, 3/12/26:1,5; Catledge wrote a day earlier for the *Memphis Commercial Appeal.* See *Commercial Appeal*, circa 3/11/26, housed in the Borden folder in the special collections department of the Mitchell Memorial Library, Mississippi State University. Also see *Modern Farmer*, 4/15/26:2.

17. *SN*, 3/12/26:1.

18. *SN*, 3/12/26:1 and 4/16/26:4.

19. *SR*, 7/1/26:10–11.

20. *RNY*, 1926:1018.

21. *MR*, 6/26:1.

22. *SA*, 9/15/26:24.

23. *SN*, 3/26/26:1, 4/2/26:1, and 4/9/26:1; WT, 4/23/26:1.

24. *SN*, 5/21/26:1 and 6/4/26:1,12; *CL*, 6/4/26:7 and 10/15/26:19; *CP*, 6/18/26:2; *WCJ*, 6/18/26:1.

25. *WT*, 5/22/25:1, 6/11/26:6, and 7/2/26:2; *CP*, 5/21/26:1; *SCN*, 5/20/26:4; *CL*, 9/30/26:5.

26. "Facts Considering Oktibbeha County and Starkville Mississippi," pamphlet authored by the Oktibbeha Chamber of Commerce and printed by the *SN*, June 1926, housed in the Borden folder in the special collections department of the Mitchell Memorial Library, Mississippi State University; *SN*, 6/18/26:1,2 and 6/25/26:1. For a history of persons visiting the South for edification, see Karen L. Cox, ed., *Destination Dixie: Tourism and Southern History* (Gainesville: University Press of Florida, 2012).

27. "Facts #2 Considering Oktibbeha County and Starkville Mississippi," pamphlet authored by the Oktibbeha Chamber of Commerce and printed by the *SN*, June 1926, housed in the Borden folder in the special collections department of the Mitchell Memorial Library, Mississippi State University; *SN*, 6/4/26:1, 6/11/26:1, 6/18/26:1, 6/25/26:1, and 7/2/26:1; *CL*, 8/6/26:7 and 9/21/26:9.

28. *SN*, 6/25/26:1,8 and 7/2/26:1; CD 10/1/26:5.

29. *CL*, 7/20/26:3.

30. *Comet*, 3/4/1882:4; *MB*, 9/13/1879:3, 9/4/1886:2, 8/20/1898:3, and "Obituary-Capt. Mat Mahorner," 11/6/09:1; *Mississippian*, 5/2/1882:4; *Aberdeen Examiner*, 4/24/1884:1. *CL*, 1/16/1884:4; *Weekly Clarion*, 4/26/1882:1.

31. *SN*, 3/26/26:1; *TJ*, 8/22/26:1,5 and 8/25/26:1; *CL*, 2/16/27:10.

32. *TJ*, 6/20/26:1,8, 9/22/26:4, 2/2/27:2, and 2/16/27:1; *WSJ*, 4/21/27:1.

33. *NR*, 11/25/26:2.

34. *TJ*, 9/8/26:9 and 9/29/26:4.

35. *GC*, 10/1/26:8; *TJ*, 8/22/26:1,5.

36. *TJ*, 1/11/27:1 and 1/16/26:1; *CP*, 1/21/27:1.

37. *TJ*, 1/11/27:3.

38. *WT*, 4/1/27:2 and 5/20/27:2; *TJ*, 1/26/27:1 and 1/30/27:2.

39. *TJ*, 4/24/27:2.

40. *CPR*, 5/14/27:2; *TC*, 5/16/27:1; *CD*, 5/15/27:4.

41. *SCE*, 10/13/27:1; *SN*, 5/20/27:1, 9/30/27:6, 10/7/27:2, 11/4/27:1, and 11/25/27:1; *CD*, 9/21/28:1.

42. *WT*, 1/28/27:2 and 2/18/27:2; *CP*, 3/4/27:2.

43. *CL*, 7/10/26:5 and 1/28/27:5; *MS-S*, 6/23/27:1.

44. *WT*, 1/28/27:2; *Winston County Enterprise*, 12/3/26:8; *WCJ*, 7/2/26:4 and 10/22/26:1.

45. *CL*, 2/17/27:5; *WT*, 2/18/27:2, 2/25/27:3, 3/25/27:2, 4/15/27:8, 6/10/27:2, and 6/24/27:1.

46. *WT*, 6/17/27:1 and 7/8/27:1; *SCE*, 7/7/27:5.

47. *CL*, 6/28/27:2, 7/8/27:3, and 7/16/27:8; *GC*, 7/16/27:1; *WT*, 7/1/27:1, 7/15/27:1, and 7/22/27:1; *SCN*, 8/4/27:2; *WCJ*, 7/8/27:1, 8/5/27:1, and 8/12/27:1; *CD*, 7/17/27:1, 8/7/27:1, and 9/16/27:1; *NB*, 9/11/27:20; *TC*, 6/30/27:1, 7/1/27:1, and 7/19/28:2; *NR*, 7/28/27:1.

48. "Mississippi Town Gets Pet Milk Branch," an editorial from the *Star Herald*, reprinted in *NB*, 8/21/27:32; *CD*, 8/26/28:6 and 8/30/28:1; *TC*, 6/7/28:2 and 6/14/28:1.

49. *CPR*, 7/15/27:1, 7/23/27:2, and 7/25/27:2; *MS-S*, 11/24/27:6; *UA*, 7/14/27:2; *CD*, 7/26/27:4.

50. *MS-S*, 7/21/27:1, 7/28/27:4, 9/8/27:1, 9/15/27:4, 10/27/27:1, 11/17/27:1, and 12/29/27:1,4. For rural electrification, see Kline, *Consumers in the Countryside*.

51. *ND*, 7/12/28:1.

52. *WCJ*, 7/29/27:8; *CL*, 8/6/27:5; *CPR*, 8/29/27:2; *WT*, 7/15/27:4; *YCH*, 7/12/27:1; *SN*, 10/7/27:1,8.

53. *NR*, 7/28/27:1; *MS-S*, 7/14/27:1 and 9/15/27:7; *CL*, 9/10/27:4; *NR*, 2/2/28:1; *TN*, 3/29/28:1; *Mountain Eagle* (Jaspar, AL), 5/9/28:4.

54. *CD*, 8/19/26:1; *WCJ*, 7/22/27:1; *CL*, 5/25/27:2; *GC*, 12/12/27:4.

55. *WPL*, 4/15/27:1; *WCJ*, 6/18/26:1, 8/18/27:1; 12/15/27:9, and 12/16/27:1; *SCE*, 9/22/27:1; *CL*, 7/28/27:3; *SCN*, 12/8/27:2; *WSJ*, 3/17/28:10.

56. *S-WJ*, 11/23/27:2.

57. *WT*, 8/13/28:3; *NR*, 8/25/27:1; *WCJ*, 4/27/28:1 and 7/15/27:1.

58. *ICM*, 1/28:12–16.

59. *S-WJ*, 8/3/27:1; *CD*, 7/27/27:1 and 10/17/28:1; *CL*, 8/15/27:12 and 11/16/27:5; *SCE*, 9/22/27:6; *MS-S*, 11/10/27:1; *GC*, 6/5/28:5; *WPL*, 5/6/27:2 and 2/20/28:1; *TC*, 6/7/28:1.

60. *GC*, 8/20/27:2 and 10/10/28:5; *CL*, 5/3/28:9; I*ndianola Enterprise*, 9/29/27:4; *S-WJ*, 7/27/27:1, 8/17/27:4, and 11/30/27:2; *ND*, 8/29/28:1; *Boston Herald*, "The Newer South," reprinted in *WT*, 8/31/28:3; *CMPM*, 9/27:60 and 12/28:78; *SR*, 10/1/26:8; *SN*, 12/3/26:1; *CD*, 8/16/27:1.

61. *CL*, 1/21/28:7; *GC*, 4/25/29:2; *CP*, 3/4/27:2; *CMPM*, 3/28:40; Ben Hilbun, "Magnolia State Dotted With Milk Plants," *Commercial Appeal*, January 29, 1928, reprinted in *SN*, 2/10/28:4.

62. *GC*, 12/14/27:2.

63. *CL*, 8/28/27:14, 10/23/27:6, 10/25/27:12, and 11/8/29:16.

64. *CD*, 3/29/25:4, 8/2/25:1, 8/23/25:1, 2/24/26:1, 4/11/26:4, 9/24/26:6, 11/24/26:4, 11/28/26:4, 1/25/27:1, 6/28/27:1, 8/22/27:1, and 8/31/27:4. *GC*, 12/7/27:4; *CPR*, 10/10/27:2; *CL*, 8/6/27:3.

65. *S-WJ*, 1/26/27:2, 10/29/27:1, and 12/28/27:1; *GC*, 1/17/29:4 and 6/11/29:6; *CL*, 9/13/27:2.

66. *GC*, 1/12/28:7. Also see *MA*, 1/16/28:4; *NB*, 1/22/28:34.

CHAPTER SEVEN

1. *Cong. Rec.* 70th Cong., 1st ses, 1928, 1096–97; *S-WJ*, 2/8/26:5.

2. *Boston Herald*, "The Newer South," reprinted in *WT*, 8/31/28:3.

3. *NB*, 11/20/27:40.

4. *Ashville Citizen*, "Mississippi Progress," reprinted in *WT*, 8/31/28:3.

5. *CL*, 10/14/27:22–23.

6. *Memphis Commercial Appeal*, reprinted in *Madill Record* (OK) 3/15/29:3.

7. *SCN*, 9/19/29:1.

8. *NT*, 5/17/26:5.

9. *NT*, 8/28/26:4.

10. *NT*, 5/19/26:16, 7/12/26:5, 7/30/26:3, and 7/31/26:10; *NB*, 8/1/26:19; *LCN*, 3/31/27:1.

11. *DGM*, 8/18/26:3.

12. *NT*, 8/22/26:14 and 8/23/26:5; *TN*, 1/25/27:4.

13. *MR*, 8/26:14 and 8/27/26:4; *NT*, 8/27/26:1.

14. *NT*, 8/28/26:4 and 8/29/26:29.

15. *NT*, 8/30/26:1, 1/19/27:9, and 1/24/27:7; *JCSN*, 2/22/27:7; *LCN*, 2/24/27:1 and 6/9/27:13; *DNJ*, 5/6/27:5; *CDT*, 6/9/27:2; *NB*, 1/25/27:42 and 6/11/27:9.

16. *NT*, 9/6/26:5, 9/18/26:7, 9/19/26:5, 9/26/26:32, 10/3/26:29, 10/5/26:11, 10/17/26:1, 10/18/26:6, and 10/27/26:6; *NB*, 9/22/26:1, 9/26/26:10, and 9/30/26:20; *SA*, 9/15/26:1; *CN*, 10/26/26:10.

17. *NT*, 12/9/26:1, 12/10/26:15, 12/11/26:9, 12/12/26:1, 12/14/26:4, 12/19/26:12, and 4/5/27:5; *JCC*, 12/10/26:12; *JCS-N*, 12/9/26:12; *KJ*, 12/12/26:15; *CDT*, 12/13/26:2; *Daily News-Journal*, 4/12/27:4; *CT*, 12/13/26:2; *NB*, 12/9/26:1 and 12/12/26:1; *CN*, 12/13/26:11.

18. *DNJ*, 5/10/27:4; *NT*, 4/23/27:8.

19. *CDT*, 5/23/27:8; *CN*, 5/23/27:3; *DNJ*, 5/25/27:4 and 3/20/28:2; *NT*, 5/25/27:8.

20. *LCN*, 6/9/27:16; *CDT*, 6/13/27:8; *NB*, 5/12/27:12; *MR*,12/26:8; *NT*, 3/27/27:29.

21. *LCN*, 6/9/27:18; *NB*, 6/5/27:1.

22. *KN-S*, 7/6/27:21, 7/13/27:3, 7/25/27:7, 7/26/27:4, 9/11/27:6, and 11/23/27:3; *KJ*, 7/7/27:5; *NB*, 9/3/27:1.

23. *GDS*, 6/10/27:1 and 6/29/27:1,6; *NB*, 6/19/27:20.

24. *GDS*, 5/20/27:1; *DGM*, 7/21/27:1.

25. *GDS*, 6/18/27:1,3, 6/20/27:1, 6/29/27:1, 7/11/27:1, 7/18/27:1, 7/19/27:1, 7/20/27:1, 9/1/27:1, 10/26/27:1, 11/5/27:1, and 4/11/28:1; *NB*, 12/9/27:14; *KJ*, 7/14/27:2; *JCSN*, 8/4/27:4 and 8/16/27:6; *DGM*, 9/20/27:4; *JCC*, 11/9/27:6; *NB*, 11/18/27:17; *KJ*, 6/19/27:11.

26. *JCC*, 11/12/27:6; *BH*, 3/12/28:10; *NB*, 3/25/28:16; *KJ*, 4/8/28:7; *GDS*, 3/14/28:1, 4/10/28:1, 8/14/28:1, and 8/30/28:1; *Erwin Record*, 7/20/28:1; *Morristown Gazette and Mail*, 12/31/28:1.

27. *JCC*, 4/6/28:8; *JCSN*, 4/12/28:12; *GDS*, 4/11/28:1 and 4/16/28:10. The *Greeneville Sun* did an historical retrospective. See 10/12/2015:1.

28. *NT*, 6/10/27:1,5, 6/11/27:1, NT 6/12/27:1,5, and 10/8/27:1,8; *CN*, 10/5/27:15; *DNJ*, 10/7/27:1,8; *LCN*, 5/5/27:1 and 6/16/27:1; *NB*, 6/5/27:4, 6/11/27:1,3, and 10/5/27:2.

29. *GDS*, 4/11/28:5, 5/25/28:1, and 7/19/27:1; *NB*, 5/20/28:39.

30. *NT*, 8/29/27:2, 9/13/27:2, 10/11/27:2, 11/17/27:15, and 11/30/27:2; *NB*, 7/3/27:36 and *NB*, 7/17/27:38.

31. *DNJ*, 7/28/27:1; *NT*, 1/18/26:1,5, 5/25/27:8, 6/10/27:18, 6/12/27:34, and 4/2/28:10; *NB*, 7/10/27:1,4 and 8/15/27:16.

32. *NT*, 5/2/27:6; *KJ*, 11/11/27:3; *KN-S*, 11/13/27:7; *BH*, 3/30/27:1; *NB*, 6/19/27:20 and 11/20/27:40.

33. *CDT*, 11/24/27:11.

34. *NB*, 9/3/29:6.

35. *MA*,12/2/23:4 and 10/30/25:4; *Huntsville Daily Times*, 11/23/23:7; *STJ*, 9/9/23:6 and 11/23/23:10.

36. *MA*, 8/8/24:2 and 8/17/24:7.

37. *MA*, 9/3/25:1–2; *BN*, 6/1/26:1 and 9/3/25:1.

38. *Escambia Record*, 10/1/25:1.

39. *SN*, 3/19/26:1.

40. *MA*, 11/14/24:4; *STJ*, 1/15/23:3; *PCH*, 9/27/23:6, 8/13/25:3, and 10/1/25:5; *Democrat-Reporter* (Linden, AL), 4/26/23:1; *TN*, 1/13/24:5; DT 1/3/24:2; *TN*, 1/20/24:1, 1/22/24:1,4, and 10/9/25:9.

41. *TN*, 7/1/26:8.

42. *TN*, 11/23/26:1, 11/28/26:2, 12/14/26:1, and 11/7/28:1.

43. *TN*, 1/20/27:4.

44. *TN*, 2/22/27:1,8.

45. *CN*, 3/2/27:3; *Huntsville Times*, 3/25/27:1 and 4/15/28:1.

46. *TN*, 3/22/27:1, 4/10/27:1, 4/17/27:4, 5/24/27:1,10, 5/29/27:1, 6/6/27:4, and 11/7/28:1; *STJ*, 4/16/27:2.

47. *TN*, 6/8/27:3, 6/28/27:7, and 6/29/27:3.

48. *TN*, 7/14/27:4,6 and 7/15/27:4; *CD*, 7/25/27:4.

49. *TN*, 7/17/27:3, 7/19/27:4, 7/22/27:3, and 7/31/27:4.

50. *TN*, 8/10/27:4 and 8/12/27:4.

51. *TN*, 8/9/27:1,8, 8/14/27:2, and 8/23/27:1.

52. *TN*, 8/15/27:4, 8/17/27:4, 8/25/27:8, 8/26/27:3, 8/28/27:9; 8/31/27:5, 9/13/27:1,3,10, 9/14/27:8, 9/15/27:1; 9/16/27:1, and 9/29/27:1,3,4.

53. *TN,* 8/25/27:10, *TN,* 9/7/27:8, 9/18/27:18; 9/21/27:4, 9/23/27:1, and 9/27/27:1,8; *PCH,* 9/29/27:1.

54. *TN,* 9/20/27:1,8.

55. *TN,* 9/4/27:4, 9/30/27:1, 10/2/27:1, 10/3/27:1,4, and 10/24/27:8; *Sumter County Journal,* 10/6/27:2; *PCH,* 10/13/27:1 and 10/20/27:6.

56. *TN,* 10/9/27:1, 10/14/27:10, 10/16/27:2, 10/17/27:1,4, 10/18/27:1, and 10/19/27:4.

57. *TN,* 11/3/27:4, 11/7/27:1, 11/11/27:1, 11/15/27:3, 11/16/27:1, 11/20/27:1, 11/22/27:1, and 11/23/27:6.

58. *TN,* 12/2/27:3,10, 12/5/27:8, 12/6/27:1,8, 12/7/27:1, 12/8/27:1, 12/9/27:1,3, 12/11/27:4, 12/13/27:1, 12/16/27:1,12, 12/23/27:1, and 12/29/27:3; *PCH,* 12/29/27:1; *CD,* 12/28/27:3.

59. *TN,* 1/3/28:8, 1/8/28:1 and 1/10/28:1,8.

60. *TN,* 1/17/28:1, 1/24/28:1, 1/29/28:1, 2/1/28:1,8, 2/2/28:1, 2/2/28:4, 2/5/28:1,5, and 4/29/28:4; *PCH,* 1/26/28:1 and 2/2/28:5.

61. *PCH,* 1/5/28:1 and 1/12/28:1.

62. *TN,* 2/12/28:1,8, 2/14/28:1, 2/20/28:1, 2/21/28:4, 2/22/28:5, 2/23/28:1, 2/24/28:1, 2/26/28:1, 2/27/28:8, 2/28/28:1, and 2/29/28:1; *MA,* 2/25/28:3 and 2/20/28:9.

63. *TN,* 2/6/28:1, 2/13/28:1,4, and 2/14/28:1.

64. *TN,* 2/17/28:1; *CL,* 2/18/28:9.

65. *TN,* 2/19/28:1; *SN,* 3/3/28:1.

66. *TN,* 3/1/28:1, 3/2/28:1, 3/12/28:8, 3/15/28:1, 3/19/28:1,3, 3/26/28:3, 4/1/28:9, 4/13/28:1, 4/17/28:1, 6/18/28:1, 7/1/28:1, 9/2/28:1, and 11/2/28:10. "For the Farmers," *TN,* 3/6/28:8, 3/7/28:4, 3/8/28:8, 3/12/28:3, 3/25/28:14, 4/2/28:3, 4/4/28:4, 4/12/28:3, 4/16/28:3, 4/18/28:3, 4/22/28:3, 4/25/28:3, 4/26/28:3, 4/27/28:3, 4/29/28:1, and 4/30/28:3.

67. *TN,* 3/18/28:1, 3/26/28:1, 3/28/28:1, 3/29/28:1,8, and 4/2/28:2.

68. *TN,* 3/4/28:1, 4/8/28:1, 4/11/28:1, 4/13/28:1, and 4/15/28:1; *PCH,* 4/12/28:1.

69. *TN,* 4/27/28:1, 6/13/28:1, 6/14/28:1, and 6/15/28:1; *PCH,* 5/3/28:1; "For The Farmer," 6/5/28:3, 6/12/28:4, and 6/18/28:3.

70. *TN,* 4/13/28:1, 8/5/28:9, 8/9/28:10, and 8/12/28:16.

71. *TN,* 5/13/28:9; *Birmingham Iron Age,* 5/22/1878:2; "Hon. T. J. Patton," *EWO,* 6/14/1883:3 and 11/5/1885:3.

72. *TN,* 7/9/28:3, 8/12/28:3, 8/19/28:1, and 8/29/28:1.

73. *OMH,* 8/15/28:2, 8/22/28:4, 8/29/28:2, and 9/5/28:1; *TN,* 8/12/28:1, 8/13/28:1, and 8/14/28:8; *Roanoke Leader,* 9/26/28:3; *Anniston Star* (Anniston, AL), 11/10/28:4; *DD,* 11/13/28:4.

74. *TN,* 6/10/28:2, 7/26/28:9, 8/23/28:1, and 10/14/28:1.

75. "For the Farmers," *TN,* 11/1/28:7,10, 11/5/28:4, 11/13/28:4, 11/18/28:11, 11/22/28:3, 11/27/28:4, 11/29/28:10, 11/30/28:7, 12/2/28:18, 12/4/28:8, 12/9/28:7, 12/13/28:3, 12/17/28:4, 12/18/28:8, 12/20/28:14, 12/23/28:8, 12/24/28:10, and 12/3028:13; *TN,* 12/27/28:1; *Fayette Banner* (Fayette, AL), 11/8/28:5; *TN,* 11/8/28:12, 11/14/28:3, TN 11/18/28:4, 11/22/28:1, TN 11/28/28:3, 12/6/28:3, 12/9/28:1, and 12/16/28:1.

76. *TN,* 10/17/28:4, 11/7/28:1, 11/8/28:1, 11/11/28:1, *TN,* 11/12/28:1,8, and 11/13/28:1.

77. *TN,* 11/14/28:1,8.

78. *TN,* 12/23/28:1,8.

CHAPTER EIGHT

1. *AM,* 3/14/25:6.

2. Strom, *Making Catfish Bait.* Also see Ott, "Open Range Cattle-Ranching."

3. *DA,* 8/29/27:3.

4. *TG,* 4/9/26:2.

5. "Milk and Mississippi," from *New Orleans Item-Tribune,* reprinted in *SN,* 3/19/26:1,12; "It Might Have Been," from *New Orleans Times-Picayune,* reprinted in *TT,* 7/17/26:6.

6. *CDS,* 10/24/27:2; *TT,* 3/3/28:2.

7. *CDS,* 8/15/28:2; *DA,* 4/26/27:7.

8. *AP,* 10/30/26:2 and 8/6/27:2; *TT,* 10/5/27:1.

9. *MNS,* 8/12/26:5 and 8/18/26:12; *SJ,* 8/30/26:7 and 9/25/26:6; *ST,* 8/13/26:3.

10. *Eunice News,* 12/2/27:12; *TT,* 9/15/27:4, 10/8/27:2, 10/27/27:6, 12/19/27:11, 2/21/28:6, and 2/28/28:4; *MNS,* 10/15/27:4 and 5/4/28:1; *ST,* 10/27/27:35,38; *AP,* 8/6/27:1; *CDS,* 10/22/27:2 and 12/18/27:2; *DA,* 9/17/27:8; *NE,* 3/2/28:1,6; *Times,* 2/25/28:3.

11. *CL,* 3/31/28:6 and 6/16/28:2; *C-P,* 2/10/28:1,3; *GC,* 3/16/28:2; *SN,* 6/15/28:1; *RB,* 8/18/28:1; *AM,* 12/22/28:3; *Opelousas News,* 8/16/28:1; *TT,* 1/5/28:9, 8/11/28:1, and 10/27/28:10; *CDS,* 6/28/28:2, 8/15/28:2, 11/17/28:6, and 12/12/28:5.

12. *CDS,* 12/7/27:2 and 4/30/28:2; *TT,* 8/27/27:2, 1/6/28:8, and 8/24/28:1; *DA,* 8/17/27:6; *RB,* 8/4/28:1 and 11/3/28:3.

13. *TG,* 2/3/28:2; *C-P,* 8/24/28:1; *NE,* 8/24/28:2; *TT,* 7/19/28:1, 7/20/28:16, 7/21/28:3, 7/28/28:10, 8/4/28:4, and 8/18/28:5; *DA,* 10/18/28:10; *CDS,* 12/18/28:1,6; *RB,* 10/27/28:5.

14. *RT,* 3/13/28:7 and 9/15/28:2; *TT,* 7/21/28:10 and 12/29/28:5; *DA,* 10/20/28:10 and 10/24/28:10.

15. *TT,* 11/24/28:8. Also see *NE,* 11/2/28:1,6.

16. Pasquill Jr., "Arsenic and Old Bovine Lace." Also see *NE,* 4/27/28:10; *CDS,* 2/18/28:2; *AP,* 1/28/28:2; *RB,* 8/11/28:2; *RT,* 10/20/28:4; *TT,* 1/21/28:2, 2/18/28:2, 6/25/28:6, 7/21/28:2, 8/18/28:2, 8/27/28:1, 9/15/28:8, and 12/15/28:5.

17. *FWR,* 1/9/25:7, 8/2/25:36, and 8/6/25:2; *MN,* 9/24/25:6; *FWST,* 12/21/25:10; *AS,* 2/8/25:44.

18. *FWST,* 4/15/26:11.

19. *MN,* 9/1/26:6, 9/12/26:4, and 9/25/26:1; *MM,* 10/12/26:1.

20. *MM,* 6/25/26:1, 10/18/26:5, 11/3/26:1–2, 6/14/27:1, 6/27/27:6, 6/28/27:4, and 6/29/27:6.

21. *MM,* 7/7/27:5, 7/13/27:2, 7/19/27:4, 7/20/27:1, and 7/25/27:5; *MN,* 6/11/27:5.

22. *MN,* 7/29/27:11, 8/6/27:5, and 8/9/27:4; *MM,* 8/5/27:1, 8/11/27:2, and 8/12/27:6.

23. *MM,* 9/8/27:4, 9/14/27:5, and 10/3/27:1.

24. *McKinney Weekly Democrat-Gazette,* 10/6/27:4; *FWST,* 6/6/27:13, 6/25/27:25, and 8/15/27:16; *WS,* 9/1/27:1 and 1/19/28:1. Soon after the plant opened, Chamber members went to Starkville to learn about dairying. See *SN,* 3/16/28:1.

25. *MM,* 10/4/27:6, 10/6/27:6, 10/15/27:4, 10/25/27:4, 11/18/27:1,7, 11/25/27:1, 11/28/27:1,5, and 12/6/27:1; *MN,* 7/20/28:1 and 7/22/28:1,4.

26. *MN,* 7/20/28:4.

27. *WNT,* 10/27/26:2, 11/24/26:10, 12/29/26:3, 1/5/27:11, 1/30/27:1–2, 2/1/27:12, 2/2/27:10, 2/5/27:7, and 2/9/27:10.

28. *WNT,* 2/4/27:2, 2/11/27:8, 2/22/27:10, 2/25/27:10, and 9/25/27:11.

29. *WNT,* 3/7/27:8, 4/28/27:1, and 4/14/27:11.

30. *WNT,* 8/22/27:1, 8/27/27:12, 8/31/27:5, 9/2/27:12, 9/8/27:12, 9/9/27:10, 9/11/27:7, 9/20/27:10, and 9/24/27:8.

31. *WNT,* 7/27/27:1,9, 9/28/27:10, 9/29/27:12, and 10/4/27:12.

32. *WNT,* 10/13/27:10 and 10/14/27:12.

33. *WNT,* 10/19/27:13.

34. *WNT,* 4/5/28:12, 4/11/28:14, 5/4/28:14, and 5/10/28:14.

35. *WNT,* 5/30/28:10, 6/1/28:14, 6/2/28:12, and 6/5/28:10.

36. *WNT,* 6/26/28:12.

37. *WNT,* 6/28/28:10 and 6/30/28:1,12.

38. WNT, 7/1/28:11,14,39, 7/2/28:3, 7/5/28:7, 7/8/28:10,11, 7/10/28:5, 7/11/28:10,12, 7/12/28:3,5, 7/13/28:10, 7/15/28:12, 7/17/28:4, and 8/21/28:10.

39. *WNT,* 11/20/28:1–2,3,8.

40. *WNT,* 11/8/28:1,3, 11/10/28:6, 11/20/28:1,3, 11/23/28:1,11, 11/24/28:12, 11/26/28:9, 11/27/28:5, and 11/29/28:4.

41. *WNT,* 12/7/28:10, 12/19/28:1, 2/17/29:13; 2/18/29:5, 5/21/29:1, and 6/13/29:12; *AS,* 1/16/29:4 and 7/11/29:12; *Bryan Daily Eagle,* 1/9/29:2; *Cameron Herald,* 1/24/29:19.

42. *WNT,* 11/20/28:2.

43. *AS,* 7/12/29:1.

44. *WNT,* 3/31/29:11; *Victoria Advocate,* 3/21/29:2.

45. *FWST,* 3/25/28:24, 10/7/28:73, and 11/18/28:39; *WS,* 1/26/28:6, 3/22/28:1, and 4/12/28:2; *AS,* 4/8/28:33, 12/7/28:4, 12/9/28:4, and 12/16/28:1; *WSJ,* 12/17/28:18; *ST,* 10/5/28:5; *Longview Daily News,* 5/9/28:1,5; *Waxahachie Daily Light,* 3/8/28:4.

46. *AS,* 3/21/29:4.

47. *Daily Oklahoman* (Oklahoma City, OK), 8/27/29:6; *Charlotte News,* 7/19/26:29; *Greenville News (Greenville, SC),* 10/16/27:4; *AC,* 4/18/26:10,14 and 1/14/28:8; *Chillicothe Constitution (Chillicothe, MO),* 7/28/27:1.

48. *MA,* 8/28/29:4. The *Arkansas Gazette* story is printed there; "Goes Calling on the Cows," *SR,* 10/15/29:14; *TT,* 7/13/29:8. Sudduth's visit to the convention and speech are here. "Learning from Mississippi," *SN,* 5/4/28:3 and *CL,* 7/17/28:5.

CHAPTER NINE

1. *Kenosha Evening News,* 7/31/05:2; *AC,* 11/26/26:7; *CT,* 4/10/27:45; *CL,* 8/17/27:6; *Courier* (Waterloo, IA), 12/10/26:25; *SN,* 5/13/27:10.

2. *SR,* 9/15/27:1 and 12/15/27:14; *SA,* 11/15/27:2; *CMPM,* 5/27:18–19 and 11/27:37–38; *WPL,* 5/20/27:1.

3. *Baxter Bulletin* (Mountain Home, AR), 9/30/27:2; *Florence Herald* (Florence, AL), 7/1/27:15; *WCJ*, 10/7/27:1; *CD*, 7/7/27:1 and 9/28/27:2; *SA*, 10/1/27:12; *GC*, 10/31/27:2.

4. *CD*, 6/15/27:1, 7/19/27:1, 7/31/27:1, 8/14/27:1,5, 8/22/27:1, and 8/28/27:1; *CL*, 8/9/27:7 and 8/23/27:3.

5. *SN*, 7/15/27:1 and 10/21/27:1; *CD*, 10/16/27:4 and 10/17/27:4; *CL*, 10/20/27:4.

6. *SN*, 11/4/27:1; *SR*, 11/11/27:14; *TT*, 10/28/27:16; *TJ*, 2/22/28:1; *CSM*, 8/28/28:3.

7. *RNY*, 7/17/26:1017–18; *CMPM*, 7/28:31 and 11/28:92–93.

8. *NYPRAC*, 1/26/27:464.

9. *NYPRAC*, 1/26/27:464; *NYT*, 12/30/28:27; *WSJ*, 12/31/28:3 and 4/29/29:5; *St. Louis Globe-Democrat*, 7/12/28:24; *Sacramento Bee*, 5/8/29:1; *BTU*, 7/12/29:12; *CMPM*, 3/28:82–84 and 7/28:72. For the 1920s merger mania, see Eis:267–96; Gulick et al., "Modern Merger Movement"; White, "Merger Movement in Banking.

10. *WSJ*, 11/5/27:1, 12/14/27:9, 3/6/29:2, 1/25/30:1, and 3/12/30:5; Borden actions were characteristic. See *NYT*, 11/22/25:X17; *MR*, 2/26:1;8,13.

11. *SN*, 1/18/29:1; *CD*, 5/5/29:1 and 5/6/29:4; *CL*, 5/5/29:12.

12. *DD*, 7/18/28:1; *WPL*, 3/10/28:3.

13. *HC*, 6/28/28:18; *Onlooker* (Foley, AL), 7/19/28:3; *Journal and Courier* (Lafayette, IN), 1/15/27:11; *BG*, 11/21/29:19; *Muncie Star*, 8/1/27:8; *AC*, 10/17/27:4; *NYT*, 7/29/27:22; *WP*, 7/21/29:51; *CD*, 10/3/28:4.

14. *Advertiser* (Moulton, AL), 7/19/28:4.

15. *Anniston Star*, 10/27/27:4; *NE*, 2/10/28:8; *SC*, 9/1/27:12; *CT*, 4/15/27:30.

16. *MC*, 3/22/28:6; *GC*, 3/27/28:2; *SCE*, 3/29/28:13–14; *DD*, 9/13/28:2; *CD*, 3/3/29:4, 4/25/29:4, and 7/17/28:4; *ND*, 4/5/28:8. For 1920s rural industrialism, see Danbom, *Resisted Revolution*, 120ff.

17. *DD*, 7/29/29:4; *BDU*, 4/8/28:50; *SA*, 4/1/28:4 and 9/1/28:6; *CT*, 4/7/29:B7.

18. *Weekly Gazette* (Ville Platte, LA), 9/28/29:1,7.

19. *SN*, 12/23/27:6, 5/3/29:8, and 5/10/29:8; *CD*, 8/2/28:4; *CL*, 2/13/29:3.

20. *CD*, 6/22/27:1 and 11/16/28:1; *CL*, 9/18/27:3 and 6/17/30:7; *CPR*, 7/18/29:3.

21. *CD*, 11/15/28:2.

22. *SN*, 10/5/28:8; *CD*, 6/28/27:2.

23. *SN*, 1/7/27:1, 6/3/27:1, 6/17/27:1, 8/5/27:4, and 3/1/29:1.

24. *SN*, 11/19/26:1, 12/17/26:1, 1/21/27:1, 2/25/27:1,4, 3/4/27:1, 3/11/27:1,4, 3/18/27:1, 4/28/27:4, 7/1/27:6, 8/5/27:4, 11/25/27:6, 8/3/28:3, 6/15/28:8, and 10/12/28:4; *CD*, 10/18/28:1.

25. *SN*, 3/18/27:1 and 1/6/28:4; *CD*, 2/18/29:6, 3/21/27:8, 6/15/27:1, and 2/13/29:1,3.

26. *SN*, 1/7/27:1,5, 3/4/27:1, 10/14/27:1, 1/11/29:1,8, and 9/28/28:1; *CD*, 2/14/27:5.

27. *SN*, 1/28/27:2, 3/11/27:3, 10/21/27:1, 12/9/27:1, 1/27/28:1, 4/13/28:1, and 4/27/28:1.

28. *CD*, 6/2/27:1; *SN*, 8/5/27:4 and 11/1/29:8.

29. *SN*, 10/7/27:1,8, 10/14/27:1, 10/21/27:1, 11/11/27:1,4, 11/18/27:8, 11/25/27:1, 12/9/27:1, 9/7/28:6, 10/5/28:1, 12/14/28:1,4, and 4/4/29:1; *CD*, 9/17/28:6, 9/21/28:3, and 4/12/29:4; *WCJ*, 6/29/28:1.

30. *SN*, 8/12/27:1, 8/19/27:1,6, and 11/11/27:4.

31. *CD*, 8/20/28:4 and 9/21/28:1.

32. *SN*, 11/11/26:1, 2/4/27:1, and 7/8/27:1,4.

33. *SN*, 3/4/27:4, 8/5/27:4, and 12/9/27:4. Of interest is Daniel Immerwahr, *Thinking Small: The United States and the Lure of Community Development* (Cambridge: Harvard University Press, 2014).

34. *SN*, 3/11/27:5.

35. *SN*, 9/20/29:4.

36. *SN*, 7/20/28:6; *CD*, 11/21/28:4 and 5/20/29:4.

37. *SN*, 7/20/28:1.

38. *SN*, 9/7/28:1–2.

39. *SN*, 9/7/28:4.

40. "Raymond J. Goodman," *CL*, 3/7/71:12; *SN*, 9/7/28:1,12.

41. *SN*, 9/14/28:1. The *Commercial Dispatch*, which considered Starkville in its orbit, made a similar argument. See *CD*, 5/24/29:4. See also *CD*, 4/12/29:4; *WCJ*, 2/24/28:1.

42. *SN*, 9/21/28:1, 9/28/28:1, and 10/5/28:16; *CD*, 9/21/28:2.

43. From the *New York Sun*, reprinted in *CD*, 9/2/26:6; *CD*, 12/14/27:4 and 8/23/28:4; *CL*, 12/8/26:1–2 and 10/29/29:12.

44. *SN*, 1/1/29:1.

45. *SN*, 10/26/28:4, 11/16/28:4, and 3/1/29:4; *CD*, 8/9/28:1, 12/6/28:1, 1/2/29:1, and 2/6/29:6; *CL*, 8/4/29:3. "For Colored Farmers and Dairymen," *SN*, 9/21/28:6, 10/5/28:6, 11/16/28:4, and 11/22/29:2.

46. *CL*, 1/10/28:3; *SN*, 12/21/28:1 and 1/11/29:1.

47. *CL*, 10/15/26:16 and 7/5/27:8; *SN*, 5/17/29:8, 5/24/29:6, and 6/21/29:1.

48. *CD*, 2/11/29:1 and 2/21/29:1; *SN*, 10/5/28:1,16, 7/26/29:1, and 8/16/29:1,9; *CL*, 4/4/29:11.

49. *SN*, 3/1/29:1,4 and 3/15/29:1.

50. *SN*, 4/12/29:1 and 4/19/29:6.

51. *CL*, 3/3/29:9 and 4/25/29:4; *SN*, 4/19/29:4.

52. *SN*, 3/1/29:1.

53. *SN*, 3/22/29:1, 3/29/29:1,4, and 4/5/29:1.

54. *SN*, 3/29/29:8 and 4/26/29:1.

55. "Borden Vertical File," Special Collections Department, Mississippi State University Library, material dated 4/26/1929; *SN*, 4/26/29:4; *CD*, 4/26/29:4.

56. *SN*, 8/23/28:1–2 and 3/1/29:12.

57. *SN*, 11/1/29:1.

58. *CL*, 5/7/29:28.

EPILOGUE

1. Clyde F. Kohn, "Development of Dairy Farming in Mississippi," *Economic Geography* 4/43:188–195; Marvin Guin, "An Economic Study of Dairy Farming in Oktibbeha and Lowndes Counties, Mississippi 1936–1937," *Mississippi Agricultural Experiment Station Bulletin* No. 324 (10/38).

2. *SN*, 1/15/37:1, 3/5/37:4, and 3/19/37:1,4.

SELECTED BIBLIOGRAPHY OF CITED SECONDARY SOURCES

Baritz, Loren. *The Servants of Power: A History of the Use of Social Science in American Industry.* Middletown, CT: Wesleyan University Press, 1960.

Bell, Martin L. *A Portrait of Progress. A Business History of Pet Milk Company From 1885 to 1960.* St. Louis: Pet Milk, 1962.

Dairymen's League Co-operative Association. *The Fifty Year Battle for A Living Price for Milk: A History of the Dairymen's League.* New York: Dairymen's League Co-operative Association, 1939.

Danbom, David B. *The Resisted Revolution: Urban America and the Industrialization of Agriculture, 1900–1930.* Ames: Iowa State University Press, 1979.

———. *Born in the Country: A History of Rural America,* 3rd ed. Baltimore: Johns Hopkins University Press, 2017.

Dillon, John J. *Seven Decades of Milk: A History of New York's Dairy Industry.* New York: Orange Judd Publishing, 1941.

Eis, Carl. "The 1919–1930 Merger Movement in American Industry." *Journal of Law and Economics* (1969): 267–96.

English, Beth. *A Common Thread: Labor, Politics, and Capital Mobility in the Textile Industry.* Athens: University of Georgia Press, 2006.

Fite, Gilbert C. *Cotton Fields No More: Southern Agriculture, 1865–1980.* Lexington: University of Kentucky Press, 1984.

Fitzgerald, Deborah. *Every Farm a Factory: The Industrial Ideal in American Agriculture.* New Haven: Yale University Press, 2003.

Frantz, Joe B. *Gail Borden: Dairyman to a Nation.* Norman: University of Oklahoma Press, 1951.

Fried, Richard M. *The Man Everybody Knew: Bruce Barton and the Making of Modern America.* Chicago: Ivan R. Dee, 2005.

Gertner, Jon. *The Idea Factory: Bell Labs and the Great Age of Innovation.* New York: Penguin Press, 2012.

Giesen, James C. *Boll Weevil Blues: Cotton, Myth, and Power in the American South.* Chicago: University of Chicago Press, 2011.

Gulick, Charles A., et al. "The Modern Merger Movement." *American Economic Review,* Supplement Papers of the Forty-Third Annual Meeting of the American Economics Association (1931): 90–103.

Guth, James L. "Herbert Hoover, the U.S. Food Administration, and the Dairy Industry, 1917–1918." *Business History Review.* 1981: 170–87.

Hounshell, David A. *From the American System to Mass Production, 1800–1932: The Development of Manufacturing Technology in the United States.* Baltimore: Johns Hopkins University Press, 1985.

Hunziker, Otto Frederick. *Condensed Milk and Milk Powder.* Lafayette, IN: Otto F. Hunziker, 1914.

Hurt, R. Douglas. *Problems of Plenty: The American Farmer in the Twentieth Century.* Chicago: Ivan R. Dee, 2002.

Kline, Ronald R. *Consumers in the Country: Technology and Local Change in Rural America.* Baltimore: Johns Hopkins University Press, 2000.

Kohn, Clyde F. "Development of Dairy Farming in Mississippi." *Economic Geography* (1943): 188–95.

Marchand, Roland. *Advertising the American Dream, Making Way for Modernity, 1920–1940.* Berkeley: University of California Press, 1985.

Marcus, Alan I. "'Would You Like Fries with That, Sir?' The Evolution of Management Theories and the Rise and Fall of Total Quality Management Within the American Federal Government." *Management and Organizational History* (2008): 311–37.

Marcus, Alan I., and Howard P. Segal. *Technology in America: A Brief History,* 3rd ed. New York: Red Globe Press, 2018.

Markham, Jesse W. "Survey of the Evidence and Findings on Mergers." In Universities-National Bureau, *Business Concentration and Public Policy.* Princeton: Princeton University Press, 1955: 141–212.

Marshall, James. *Elbridge A. Stuart, Founder of Carnation Company.* Los Angeles: Carnation Company, 1949.

Mueller, Dennis C. *The Corporation: Growth, Diversification and Mergers.* New York: Harwood Academic Publishers, 1987.

Olmstead, Alan L., and Paul W. Rhode. "An Impossible Undertaking: The Eradication of Bovine Tuberculosis in the United States." *Journal of Economic History* (2004): 734–72.

Osborn, George C. "The Southern Agricultural Press and Some Significant Rural Problems, 1900–1940." *Agricultural History* (1955): 115–22.

Ott, John Solomon. "Open Range Cattle-Ranching in the Florida Pinewoods: A Problem in Comparative Agricultural History." *Proceedings of the American Philosophical Society* (1986): 312–24.

Pasquill, Robert G., Jr. *Arsenic and Old Bovine Lace–History of the Cattle Tick Eradication Program in the South,* found at http://www.fs.usda.gov/Internet/FSE _DOCUMENTS/stelprdb5396091. PDF, accessed August 27, 2020.

Reich, Leonard S. *The Making of American Industrial Research: Science and Business at GE and Bell, 1876–1926.* New York: Cambridge University Press, 1985.

Rieser, Andrew C. *The Chautauqua Moment: Protestants, Progressives, and the Culture of Modern Liberalism.* New York: Columbia University Press, 2003.

Rosenberg, Gabriel N. "No Scrubs: Livestock Breeding, Eugenics, and the State in the Early Twentieth-Century United States." *Journal of American History* (2020): 362–87.

Scott, Roy V. *Railroad Development Programs in the Twentieth Century.* Ames: Iowa State University Press, 1985.

Sloan, Alfred P., Jr. *My Years with General Motors.* Garden City, NY: Doubleday, 1964.

Strom, Claire. *Making Catfish Bait Out of Government Boys: The Fight Against Cattle Ticks and the Transformation of the Yeoman South.* Athens: University of Georgia Press, 2009.

True, Alfred C. *A History of Agricultural Extension Work in the United States, 1785–1923.* Washington, DC: Government Printing Office, 1928.

White, Eugene Nelson. "The Merger Movement in Banking, 1919–1933." *Journal of Economic History* (1985): 285–91.

INDEX

census, US (1920), 98–100
censuses of cows. *See* cow censuses
Central Union of Fort Scott, 48
Charleston, MS, 171–72
Chattanooga, TN, 183
cheese factories: Bristol, TN, 191; Columbus, MS, 177, 209; Dairymen's League Cooperative Association and, 39; Fort Scott, KS, and, 15; in Mississippi, 164, 169–70, 173–74, 176, 180; taken over by condenseries, 11
Chicago Producers' Association, 16–18, 20–21
Choctaw, 154–55
Citizens' Bank, 190–91
Citizens League of Sturgis, 100
Clarksdale, MS, 170–71
Clarksville, TN, 193
Clemson College, 68–69
Cobb, Cully, 156, 238, 287n3
collectivism: Chicago Producers' Association, 16–18, 20–21; corporate fear of, 8–9, 22–23; Dairymen's League (New York City), 18–20, 22, 37–40; fluid milk vs. condensed milk and, 22–23; Independent Milk Workers' Union, 44; Milk Producers Association (Chicago), 9–10, 17; Starkville civic organizations and, 146
Collingwood, Herbert W., 70–71, 110, 119, 124–25, 156, 241–42
Collins, James H., 151
Columbia, TN, 122, 140, 184, 185, 188
Columbus, MS, 110, 140, 177, 205, 209, 239
condensed milk industry: Borden's dominant place in, 6; industrial production methods, 11; Kansas condenseries, 12–16, 46–53; post-WWI surpluses, 37–38, 50; safety and flavor issues, 11; WWI boom, 10–11, 13. *See also* Borden Condensed Milk Company
condenseries. *See specific locations*
cooperative creamery, Starkville. *See* Mississippi Agricultural College cooperative creamery

Corinth, MS, 176
cotton agriculture: cow dung and, 164; in Greenwood, 176–77; in Marshall, TX, 226; mills, 80, 192, 236, 251, 259, 261, 263, 266–67, 271–72; in Oktibbeha County, MS, 77–81, 83–84, 98, 99, 109, 111–12, 114, 164; southern, 56–57, 64, 67–70
Cover, Frank G., 37, 43
cow censuses: Greeneville, TN, 189; Lee County, MS, 165; Lewisburg, TN, 185; Marshall, TX, 225; Pulaski, TN, 184; Starkville, MS, 121–22, 124; Tuscaloosa, AL, 201; Waco, TX, 230–31
cow testing: about, 47; A&M College and, 94; in Oktibbeha County, 109–11, 252; in Waco, TX, 230
creameries: established in Oktibbeha County during WWI, 88–89; Fort Scott, KS, and, 15; Montgomery, Jerseys, and, 79–80; Murfreesboro, TN, 187–88; southern history of, 72–73; taken over by condenseries, in WWI, 11; Waco, TX, 227–28
Crystal Springs Chautauqua, 66
Cunningham, Nar McArthur, 163
Curtis, V. C., 141, 149

dairy industry. *See specific topics and locations, such as* Borden Company *or* Starkville
Dairymen's League (New York City), 18–20, 22, 37–40
Dairymen's League Cooperative Association, 38–40, 45
Dallas County, AL, 194
Daniel, D. A., 90
Daniel, G. Odie, 94, 135
Davis, Whitman, 253–54
demonstration farms, 57–58, 63, 85, 92
DeMotte, John B., 95, 101–4, 106–7
Deute, A. H., 31–32, 37
Dillon, John J., 18–19
Dixon, IL, 13, 122–24, 126–27, 193

www.ingramcontent.com/pod-product-compliance
Lightning Source LLC
Chambersburg PA
CBHW030047050126
PP17639900002B/1